D0368819

UFOs & ALIEN CONTACT

UFOs & ALIEN CONTACT

Two Centuries of Mystery

ROBERT E. BARTHOLOMEW
& GEORGE S. HOWARD

Prometheus Books
59 John Glenn Drive
Amherst, New York 14228-2197

Published 1998 by Prometheus Books

02 01 00 99 98 5 4 3 2 1

Library of Congress Cataloging-in-Publication Data

Bartholomew, Robert E.
UFOs & alien contact : two centuries of mystery / Robert E. Bartholomew and George S. Howard.
p. cm.
Includes bibliographical references and index.
ISBN 1-57392–200–5 (alk. paper)
1. Unidentified flying objects. 2. Human-alien encounters. I. Howard, George S. II. Title.
TL789.B324 1998
001.942—dc21 97–48845
CIP

Printed in the United States of America on acid-free paper.

In the twenty-first century the greatest progress in civilization will be made not through science and technology, but in the understanding of what it means to be human.

—John Naisbitt

This book is dedicated to Robert C. Girard and Thomas Bullard, UFO pioneers.

Contents

Part II. Strange Experiences: Real or Fantasized?

Acknowledgments

This book could not have been written without several people who contributed rare newspaper clippings on UFO sighting waves. Foremost is Thomas E. Bullard at the department of folklore, Indiana University at Bloomington, Indiana, for providing a treasure trove of press accounts for most UFO sighting episodes in this book. For providing British press reports on UFO sightings, we are indebted to Nigel Watson, Granville Oldroyd, and David Clarke; also to Naomi Miller of the British Columbia Historical Federation.

Clas Svahn and Anders Liljegren sifted through thousands of documents from the Swedish ghost rocket wave of 1946. New Zealand press accounts were provided by several UFO researchers: Bryan Dickeson and Murray Bott, head of New Zealand's Mutual UFO Network. Other New Zealand UFO researchers who provided material are Peter Hassall, Bill Mercer, and Angie Moore. I am grateful to Jan L. Aldrich, who provided press accounts of phantom airplanes over Delaware in 1916.

A portion of chapter 10 first appeared in R. E. Bartholomew, "Collective Delusions: A Skeptic's Guide," *Skeptical Inquirer* 31, no. 3 (1997): 29–33. Some of the material in chapter 12 was first published in R. E. Bartholomew, K. Basterfield, and G. S. Howard, "UFO 'Abductees' and 'Contactees': Psychopathology or Fantasy Proneness?" *Professional Psychology: Research and Practice* 22, no. 3 (1991): 215–22. It is reproduced with permission of the American Psychological Association.

For all of those who contributed information or collaborated on chapters, we acknowledge that you may not necessarily concur with our interpretation of the material, which is the sole responsibility of Robert Bartholomew and George Howard.

We would like to thank the Prometheus team who worked closely and professionally with us at every stage, on what was a challenging manuscript to edit: editor-in-chief Steven L. Mitchell, freelance copyeditor Michele Pelton-Fall, typesetter Bruce Carle, freelance proofreader Nicholas A. Read, and especially associate editor Mary A. Read.

Prologue

Sky Searches Marked Last Days

SAN DIEGO (AP)—For months, the thirty-nine members of Heaven's Gate climbed a sci-fi stairway to Paradise, step by faithful step. Up before dawn, they prayed and then trained a telescope on the sky to look for the UFO they believed would whisk them away from Earth's tribulations. In March, as the Hale-Bopp comet swooped to within 122 million miles of Earth, they got the signal. Time to go. Suddenly, their daily regimen switched from holistic hokum to recipe for destruction as they leaped into the void fueled by a cocktail of pudding, sedatives, and vodka, confident to the end that cosmic salvation beckoned.

"We know whatever happens to us after we leave our bodies is a step forward," said Marshall Applewhite, glassy-eyed leader of Heaven's Gate, in a videotaped message.

Last October, the group known as Heaven's Gate moved into the sprawling mansion that would eventually become their high-priced mausoleum. Here, according to people who knew them through their business incarnation of Web site designers, Higher Source Contract Enterprises, group members followed a schedule of almost military precision. They got up at 3 A.M. for prayers, searched the sky at 4 A.M., ate a communal meal at 5. The rest of the day it was work and more work . . .

They wore black and kept their hair trimmed to marine recruit length. They didn't drink alcohol. They didn't do drugs. They didn't have sex. Some of the men had taken celibacy to the extreme: castration.

"I have the same kind of penetrating questions that you have: Who or what would make thirty-nine people take their life in this manner?" asked Sheriff Bill Kolender at a news conference describing the deaths. In mid-November, a rumor began to circulate that there was a spaceship lurking behind Hale-Bopp. On their Web site, cult members made references to the ghost ship. But they said it was irrelevant, because the comet signaled it was time for "the arrival of the space-craft from the Level Above Human to take us home to 'Their World.' " . . .

On Friday, March 21, the ball of frozen gas and dust known as Hale-Bopp made its closest pass to Earth. The Heaven's Gate Web site was updated one last time at 10:26 Pacific time. In its final version, the page carried a flashing logo borrowed from *Star Trek.* "Red Alert, Hale-Bopp Brings Closure to Heaven's Gate."

"Take the little package of pudding or applesauce and eat a couple of tablespoons. Pour the medicine in and stir it up. Eat it fairly quickly and then drink the vodka beverage. Then lie back and rest quietly"—suicide instructions as read by the medical examiner.

Notes, a trash can full of plastic bags, and medical evidence indicate the final hours of Heaven's Gate was a calmly choreographed dance of death. Members put on a uniform of long black pants, oversized black shirts and brand-new black Nike sneakers emblazoned with the shoemaker's cometlike white "swoosh" trademark.

All but one group member had left a final message on videotape. Most tucked identification into their shirt pockets along with a $5 bill and some quarters. They packed suitcases or canvas grips and stowed the luggage neatly at the foot of their beds.[1]

* * *

What are we to make of this bizarre event? Is it best understood as an extremist religious cult—like David Koresh's Branch Davidians of Waco, Texas, or Jim Jones's mass suicide in Jonestown, Guyana? In 1993 the Davidians perished after turning their compound into a hellish inferno to avoid capture by advancing police. On November 18, 1978, about nine hundred of Jones's followers swallowed a lethal mix of cyanide-laced Kool Aid—many willingly, some unwillingly—or were shot. Perhaps the San Diego tragedy is more representative of what occurs when a group of UFO enthusiasts becomes completely unglued. Or it can be seen as the first in a series of events that shows what happens to people who spend too much time in cyberspace and not enough time in the world of real people and social relationships. How are we to understand the events that led to the largest mass suicide in the history of the United States?

This book represents a social history that will lead directly to an understanding of the Heaven's Gate tragedy. After reading the book you will be in a better position to judge: Is this episode the logical extension of a century of UFO sightings, or is it better understood as a cult religion, or a cyberspace psychosis? *UFOs and Alien Contact* extracts the messages that can be gleaned from a century of people who see strange things in the skies. But first we must be completely honest with our readers about where we stand on the possibility of UFOs and alien contact.

Do You Believe in UFOs?

Consider the following imaginary encounter:

"Professor Robert Bartholomew?"

"Yes. How can I help you?"

"My name is Claire Martin. I live near Sydney. I've sought you out because I understand that you study people who have had encounters with UFOs. Is this a convenient time to talk?"

"Yes, it is. Have you had an encounter with a UFO?"

"Yes, I have. But first tell me, do you believe that aliens sometimes contact humans?"

"Well, Claire, that's a tough question. I would be lying to you if I said I think we have been contacted. I simply don't know. I do think it's an important topic for serious study, and I consider myself open-minded and genuinely willing to listen to people's claims. I think it *is* possible. The universe is an awfully big place, and it appears to have millions upon millions of galaxies like our own—and that could translate into billions of planets. It would not surprise me if the universe is teeming with life.

"I really do hope that we've been contacted, Claire. I must admit that when I'm alone in the Australian outback and gaze up at the stars on a pitch-black night, the thought of alien contact sends chills up my spine. But just when I almost believe it's true, a little voice inside my head—my scientist half—spoils the excitement by asking some nagging questions: Why has there never been any unambiguous physical evidence? Why is it that most of the UFO photos I've seen either look too good—as if the aliens were posing—or seem to be just a blur of light? And why do they always seem to land in some farmer's field?

"So to answer your question, Claire, I'm not sure, but as a scientist I try to be a bit like Mr. Spock on 'Star Trek.' I try to suppress my emotional side and examine the evidence in a logical, systematic fashion. Otherwise, we can throw science books out the window. If all scientists went on gut feelings, we would be living in the Dark Ages again. Remember, in the nineteenth century, a lot of famous scientists believed in the existence of witches and fairies. So far I have examined a lot of interesting, even compelling, cases, but nothing so clear-cut as to represent obvious proof. As a scientist, I have to ignore what my heart says and go on the evidence."

"But Professor Bartholomew," Claire objected, "there are so many unexplained cases. Aren't you being somewhat arrogant and close-minded to dismiss them all?"

"Claire, you have to realize that there are thousands of reports worldwide every year. It's just not possible for any one person to be familiar with all of them. Some UFO investigators have spent years examining a single case. What I'm looking for is the broad picture. Remember, in the nineteenth century alone there were tens of thousands of fairy sightings and contact claims. So it is important to keep things in historical perspective and not get too carried away by our emotions. Before we discuss this further I'd like to introduce you to a colleague from the United States, George

Howard, who is spending a sabbatical in Australia. George is a psychologist with an interest in UFO percipients—people who claim to have had contact with aliens. I'd like to ask him to join us, if you don't mind."

Claire nods her acquiescence, and Bob uses the intercom to invite his colleague in the next office to join them. George quickly arrives.

"George, this is Claire Martin. She tells me she has had an experience with a UFO. I've briefly summarized my beliefs about aliens, and I'd like you to share your perspective on this topic also. Then, I think, we'll be in a position to hear her story."

"Okay, Bob," George begins. "To this point in time I've led an extremely boring life. I've never been contacted by aliens, nor (for that matter) have I ever been contacted by God! Every experience in my life seems to me to have had a natural or an ordinary explanation. So while I now study the possibility of the existence of God and of alien visitors, honesty demands that I tell you that my experience in life strongly suggests that there are natural explanations for everything that has happened to me."

"Professor Howard," Claire asked, "since you've had no experience with UFOs or aliens, does that mean you don't believe in them?"

"Absolutely not, Claire. A parallel argument would be that since I have had no supernatural or religious experience I therefore believe there is no God. That represents a flawed inference that I would never draw. Rather, if you are looking for evidence of the existence of God (or aliens), my life and experiences simply represent a bad place to look. At this point in time, my life and experiences simply have nothing to say on that topic. If God wants me to believe in Him more concretely, He will simply have to call to me a bit more forcefully. Similarly, if aliens want me to believe in them, then they'll have to first get in touch with me. So far neither gods nor aliens have seen fit to attract my attention to themselves, but that poses no particular problem to me.

"However, there are a lot of people in my position (people with no experience of God or aliens) who have the pomposity to think that their lack of contact proves the nonexistence of God or aliens. In my judgment, that position represents a flawed logic and bad science. So when someone asks if I believe in God or in aliens, I give the same answer: 'I have no idea!' My experiences in life do not furnish good ground for either belief or disbelief in God or aliens. And Claire, that's precisely why I talk to theists and UFO contactees. I'd like to examine someone else's experiences that might have something important to say about the existence (or lack thereof) of God or aliens."

Claire looked suspiciously at Professor Howard and then asked slowly, "Are you saying that you don't care whether or not God or aliens exist?"

George laughed nervously before continuing. "No, Claire, I care very deeply about the existence of God and aliens. That's precisely why I spend so much time conversing with people like you. Think about it. Suppose we found some incontrovertible proof that there was or was not a God. How could that knowledge leave any of us unmoved? Similarly, as a citizen of this planet, I would be affected by proof that we humans either are or are not the only intelligent life in this otherwise cold and lonely universe.

"But when I'm in my role as a psychologist, my hopes and fears function slightly differently. For example, psychologically speaking, your experience with aliens becomes much less interesting to me if we find proof of the existence of your aliens. Then your experiences would represent a simple report of what happened to you—it would be a lot like telling me what you ate for breakfast. Who cares? Such reports have no particular psychological interest, if they actually occurred. Reports of alien contact have psychological importance only if there are no aliens. In this case, humans would have created an experience for themselves. Why would people do this? How could they bring this about psychologically? What is the impact of this new belief on the quality of their lives? These are the sorts of questions that grab a psychologist's attention. Please don't take this personally, Claire, but if we obtain rock-solid proof of the existence of your aliens, as a psychologist I lose interest in you and your experience very quickly—because you're just reporting what happened to you! That's pretty ordinary stuff. In that case, Claire, both as a psychologist and as a citizen of the universe, I'd like to talk with the aliens—not with you. Can you blame me?"

Claire laughed and replied, "Not really! Well, at least I now know where both of you stand on alien contact. So I'll tell you my story. My experience with aliens began one night two months ago as I was driving from Sydney to Murray Bridge . . ."

Note

1. Michelle Locke, *South Bend Tribune,* March 31, 1997, p. 1.

Part I

Strange Things Seen in the Sky

Thousands of people have seen things in the sky that they took to be alien spacecraft. These UFO sightings did not suddenly appear overnight. Rather, they are logical extensions of a social phenomenon that has been emerging for more than one hundred years—our tendency to see strange things in the sky.

1

Wishful Thinking: The Great American Airship Mania of 1896–97

> Let us hope that the advent of a successful flying machine . . . will bring nothing but good into the world; that it shall abridge distance, make all parts of the globe accessible, bring men into closer relation with each other, advance civilization, and hasten the promised era in which there shall be nothing but peace and good-will among all men.
>
> —Octave Chanute[1]

During the last decade of the nineteenth century, a remarkable social delusion swept across the United States. Amid rumors that an American inventor had perfected the world's first heavier-than-air flying machine, "airship fever" gripped the country as tens of thousands of citizens reported seeing a nonexistent airship. It was typically described as cigar-shaped, having wings or propellers and an attached undercarriage, resembling a crude, smaller version of a modern blimp. The vessel was usually described as having a powerful headlight and giant fans or wings protruding from both sides. Some witnesses claimed that the wings slowly flapped up and down in a birdlike motion.

The airship sightings took place between November 17, 1896,

and mid-May 1897, during which time it was seen in most states. During the 1890s, Americans were enchanted by literature on science and invention, which had become something of a national obsession. This was "an age that was in love with the great wonders of science."[2] The sightings occurred during a period of great social and technological change that fostered the widespread belief that almost any invention was possible. The second half of the nineteenth century was marked by a series of revolutionary inventions that would permanently alter people's lifestyles. These included the telephone (1876), gramophone (1877), filament lamp (1879), motor car (1884), steam turbine (1884), diesel engine (1893), X-rays (1895), and radio (1896), to name a few. Of particular in-

This illustration of how the airship reflected the hope of rapid technological advancement appeared on the front page of the Denver, Colorado, newspaper the *Rocky Mountain News*, May 9, 1897.

terest was the age-old dream of heavier-than-air flight, for during this period "magazines devoted to science and engineering vied with Jules Verne's *Robur the Conquerer* and other fictional publications to describe the flier which would soon succeed."[3] The voluminous literature on aviation "fed the public a steady diet of aeronautical speculation and news to prime people for the day when the riddle of aerial navigation finally would receive a solution."[4] This social climate fostered an exaggerated optimism in the belief that the perfection of the world's first heavier-than-air flying machine was imminent.

In terms of historical context, however, nineteenth-century science lacked the technological sophistication to navigate heavier-than-air machines.[5] In practical terms, this technology was several years away, and when it was invented, it was a very modest achievement by modern standards. The first recorded piloted self-powered flights of Orville and Wilbur Wright at Kitty Hawk, North Carolina, did not occur until December 17, 1903, and consisted of four brief "hops" totaling just ninety-seven seconds. While an array of crude prototypes was developed during this period, they held little practical value. Aerial navigation over the next decade was a dangerous occupation, as a sudden wind gust could easily bring down the fragile, clumsy airplanes of the era, and night flying was tantamount to suicide. Despite heavy press coverage of the numerous flight trials during this time, most were abysmal failures. Albert and Gaston Tissandier's electric motor-driven dirigible of 1883 and 1884 in France was hailed as successful, yet it was unable to maintain itself even against a current of wind.[6] Eminent British aviation historian Charles H. Gibbs-Smith, a specialist in aeronautical flight before 1910, is emphatic in his view that the airships sighted during 1896 and 1897 were not feasible.

> I can say with certainty that the only airborne vehicles, carrying passengers, which could possibly have been seen anywhere in North America . . . were free-flying spherical balloons, and it is highly unlikely for these to be mistaken for anything else. No form of dirigible . . . or heavier-than-air flying machine was flying—or indeed could fly—at this time.[7]

During the 1880s and 1890s, numerous backyard tinkerers in America and Europe claimed to be perfecting the first practical airship, and they were typically afforded hero or adventurer status, their exploits glorified in the press and by science-fiction writers. There was intense competition to be the first to patent such a vessel, resulting in a flurry of submissions to the Washington, D.C., patent office, and a shroud of secrecy prevailed, as many inventors withheld vital data on their patents and experimental craft.[8] This veil of mystery surrounding the state of aerial development further fostered public belief that a practical airship had been developed.

> In the late 1890s many people in the United States obtained patents for proposed airships. Most people believed someone would soon invent a flying machine, and many wanted to capitalize on the fame and fortune that would certainly come to the first person to launch an American into the skies. As soon as someone had a glimmer of an airship design, he immediately applied for a patent. These would-be inventors constantly worried over possible theft or plagiarism . . . [and] most people kept their patents secret. Given this atmosphere and the numerous European and American experiments with flight, it is not surprising that secret inventor stories so captured the public imagination and seemed such a logical explanation for the airship mystery.[9]

It was within this context that a telegram appeared in the *Sacramento Evening Bee* of Tuesday, November 17, 1896, in which a New York entrepreneur claimed that he would pilot his newly invented airship to California, which he vowed to reach within two days. That very evening the first recorded sightings of the cigar-shaped airship occurred as hundreds of Sacramento residents reported seeing it.[10] The incident took place between six and seven P.M. as a brilliant bobbing light was seen on the eastern horizon, drifting to the southwest, and it caused a sensation across California. As word of the spectacle spread rapidly throughout Sacramento, residents on sidewalks began gazing skyward. At one point the glittering light appeared to descend near the distant housetops, and people maintained they heard faint voices warning: "Lift her up quick! You are making directly for that steeple!"[11] A group of electric railway workers reported that while passing near East Park, music and human voices seemed to emanate from the sky.[12] Railcar operator R. L. Lowry described the craft "as an oblong mass, propelled by fanlike wheels operated by four men, who worked as if on bicycles."[13]

The popular folk theory that the first practical airship had been perfected and was being secretly tested by a local inventor on the West coast under cover of darkness gained credence in the intense press debate that followed. Some newspapers treated the Sacramento sighting as due to overactive imaginations or a hoax,[14] while others described the incident as plausible or factual.[15] One press account aptly summed up the conflicting public mood: "What is probably one of the greatest hoaxes that has ever been sprung on any community has been started in this city, and yet . . . it is hard to account for the evident sincerity of those who claim they saw the machine and heard the voices."[16]

In the days following the sensational Sacramento sighting, hun-

An eyewitness sketch of an airship sighted over Sacramento, California on the evening of November 17, 1896.

Sketch of an airship reported by scores of people as it hovered over St. Mary's College in Oakland, California near dusk on November 21, 1896. The picture appeared the next day in the *San Francisco Call*.

dreds of descriptions of the airship appeared in the California press as the vessel's existence became widely perceived as real and was reported as such. Newspaper coverage in the San Francisco *Call* typifies this transition from possibility to probability. On November 18, it reported that people saw "what appeared to them to be . . . an electric arc lamp." On the nineteenth, there was discussion of "the reported appearance of an airship." The November 21 edition states that "scores of residents . . . are . . . convinced that it is an airship . . . making nightly trial trips through the surrounding heavens." By November 22, a journalist writes that "someone must be operating an airship in this portion of the State." On the twenty-third, in the wake of continued sightings, the following headline appeared: "Exclusive Account of the Greatest Invention of the Age Is Now Corroborated by Thousands."

Sightings were so massive and widespread that one press source described them as "thick as geese,"[17] while another journalist quipped: "The man who has not an airship in his backyard in these days is poor indeed . . . [and] has left California ashamed of himself."[18] The deluge began two days after the initial sighting when, on Thursday, November 19, the mysterious light of a possible airship was seen near Eureka, California.[19] By Friday afternoon the airship was spotted over an orchard near Tulare.[20] That evening numerous Sacramento residents again observed what appeared to be a light "attached to some aircraft" pass over the city

Another sketch of the majestic, birdlike airship reported by thousands of residents in Oakland, San Francisco, and Sacramento during late November 1896. Source: *San Francisco Call*, November 23, 1896, page 1.

Blowup of a sketch of an airship seen near the state capitol in Sacramento during late November 1896. Source: *San Francisco Call,* November 29, 1896, page 1.

at a distance,[21] while in Oakland scores of people reported seeing the airship, and some claimed to discern huge fanlike propellers, while others said they saw giant wings attached to each side.[22] On

November 22 between 5 and 6 P.M., hundreds of Sacramento residents watched what they thought was an airship with a brilliant arc lamp pass to the southwest.[23]

During the last week of November and the first week of December it was reported in dozens of California communities, including Red Bluff,[24] Riverside,[25] Antioch,[26] Chico,[27] Visalia,[28] Hanford,[29] Ferndale,[30] Box Springs,[31] Salinas,[32] Maxwell,[33] Tulare,[34] Merced,[35] Fresno,[36] and Pennington[37] to name just a few. There were scattered sightings in the adjacent states of Oregon,[38] Washington,[39] Nevada,[40] and Arizona[41] during the episode, although they

Artist's rendition of the airship passing near the dome of the state capitol building in Sacramento, California during late November 1896. It appeared on the front page of the *San Francisco Call*, November 29, 1896.

received minor press coverage. The wave was almost exclusively a California phenomenon, where widespread sightings continued until dramatically declining by mid-December, with the exception of a few intermittent cases from around the state.

An interesting feature of the California episode were several reports of close encounters with airship pilots or crew. Several days after the California sightings began, William Jordan claimed that while deer hunting in the mountains near Bolinas Bay the previous August, he had stumbled upon several men working on a nearly completed airship and was sworn to secrecy.[42] On November 25, 1896, two men riding on horseback near Lodi said they encountered what appeared to be three Martians, each about seven feet tall with slender builds, hairless faces, and huge feet. Each used a nozzle attached to a bag to breathe. As they floated through the atmosphere their feet touched the ground every fifteen feet before retreating into an "immense airship," which flew off. The

The *New York Morning Journal* of Sunday, November 28, 1896, published this illustration of "The Great California Airship" based on witness descriptions.

vessel "was pointed at both ends," had a large steering rudder, and "expanded and contracted with a muscular motion."[43] The next day, a San Jose electrician, John A. Horen, told journalists that he was approached by the airship inventor, who took him on horseback to a secluded spot where Horen installed his newly perfected sparking apparatus to the airship's motor. Horen said that the grateful inventor rewarded him with a three-day ride to Hawaii and back on the airship.[44] On November 29, Joel Flynn of Barry Creek reported that he too was given a ride on the ship after the inventor landed near his farm.[45] Fishermen Giuseppe Valinziano and Luigi Valdivia claimed that early on the morning of December 2, an airship landed in the ocean near their boat some fifteen miles north of Pacific Grove, and they were allowed to examine the ship from afar.[46] The following night sailor William Gordon said he was given a ride on an airship near San Luis Obispo by a pilot who spoke Spanish to his lone female companion.[47] Finally, James Lewis said he was taken for a ride in the vessel near San Diego, in which he visited heaven.[48]

1897: The Sightings Rekindle Nationwide

Starting with a trickle of reports in mid-January 1897 and climaxing during April before petering out in May, speculative stories about the possible existence of an airship and inventors, in addition to reports of other sightings, appeared in almost every state. Most of the airship sightings closely paralleled popular literature of early heavier-than-air flight attempts. An examination of over one thousand sighting reports shows that whenever specific airship descriptions were given, beyond ambiguous nocturnal aerial lights, eyewitness accounts vacillated between two craft types. One was a large oblong or egg-shaped main structure having two winglike appendages resembling those of a bird. The second type also consisted of a large central portion but sported propellers or fanlike wheels. Both types were said to possess powerful searchlights and some form of motor-driven propulsion system, often having a carriage suspended beneath the main structure.

Press sensationalism appears to have played a major role in

creating and perpetuating the hysterical social climate, first in California and later across the United States. Sensationalistic yellow journalism typified the period just prior to and encompassing the sightings, as it was not unusual for newspapers to publish highly speculative or even fabricated stories in attempts to secure wider readership, especially on slow news days.[49] Amid intense public interest in airship development, newspaper editors published a barrage of articles speculating as to whether someone had invented the world's first practical airship. Publisher William Randolph Hearst noted this in an editorial attacking such tactics:

> "Fake journalism" has a good deal to answer for, but we do not recall a more discernible exploit in that line than the persistent

Walter McCann claims to have used a box camera to take this photo of an airship passing over Chicago during April 1897. In reprinting the photo, many newspapers failed to note that the original object in the photo was very vague and the "airship" had to be enhanced by a sketch artist.

> attempt to make the public believe that the air in this vicinity is populated with airships. It has been manifest for weeks that the whole airship story is pure myth.[50]

Other editors attacked the initial sensationalism of the airship rumors and sightings by portions of the California press.[51] One editor noted that the California press was notorious for propagating "the fake," which "at its best is a lie well told; that is, a piece of pure fiction dressed up with an air of probability and presented as truth."[52] It would be a mistake, however, to conclude that the airship wave was a hoax. While yellow journalism was instrumental in propagating the episode, witnesses were usually seeing something (e.g., stars, planets).

Within this context of newspaper saturation and public enchantment with aeronautics, and in conjunction with this new definition of plausible reality, past and concurrent events, objects and circumstances were reinterpreted relative to the newly ascribed meaning. On numerous occasions, even ambiguous noises or voices in remote areas were attributed to the airship's engine or occupants.[53] The following account is typical:

> Mr. Johnson, foreman of the Haggin ranch, in company with another gentleman, was driving across the bare plains adjacent to the city last Tuesday night, when they plainly heard a merry chorus of human voices. The thing was uncanny and unreal. They were entirely alone and on all sides stretched bare fields without a brush or fence, no human being was visible, . . . and yet the merry chorus rang out distinct, but faint. They stopped their team and listened and looked, saw the clear bright light high over their heads, but did not dream that . . . above them human beings were floating.[54]

Several newspaper editors and public figures reinforced the airship's plausibility by speculating about the inventor's identity. A typical aeronautical inventor profile portrayed a fiercely independent, wealthy eccentric. A Nebraska newspaper reported that local man Clinton Case was the presumed inventor as he was known to have possessed complicated blueprints for aerial navigation.[55] Speculation also turned to John Preast, an educated recluse residing on the outskirts of Omaha.[56] As further confirming evidence, the press reported: "The two times in the past week that the [airship] light has been seen at Omaha it disappeared near Preast's home." In Montana it was said to be Albert Zoske.[57] In Savannah, Ohio, the inventor was identified as a wealthy genius,[58] while in western Missouri suspicion fell on G. D. Schultz, "a retired capitalist of decidedly sedentary habits."[59] Perhaps the most scrutinized individual was California dentist E. H. Benjamin.[60]

> This gentleman is six feet in height, about forty years of age, and as far as his mysterious habits are concerned [Mr.] Keiser said last night: "We have had him in the house for two years and don't know any more about him than on the day he came in. He goes away every little while on trips to Oroville, Sacramento and Stockton, sometimes staying a few days, sometimes a month. He has plenty of means and fills his time when at his room experimenting with various metals, principally aluminum and sheet copper.
>
> "He is a dentist by profession, I think. I know he has friends and one relative in Oroville who are experimenting on some invention or other, but what it is I don't know. He has told me once or twice that attorney Collins does his law business for him, and I have often wondered what law business a dentist in a small way would be likely to have."
>
> "Dr." Benjamin's name is not in the directory, nor in the list of dentists in the city. Nobody could be found last night who had ever heard of him practicing his profession. His room contains very little to show what his real business is. There are a few drawings and charts scattered around bearing trigonometrical figures, two very ancient teeth on the mantle shelf and a litter of aluminum and copper shavings all over the carpet.
>
> According to Keiser's statements of his late movements, he was in Sacramento twice last week, has been out very late at night during the last month and has not been home more than a few hours in the last two days—a record that fits in seemingly with the stories of the airship's movements. Up to two o'clock this morning Benjamin had not returned to his room, and the flying machine was at latest reports being steered by its proprietor over localities several miles away from Ellis Street.[61]

Dozens of stories were reported by citizens who had seen something unusual in the sky in the weeks prior to the first publicized sightings and who were now reinterpreting this activity as originating from the airship.[62] One newspaper reported an account of a woman in Oakland, California, who had seen "a strange looking object in the sky" six weeks earlier. As it had "a powerful headlight" the newspaper concurred that an airship was the most likely explanation.[63] The night prior to the first publicized sighting over Sacramento, Mr. and Mrs. George Plummer of Alameda, California, spotted an apparent fire balloon.[64] In light of the airship publicity, however, George Plummer believed it was an airship.[65]

The rationalistic subculture of scientism fostered a prevalent view that witness reports were due to irrationality or mental disturbance, for the consensus among scientists was that "mob" behavior was abnormal, a view that remains true among a few influential collective behavior theorists in more recent times.[66] Witnesses were believed to have succumbed to instinctive, regressive, irrational thinking. The airship sightings were typically described as a "craze," spreading like a disease, reflecting French psychologist Gustave LeBon's popular notion of crowd pathology.[67] Humans under "the herd" influence were believed to degenerate and regress to primitive, illogical thought patterns. Irrationality was widely viewed within a contagious-disease model. Thus, the *San Francisco Examiner* blamed newspaper sensationalism for trying to "infect its readers with a silly craze." This belief, espoused by both popular writers and social scientists, held that mass behavior resulted from an abnormal stimulus, and it was deemed impossible for reasonable people to view anomalies such as flying machines. If witnesses were of good repute or education, it was assumed that substances such as alcohol had deluded their thinking. It is within this context that *delirium tremens*[68] was implicated in sightings by several Hastings, Nebraska, residents who were described as having a "bad case of 'em,"[69] while in Elko, Nevada, witnesses were said to "have 'em in a mild form."[70] In Omaha, Nebraska, sightings were attributed to the "wrong kind o' booze,"[71] and in response to a prominent citizen's sighting in Topeka, Kansas, a reporter inquired as to his "brand of soothing syrup."[72] In Kearney, Nebraska, a jailer wrote a witness-ridiculing poem, attributing reports to alcoholic visions,[73] while the *St. Louis Post-Dispatch* of April 12, 1897, printed a front-page airship cartoon depicting an insect viewed through empty wine and liquor bottles.

To document the thousands of observations from nearly every state could easily fill several hundred pages. In order to provide a flavor of the airship reports as they spread across the United States, we will document sighting waves in five representative states: Wisconsin, Michigan, Kentucky, Indiana, and Minnesota.

The Airship in Wisconsin

With the exception of one report in 1896, all of the Wisconsin sightings were confined to late March and April of 1897. The first report occurred in Milwaukee on Sunday afternoon, December 6, 1896, as hundreds of residents were greatly excited after spotting what appeared to be a flying machine high above the bay. The incident began when local millionaire Herman Nunnemacher was sitting in his room at the Pfister Hotel and saw an object in the sky. Grabbing a field glass, he saw not only that it appeared to be an airship, but also that there seemed "to be a man working the wings." He

A skeptical view of airships taken by a cartoonist. This picture shows residents viewing the airship through empty alcohol bottles. It appeared on page 1 of the *St. Louis Post-Dispatch*, April 12, 1897, after a spate of sightings in the state.

Cartoonist's illustration of a drunk seeing airships. Source: *St. Louis Post-Dispatch*, April 18, 1897, page 1.

dashed down to the lobby, exclaiming, "It is a flying machine!"[74] This aroused considerable excitement as more and more people saw it. However, it was later determined that the object was an experimental kite that the army was testing.[75]

The first sighting of 1897 was recorded on April 8 at 9 P.M. by "a number of reliable people" in the village of Lake Mills, including well-known baseball player Lynn Mills.[76] It carried "a great red light, moving up and down as if on wings" as it traveled westward before disappearing behind the woods on the western shore of Rock Lake.[77] At 10 P.M. about fifty residents in Wausaw claimed to see an illuminated aerial craft pass over the city and head northwest. "A dim outline of it could be seen which appeared to be shaped like an egg. The main talk of the city today is about the airship."[78] The next night about twelve people in Kenosha saw a greenish light in the clear skies and believed it to be the airship.[79] It was also seen moving westward by citizens in Oshkosh at 8:30 P.M. John C. Thompson said that he could plainly see the outline of the flying machine—"the forward portion being cigar-shaped and the rear part square or box-shaped."[80]

On the night of April 10, an airship was spotted near Marshfield just after sunset as hundreds of residents poured onto the streets. When viewed with binoculars, it appeared to be cone-shaped with a powerful headlight.[81] It was also seen in Manitowoc.[82] At about 10 P.M., the following account was recorded in Green Bay of an object that was viewed for thirty minutes:

> Residents of this city are intensely excited over the appearance, to-night, of what is supposed to be the airship which has been seen near Chicago and elsewhere. Many prominent people of the city saw it distinctly, among them being attorney H. G. Fairchild, clerk E. J. Carroll of the Hotel Straubel, and many other citizens whose veracity is beyond question. It was first seen high up in the heavens, the light shown being of a reddish color, and larger than a star. . . .
>
> News of its appearance spread rapidly over the city. . . . [Several people using night glasses] . . . claimed that a large cigar-shaped body could be seen projecting back out of the large light, which was on the forward end of the machine.[83]

Some press accounts openly ridiculed the Green Bay sightings on the grounds that it had all been a practical joke caused by a twelve-foot-high fire balloon made of tissue paper with a rod across the bottom from which hung two Chinese lanterns. Its remains were later found in the barnyard of Fred Reschke.[84]

The airship was also observed by several people at Fond du Lac between 10 P.M. on the tenth and 3 P.M. on the eleventh, and some observers claimed to see the guy ropes on the vessel.[85] One press account was highly skeptical, noting that "their visions were so acute that they clearly distinguished the stern light which was green, from the fore light which was red."[86] At about midnight on the tenth it was seen by Racine resident Silas Bilderback, who saw a variety of colored lights—red, blue, yellow—"attached to some apparatus or machine," of which only a dim outline could be seen. He also claimed to hear what sounded like faint voices "uttered in authoritative and commanding tones, as of a captain giving orders to sailors," although he could not discern what they were saying. The object slowly faded off to the northwest.[87] The airship was also spotted on the evening of April 11 in Appleton,[88] and on both the eleventh[89] and twelfth[90] in Kenosha.

The airship hysteria peaked between April 11 and 12, as it was appearing everywhere at once. The following reports illustrate the scale of the sightings:

Ripon, Wis., April 12—Claim is made that fully one-twentieth of Ripon's entire population saw the now celebrated airship last night . . .

Eau Claire, Wis., April 12—About 150 persons were assembled at the Omaha depot about midnight last night by a report received there from Nerrillan that the airship was coming. The telegraph operator and others saw it through field glasses and vividly described it to the crowd, several of whom saw it also. The strange visitor caused considerable excitement.

Rio, Wis., April 12—The airship was seen passing over this place at 8:45 last evening. Several persons saw a white and red light apparently about three hundred feet above the earth, moving swiftly in a northwesterly direction.

West Superior, Wis., April 12—The airship is reported to have been seen here, circling about the head of the lakes.

Darlington, Wis., April 12—The airship was seen passing over west of here this evening. It appeared to be a large, bright light and moved off in a northwesterly direction.

Madison, Wis., April 12—A great many Madison persons are confident that they saw the "airship" last night.

Lodi, Wis., April 12—James Wilson and many others say they saw the airship here to-night between 10:20 and 11 o'clock. It seemed quite low and was passing from a southeasterly to a northeasterly direction.[91]

The following account captures the intense excitement during a mass sighting near Milwaukee on the eleventh:

Every adult citizen of Milwaukee . . . swept the "infinite meadow of heaven" last night in search for the mysterious airship. . . .

"Have you seen the airship!" took the place of the conventional "Good evening," when two friends met upon the street, and they immediately took a look . . . in hopes of discovering the aerial navigator. . . . People coming out of the churches lost the inspiration of the prayer and the praise service as they sought out the invention of the man amid the handiwork of the Creator in space. Audiences coming from the theaters halted upon the street to cast aloft a searching glance, and they discussed the craze that is sweeping over the country.[92]

The reports rapidly declined and ceased altogether by the end of the month. On the night of the thirteenth the vessel was seen at Portage at about 8 P.M.,[93] and by hundreds in Racine on the fourteenth where some of the most enthusiastic declared they could see the outline of the mysterious ship, and some even went so far as to state that they could hear voices.[94] It was also seen on the night of the eighteenth near Beloit.[95]

As the sightings continued, many newspapers became increasingly incredulous. The *Wisconsin State Journal* remarked that "every bird that essays the zenith these days incurs the imputation of being an airship."[96] Many papers equated the airship with the sea serpent sightings during the "silly season."[97] The *Evening Wisconsin* suggested two possible explanations: "One is that all the air is full of airships. The other is that a good many people are lying." It concluded by saying there was much evidence "in favor of the latter."[98] When the ship was seen at Lancaster on Saturday night, April 10, one press report proclaimed, "Fake airship at Lancaster," suggesting that it was another tissue balloon.[99]

Perhaps the most sensational report was from the town of Norway, where there was "great excitement" after a small boy swore that he saw the ship alight on the John Johnson farm, where its occupants took water aboard that was poured into the vessel's boiler. After telling the story, the boy "was taken down cellar and spanked by his mother."[100] There were other reports of contact with the pilots and their crew at remote sites near Rice Lake on April 12,[101] while at Potosi two airship occupants were seen sitting on the rail track smoking cigarettes before jumping into the craft and flying off after being startled by local resident John MacGuire.[102] Near the end of the episode, a woman rushed into the offices of a local newspaper in Racine in a state of great excitement and holding a wooden arrow that she said she found in the street. On the end was attached a note: "Airship S & G, dropped from a distance of two miles in the air." While her faith that it had fallen from an airship could not be shaken, an investigation revealed that it was a publicity stunt by the firm of Silber and Griswold.[103]

Michigan

The episode of phantom airship sightings in Michigan occurred between April and May of 1897 following a flurry of sightings in nearby Iowa and Missouri.[104] During the last week of March there were several reports of mysterious aerial lights in Michigan, but these were interpreted as either a strange "meteor" that was seen for an hour in Holland[105] or "ghost lights" on Boughner and Mills Lakes near the village of Shearer, which resulted in several inhabitants' leaving the vicinity due to the "ghost scare."[106] A similar episode was reported in the bay off Caseville, where a fluttering light was thought to be ghosts from the steamer Oconte, which sank near Big Charity Island several years earlier.[107] A mysterious nocturnal light seen by Rodney Heddon near his farm in Byron was attributed to the ghost of his deceased father.[108]

The first Michigan airship sighting took place in the village of Alma on Saturday evening, April 10, in the western sky.[109] At Benton Harbor at 7:45 P.M. on the following night it was watched for fifteen minutes flying high above Lake Michigan by a group of residents on Morton Hill, before it faded off to the northwest.[110] The vessel was described as having red, green, and blue flickering lights, and was also seen at St. Joseph at about the same time.[111] An hour later several hundred people saw the aerial "machine" floating above Black Lake near Holland, including prominent citizens Dr. J. D. Wetmore and Mr. C. L. King, manager of the large King Basket Factory.[112] Near Niles, Michigan, two men saw bright aerial lights during the evening, of what may have been the airship,[113] while at 10 P.M. it was seen by three Mendon residents.[114] On April 12, some twenty "reputable citizens" in Battle Creek claimed to watch the vessel pass two miles west of the city at 8:55 P.M. "Sparks flew forth and the ship began to slowly settle to within about half a mile from the earth."[115] It was twenty-five to thirty feet long and hovered near the ground a few moments, when a buzzing noise was heard. "Again the sparks flew out as if from an emery wheel and the machine began to rise slowly . . . [and] the lights went out."[116] Some witnesses even claimed they could discern faint voices coming from the "craft."[117] The object disappeared to the southwest.[118] When the brilliantly illuminated airship was spotted by several residents of Kalamazoo on the same evening, it was said to be moving about fifty miles per hour as it passed northwesterly. The editor of the *Kalamazoo Gazette*, Andrew J. Shakespeare, also observed it.[119] The most sensational report of the evening was from the town of Pavillion, where residents George W. Somers and William Chadburn saw an illuminated object explode in the air, leading them to assume that the airship had blown up. Several other residents heard the noise but saw nothing. When part of an electric appliance was found lying on the ground the next morning, it was thought to have come from the airship, as were mysterious tiny fragments of an unknown material found scattered near a barn in the town of Comstock.[120]

On Tuesday night, April 13, the airship mania continued. When a mysterious glow was noticed in the southern sky over Kalamazoo, the cry of airship immediately went up, but the illumination was a reflection from Thomas Moore's barn burning down on South Burdick Street.[121] Meanwhile, George Parks and his wife reported that an airship swooped to within one hundred feet of a field on their Pennfield farm, five miles north of Battle Creek, and claimed that a wheel fell off, embedding itself in the ground. The wheel was three feet in diameter and was put on display at their farm.[122]

As the sightings continued, press editors grew increasingly incredulous as numerous hoaxes came to light, and stories grew more outlandish. A carrier boy for the *Battle Creek Daily Moon* claimed to have found a letter dropped from the vessel.[123] There was a sensation in Pontiac on the evening of the fifteenth as hundreds of persons were certain that the airship had passed about 250 feet above Saginaw Street, but were disgusted upon realizing that enterprising students had hauled lanterns up on the flagpole of the school.[124] On the same evening, hundreds of Lansing residents reported seeing the airship, which was later identified as a toy balloon.[125]

On April 16, a man near Lansing claimed to have accepted a ride in a cigar-shaped airship with large wings and conversed with the "professor" who invented it and said he was flying it across the country.[126] Meanwhile, at Pine Lake, it reportedly alighted and obtained food from William McGiveron.[127]

By mid-April, the airship episode peaked. The following excerpt from the *Saginaw Courier-Herald* gives a flavor as to the widespread nature of the sightings:

> Corroboration of the visit of the flying air-ship to this city [Saginaw] yesterday morning has been received from many sources. . . .
>
> Charlotte, Mich., April 16—The mysterious air ship was seen by many people last night.
>
> Hudson, April 16—This morning's Hudson Gazette contained an account of the passage of the airship over this city . . . last night. It . . . was also seen at Pittsford, Clayton and Cadmus.
>
> Hart, April 16—A large crowd witnessed a strange sight Wednesday night. Something floated over Shelby . . .
>
> Olivet, April 16—The airship was observed here Wednesday night by a large crowd.

A NIGHT SCENE IN ST. LOUIS

A skeptic's humorous interpretation of the airship, comparing local sightings to sea serpent reports. It appeared on page 1 of the *St. Louis Republic*, April 16, 1897.

Battle Creek, April 16—The aerial phenomenon, construed by some to be an airship, was seen by many persons here Wednesday evening.

Middleville, April 16.—This village takes the cake in regard to airships. Several responsible residents claim to have seen two of them Wednesday evening. . . . A car attachment had colored lights and scattered sparks, and what was supposed to be smoke.

Lansing, April 16.—Many citizens of Lansing are willing to swear that they saw the airship last evening.[128]

From this point on, witnesses were mercilessly ridiculed in most press accounts, although sightings continued until early May when they tapered out, with reports in Manistee,[129] Saginaw,[130]

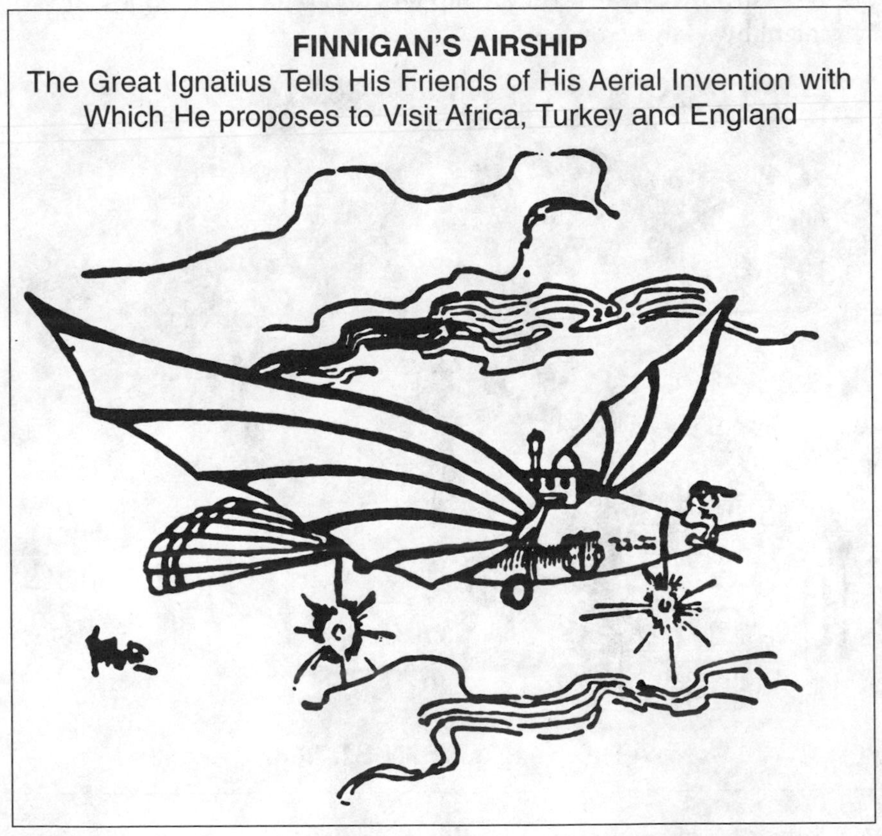

Spoof sketch of the airship published in the *St. Louis Republic*, April 29, 1897, page 9.

Many advertisers jumped on the airship theme in order to sell their products, often humorously. This ad appeared in the *Rocky Mountain Daily News* on April 14, 1897, to pitch the popularity of "News Small Ads."

Davison,[131] Three Rivers,[132] Saline,[133] Grant,[134] Marquette,[135] Marshall,[136] Geneseeville,[137] Sidnaw,[138] Dayton,[139] and Flint.[140] After a report by several people in Wyandotte, it was noted that beer season was open.[141] One journalist quipped that an American had "the same right to see airships that he has to see pink-winged elephants and man-eating cockroaches."[142] Another reporter warned that if the sightings did not abate soon, large numbers of citizens were in danger of getting cricks in their necks. One newspaper reported that "the sea serpent was green with envy over the notoriety being enjoyed just now by its rival the airship."[143] Meanwhile, the *Saginaw Globe* commented that future historians should note "the fact that the airship is always seen on Saturday night, when a large portion of the population is in a proper mood to see such things."[144] One writer told of being pleased by three consecutive days of rain, since during this time "nobody claims to have seen the airship."[145] A press editor sarcastically urged sinners to repent, noting that the Bible predicts the appearance of strange signs and wonders during the Last Days, and that the airship may portend that "the day of judgment draws near."[146]

A humorous incident was recounted near Galesburg, when a hunter came upon a hole which appeared to contain a metal instrument. "Visions of airships and grappling hooks arose before him and he made all speed to town" to relay his finding to the local newspaper office. While the paper reported that an anchor dropped from the airship had made a deep hole, a subsequent investigation revealed "a steel trap in the entrance of a skunk's dwelling place."[147]

Indiana

The Indiana airship mania lasted from early April until mid-May of 1897. The first sighting was recorded on the evening of Friday, April 9, when several "reputable citizens," including deputy postmaster D. A. Gibbons, saw what appeared to be an airship pass to the north of Newport. It was visible for twenty minutes and had a reddish color.[148] At 1 A.M. on the tenth, Mrs. William Marsh of Anderson went to fetch water from an outside hand pump when she was startled by a powerful headlight overhead. She roused her husband and neighbors, and they watched as it appeared to circle around before attaining great height and flying southward. At one point they claimed to hear what sounded like its wings flapping.[149] Meanwhile, at about this time, farmers north of Anderson reported seeing a "crazy star,"[150] and in Lowell, it was seen by the Elliot family.[151]

On the night of the eleventh, it was spotted across the state. The airship light was seen at about 7:30 at Warsaw, swaying in the distance as it traveled to the northwest.[152] At least one hundred residents in New Carlisle claimed to have watched it pass by at 8:30, its lights "distinguished from a dark object far up in the heavens."[153] It had a green light in the front and a red light at the rear.[154] At nine o'clock it reportedly passed over Plymouth,[155] while in LaGrange "great excitement" prevailed after it was observed by numerous people at 9:30 before fading away after forty minutes.[156] It was reported at Elkhart about ten o'clock,[157] and by 11 P.M. several prominent citizens of Logansport saw the airship, including Henry Poit of Porter's Drug Store and Al Anderson of Kraut's Barber Shop. It appeared to have red and green lights. One witness, Charles Knowlton of Lock Mills, claimed that there was a man in the vessel who projected "magic lantern" pictures[158] onto the side of his barn.[159] Meanwhile, on the following night, residents along South 10th Street in Terre Haute were excited by "a powerful revolving searchlight with a dark object behind it."[160] In Danville on the evening of the thirteenth, Green Burris, John Tinder, and Livingstone Rankin claimed not only that it passed overhead, but that they could hear singing and talking coming from the vessel.[161] At about 9 P.M., it flew just a few hundred feet above Michigan City.[162] At the same time, near Brook numerous residents saw the illuminated airship whose wings "flopped slowly" and majestically. Some could even see a propeller that made "a loud whirring noise."[163]

During midafternoon on the fourteenth, several residents in Gas City reported seeing a cigar-shaped airship with broad canvas wings land in a corn field on the John Roush farm, but that it flew off before they were able to reach it. There appeared to be six men on board.[164] Also on the fourteenth, "a strange craft" was seen to pass by Middlefork,[165] and there was a sensation in Valparaiso when the airship was sighted at about eight o'clock. "In less than ten minutes nearly half the population . . . was on the streets and on top of buildings watching its movements." It disappeared after thirty minutes.[166] It was also observed at Princeton at about the same time, where there "was great excitement,"[167] and in the countryside near Frankfort, where it passed over the treetops and was described as "cigar-shaped and rigged with wings or fins."[168] Also on the night of the fourteenth, a vivid encounter was reported near Shelburn by Mr. I. H. Woolsey, T. J. Cushman, and Edward Woods, who were returning from Currysville at about 11:30. They reported that a brilliantly illuminated airship passed overhead about two hundred feet above the ground. It was barrel-shaped with a point in the front and "was bound by heavy bands and had the steering apparatus in the rear."[169]

A sighting by three Fort Wayne residents on the fourteenth, provides insight into the influence of the mass media on airship accounts, making it clear that residents were scanning the skies in hopes of glimpsing the craft.

> Telegrams from various places have told about the sight of this strange light and Fort Wayne people have been on the lookout for it. For several nights telescopes have been directed toward the heavens of the northwest, and at last F. Crocker and R. J. and J. L. Tretheway have been rewarded. . . .
>
> Mr. Crocker, who lives at 56 Barr street, was the first man to see it, and after watching the light for some time, called his wife . . . [and neighbors] . . .
>
> When asked to describe what he saw, Mr. Crocker said: "I had taken a great deal of interest in the stories printed in the newspapers about this star or airship, and was standing at the window of my flat endeavoring to get a glimpse of it. In a short time I was rewarded . . ."
>
> So far as is known no other Fort Wayne people have seen the light, but many are on the lookout for it.[170]

During mid-April there were wild rumors that the airship had alighted for repairs atop Weed Patch Hill in Brown County, after two farmers claimed that they had seen it anchored there. As a result, a number of residents, mainly from Martinsville, became excited and trekked to the hill, only to be disappointed when they could not locate the ship, and locals had no idea what they were talking about.[171]

On April 15 it was sighted by several citizens of Albany,[172] the same day that Mrs. C. Strock of St. Joseph Street in Elkhart said she found a note dropped from the airship in which it was claimed the vessel would pass back over the city on a return trip Friday night. As a result "several parties have been formed here to watch for the return trip of the machine."[173] On the next evening of the sixteenth, over twenty residents of Vincennes saw a "strange body" at great altitude fly over the city.[174] There was pandemonium in Muncie on April 17 as several thousand Saturday-night shoppers were certain that an aerial craft passed near the city low to the ground. It was later revealed to have been four hot-air balloons tied together and attached to lanterns with colored globes which were sent up by two mischievous reporters.[175]

On the night of April 21, several members of the First Spiritual Circle saw the airship as they exited their meeting hall, at which time one member returned to the building and went into a trance. He claimed that the vessel was occupied by two men and a dog.[176] On Saturday evening, April 24, several East Greenfield residents reported that the vessel hovered above the filter at the Greenfield paper mill, and a man was clearly visible and standing in front of a boat-shaped undercarriage.[177]

As was typical of the reports across the country, as the sightings continued, press accounts, which were often positive near the beginning of the episode, grew increasingly skeptical. The editors of the *Indianapolis Journal* remarked that the description of the airship seemed to vary depending as to whether it was "viewed through a common tumbler, a champagne glass, a demi john or a quart bottle."[178] In describing a sighting at Terre Haute, a reporter noted, "They looked through all kinds of glasses . . . field glasses, beer glasses and whiskey glasses in use."[179] Another editor noted that the widespread sightings indicated that either an airship was afloat or "alcoholic visions have become epidemic."[180] One journalist asserted: "If you haven't seen the air ship yet you are behind the time."[181] Another observed that the airship far exceeded the powers of the sea serpent, as "an inland town has the same show as a fishing village on the coast."[182] The editors of the *Evening Republican* expressed displeasure at having "been slighted" since the vessel had not yet been viewed in Columbus, and wondered why the tiny community of New Carlisle should be favored, as it "never did anything to entitle it to any distinction."[183] The *Ligonier Banner* editor sarcastically wrote, "If you want to know anything about the airship that passed over here Saturday night ask Operator Schwab and he will tell you all about it."[184]

Just before the sightings ceased altogether, press accounts became noticeably shorter as a flurry of reports appeared attributing several recent observations to hoax balloons sent aloft by pranksters,[185] and some press accounts were acerbic in their reporting of alleged incidents. For instance, after a sighting near Seymour on May 7, one newspaper headline stated: "Sure it was the air ship."[186] Following another incident, a paper used the rather blunt headline "The Airship Fake."[187] When the vessel was spotted near Angola on April 18, a local paper gave the incident a two-sentence report, beginning with, "Some of our citizens thought they saw an air ship Sunday night."[188] After several Lake Station residents claimed to see the flying machine, a local paper afforded the event a single sentence: "Some of the Lake people have sighted the airship, or claim they have."[189] When it was seen near Rensselaer, the press account began "Of course somebody in Rensselaer had to see the airship."[190] After a mass sighting at Mitchell, an article concluded by noting: "They don't pretend to say that it was an air ship but they do know that it was something unusual."[191]

Some newspapers clearly stoked the embers of the craze, perhaps in hopes of selling copies. The editor of the *Greensburg Review* was furious over a lengthy article about his city that appeared in the *Chicago Chronicle* of April 14th.

> Greensburg, Ind., April 13—The skeptics of this city who have read the accounts of the airship . . . now no longer doubt its reality, since the machine itself was seen here this evening. The airship made its appearance in this county about 6:30 o'clock and was seen by several hundred people. One hundred fifty-six prominent citizens of the city and county are willing to make sworn statements that they saw the strange machine.
>
> The news of the sighting of the airship spread like wildfire, and it is the sole topic of conversation on the streets tonight. . . . Three or four hundred people were immediately on the streets, when, in a few minutes, the strange object made its appearance. . . .
>
> The article goes on to describe the anxiety of Prof. Keeley and our people concerning the clothing worn by the men in the air ship, and closes as follows:
>
> > One disastrous result of the airship's visit came to the famous Greensburg goat. Billy saw the strange thing in the heavens and immediately becoming frantic, commenced to butt the northeast corner of the Reformed Presbyterian Church. Finally he took another despairing look at the heavens. The lights in the airship changed color at that instant, and Billy frothed at the mouth and went against the corner of the church a seventh time,

> when his left horn broke off near its base. He is now under the care of a veterinarian.[192]

The *Greensburg Review* editor condemned the *Chicago Chronicle* for making Greensburg and its inhabitants "appear silly and ridiculous."[193]

Several Indiana residents claimed to have talked with the airship occupants in remote locations at night. The vessel and its three occupants allegedly landed near the Monon depot and alighted in order to make minor repairs to the motor.[194] On the evening of April 17, it reportedly landed near Charles Brown's feed mill near Upland, where a quantity of ground cattle feed was purchased by its lone occupant—a stout man with long flowing whiskers who spoke good English. The man then got into his cab, pressed a button, and the craft rose above the treetops and sailed off.[195] At Hodge's Branch near Rushville Charles Worthington and John Rodabaugh claimed they saw an airship with enormous wings alight, its three occupants taking water aboard before the craft flew off to the northeast.[196] George Haskell, a farmer living just east of Muncie, told that while he was milking his cows at night, an airship landed in his barnyard. "One of the occupants stepped from the car attached to the ship and asked for some milk. After receiving a pail full, the man pulled on a cord and it flew off."[197] In northern Hamilton county the airship reportedly alighted to take on provisions which were paid for with a gold coin.[198] Finally, the airship purportedly landed under cover of darkness near a mine shaft, where two men took on a quantity of coal and conversed with a bystander, before taking off.[199]

The reports continued to decline during the latter part of April until they ceased altogether by mid-May. During this period there were sightings on the twenty-first at Terre Haute,[200] reports by several witnesses, including police officers, at Kokomo[201] and Logansport[202] on the twenty-second, sightings at Cannelton on the twenty-third,[203] Logansport and Greenfield on the twenty-fourth,[204] Logansport again on the twenty-fifth,[205] and Auburn on the twenty-eighth.[206] One of the last sightings was at Seymour on May seventh.[207]

Minnesota

Minnesota was inundated with airship reports during a two-week period in April 1897. The first sighting was in the city of Albert Lea at 11:00 P.M. on Friday, April 8, when a bright object that "seemed to be under perfect control" and that was carrying red and white lights was seen traveling northward.[208] Residents were greatly excited.[209] It was also seen about ten minutes later at Waseca.[210] On April 10, a peculiar square-shaped reddish light was spotted by several Minneapolis residents at about 9:25 P.M. It was estimated to have been half a mile high and nine miles in the distance before disappearing and then reappearing.[211] The vessel was also witnessed by a large number of residents as it again hovered over Albert Lea. Among the observers was ex-mayor Gillrup.[212] It was first seen at about 9 P.M. and was visible for twenty-five minutes before vanishing to the north.[213]

On Sunday the eleventh, it was observed by at least a thousand people in Minneapolis and Minnetonka between 8 P.M. and midnight. R. G. Adams gave a particularly vivid description. He said it was cigar-shaped, eighteen to twenty feet long and had square lights attached to the top and middle portions. "I could distinctly see the vague outlines of the craft,"[214] he reported. An even more sensational description was provided by Stuart Mackroth, an employee of the Flour City National Bank. While riding his bicycle behind the Minnetonka hills on his way to Minneapolis, he said that a boat-shaped flying machine with an array of lights appeared a quarter of a mile overhead. He claimed to be able to discern "men, women and children . . . [who] were moving about as if very busy."[215] Also that evening, a large crowd assembled atop the Commercial Hotel in Anoka when the airship was sighted between 9:30 and 10 P.M.[216] On April 12, the editors of the *Minneapolis Tribune* summed up the public mood:

> "Where there is so much smoke there must be fire." The persistent reports of a sighting of a queer craft sailing about in the sky, apparently under perfect control of some intelligent power, suggest a possibility, that at last the problem of aerial navigation has been solved, and that the world may be astonished with the most wonderful invention of this or any other age .[217]

By April 12, several Duluth residents sat on the rooftops of buildings in the business block with binoculars, refreshments, and cigars, hoping to glimpse the much talked about vessel. Observations were confined to several lights in the distance.[218] On the night of the thirteenth, it was seen near Stillwater, while the outline of the craft was spotted by fifty residents in Rogalton and near Winona.[219] At this point the press grew more skeptical, even blatantly cynical in reporting claims. The *St. Paul Pioneer-Press* described these sightings with the headline "Of Course They Saw It."[220]

On the evening of the fourteenth, thousands of people in Minneapolis were greatly excited, gathering at various points throughout the city in expectation of seeing the airship. One journalist noted that "groups were at every street corner; passengers awaiting electric cars scanned the heavens."[221] At the corner of Nicollet and Washington Avenues about two hundred citizens congregated, while a similar scene was occurring one block over at Hennepin Avenue. Many believed they had seen the vessel, including chief of detectives Schweitzer,[222] although one editor said that they were simply watching Venus "slowly sinking to the horizon."[223] The same paper published a cartoon depicting two intoxicated citizens discussing the airship.[224] Another editor scoffed at the reports, stating that they were "simply the star 'Alpha Orionis,' which has been wandering about the heavens for ten million years" and was now prominent.[225] Yet another editor jokingly warned that witnesses were "wrecking the church standing of more than one . . . truthful citizen."[226] After the night of the fifteenth when the flying machine was observed over Glencoe and Howard Lake,[227] the reports died out completely.

Kentucky

The Kentucky sightings persisted from mid-April to mid-May, and just before they began, at least one resident in Morganfield was holding nightly parties on the roof of his house in expectation of seeing the airship that had been reported in other parts of the country.[228] The first sighting occurred on Monday evening, April 12, near Adairsville, in Robertson County. The airship caused a sensation among the inhabitants when it was spotted at 8:30 P.M. nearly a mile high. It had a bright headlight attached to a steel body twenty-five to thirty feet long that sported wings or propellers and a red lantern on the tail.[229] Many people panicked at the sight and "shouted and prayed as if they thought the millennium was at hand."[230] Early the next morning, two miles south of Louisville, farmer Augustus Rodgers claimed to observe an illuminated oblong-shaped airship traveling about one hundred miles per hour just four hundred feet above the ground. Rodgers called to his wife, and they "saw a form, like that of a man, standing at the front of the ship and directing its course," and the vessel soon disappeared to the southeast.[231] At about the same time, John S. McCollough, who resided near Churchill Downs, reported that a brilliantly lighted airship passed overhead while he was traveling near the city and that a piece of half-burned coal fell from it.[232]

On the evening of April 15, several Russellville residents saw the airship "plainly and distinctly," including Mayor Andrews and prominent dry goods merchant Colonel James McCutchens. The illuminated object sailed out of sight westward.[233] It was also spotted that night by many people in the communities of Todd,[234] Clarksville,[235] and Hopkinsville.[236] The following day, the managers of the Nashville Centennial Exposition used the growing public interest in the airship to their advantage to gain free publicity by claiming that the vessel was real and the owners were under contract to put it on display.[237] On the sixteenth at 8:30 P.M., hundreds of people in Cairo saw the airship pass slowly just above the western horizon.[238] At about this time, Samuel Bunnel of Mercer County made perhaps the most incredulous report when he claimed to have viewed the airship through his telescope and saw that it contained exquisitely garbed, winged angels.[239]

On April 18 scores of people in Bowling Green saw a large moving light in the western sky for about an hour, which was widely assumed to have been the airship.[240] There was "great excitement" in Madisonville on the night of April 20 as "the streets were crowded with people watching the aerial wonder," among them Mayor Holeman A. Worley.[241] On the same evening, it was seen passing over Rich Pond, and well-known merchant H. F. Jordan proclaimed: "I saw the airship and it was a beautiful sight."[242] By April 20, the craze had reached such proportions that newspapers were carrying airship-related advertisements. For instance, one ad read: "The Airship a Certainty—Make this doubly sure by buying one of our choice carpets, and your 'HEIRSHIP' will not be questioned."[243] Another proclaimed that the airship had been seen with two men on board, one of whom dropped a message that urged people to attend a local sale.[244]

On the twenty-first several Louisville policemen and citizens spotted a brilliant aerial light, which many assumed to be a flying machine. Captain John Tully and his entire company of firefighters also witnessed the light upon returning from a fire call. "One of the men called attention to the peculiar sight, and the men at once concluded that it was the air ship," which disappeared to the northwest.[245] At about this time, three men in Berea claimed the airship passed overhead at about 10 P.M.[246] On April 23, numerous residents in Lewisburg were convinced that they saw the craft pass to the southwest: "Its outlines were plainly observed and many good citizens will swear that it was the aerial flyer."[247] One newspaper reported the incident as follows:

> Lewisburg, April 24—A profound sensation was created here last night by the discovery of the lights of an airship moving in a south of west course and at a great height. It was witnessed by a great number of our most reputable citizens. There can be no doubt whatever that it was the airship that is said to have been seen in so many places.[248]

Also on the night of April 24, a Louisville man gave a particularly vivid description of the vessel. Thomas J. Casey stated that he was behind his home at 1237 13th Street when he heard a buzzing sound and saw the cigar-shaped ship about two hundred feet up.[249] He saw the outline of a man standing in the lower rear section: "He looked at me and I waved my hat. Two other men were sitting in the helm."[250] The object rapidly disappeared to the south. Station keeper Thomas O'Neil of the central police station also reported seeing the airship at about the same time.[251] The ship which "carried a very bright light" was again sighted by Clarksville residents on Sunday evening, April 25, flying half a mile high to the southwest.[252]

There were other reports of close encounters with the airship's occupants:

> Tuesday night about 7 o'clock as a family living south of town were sitting at the supper-table, they were suddenly startled by the furious barking of the ever-faithful watchdog, and as is usual with children, they all rushed out to see what had caused the excitement of the canine. They all rushed back pell-mel, head-over-heels, exclaiming: "Jack-o' lantern in the sky, mamma! Jack-o' lantern in the sky!" The wiser heads of the family, after close inspection . . . [described seeing] a large cigar-shaped affair, with immense white wings. It was not very high and the guy ropes and rods could be seen plainly. Three men were visible and they frantically waved their hands as they passed. The machine had a zig-zag course and seemed to be out of working order.
>
> Any further information will be gladly furnished by Miss Katie Barnes, Elkton, Ky.[253]

Meanwhile, on the evening of April 17, three men in Lexington claimed to have met an airship occupant, about forty years of age, who emerged from the vessel with a bucket. After filling it with water from a nearby stream, he declined to answer any questions and sailed off.[254]

Many newspaper editors were skeptical, attributing the observations either to irrationality precipitated by emotional excitement, or to alcohol or opium intake. The editors of the Paducah *Daily News* ridiculed witnesses, referring to them as "rubbernecks" and to the airship as a "queer aerial voyager" and "strange lightening bug."[255] When hometown lawyers Tom Wallace and Jess Scott said they watched the airship fly over Mayfield on April 14, the *Mayfield Mirror* quipped that they must have been viewing the vessel "through a bottle."[256] The *Louisville Courier-Journal* sarcastically suggested that there must be an "aerial flotilla" due to the volume of sightings.[257]

During late April the episode peaked, at which time the claims grew more sensational, and the belief in the flying machine's existence began to rapidly erode. As had occurred in other parts of the country, some Kentucky residents maintained that they found letters dropped from the airship.[258] In Corbin, a businessman who also served as a church deacon claimed to be in possession of a piece of metal that he said had fallen from the airship.[259] By April 30, the sightings had declined dramatically. One of the last observations was recorded on the thirtieth when Gillis Hendricks, a section foreman with the Louisville and Nashville railroad, reported seeing a cone-shaped airship with blue and white signal lights. The account states that "Hendricks' story is laughed at."[260]

The Social Psychology of Airships

While it is tempting to conclude that these witnesses were acting irrationally or exhibiting signs of mental disturbance, the airship sightings are explainable using mainstream theories of social psychology. In examining the episode, we are essentially left with eyewitness testimony, which is notoriously unreliable and subject to error.[261] Further, under ambiguous circumstances, such as looking at the nighttime sky, stars can appear to change color, flicker, and move.[262] A person's mental set or frame of reference has a strong influence on how external events are interpreted and internalized as reality.[263] A classic illustration of this occurred on March 3, 1968, as the Russian *Zond* 4 moon probe plunged into the atmosphere, resulting in the appearance of several "man-made meteors" in the northeastern United States.[264] After witnessing the reentry, one witness told Air Force investigators:

> It appeared to have square-shaped windows along the side that was facing us. It appeared to me that the fuselage was constructed of many pieces of flat sheets of metal-like material with [a] "riveted-together look . . ." The many windows seemed to be lit up from the inside of the fuselage. . . .
>
> When the craft was flying near us, it did seem to travel in a flat trajectory. I toyed with the idea that it even slowed down somewhat, for how else could we observe so much detail in a mere flash across the sky? All three of us agreed that we had seen something other than any planes we had seen or read about from our Earth, or that we had seen a "craft from Outer Space."[265]

Since an observer's mental outlook at the time of the sighting is of key importance, the context of the episode is very significant. The 1896–97 airship sightings occurred amid widespread rumors that a flying machine was on the verge of being perfected. Many Americans believed that such a dramatic achievement was at hand, and their emotions were stoked by speculative and often fabricated newspaper stories. As people began searching the skies for confirmation of the airship-invention stories, they expected to see airships, and did see them. Whereas modern sightings consist almost exclusively of "flying saucers" from outer space, citizens in 1896–97 were predisposed by popular literature of the era to see airships. The overwhelming majority of reports occurred at night and described ambiguous lights viewed at a distance. It is not surprising that given these circumstances, residents interpreted information in ways that were consistent with their view of the world.

Studies on the fallible nature of human perception and the tendency for people in group settings to conform are especially applicable.[266] The human mind does not gather information like a videotape recorder. Humans interpret events as they perceive the world and often come to opposite interpretations of the same event witnessed under nearly identical circumstances, as anyone who has watched a hotly contested sporting event can attest. Perception is sometimes based more on inference than on reality, allowing for interpretations that often differ substantially from what actually exists. Research on autokinetic movement is applicable to such situations, as it concerns problem-solving dynamics.[267] The variance of interpretations from what actually exists is especially noticeable with the perception of ambiguous stimuli or conflicting patterns of information within a group setting, which will result in members developing an increased need to define the situation, depending less on their own judgment for reality validation and more on the judgment of others for reality testing.

> When the stimulus situation lacks objective structure, the effect of the other's judgement is . . . pronounced. . . . In one . . . study of social factors in perception utilizing the autokinetic phenomenon, an individual judged distances of apparent movement first alone and then with two or three other subjects. This unstruc-

> tured situation arouses considerable uncertainty. Even though they were not told to agree and were cautioned against being influenced, the individuals in togetherness situations shifted their judgement toward a common standard or norm of judgement. . . . The influence of various individuals differed, and the emerging common norm for judgement was in various instances above or below the average of individual judgements in the initial session alone.[268]

Research on the "autokinetic effect" is of more specific interest as it has been shown that individual judgments tend to agree in a group setting while observing the common stimulus of a pinpoint of light within a dark environment. This effect is well known among social psychologists and was first demonstrated in 1936.[269] Individuals in situations lacking stable perceptual anchors begin to feel a sense of uneasiness, then anxiety as they have a heightened need to visually define or make sense of the light. In group settings, individuals will attempt to reduce the anxieties created by an uncertain situation.

> A viewer in a completely dark room seeing one pinpoint of light experiences a visual stimulus without its normal attendant visual context. Up, down, back, forward, far and near, exist in relation to other stimuli and when this frame of reference is missing, the light is free to roam in one's perceptual field. It is for this reason that considerable random motion will be experienced by anyone viewing the light.[270]

During highly ambiguous situations, such as people scanning the nighttime skies for an imaginary but plausible airship, "inference can perform the work of perception by filling in missing information in instances where perception is either inefficient or inadequate."[271]

Encounters with Airship Pilots and Crew

An interesting aspect of the airship wave were several dozen encounters involving people who were usually alone in rural areas and claimed to have conversed with the airship pilots or crew. However, unlike modern descriptions of diminutive extraterrestrials emerging from flying saucers, most witnesses described occupants who claimed to be Americans and who had perfected an airship that would revolutionize travel.[272] Pilot-inventors and their crews typically alighted in remote sections of the country in order to make repairs or obtain provisions. In Chillicothe, Missouri, electrician Walter Baker said a stranger woke him at 3:30 A.M. and took him to the nearby airship to help recharge its fuel supply.[273] Near Nora, Illinois, railroad worker Daniel Manley claimed to have helped airship occupants repair a faulty steering apparatus.[274] A Detroit man observed an occupant "dressed in a checked hunting suit and wearing a long peaked cap" fishing from an airship.[275] In Woodson County, Kansas, farmer Alexander Hamilton and his family reported a cigar-shaped airship three hundred feet long hovering over their cattle at 10 P.M. They saw a cable extending down from the vessel and tied around a heifer's neck. They "stood in amazement to see ship, cow and all rise slowly and sail off." Its hide, legs, and head were found in a nearby field by a farmer the next day.[276]

Of course, our interest with these contact cases is in the narrative content of the stories, and not their truth or falsity per se, although clearly they were fictional. When persons perpetrate hoaxes, tell "tall tales," experience hallucinations or vivid fantasies, the context of these occurrences is shaped by their social and cultural background. This is evident in the airship close-encounter stories, as none remotely resemble modern-day flying saucer occupant contacts. A typical case was that of farmer Frank Nichols of Josserand, Texas, who reported that an airship landed in his field and two men with buckets emerged and asked permission to draw water. After readily granting them permission,

> Mr. Nichols was kindly invited to accompany them to the ship. He conversed freely with the crew, composed of six or eight individuals, about the ship. The machinery was so complicated that in his short interview he could gain no knowledge of its workings. However, one of the crew told him the problem of aerial navigation had been solved. The ship or car is built from a newly

discovered material that has the property of self-sustenance in the air, and the motive power is highly condensed electricity. He was informed that five of these ships were built in a small town in Iowa. Soon the invention will be given to the public. An immense stock company is now being formed and within the next year the machine will be in general use.

Mr. Nichols lives at Josserand, Trinity County, Texas, and will convince any incredulous one by showing the place where the ship rested.[277]

The small number of alleged encounters with extraterrestrials in this era involved occupants in wooden and metallic airships sporting wings or propellers.[278] When their origin is mentioned, it is always said to be Mars, reflecting popular interests of the period. The writings of American astronomer Percival Lowell (1855–1916) discussed the artificial Martian canal system. His theories of intelligent Martian life were widely known, and public acceptance of the existence of such beings was high. Life on Mars was also consistent with the popular mechanistic stories of Jules Verne. On the night of April 21, a man walking home near Ogdin, West Virginia, said he saw an illuminated craft with propellers land nearby. Eight Martians standing eleven to twelve feet tall embarked from the ship. The creatures had huge heads, and said they were exploring Earth, subsisting on small pills. They did not carry water but "drank air." An hour later they flew off.[279] The following report is typical, and involved W. H. Hopkins of St. Louis, who claimed to have met two naked Martians while he was walking through the hills east of Springfield, Missouri.

. . . coming to the brow of a hill overlooking a small . . . clearing rested a vessel similar in outline to the airship shown in the Post-Dispatch of a few days ago. . . . The vessel itself was about twenty feet long and eight feet in diameter and the propellers about six feet in diameter.

Near the vessel was the most beautiful being I ever beheld. She was rather under medium size, but of the most exquisite form and features such as would put to shame the forms as sculptured by the ancient Greeks. She was dressed in nature's garb and her golden hair, wavy and glossy, hung to her waist,

> unconfined excepting by a band of glistening jewels that bound it back from her forehead. . . . In one hand she carried a fan of curious design that she fanned herself vigorously with, though to me the air was not warm and I wore an overcoat.
>
> In the shade of the vessel lay a man of noble proportions and majestic countenance. His hair of dark auburn fell to his shoulders in wavy masses and his full beard of the same color, but lighter in shade, reached to his breast. He also was fanning himself . . . as if the heat oppressed him.
>
> I tried by signs to make them understand I meant no harm. Finally his face lighted up with pleasure, and he turned and spoke to the woman. She came hesitatingly forward. . . . I took her hand and kissed it fervently. The color rose to her cheeks and she drew it hastily away.
>
> I asked them by signs where they came from . . . [and they pronounced a word that] sounded like Mars. I pointed to the ship and expressed my wonder in my countenance. He took me by the hand and led me towards it. In the side was a small door. I looked in. There was a luxurious couch. . . .
>
> I pointed to the balls attached to the propellers. He gave each of the strips of metal a rap, those attached to the propellers under the vessel first. The balls began to revolve rapidly, and I felt the vessel begin to rise, and I sprang out, and none too soon, for the vessel rose as lightly as a bird, and shot away like an arrow . . . out of sight. The two stood laughing and waving their hands at me.[280]

One miscellaneous contact claim involved inhabitants from the North Pole, which was considered the Holy Grail of the era, one part of Earth that had been inaccessible to explorers despite many well-publicized attempts. Swedish explorer Salomon Andree's unsuccessful balloon expeditions to the pole in 1896, and a subsequent fatal attempt in 1897, generated intense global interest. Correspondingly, two men fishing by a creek near Waxachie, Texas, reportedly encountered "North Pole people" resting on "furs" and "smoking pipes" near a cigar-shaped airship. The men said they learned to speak English from a polar expedition in 1553, which was believed lost. The buildings and soil of the North Pole were heated by pipes containing steam, and the country was "lighted by electricity" generated by melting icebergs.[281]

The Symbolism of Airships

When we compare the events of the airship episode with contemporary UFO and flying saucer sighting waves, the similarities are striking. Perhaps most conspicuous is the complete absence of flying saucers or tiny extraterrestrials with technology far in advance of our own. What people claim to observe and experience are reflections of popular social and cultural expectations of a particular era. It is important to remember that humans are meaning-oriented beings capable of adapting to changes in their environment in a myriad of creative and often unprecedented ways. New coping strategies and methods of ordering reality provide meaning and stability. The emergence of the plausible existence of the world's first practical airship in America during the late nineteenth century embodied the promise of "magical" science during a secular age. The airship itself seemed to have quasi-supernatural qualities as it appeared to be omnipresent and often performed maneuvers beyond the capability of our most sophisticated modern aircraft.

Aircraft occupants often gave predictions mirroring divine revelations in a different functional guise. While the mere presence of the airship implicitly portends a dawning futuristic world revolutionized by science and technology, occupants eagerly provided vivid accounts of these secular images. Within this context, one airship pilot predicted that "all principal points in the world" would soon be connected by aerial navigation, implying that the inventor would accomplish this through a capitalistic venture.[282] Another pilot claimed to have invented "perpetual motion," which would soon be revealed, but only after securing patents in every country.[283] A prominent Harrisburg, Arkansas, resident reported that an airship had landed near his home and discussed the possibility of using an antigravity invention to "kill off the Spanish" in Cuba.[284] Instead of dynamite, the craft carried a newly perfected weapon and gravitational control device, the description of which sounds supernatural:

> Weight is no object to me. I suspend all gravitation by placing a small wire around the object. You see I have a four-ton improved

> Hotchkiss gun on board, . . . we only have to pour the cartridges into the hopper and press a button and it fires 53,000 times per minute . . . place my wire across this four-ton gun and hold it out with one hand and take aim.[285]

These inventors were refined, gentlemanly, intellectual, and civilized, offering a glimpse of the impending semiutopian social order that was believed to be evolving rapidly through adherence to secular philosophies. The narrative imagery of these reports underscores the boundless faith that Americans placed in the rapidly evolving trinity of science, technology, and rationalism. It would take the passage of fifty years, two world wars, and a depression before a similar optimism reappeared. The immediate postwar era was another period of "magical" science where nearly all things seemed possible, paving the way for a symbol far exceeding the power and function of the airship—the flying saucer.

While it was an era of great advancements in science and technology, there was also considerable uncertainty and anxiety. The airship sightings and reported encounters with occupants appear to have served a useful function as a reassuring symbol. Science-fiction stories were predicting the day when flying vessels would drop bombs from above. It was comforting to believe that Americans were in control of this technology. Perhaps the most extraordinary aspect of the airship episode was the sheer volume of reported observations and encounters. As one newspaper editor commented, "This has certainly been one of the most remarkable crazes in the history of human delusions."[286]

Notes

1. Quoted in 1893 in C. H. Gibbs-Smith, *Aviation: An Historical Survey from Its Origins to the End of World War II* (London: Her Majesty's Stationery Office, 1985), p. 221.

2. I. F. Clarke, "American Anticipations: The First of the Futurists," *Futures* 18 (1986): 584–96. See p. 589.

3. T. E. Bullard, "Mysteries in the Eye of the Beholder: UFOs and Their Correlates as a Folkloric Theme Past and Present" (Ph.D. diss., Indiana University Folklore Department, 1982), p. 203.

4. Ibid.

5. V. Sanarov, "On the Nature and Origin of Flying Saucers and Little Green Men," *Current Anthropology* 22 (1981): 163–67; C. H. Gibbs-Smith, *The Aeroplane: An Historical Survey of Its Origins and Development* (London: Her Majesty's Stationery Office, 1960); Gibbs-Smith, *Aviation.*

6. D. M. Jacobs, *The UFO Controversy in America* (New York: Signet, 1975), pp. 27–28.

7. J. Clark and L. Coleman, *The Unidentified: Notes Toward Solving the UFO Mystery* (New York: Warner, 1975), p. 133.

8. For actual reproductions of some of the original patents, see G. Lore and H. Deneault, *Mysteries of the Skies: UFOs in Perspective* (Englewood Cliffs, N.J.: Prentice-Hall, 1968), pp. 16–17, 38–39.

9. D. Jacobs, *The UFO Controversy in America,* pp. 27–28.

10. "Voices in the Sky . . . People Declare They Heard Them and Saw a Light," *Sacramento Evening Bee,* November 18, 1896, p. 1.

11. Ibid.

12. Ibid.

13. "A Lawyer's Word for That Airship," *San Francisco Chronicle,* November 22, 1896, p. 16.

14. "More of a Hoax Than an Airship," *San Francisco Chronicle,* November 20, 1896, p. 13; "The Disease Still Spreading," *San Francisco Chronicle,* November 25, 1896, p. 16; "Attractive Venus. Her Charms Still Beguiling Many of the Uninitiated," *The Call* (San Francisco), November 26, 1896, p. 1; "The Airship Craze Fast Fading Away," *San Francisco Chronicle,* November 26, 1896, p. 14; "The Scarecrow Fly-by-Night," *San Francisco Examiner,* November 26, 1896, p. 10; "A Fake," *Weekly Telegraph* (Folsom, Calif.), November 28, 1896, p. 2; "Either Mars or Venus," *Oakland Tribune,* November 30, 1896, p. 5.

15. "That Peculiar Night Visitant," *The Call* (San Francisco), November 20, 1896, p. 1; "Floating in the Air . . . All the Stories Coincide," *Oakland Tribune,* November 23, 1896, p. 1; "Body Like a Bird," *The Call* (San Francisco), November 24, 1896, p. 1; "Mission of the Aerial Ship," *The Call* (San Francisco), November 25, 1896, p. 1; "New Converts," *The Call* (San Francisco), November 26, 1896, p. 1; "Saw the Airship," *San Jose Daily Mercury,* November 26, 1896, p. 5.

16. "Strange Tale of a Flying Machine . . . ," *San Francisco Chronicle,* November 19, 1896, p. 5; "The New Air Ship," *The Mail* (Los Gatos, Calif.), November 26, 1896, p. 1.

17. "Airships Over Oakland Grouped in Flocks in the Sky," *San Francisco Examiner,* November 26, 1896, p. 10.

18. "The Scarecrow Fly-by-Night," *San Francisco Examiner*, November 26, 1896, p. 10.

19. "Singular Phenomenon," *Western Watchman* (Eureka, Calif.), November 21, 1896, p. 3; "That Mysterious March," *Western Watchman*, November 28, 1896, p. 3.

20. "Sailed High Overhead," *The Call* (San Francisco), November 22, 1896, p. 13.

21. "That Airship Again," *The Call* (San Francisco), November 21, 1896, p. 3.

22. "Saw the Mystic Flying Light," *The Call* (San Francisco), November 22, 1896, p. 13.

23. "Have We Got 'Em Again," *Sacramento Evening Bee*, November 23, 1896, p. 1.

24. "A Singular Phenomenon. Was It an Airship?" *Red Bluff Daily People's Cause*, November 24, 1896.

25. "The Airship Again," *Riverside Daily Press,* December 10, 1896, p. 5.

26. "A Strange Phantom," *Weekly Antioch Ledger*, November 28, 1896, p. 3.

27. "Seen Again. Many People of Chico Gaze at the Supposed Airship," *Morning Chronicle-Record* (Chico, Calif.), November 25, 1896, p. 3.

28. "The Air Ship," *Weekly Visalia Delta,* November 26, 1896, p. 2.

29. "Seen at Hanford," *Weekly Visalia Delta*, November 26, 1896, p. 2; "The Air Ship. The Vessel Seen Again . . . ," *Weekly Visalia Delta*, December 3, 1896, p. 1.

30. "Was It an Air-Ship?" *Ferndale Semi-Weekly Enterprise*, December 1, 1896, p. 5.

31. "The Air Ship," *Riverside Daily Press*, December 2, 1896, p. 5.

32. "Observations," *Daily Colusa*, December 1, 1896, p. 2.

33. "County News," *Daily Colusa*, December 3, 1896, p. 3.

34. "Our Neighbors," *Weekly Visalia Delta,* December 3, 1896, p. 3; "The Air Ship at Tulare," *Tulare County Times* (Visalia, Calif.), December 3, 1896, p. 4.

35. *Merced Express*, December 4, 1896, p. 3.

36. *Fresno County Enterprise* (Selma, Calif.), November 27, 1896, p. 4.

37. "Pennington Points," *Sutter County Farmer* (Yuba City, Calif.), December 4, 1896, p. 6.

38. McMinnville *Telephone-Register* (Ore.), November 26, 1896, p. 3.

39. "The Tourist of the Air," *Tacoma News* (Wash.), November 28, 1896, p. 4; "Beats the Airship," *Tacoma News* (Wash.), November 30, 1896, p. 2.

40. "The Airship of Winnemucca," *Carson City Morning Appeal*, November 26, 1896, p. 3; "The Airship," *Reno Evening Gazette*, December 3, 1896, p. 1; "The Airship Again," *Reno Evening Gazette*, December 5, 1896, p. 3; "That Airship," *Carson City Morning Appeal*, December 6, 1896, p. 2; "Airship Burned," *Carson City Morning Appeal*, December 9, 1896, p. 3; "Airship Yarns," *Territorial Enterprise* (Virginia, Nev.), December 12, 1896, p. 2; "What Could It Have Been?" *Central Nevadan*, December 10, 1896, p. 3; "The Air Ship. It Reached Carson Saturday Night," *Carson Weekly*, December 7, 1896, p. 6.

41. "Local Briefs," *Arizona Gazette* (Phoenix, Ariz.), December 4, 1896, p. 8.

42. "Others Who Saw It" (letter), *The Call* (San Francisco), November 23, 1896.

43. "Three Strange Visitors. Who Possibly Came from the Planet Mars," *Evening Mail* (Stockton, Calif.), November 27, 1896, p. 1.

44. "Piercing the Void, or on to Honolulu," *San Francisco Examiner*, December 2, 1896; "How About This. A San Josean Declares That He Traveled on the Ship," *Oakland Tribune*, December 1, 1896, p. 1; "We Are in It," *San Luis Obispo Tribune*, December 11, 1896, p. 1; *San Jose Daily Mercury*, December 1, 1896, p. 8.

45. *Marysville Daily Appeal*, December 2, 1896, p. 3.

46. "The Airship Described by Fishermen," *The Call* (San Francisco), December 3, 1896, p. 1.

47. "Strange and Circumstantial Story of a Sailor Passenger," *The Call* (San Francisco), December 5, 1896, p. 2.

48. "San Diego to Heaven," *San Diego Union*, December 10, 1896, p. 5.

49. R. Hiebert, T. Bohn, and D. Ungurait, *Mass Media III* (New York: Longman, 1982).

50. "The Airship Nuisance," *San Francisco Examiner*, December 5, 1896, p. 6.

51. "A Necessity," *San Luis Obispo Tribune*, December 18, 1896, p. 3; "California's Fake," *Dalles Times Mountaineer* (Ore.), November 28, 1896, p. 2; "A Journalistic Failure," *San Francisco Examiner*, December 6, 1896, p. 6; "Coincidents," *Roseburg Plaindealer* (Ore.), November 30, 1896, p. 6; *Merced Express* (Merced, Calif.), December 4, 1896, p. 3; "Credit Where It Is Due," *San Francisco Chronicle*, December 5, 1896, p. 6; "The Airship," *Spokane Spokesman-Review* (Wash.), April 17, 1897, p. 4; "The Airship Fake," *Daily News* (Lincoln, Nebr.), April 22, 1897, p. 4; *Daily Free Press* (Streator, Ill.), April 22, 1897, p. 2.

52. "The Liar of the Faker," *Portland Oregonian*, November 29, 1896, p. 4.

53. See, for example, *Nevada State Journal* (Reno), December 5, 1896, p. 3.

54. "A Winged Ship in the Sky," *The Call* (San Francisco), November 23, 1896, p. 1.

55. "Stories of the Airship. . . . Believe that Clinton A. Case Has Carried Out His Ideas to a Successful Conclusion," *Omaha World-Herald*, April 25, 1897, p. 12; "Says He Sailed the Airship," *Chicago Record*, April 24, 1897, p. 2.

56. *Omaha Globe-Democrat*, April 10, 1897.

57. "Local News Items," *Darby Sentinel* (Mont.), May 11, 1897, p. 1.

58. "Is It Solved?" *Salem Daily Herald* (Ohio), May 8, 1897, p. 2.

59. "An Air Ship Located. G. D. Schultz has one locked up in his barn," *Kansas City Times*, April 3, 1897, p. 1.

60. "An Air-Ship Inventor," *Weekly Visalia Delta* (Calif.), December 10, 1896, p. 4; "An Inventor. Dr. E. H. Benjamin of San Francisco in Visalis," *Tulare County Times* (Visalis, Calif.), December 10, 1896, p. 4; "Aerial Navigation," *Woodland California Daily Democrat*, November 23, 1896, p. 3.

61. *San Francisco Chronicle*, November 23, 1896, p. 12.

62. See, for example: "It Was Seen Here," *Calaveras Prospect* (San Andreas, Calif.), November 21, 1896, p. 3; "Lights Aloft," *Oakland Times*, November 25, 1896, p. 3; "Was It an Airship?" *Woodland Daily Democrat*, November 24, 1896, p. 3; "People in Winnemucca Saw the Airship One Day Before Sacramentans," *Silver State* (Winnemucca, Nev.), November 23, 1896, p. 3; "Sighted Triple Lights," *The Call* (San Francisco), November 25, 1896, p. 1.

63. "Saw the Mystic Flying Light," *The Call* (San Francisco), November 22, 1896.

64. Fire balloons were popular during this period and were typically sold at shops selling pyrotechnics. They consisted of paper balloons with candles attached near the mouth and were made buoyant by the generation of heat.

65. *San Francisco Examiner*, November 24, 1896.

66. Perhaps the most extreme position is that of mass behavior as pathological. A classic textbook in the field of collective behavior by Kurt and Gladys Lang, *Collective Dynamics* (New York: Thomas Y. Crowell, 1961), views collective behavior psychopathologically, stating: "This view that the 'crowd' brings pathological elements to the fore is more than an ideological assumption . . . especially considering that large unities often act irrationally and under the impact of emotion." The most influential and comprehensive modern collective behavior paradigm remains Neil J.

Smelser's *Theory of Collective Behavior* (Englewood Cliffs, N.J.: Prentice-Hall, 1962). In it he views mass phenomena, including sightings of phantom airships and flying saucers, as "hysterical" and irrational.

67. Gustave LeBon, *Psychologie des Foules*, 2d ed. (Paris: Felix Alcan, 1896). LeBon likened "emotional contagion" to a form of shared madness, believing that ideas, emotions and beliefs infect crowds in a contagious manner "as intense as that of microbes. . . . Cerebral disorders, like madness, are contagious. . . . One knows how frequent madness is among doctors for the insane" (pp. 113–14).

68. From the Latin, literally meaning "trembling delirium," the term refers to a violent form of delirium that is characterized by muscular tremors, frightening hallucinations, and restlessness. This condition is typically triggered by excessive, prolonged consumption of alcoholic substances.

69. "Bad Case of 'Em at Hastings," *Beatrice Weekly Express* (Nebr.), February 11, 1897, p. 4.

70. "The Air-Ship," *Nevada Morning Appeal*, December 10, 1896, p. 3.

71. "Experts on the Airship," *Omaha World-Herald* (Nebr.), March 2, 1897, p. 6.

72. "Topeka's Vision," *St. Joseph Daily Herald* (Mo.), March 30, 1897, p. 4.

73. "Tales of the Town," *Kearney Hub*, April 14, 1897, p. 2. This verse read in part: "There are airships in the sky, Rock and rye. Don't you see them as they fly, Rock and rye. . . . If you don't believe it try, Rock and rye."

74. "Milwaukee's Flying Machine," *Chicago Tribune*, December 7, 1896, p. 4.

75. Ibid.

76. "Says He Saw the Airship. Lake Mills Man Describes the Aerial Conveyance," *Milwaukee Sentinel*, April 11, 1897, p. 11.

77. "Saw the Airship. Lake Mills People Watched It Ten Minutes," *Wisconsin State Journal* (Madison), April 10, 1897, p. 1.

78. "Airship Comes North. Or Else the Citizens of Wausau Have Been Imbibing in Strong Drinks," *Milwaukee Journal*, April 9, 1897, p. 2.

79. *Evening News* (Kenosha, Wis.), April 10, 1897, p. 3.

80. "Seen in Oshkosh," *Oshkosh Daily Northwestern*, April 10, 1897, p. 1.

81. "They Saw the Airship. . . . Eminent Green Bay Citizens Willing to Make Oath," *Milwaukee Sentinel*, April 11, 1897, p. 1.

82. "The Following Dispatch Was Received by *The Sentinel* from Marshfield," *Milwaukee Sentinel*, April 11, 1897, p. 1.

83. "Here is the report from Green Bay," *Milwaukee Sentinel*, April 11, 1897, p. 1.

84. "Look for Airships. And Green Bay Always Gets What She Wants," *Green Bay Gazette*, April 12, 1897, pp. 1 and 5; "Secret of an Airship. It Was a Big Hot Air Balloon That Deceived All Green Bay," *Milwaukee Journal*, April 12, 1897, p. 2.

85. "The Fiery Airship. Fond du Lacers Have Visions of the 'Airship,' " *Daily Commonwealth* (Fond du Lac, Wis.), April 12, 1897, p. 3.

86. Ibid.

87. "Claims He Saw It," *Racine Daily Journal*, April 10, 1897, p. 5.

88. "Appleton Saw Only a Star," *Milwaukee Journal*, April 12, 1897, p. 2.

89. *Evening News* (Kenosha, Wis.), April 12, 1897, p. 3.

90. *Evening News* (Kenosha, Wis.), April 13, 1897, p. 3.

91. "Identity of 'Airship,' " *Milwaukee Sentinel*, April 13, 1897.

92. "Airship Is Seen Again," *Milwaukee Sentinel*, April 12, 1897, p. 1.

93. "City Affairs," *Daily Register* (Portage, Wis.), April 14, 1897, p. 6.

94. "They Saw the Air Ship," *Racine Daily Journal*, April 15, 1897, p. 1.

95. "Saw the 'Air Ship,' " *Beloit Weekly Free Press*, April 22, 1897, p. 3.

96. *Wisconsin State Journal*, April 13, 1897, p. 2.

97. *Wisconsin State Journal*, April 15, 1897, p. 2.

98. "The Airship Mystery," *Evening Wisconsin* (Milwaukee), April 12, 1897, p. 4.

99. *Racine Daily Journal*, April 12, 1897, p. 2.

100. "Keeps on Sailing," *Racine Daily Journal*, April 12, 1897, p. 2.

101. "A Thrilling Story," *Minneapolis Tribune*, April 13, 1897, p. 1.

102. "Proof Beyond Controversy," *The Times* (London, Ohio), April 29, 1897, p. 1, citing the *Inter Ocean* (Chicago), April 26, 1897.

103. "The Great Air Ship. The Imagination of Some People Is Remarkable," *Racine Daily Journal*, April 16, 1897, p. 1.

104. "Strange Aerial Craft," *Saginaw Courier-Herald*, April 11, 1897, p. 4.

105. "Wolverine Tidbits," *Detroit Free Press*, March 24, 1897, p. 4.

106. "Weird Lights. Seen in Two Little Lakes in Ogemaw County," *Detroit Evening News*, March 29, 1897, p. 4.

107. "Caseville Has a Mystery. Strange Light Moves at Night in the Bay . . . ," *Saginaw Globe*, March 30, 1897, p. 1.

108. "State Notes," *Detroit Free Press*, April 9, 1897, p. 3.

109. "Mysterious Airship," *Saginaw Courier-Mail*, April 14, 1897, p. 3.

110. "Airship Seen Here. It Was Moving in a Northwesterly Direction . . . ," *Benton Harbor Evening News*, April 12, 1897, p. 1.

111. "It Bore Colored Lights. Benton Harbor People Claim They Saw the Airship," *Detroit Free Press*, April 14, 1897, p. 3.

112. "Is Seen at Holland," *Benton Harbor Evening News*, April 12, 1897, p. 1; *Grand Haven Daily Tribune*, April 12, 1897, p. 1.

113. "Queer Object. Seen in the Skies Last Evening—Might Have Been Airship," *Niles Daily Star*, April 12, 1897, p. 2.

114. "All Sorts," *Evening News* (Detroit), April 15, 1897, p. 4.

115. "The Air Ship. It Was Seen to Pass Over Battle Creek Last Night," *Battle Creek Daily Moon*, April 13, 1897, p. 4; "The Airship with Us. It Was Seen by Responsible Citizens in a Number of Cities . . . ," *Saginaw Evening News*, April 13, 1897, p. 2.

116. Ibid., p. 4.

117. "High in the Air. Airship Taking Spin over Michigan. If the Testimony of Sober Men Is Accepted," *Evening News* (Detroit), April 13, 1897, p. 4.

118. "Shower of Sparks. Marks the Air Ship's Path in Michigan . . . ," *Grand Rapids Evening Press*, April 13, 1897, p. 3.

119. "Air Ship or Not," *Kalamazoo Gazette*, April 14, 1897, p. 4; "Shakespheare Saw It. The Kalamazoo Editor Gives His Version of the Air Ship," *Saginaw Evening News*, April 16, 1897, p. 1.

120. "Went to Smash. Airship Said to Be Scattered Over Kalamazoo County," *Evening News* (Detroit), April 13, 1897, p. 4.

121. "Not an Air Ship. Just a Reflection in the Sky of the Light from a Burning Barn," *Kalamazoo Gazette*, April 14, 1897, p. 1.

122. "Airship Again. Broken Wheel Dug up Near Battle Creek," *Evening News* (Detroit), April 15, 1897, p. 4; "That Airship. Well-to-Do Battle Creek Farmer Claims to Have Found a Wheel from the Mysterious Craft," *Saginaw Courier-Herald*, April 16, 1897, p. 1.

123. "Dropped from the Clouds. A Message from the Airship Picked Up on Maple Street," *Battle Creek Daily Moon*, April 16, 1897, p. 5; "Letter from Airship. Received by a paper in Battle Creek," *Evening News* (Detroit), April 16, 1897, p. 4.

124. "Trip of the Airship . . . ," *Saginaw Courier-Herald*, April 17, 1897, p. 5.

125. "Seems to be Catching. Stories Told about an Airship in Michigan," *Detroit Free Press*, April 17, 1897, p. 3.

126. *State Republican* (Lansing, Mich.), April 17, 1897, p. 1.

127. Ibid.

128. "Trip of the Airship. . . . Seen at Different Points Throughout the State as Well as in Other Parts of the Country," *Saginaw Courier-Herald*, April 17, 1897, p. 5.

129. "That Air Ship. The Cigar-Shaped Body Gives Us a Call," *Manistee Daily News*, April 17, 1897, p. 5; "Was It an Air Ship?" *Manistee Daily Advocate*, April 20, 1897, p. 1.

130. "People Who Saw It. Three Citizens of Saginaw Claim to Have Been Favored," *Saginaw Evening News*, April 17, 1897, p. 7; "That Airship Again . . . ," *Saginaw Courier-Herald*, April 21, 1897, p. 5.

131. "Are Adrift in the Air . . . ," *Flint Daily News*, April 19, 1897, p. 3.

132. "Michigan News. Some Citizens of Three Rivers Are Positive the Airship Passed Over that Place Saturday Night," *Saginaw Globe*, April 19, 1897, p. 2.

133. "Beats Any Fish Story . . . ," *Detroit Free Press*, April 20, 1897, p. 3.

134. "That Rapid Airship. Now the Citizens of Grant, Newaygo County, Claim to Have Spied It," *Muskegon Daily Chronicle*, April 20, 1897, p. 2.

135. "Air Ship Passed Over . . . ," *Daily Mining Journal* (Marquette), April 23, 1897, p. 8; "Out in Broad Daylight . . . ," *Flint Daily News*, April 24, 1897, p. 3.

136. *Daily Chronicle* (Marshall), April 27, 1897, p. 3.

137. "The Airship at Geneseeville," *Flint Daily News*, April 28, 1897, p. 2.

138. "Airship Seen at Sidnaw," *Daily Mining Journal* (Marquette), April 28, 1897, p. 8.

139. "Fragments of Flint," *Flint Daily News*, May 1, 1897, p. 3.

140. "The Airship in Flint," *Flint Daily News*, May 11, 1897, p. 3.

141. "Saw the Airship. Bock Beer Season Has Opened . . . ," *Evening News* (Detroit), April 18, 1897, p. 9.

142. Ibid., p. 2.

143. "Around the State," *Muskegon Daily Chronicle*, April 14, 1897.

144. *Saginaw Globe*, April 26, 1897, p. 2.

145. *Detroit Free Press*, May 3, 1897, p. 4.

146. *Kalamazoo Gazette*, April 23, 1897, p. 4.

147. "Stories of the State," *Evening Press* (Grand Rapids, Mich.), April 23, 1897, p. 3.

148. "Moving Lights in the Sky," *Indianapolis Journal*, April 11, 1897, p. 6; *Hoosier State* (Newport, Mich.), April 14, 1897, p. 4.

149. "Mysterious Air Ship," *Indianapolis Journal*, April 15, 1897, p. 4.

150. Ibid.

151. "Lowell Items," *Lake County Star* (Crown Point, Ind.), April 16, 1897, p. 2.

152. "Misled by a Meteor," *Indianapolis News*, April 12, 1897, p. 9.

153. "Passed Over New Carlisle," *Indianapolis News*, April 12, 1897, p. 9; "Where It Has Been," *Indianapolis Journal*, April 15, 1897, p. 4.

154. "Saw It at New Carlisle," *South-Bend Daily Tribune*, April 12, 1897, p. 1.

155. "Headed Northwest," *Indianapolis News*, April 12, 1897, p. 9; *South-Bend Daily Tribune*, April 13, 1897, p. 1.

156. "The Airship. . . . Several Towns and Villages Claim to Have Witnessed Its Flight," *Indianapolis News*, April 12, 1897, p. 9.

157. "Saw the Airship at Elkhart," *Indianapolis Journal*, April 13, 1897, p. 2.

158. Magic lanterns were a crude precursor of the modern slide projector.

159. "Mysterious Airship," *Logansport Daily Reporter*, April 12, 1897.

160. "Saw an Air Ship. Residents of South 10th Street Think They Have Seen the Electric Air Ship," *Terre Haute Evening Gazette*, April 13, 1897, p. 2.

161. "Danville Has 'Em," *Daily Banner Times* (Greencastle), April 15, 1897, p. 1; "Merry Party on the Ship," *Indianapolis Journal*, April 15, 1897, p.4.

162. "That 'Airship' Again," *Michigan City Dispatch*, April 15, 1897, p. 8; "Chesterton Chips," *Westchester Tribune*, April 17, 1897, p. 4.

163. "Air Ship Passes Over Brook," *Brook Reporter*, April 16, 1897, p. 1.

164. "Landed at Gas City," *Indianapolis Sentinel*, April 15, 1897, p. 6; "No Affidavit to This. The Mysterious Air Ship Alleged to Have Rested in a Field," *Indianapolis Journal*, April 15, 1897, p. 4; "Airship Comes to Earth," *Logansport Daily Reporter*, April 16, 1897, p. 4; "Indiana News . . . ," *Marion Daily Leader*, April 15, 1897, p. 1.

165. "The Mysterious Air Ship," *Kokomo Daily Tribune*, April 16, 1897, p. 5.

166. "Valparaiso Sees the Ship," *Indianapolis Journal*, April 15, 1897, p. 4.

167. "Passed over Princeton," *Indianapolis Sentinel*, April 15, 1897, p. 6.

168. "That Mysterious Airship," *Indianapolis Sentinel*, April 15, 1897, p. 6.

169. "Saw the Air Ship," *Terre Haute Evening Gazette*, April 15, 1897, p. 5.

170. "Sighted Here," *Fort Wayne Weekly Gazette*, April 15, 1897, p.1.

171. "The Ship," *Martinsville Republican*, April 15, 1897, p. 6; "Airship Is in Brown. It Is Waiting on Weed Patch Hill for Repairs," *Columbus*

Evening Republican, April 21, 1897, p. 1; "The Airship Located. It Is on Weed Patch Hill . . . ," *Martinsville Republican*, April 22, 1897, p. 6.

172. "Albany Gets a Sight of the Ship," *Indianapolis Journal*, April 17, 1897, p. 1.

173. "Message from the Airship. Note Tied to a Screw Found . . . ," *Indianapolis Sentinel*, April 17, 1897, p. 6.

174. "That Air Ship," *Daily Banner-Times* (Greencastle), April 17, 1897, p. 1; "They Saw a 'Strange Body,' " *Indianapolis Journal*, April 17, 1897, p. 1.

175. "The Airship Fake. Muncie People Duped by a Quartet of Balloons," *Indianapolis Sentinel*, April 19, 1897, p. 6.

176. "Two Men in the Ship . . . Spiritualists Make a Discovery," *Fort Wayne Weekly Gazette*, April 22, 1897, p. 12.

177. "The Air Ship in Greenfield," *Hancock Democrat*, April 29, 1897, p. 1.

178. "Saw the Airship . . . ," *Indianapolis Journal*, April 13, 1897, p. 2.

179. "Danville Has 'Em," *Daily Banner-Times* (Greencastle), April 15, 1897, p. 1.

180. *Indianapolis News*, April 13, 1897, p. 4.

181. "That Air Ship," *Daily Banner Times* (Greencastle), April 14, 1897, p. 1.

182. *Lebanon Patriot*, April 15, 1897, p. 8.

183. "Anent the Airship," *Evening Republican* (Columbus), April 15, 1897, p. 2.

184. "Wawaka News Nuggets," *Ligonier Banner*, April 22, 1897, p. 1.

185. See *Monticello Herald*, May 6, 1897, p. 1; "Richmond Sees the Air Ship," *Hartford City Telegram*, May 5, 1897, p. 2; "The Air Ship Is Found," *Daily Banner Times* (Greencastle), April 20, 1897, p. 4.

186. *Indianapolis Journal*, May 9, 1897, p. 2.

187. *Indianapolis Sentinel*, April 19, 1897, p. 6.

188. "Brevities of Local Interest," *Angola Herald* (Steuben City), April 21, 1897, p. 5.

189. "Lake Station," *Hobart Gazette*, April 30, 1897, p. 8.

190. *Rensselaer Republican*, April 22, 1897, p. 1.

191. "That Air Ship," *Mitchell Commercial* (Lawrence City), April 22, 1897, p. 1.

192. "The Greensburg Liar Loose Again," *Greensburg Review*, April 17, 1897, p. 1.

193. Ibid.

194. "Landed at Monon," *Indianapolis Sentinel*, April 17, 1897, p. 6.

195. *Monitor* (Upland), April 22, 1897, p. 1.

196. "Mysterious Air-Ship," *Rushville Republican*, April 20, 1897, p. 3.

197. *The Times* (London, Ohio), April 29, 1897, p. 1, citing the *Inter Ocean* (Chicago), April 26, 1897.

198. "Local News," *Hamilton County Ledger* (Noblesville), April 23, 1897, p. 8.

199. "Very Hard to Believe," *Indianapolis Sentinel*, April 21, 1897, p. 6.

200. "Saw the Air Ship," *Terre Haute Evening Gazette*, April 22, 1897, p. 4.

201. "The Mysterious Air Ship," *Kokomo Daily Tribune*, April 23, 1897, p. 4; "On Their Oaths," *Kokomo Dispatch*, April 23, 1897, p. 4.

202. "Saw the Airship," *Logansport Daily Register*, April 23, 1897.

203. "Right in the Swim," *Cannelton Inquirer*, April 24, 1897, p. 1; "An Odd Light Seen . . . Was It the Air Ship?" *Davies County Democrat* (Wash.), April 24, 1897, p. 2.

204. "Did They See It?" *Logansport Daily Reporter*, April 26, 1897, p. 5; "The Air Ship in Greenfield," *Hancock Democrat*, April 29, 1897, p. 1.

205. "Looked Like a Kite," *Logansport Daily Reporter*, April 27, 1897, p. 3.

206. "Saw the Airship," *Auburn Courier*, April 29, 1897, p. 1.

207. "Sure It Was the Air Ship," *Indianapolis Journal*, May 9, 1897, p. 2.

208. "The Wonder Grows," *Minneapolis Tribune*, April 9, 1897, p. 1.

209. "License Fluid. What Is This That Enabled Them to See the Air Ship?" *St. Paul Pioneer Press*, April 10, 1897, p. 2.

210. "The Wonder . . . ," *Minneapolis Tribune*, April 9, 1897, p. 1.

211. "Genuine! The Mysterious Airship Hovers about Minneapolis," *Minneapolis Tribune*, April 11, 1897, p. 1.

212. "That Airship Again Seen by Albert Lea Citizens," *St. Paul Pioneer Press*, April 12, 1897, p. 4.

213. "Special Telegram to the Tribune," *Minneapolis Tribune*, April 11, 1897, p. 1.

214. "Navigator of the Air Ship," *St. Paul Pioneer Press*, April 12, 1897, p. 4.

215. "Mysterious Airship seen by Stuart Mackroth," *Minneapolis Tribune*, April 13, 1897, p. 1.

216. "Anoka See the Airship," *St. Paul Dispatch*, April 12, 1897, p. 4.

217. "That Air Ship," *Minneapolis Tribune*, April 12, 1897, p. 4.

218. "Whole Fleet of Airships. Witnessed by Duluthians," *St. Paul Pioneer Press*, April 13, 1897, p. 2; "See the Air Ship," *Duluth News-Tribune*, April 17, 1897, p. 6.

219. "More of 'Em," *St. Paul Pioneer-Press*, April 15, 1897.

220. *St. Paul Pioneer-Press*, April 14, 1897, p. 2.

221. "Mystery of the Airship Yet to Be Solved," *Minneapolis Tribune*, April 14, 1897, p. 5.

222. "Schweitzer Saw It. Latest Testimony Respecting the Airship," *St. Paul Dispatch*, April 14, 1897, p. 4.

223. Ibid.

224. Ibid.

225. *Minneapolis Tribune*, April 12, 1897, p. 4.

226. "It Was . . . Scott's . . . Airship," *St. Paul Dispatch*, April 20, 1897, p. 4.

227. "The Airship Visits Portions of Minnesota Yesterday and Created Unusual Sensation," *Minneapolis Tribune*, April 16, 1897, p. 5.

228. "Party of Morganfield People Anxious to See the Airship," *Louisville Evening Post*, April 13, 1897, p. 3.

229. "The Air-Ship in Kentucky," *Louisville Courier-Journal*, April 15, 1897, p. 5.

230. Ibid.

231. "Airship Passed in the Night," *Louisville Evening Post*, April 13, 1897, p. 6.

232. Ibid.

233. "Airship. Mayor and Reputable Citizens of Russellville Saw It Last Night," *Louisville Evening Post*, April 16, 1897, p. 5. Also see: *Owensboro Daily Inquirer*, April 16, 1897, p. 1.

234. "Todd People Saw It," *Louisville Evening Post*, April 16, 1897, p. 5.

235. "Seen in Clarksville," *Louisville Evening Post*, April 16, 1897, p. 5.

236. "Seen in Christian County," *Louisville Evening Post*, April 16, 1897, p. 5.

237. "Nashville's Centennial Managers Say It Will Be Exhibited There," *Louisville Evening Post*, April 16, 1897, p. 2.

238. *The Cairo Bulletin*, April 17, 1897.

239. "Must Have Been Hitting the Pipe," *Louisville Times*, April 19, 1897, p. 2.

240. "The Airship Seen by Bowling Green People Last Night," *Louisville Evening Post*, April 19, 1897, p. 3.

241. "Flitted By," *Louisville Evening Post*, April 21, 1897, p. 2; "Madisonville's Got 'Em Now," *Louisville Courier-Journal*, April 22, 1897, p. 4.

242. "Omnipresent. That Airship Is Everywhere . . . ," *Louisville Evening Post*, April 23, 1897, p. 3.

243. *Louisville Evening Post*, April 20, 1897, p. 8.

244. *Owensville Messenger*, April 27, 1897, p. 5.

245. "Pillar of Fire. Strange Light Seen in the Northern Heavens," *Louisville Courier-Journal*, April 22, 1897, p. 9.

246. "Seeing the Airship," *Owensville Messenger*, April 24, 1897, p. 4.

247. "Aerial Flyer. Seen by Reputable Citizens of Lewisburg Last Night," *Louisville Evening Post*, April 24, 1897, p. 2.

248. "Saw the Airship," *Owensboro Daily Inquirer*, April 25, 1897, p. 1.

249. Another Press Account Gives His Address as 1227 13th Street.

250. "Saw the Air Ship," *Louisville Courier-Journal*, April 25, 1897, sec. 2, p. 6.

251. Ibid.

252. "They Saw It," *Louisville Evening Post*, April 26, 1897, p. 2.

253. "Saw the Airship," *Daily Leaf-Chronicle*, May 1, 1897, p. 2, quoting verbatim from the *Todd County Times*, April 30, 1897.

254. *Cincinnati Enquirer*, April 19, 1897, p. 5.

255. "Made of Thin Air," *Daily News*, April 19, 1897, p. 2. For similar descriptions, see "News via Airship. A Heavenly Lightning Bug . . . ," *Paducah Daily News*, April 23, 1897, p. 3.

256. *Mayfield Mirror*, April 16, 1897.

257. "Madisonville's Got 'Em Now," *Louisville Courier-Journal*, April 22, 1897, p. 4.

258. "That Air Ship," *Louisville Courier Journal*, April 30, 1897, p. 5.

259. "Dropped from the Airship as It Passes over Corbin," *Louisville Evening Post*, April 27, 1897, p. 5; "Letter. From the Navigator in the Air Ship," *Louisville Courier-Journal*, May 1, 1897, p. 9.

260. "Saw the Airship. A Middlesborough Man Willing to Make an Affidavit," *Louisville Courier-Journal*, May 2, 1897, section I, p. 10.

261. E. M. Borchard, *Convicting the Innocent: Errors of Criminal Justice* (New Haven, Conn.: Yale University Press, 1932); E. Loftus, *Eyewitness Testimony* (Cambridge, Mass.: Harvard University Press, 1979); R. Buckhout, "Nearly 2000 Witnesses Can Be Wrong," *Bulletin of the Psychonomic Society* 16 (1980): 307–10; G. Wells and J. Turtle, "Eyewitness Identification: The Importance of Lineup Models," *Psychological Bulletin* 99 (1986): 320–29; D. F. Ross, J. D. Read, and M. P. Toglia, *Adult Eyewitness Testimony: Current Trends and Developments* (Cambridge: Cambridge University Press, 1994).

262. E. U. Condon and D. S. Gillmor, eds., *Scientific Study of Unidentified Flying Objects* (New York: Bantam, 1969); W. R. Corliss, ed., *Handbook of Unusual Natural Phenomena* (Glen Arm, Md.: The Sourcebook Pro-

ject, 1977); W. R. Corliss, ed., *Mysterious Universe: A Handbook of Astronomical Anomalies* (Glen Arm, Md.: The Sourcebook Project, 1979).

263. R. Buckhout, "Eyewitness Testimony," *Scientific American* 231 (1974): 23–31.

264. P. Klass, *UFOs—Explained* (New York: Random House, 1976), pp. 14–15.

265. Bullard, *Mysteries in the Eye of the Beholder*, pp. 10–11.

266. S. E. Asch, "Studies of Independence and Conformity: A Minority of One Against a Unanimous Majority," *Psychological Monographs*, 70 (1956); D. Krech, R. S. Crutchfield, and E. L. Ballschey, *Individual and Society* (New York: McGraw-Hill, 1962).

267. R. Turner, and L. Killian, *Collective Behavior* (Englewood Cliffs, N.J.: Prentice-Hall, 1972), p. 35.

268. M. Sherif and O. J. Harvey, "A Study in Ego Functioning: Elimination of Stable Anchorages in Individual and Group Situations," *Sociometry* 15 (1952): 272–305.

269. M. Sherif, *The Psychology of Social Norms* (New York: Harper and Row, 1936).

270. R. Beeson, "The Improbable Primate and the Modern Myth," in G. Krantz and R. Sprague, eds., *The Scientist Looks at the Sasquatch II.* (Moscow, Idaho: University Press of Idaho, 1979), p. 180.

271. C. M. Massad, M. Hubbard, and D. Newston, "Selective Perception of Events," *Journal of Experimental Social Psychology* 15 (1979): 513–32.

272. For examples of "encounters" see: "The Airship," *Morning Appeal* (Carson City, Nev.), December 10, 1896, p. 3; "Joe Saw It," *Waterloo Daily Courier* (Iowa), April 10, 1897; "That Blooming Ship," *Daily Republic* (Rockford, Ill.), April 12, 1897, p. 1; "Rode in a Flying Machine," *Pittsburgh Dispatch*, April 12, 1897, p. 2; "The Aerial Mystery," *Daily Pantagraph* (Ill.), April 17, 1897, p. 5; "A Visit of the Airship," *Quincy Daily Herald* (Ill.), April 13, 1897, p. 3; "Mystery Solved," *Springfield News* (Ill.), April 15, 1897, p. 1; "Airship Story," *Decatur Evening Republican* (Ill.), April 15, 1897, p. 8; "The Airship," *Daily Picayune* (La.), April 25, 1897, p. 7; "Oft-Seen Air-Ship," *Fort Worth Register* (Tex.), April 18, 1897, p. 11; "Trip of the Airship," *Saginaw Courier-Herald*, (Mich.), April 17, 1897, p. 5; "Was Plainly Seen," *Cincinnati Commercial Tribune*, April 18, 1897, p. 20; "Air Ship in Bryan," *Bryan Texas Daily Eagle*, April 20, 1897, p. 4; "Inspected the Air Ship," *Houston Daily Post*, April 21, 1897, p. 2; "Saw the Air Ship," *Arkansas Gazette*, April 22, 1897, p. 3; "The Work of the Air Ship," *West Virginia Daily Oil News* (Sisterville), April 21, 1897, p. 2; "The Airship Located," *Martinsville Republican* (Ind.), April 22, 1897, p. 6; "The Airship in west Texas," *Galveston Daily News*, April 24, 1897, p. 3; "The

Air-Ship," *Fort Worth Register*, April 24, 1897, p. 5; "Supplies for Airship," *Houston Post*, April 25, 1897, p. 13; "Aeribarkque," *Cincinnati Enquirer*, April 25, 1897, p. 9; "Loveland Is Way Ahead," *Loveland Reporter*, April 29, 1897, p. 4; *Avalanche* (Glenwood Springs, Colo.), May 4, 1897, p. 1.

273. "Airship at Chillicothe," *Trenton Morning Tribune*, April 16, 1897, p. 3.

274. *Warren Sentinel* (Ill.), April 21, 1897.

275. "Sees Man Fishing from Air Ship," *Chicago Tribune*, April 16, 1897, p. 4.

276. "Air Ship Steals a Calf," *Kansas City Times*, April 27, 1897, p. 1.

277. "That Airship. Farmer Near Josserand Conversed with the Crew," *Houston Post*, April 26, 1897, p. 2.

278. See, for instance: "Three Strange Visitors," *Evening Mail* (Stockton, Calif.), November 27, 1896, p. 1; *St. Louis Globe-Democrat*, April 12, 1897, p. 12; "Startling!" *Bellefontaine Republican* (Ohio), May 14, 1897, p. 1.

279. "The Worst Yet," *Parsons Advocate* (W. Va.), April 23, 1897, p. 2.

280. "Golden Haired Girl Is in It. The Airship Discovered . . . ," *St. Louis Post-Dispatch*, April 19, 1897, p. 1.

281. *Dallas Morning News*, April 19, 1897, p. 5.

282. *Minneapolis Journal*, April 9, 1897, p. 2.

283. *Cincinnati Enquirer*, April 25, 1897, p. 9.

284. Cubans staged several revolts during the nineteenth century, and although there was much discussion of annexing Cuba as a state, the U.S. government declined to intervene. American sympathies strongly sided with the Cubans, as many Cuban-Americans solicited funds for arms and food shipments. Sensational newspaper stories depicting Spanish atrocities against Cubans further crystallized American sentiments.

285. *Harrisburg Modern News*, April 23, 1897, p. 2.

286. "Time for a Rest," *San Francisco Examiner*, November 26, 1896, p. 6.

2

Thomas Edison's "Electric Star" Illusion of 1897

Tain't what a man don't know that hurts him; it's what he knows that just ain't so!

—Frank McKinney Hubbard

In the waning months of the airship wave, another remarkable social delusion occurred in America. In 1885 Thomas Edison had conducted a series of experiments involving wireless telegraphy between two balloons near his laboratory in his hometown of Menlo Park, New Jersey. Achieving better results at night, he began sending balloons aloft with lights attached. As a result of press publicity surrounding these balloon experiments, sporadic rumors and sightings of the "Edison Star" were reported for years afterward.[1] An intense spate of sightings occurred between late March and mid-April of 1897, when this remarkable social delusion arose at numerous locations across the United States, tens of thousands of citizens reporting seeing what they assumed to be a giant imaginary arc lamp suspended in the sky.

During 1897, amid rumors that Edison was conducting "electric balloon" experiments with lamps of phenomenal candle power along with powerful reflectors to determine how far the light could be seen, the unusual series of reports began. On Tuesday evening, March 29, a large crowd gathered in the city of Iron Mountain, Michigan, as rumors spread that a conspicuous object in the evening sky "was an electric light hoisted two miles high over St. Paul" in the adjacent state of Minnesota. One man claimed that it consisted of a storage battery attached to a tethered balloon.[2] A story circulated that the light was sent up at about 5 P.M., was visible across the entire United States, and was taken down mid-evening. Correspondingly, many residents claimed that they could see the balloon being slowly reeled in toward the ground at about 9 P.M.[3] The following night in Portland, Maine, a large number of people gathered at various street corners and stared at Venus under the delusion that it was a "mammoth electric searchlight suspended by a block and tackle."[4] The "electric balloon" was seen in the Portland vicinity for several days in early April, and one newspaper noted that "Nine out of ten men and women who parade the streets nowadays are excited over it."[5] It was widely believed that they had observed an electric light suspended atop New Hampshire's Mount Washington, and residents in Dover and Foxcroft, Maine refused to accept that it was Venus.[6] In Bangor, Maine, one man was emphatic that he could see "by the light of the balloon, a faint outline of the frame which sustained the machinery." Meanwhile, a sensation was created in Waterville and throughout the Kennebec valley in Maine as the light was seen to suddenly move "as if it had been pulled down with a rope."[7]

During early April, rumors of the electric balloon swept across America, and it was even sighted for a week over Montreal, Canada.[8] One newspaper editor remarked that "no blizzard ... ever swept over the country with greater rapidity or more thoroughly."[9] The *Augusta Chronicle* editors commented on the extent of the delusion: "[J]ust think of the people of New England, the cultured east, in the state of Massachusetts where Boston is, taking the planet Venus for an electric light swung in the sky by Mr. Edison."[10] A Boston astronomer remarked that he was unable to work as he was inundated with queries about "Edison's experimental star."[11] In Berrien Springs, Michigan, the "electric star" was rumored to have been a monumental advertising ploy to promote a popular brand of soap manufactured in Michigan City. In supporting this story, one press account stated that "we all now know that many things are possible to electrical engineers."[12]

To understand the sightings, we need to examine their context in relation to the events in America during the latter nineteenth century. It was the same context that engendered the phantom airship sightings—only this time the image had changed. The period between 1850 and 1897 was marked by unprecedented technological changes,[13] the most visible highlight of which was the installation of electric lights that were dotting the countryside and quickly changing lifestyles forever; a marvelous and practical example of the Enlightenment faith in science and technology. The sightings were a symbolic projection of the prevailing technological mania and seemingly limitless faith in science and inventions that was sweeping America.

In his biography of Thomas Edison, Francis Jones commented that Edison "often had a quiet chuckle" over the stories of his experimental light. Edison "received many letters on the subject, but he never replied to them, hoping that the absurd story would die a natural death," which it eventually did.[14] A quasi-religious mythos surrounded Edison, who was appropriately dubbed "the Wizard." According to Edison biographer Matthew Josephson,

> the rustic neighbors of Menlo Park and nearby Metuchen gossiped about his having machines that could overhear farmers talking or even cows munching the grass in the fields a mile away. It was said that he had another machine which was supposed to measure the heat of the stars; and that illuminations of meteoric brilliance were seen blazing up through the windows of his laboratory and were extinguished as suddenly and mysteriously as they had appeared. Catching glimpses of figures gliding about the fields near his laboratory at midnight with lights and equipment, bent on missions none of them could understand. . . .[15]

What can be learned from the episode of the "Edison Star" and other attempts to superimpose magical qualities to his abilities and inventions? We should be mindful that history repeats itself. During the late nineteenth century, astronomer Percival Lowell, blinded by the hope of extraterrestrial life, was certain that he could see through his telescope a complex system of Martian-made canals on the surface of Mars. As new inventors arrive on our modern scene and new technologies are developed, it will be interesting to observe what social delusions they will engender. During the past two centuries, the rise of secularized governments and technological innovations has coincided with a growing hope that science and technology will provide humanity with answers to questions that have until recently been the exclusive domain of magic and religion. As the world grows ever more technologically sophisticated, people will increasingly turn to science for the answers to religious and philosophical questions. In this regard it may be prudent to recall the words of the late astronomer Carl Sagan: "Wherever we have strong emotions we are liable to fool ourselves."[16]

Notes

We acknowledge our indebtedness to Thomas E. Bullard, who provided the press accounts about the "Edison Star," and who indicated specific references about this social delusion, in biographies of Edison.

1. R. Conot, *A Streak of Luck* (New York: Seaview, 1979).
2. "There Is No String to It. Venus, the Evening Star . . . ," *Daily Tribune* (Iron Mountain, Mich.), March 30, 1897, p. 3.
3. Ibid.
4. "Venus Was Bright," *Daily Eastern Argus*, March 31, 1897, p. 3.
5. "See That Balloon? Everybody Is Staring at Venus and Venus Is Fooling Everybody . . . ," *Bangor Daily Commercial*, April 3, 1897, p. 3.
6. "Dover and Foxcroft Locals," *Bangor Daily Commercial*, April 2, 1897, p. 7.
7. Ibid.
8. "Puzzled Over a Light. Citizens of Montreal See a Strange Star and Wonder Increases," *Piedmont Herald* (W.Va.), April 16, 1897.
9. "Venus Maligned," *Milwaukee Journal*, April 6, 1897, p. 4.
10. "A Light in the East," *Times and Democrat* (Orangeburg, S.C.), April 7, 1897, p. 4, citing verbatim from the *Augusta Chronicle* (Maine).
11. "That Experimental Star," *Boston Evening Transcript*, April 15, 1897, p. 4.
12. "It Is No Fake," *Berrien Springs Era* (Mich.), April 7, 1897, p. 3.

13. E. de Bono, *Eureka! An Illustrated History of Inventions from the Wheel to the Computer* (London: Thames and Hudson, 1979).

14. F. A. Jones, *The Life Story of Thomas Alva Edison* (New York: Grosset & Dunlap, 1931), pp. 174–75.

15. M. Josephson, *Edison: A Biography* (London: Eyre & Spottiswoode, 1961), p. 170.

16. C. Sagan, *Cosmos* (London: Macdonald Futura, 1981).

3

When Believing Is Seeing: Canada's Ghost Balloons of 1896–97

> It is difficult to imagine today the enthusiasm of those who hailed the miracle [of balloon flight] come true.
>
> —J. Jobe[1]

As we discussed in chapter 1, numerous experimental studies attest to the notorious unreliability of human perception, including the effect of an individual's mental set or frame of reference in significantly influencing his or her interpretation of visual stimuli. For instance, on the evening of October 30, 1938, many Americans panicked after listening to a realistic radio play directed by Orson Welles depicting a Martian invasion of New Jersey.[2] Several New Jersey residents telephoned police to report their observations "of Martians on their giant machines poised on the Jersey Palisades."[3] An interesting historical example of this process occurred over western Canada during 1896–97, coinciding with heavy press coverage of daring plans by Swedish scientist Salomon Andree to navigate a balloon to the North Pole.

During the eighteenth and nineteenth centuries, popular interest in ballooning and various record-setting feats attempted by their pilots and crews captivated much of Europe and North

America, culminating in Andree's penultimate exploit of attempting to reach the Pole.[4] Andree's announcement in 1893 that he had received sufficient funds to undertake the journey was afforded spectacular press coverage. Such a voyage to this uncharted territory was considered to be one of the last great challenges. Meticulous planning went into the trip and constructing the balloon, the *Ornen* ("Eagle"). Andree's preparations made headlines around the world from 1893 until he and his two crewmen froze to death in 1897, without ever reaching the Pole.

This is only part of a more fascinating story. In 1896, the year before his death, Andree and his crew traveled to Danes Island on the northwestern tip of Spitzbergen, where he had ordered the construction of a giant building to shelter his balloon from the harsh elements so it would be in optimum condition for the ascent. Andree had originally intended to make his polar expedition in 1896, and on June 30 of that year, the balloon was inflated inside the shelter as he and the crew waited for favorable weather conditions. The world's attention was focused on Andree, and governments with territory in the polar regions were asked to inform their citizens of the event and to render any assistance to the balloonists should they land there. The Canadian government and the Hudson Bay Company publicized to Native Canadian peoples that "it was probable the aerial voyagers might be driven southerly" and stray into western Canada.[5] But the balloonists waited until mid-August, at which time they abandoned the attempt due to poor weather. However, the isolated communities in northwestern Canada were not immediately informed of the expedition's cancellation, and they remained on the lookout for his famous balloon.

Reports of phantom balloon sightings began on the afternoon of July 1, 1896, when residents of Winnipeg, Manitoba, claimed to see a balloon flying rapidly in the distance.[6] While several observers thought "that it was Andree's balloon," they were subsequently informed of the latest reports indicating that Andree had yet to depart. Once they realized this, there was some discussion that the sighting could have been of a "toy balloon sent up in honor of the Confederation holiday." The press report concluded by noting that "whether miniature or real, the passage of the mysterious balloon caused a good deal of talk among citizens last night."[7]

On August 12, a sensational story appeared in the press, discussing an apparent sighting of Andree's balloon. The government office in Ottawa received a telegram on August 11 from the Superintendent of Indian Affairs in British Columbia, A. W. Vowell. It stated: "Credible information received by Agent Lomas from two Indian parties, separated by long distance at time of observation, that the Andree balloon had been sighted in latitude 55.15, longitude 127.40, pursuing a northerly course."[8] The location described in Vowell's dispatch would have placed the sighting about one hundred miles up the Skeena River, some five hundred miles north of Victoria. At the time of the observation, local residents were unaware that Andree had not begun his voyage.[9]

The following day, August 13, more details of the dispatch became public. Dated July 3, it was sent from Hazelton and told of a boy who reported seeing a semicircular black object near the setting sun, which disappeared about forty feet above the timber line. The dispatch, sent to Vowell by agent R. E. Loring, concluded by noting that "the boy's description of the balloon and its action leaves no doubt as to its reality, and is no doubt Andree's balloon expected to have left Spitzbergen for the north pole" on July 1.[10] A second dispatch was also detailed in the same press account, again sent by Loring to Vowell from Hazelton on July 10. He wrote that Ghali, chief of the Kispiox, had seen a balloonlike object while trapping with a group of Indians on Blackwater Lake, above the head waters of the Skeena on the evening of July 3. The object was brightly illuminated and traveling almost due north. Loring also noted that the Indians living along the Skeena "were made aware that they were liable to see during the beginning of this month, a balloon going north, and of the purpose of its occupants, etc., and to report to me anything noticed by them of that description."[11]

The 1897 Episode

Andree's second and final attempt to reach the North Pole transpired on July 11, 1897, when he ascended from Danes Island. The exact details of his demise were not known until 1930, when sailors stopping at White Island discovered the expedition's remains, including undeveloped film and notes describing the tragedy that befell them. Sixty-five hours after taking off, Andree was forced to land just three hundred miles from his departure point after an ice coating formed on the balloon. He and his crew died on the arduous trek back to civilization. It was not until thirty-three years after the event, however, that the world learned his fate. In the days and weeks after Andree and his crew sailed into oblivion, his whereabouts were again the subject of intense press discussion, and those living in northern countries were told to keep a watch for his balloon.

The first sighting of the 1897 episode was reported in northern British Columbia by Rivers Inlet fisherman W. S. Fitzgerald, who was salmon fishing with a companion on the morning of July 10. At about 2:45 A.M. they spotted a "great balloon-shaped body" that was "powerfully illuminated" floating about a mile above a mountain range, when "all at once the thought burst upon us that it was a balloon and none other than Andree's."[12] The light appeared to drift southwest for about two hours, when it faded out of sight.[13] On July 12, several residents of a nursing home at Kamlooms, British Columbia, reported a similar illuminated object "fluttering" for over two hours before disappearing to the southwest.[14] Over the course of several days between the last week of July and August 3, several sightings of a "mysterious balloon or pillar of fire" were recorded in Victoria, British Columbia, including by three women camping at Sidney, who watched it drift north over Salt Spring Island.[15] On early Sunday morning, August 1, three young men camping near Goldstream also reported what appeared to be "a brilliantly lighted balloon."[16]

On August 5 at Douglas, Manitoba, several residents watched an illuminated object at about 11 P.M., swaying in the sky, "resembling the shape of a massive balloon." It was traveling northward, disappeared after forty-five minutes, and was assumed to be Andree's balloon.[17] During the early morning hours of August 6, two firemen on the Victoria city brigade observed a bright aerial light hovering above Discovery Island for over two hours, moving in a general western direction. At one point the pair thought they could discern "a dark body outlined behind the circle of intense light."[18] When the observation was denounced as the likely misperception of a toy balloon,[19] several local residents wrote in to support their claims.[20] On August 8 at 12:30 A.M., a family living on the outskirts of Winnipeg also thought they saw Andree's balloon shining a bright light as it disappeared to the northwest after forty-five minutes.[21] On August 13 at about 9 P.M., "a very bright red star surrounded by a luminous halo" swiftly traversing the southern sky was seen for nearly fifteen minutes by thousands of Vancouver residents. This followed a sighting by several prominent citizens of Rossland, who watched it hover for some time before fading from sight to the south.[22]

There were two final reports in September. The first occurred on the evening of the seventeenth, as several farmers residing near Souris, Manitoba, "distinctly saw a balloon floating over them at considerable height" traveling southwesterly. It was in sight for five minutes, and the farmers were certain that a flag was protruding from the top of the vessel, suggesting that Andree was making a triumphant return.[23] Coincidentally, at this time there was much speculation that Andree may have already reached the North Pole and was heading back, although he planned to trek back on foot. The last report was by William Graham of Honora, Manitoulin Island in Lake Huron, who stated that on September 11 at 10 P.M., he and several neighbors saw an illuminated object change from red to white to blue, which was also seen at nearby Gore Bay. Graham suggested that the object was Andree's balloon.[24]

It must be emphasized that almost certainly no one could or would have been able to fly in a balloon above Canada at this time, particularly under the conditions observed. First, most balloons were tethered to a rope and used for show purposes. A so-called "free-flying" balloon traveling in such northern regions, and at night, would have been almost certainly suicidal and would have required considerable investment of time and money, yet no attempt at such was ever recorded.

Contemporary Canadian Anomalies

The phantom sightings of Andree's balloon are a classic example of the power expectation has over perception. The sky became a

Rorschach inkblot test, mirroring the social expectations. Contemporary waves of claims and public discourse surrounding observations of other strange aerial phenomena across Canada continue today, such as thunderbirds and flying saucers. While eyewitnesses are often stereotyped by scientists and the public as mentally disturbed, in both instances there are social and cultural traditions that observers are usually aware of that influence their perceptual orientations. For instance, the Ojibway Indians of Ontario continue to see "thunderbirds" the size of airplanes, which is entirely consistent with their cultural worldview.[25] These folk beliefs are often reinforced through oral traditions, the mass media, and popular literature.

Notes

1. J. Jobe, preface to *The Romance of Ballooning: The Story of the Early Aeronauts*, by P. Stephens and E. Lausanne (London: Patrick Stevens, 1971), p. 11.

2. H. Cantril, *The Invasion from Mars: A Study in the Psychology of Panic* (Princeton, N.J.: Princeton University Press, 1940).

3. R.E. Markush, "Mental Epidemics: A Review of the Old to Prepare for the New," *Public Health Reviews* 2 (1973): 353–442. See p. 379.

4. L. Rolt, *The Aeronauts: A History of Ballooning 1783–1903* (London: Longmans, 1966).

5. "Can It Be Andree? British Columbia Indians Saw a Balloon . . . The Explorers Driven Far Out of Their Course . . . ," *Manitoba Morning Free Press*, August 12, 1896, p. 1.

6. "A Mysterious Balloon. Where Was It from and Whither Bound?" *Manitoba Morning Free Press*, July 2, 1896, p. 4.

7. Ibid.

8. "Can it Be Andree . . . ," *Manitoba Morning Free Press*, August 12, 1896, p. 1.

9. Ibid.

10. "It Was No Dream. The Ghostly Balloon Seen by Winnipeggers," *Manitoba Morning Free Press*, August 13, 1896, p. 2.

11. Ibid.

12. "That Pillar of Fire. The Mysterious Visitor Seen Again Drifting over Northern British Columbia . . . ," *Victoria Daily Colonist* (British

Columbia), July 18, 1897, p. 5; "Aerial Mystery. The Wonderful Sight Witnessed by Two Fishermen . . . ," *Manitoba Free Press*, July 20, 1897, p. 1.

13. "Aerial Mystery . . . ," *Manitoba Free Press*, July 20, 1897, p. 1.

14. "What Is It?" *Daily Colonist*, July 20, 1897, p. 4.

15. "Victoria News," *Daily News-Advertiser*, August 3, 1897, p. 5.

16. Ibid.

17. "Again the Airship. Can Andree's Balloon Be Visiting These Parts . . . ," *Manitoba Free Press*, August 9, 1897, p. 3.

18. "That Light in the Air . . . ," *Victoria Daily Colonist*, August 7, 1897, p. 7.

19. "The Ruddy Moon. Late Hours Prove Too Much . . . ," *Victoria Daily Colonist*, August 8, 1897, p. 2.

20. "That Morning Mystery," *Victoria Daily Colonist*, August 12, 1897, p. 6.

21. "Another Aerial Visitor," *Manitoba Morning Free Press*, August 10, 1897, p. 5.

22. "News from the Province," *Daily News-Advertiser*, August 15, 1897, p. 6.

23. "A Balloon Again. This Time One Is Seen Near Souris," *Manitoba Free Press*, September 20, 1897, p. 8.

24. "Another Andree Mystery," *Manitoba Morning Free Press*, September 28, 1897, p. 4.

25. For an account of a contemporary sighting, see: J. Bord and C. Bord, *Alien Animals* (Granada: London, 1985), p. 116.

4

The New Zealand Zeppelin Scare of 1909

in collaboration with Bryan Dickeson

In 1908 a frightening realization became evident in political circles across the United Kingdom, which soon sent shock waves to British subjects throughout the Commonwealth in the form of press reports, commentaries, and debates. For centuries British citizens had slept peacefully, knowing that they possessed the world's unrivaled naval power and that an invasion of the motherland was inconceivable. The security of Britain's naval dominance was also felt in its colonies around the world. Yet suddenly in 1908 this image of security and stability was shattered. In the wake of rapid aeronautical advancements, coupled with Germany's Zeppelin development, the British Empire was vulnerable to attack by air.

The year 1909 was a turbulent year in New Zealand's history, characterized by enthusiasm over rapid and dramatic aeronautical achievements, xenophobia, fears of invasion, and a sudden perception of vulnerability. Amid this setting, a remarkable event occurred. Between Sunday evening, July 11, and September 2, tens of thousands of New Zealanders reported seeing Zeppelin-type dirigibles. Equally remarkable is that the episode has yet to be thoroughly documented[1] and has been virtually forgotten by contemporary scholars.

Two subjects dominated New Zealand newspaper headlines prior to the sightings: rapid aviation advancement and concern over the adequacy of the country's defense from a potential German invasion. While in early 1909 press discussion focused on the likelihood of Germany's directly attacking the British Isles, by midyear there was concern that they might instead attack the Empire's more vulnerable, remote outposts, which engendered considerable anxiety, especially in distant New Zealand. New Zealand had one of the world's most dynamic economies, with such natural resources as gold, minerals, timber, beef, sheep, wool, hides, forestry products, and farm and refrigerated produce, which likely fostered a perception by many of its citizens that it was a prime German target.

In the months prior to and encompassing the sightings, invasion fears intensified as New Zealand newspapers described "the wild rate at which shipbuilding is proceeding in Germany and England."[2] Responding to fears that the German military would soon supersede Britain's long-held naval superiority, the British concentrated its naval fleet near the motherland, further fostering perceptions that Australia and New Zealand were vulnerable to potentially hostile foreign powers. The former commander of the Australasian naval force, British Admiral Bowden Smith, summarized the situation:

> I think New Zealand and Australia should be awakened to the matter of defense. We have withdrawn our ships . . . from foreign stations, and concentrated them round . . . Britain. We all know . . . [why]. Germany is showing such a feverish haste to build up a big navy. . . . In the event of attack by armed fleets New Zealand and Australia would have nothing to show against them.[3]

Heavy press coverage detailing the inadequacy of British defenses and the German military buildup began on March 22, when the New Zealand government made a heavily publicized decision to offer Britain funding for one and possibly two dreadnought battleships to bolster its defenses. Throughout this time until June 14, when Parliament approved the offer, there was virtually daily press coverage of the issue and the general inadequacy of New Zealand defenses.

The dreadnought offer kindled patriotic feelings toward the motherland, and the New Zealand government began holding public meetings to debate the suitability of compulsory military conscription in response to the perceived threat. On May 12, the New Zealand press reported on the British House of Commons's "Great Debate" on military strategy for Empire defense. A New Zealand correspondent in attendance reported on the sense of "semi-hysteria."[4] Similar patriotic fervor was expressed at town meetings across New Zealand as citizens debated the conscription issue. The following display of emotionalism at one meeting was typical: "The resolution was received with loud applause, mingled with hooting. A few of the audience commenced to sing 'Rule Britannia,' but their voices became inaudible when a score or two Socialists sang a few lines of 'The Red Flag.' "[5]

From Dreadnoughts to Zeppelins: The Plausible Threat Solidifies

Simultaneous with the press accounts describing Germany's threat to the British Isles, and New Zealand in particular, numerous reports detailed rapid aviation advancements. At the forefront of this technology was the Zeppelin, which remained impractical but was slowly gaining in scope and capability. During 1909 "the aeroplane came of age" with French aeronaut Louis Bleriot's dramatic flight across the English Channel on July 25, and gained rapid acceptance as a potentially practical device for long-distance transportation.[6] Then suddenly, on May 19, it was widely reported that Germany was contemplating a shift in its military strategy away from naval warship construction and toward producing a fleet of Zeppelins capable of traveling long distances in short periods while transporting soldiers and ordnance.[7] Some letters from worried citizens appeared in the press, supporting earlier accounts exaggerating the German threat. Once the danger was defined as real and the belief that the British defense scheme was inadequate, citizens began redefining what had once been perceived as an adequate local defense force. For example, in mid-September 1908, the annual report of New Zealand's chief artillery instructor noted that despite deficiencies, "the records of the field garrison artillery volunteers show that considerable progress has been made in both efficiency and shooting.... [A]rtillery volunteers throughout the Dominion were never more efficient than they are now."[8] However, the dominion's military capability was still viewed as ill-prepared and inadequate, a position espoused in many editorials. For instance, one newspaper editor stated that defenses were insufficient to repel a single "good" enemy ship and complained of insufficient artillery, ammunition, manpower, and searchlights in Auckland Harbour, concluding by saying that "citizens may well wonder what the Government has been doing that it should have left the country in such a defenseless state."[9]

From about 1880 to the early twentieth century, a wave of popular science-fiction literature appeared on the scene, trumpeting the wonders of science and technology.[10] But during the first decade of the twentieth century, amid rapid aviation advances, Germany's growing naval prowess and its leadership in aerial technology, popular fiction took on a more dark and sinister tone. The notion of aerial warfare became a popular science-fiction theme,[11] following the widespread press discussion of the likelihood that aircraft would soon play a major part in a looming confrontation with Germany. In 1908 the influential H. G. Wells novel *The War in the Air* was published and serialized in *Pall Mall Magazine*. In the book airships inflicted horrific damage on New York by dropping bombs. Literary serials sharing a similar theme were common. For instance, *Chums* published a lengthy series of stories by Captain Frank Shaw in 1908, *The Peril of the Motherland,* in which Russia declared war on Britain, wreaking havoc with a fleet of airships. It was within this sociopolitical context that Zeppelin invasion rumors circulated across New Zealand and the first sightings occurred.[12]

The Zeppelin Sightings

The episode began on the evening of July 11 on the south island, when several Kaitangata residents reported seeing the mysterious light of a possible airship for thirty minutes as it bobbed in and out of view to the east over the Wangaloa Hills. The witnesses were prepared to sign an affidavit as to their veracity.[13] It was widely rumored that the German vessel *Seestern,* which had recently left Brisbane, was somewhere off the south island where it had "set the airship free" for secret aerial reconnaissance flights.[14]

On July 19, a mysterious flickering light was reported by three residents in Oamaru.[15] Widespread sightings began on the twenty-fourth, the day after a spectacular daylight incident at Kelso, where twenty-three schoolchildren and an adult described a Zeppelin-type airship that swooped low over the township. Four detailed sketches were made by witnesses, and an excited reporter proclaimed it to be "nothing short of dumbfounding."

> Thomas Jenkins gave a very clear account of the whole incident. He saw the vessel first at 12 o'clock as he was going home from school. It had come over the hill on the east side of the school . . . and sailed across the plain to the gorge on the other side. He watched it all the time, and saw it altogether about ten minutes. . . . As it passed over he saw that it had supports on each side . . . but these sails did not move. There was a wheel at the rear revolving very rapidly. There was a box beneath the body of the ship. . . . The vessel was entirely black in color. . . .
>
> Cyril Falconer was with other boys on the school ground when the airship passed over. A big wheel was revolving at the rear. He saw this reversed, and the vessel suddenly turned. . . . This boy drew an angular picture, which appeared to represent the ship as it was turning, with a wheel at the back. Other children saw it but these gave the clearest accounts.
>
> Mrs. Russell, evidently the only adult who saw the phenomenon, said she . . . saw a streak of blackness shoot over the hill on the left and apparently come straight towards her. Then it suddenly turned and swerved away over some trees out of her sight. . . . In appearance it was just like a boat. It was black in colour. She saw it for just a few minutes. It was travelling very fast at first, but when it turned it came lower and went somewhat slower. She did not notice any wheel at the rear or any sails, but was very flustered, as she thought the end of the world had come.[16]

On Friday, July 23, 1909, twenty-three schoolchildren and a teacher in Kelso reported seeing a Zeppelin-type dirigible flying low near the school. It was seen in broad daylight and caused a sensation across the country. The three drawings below all appeared in the *Otago Daily Times*, August 4, 1909.

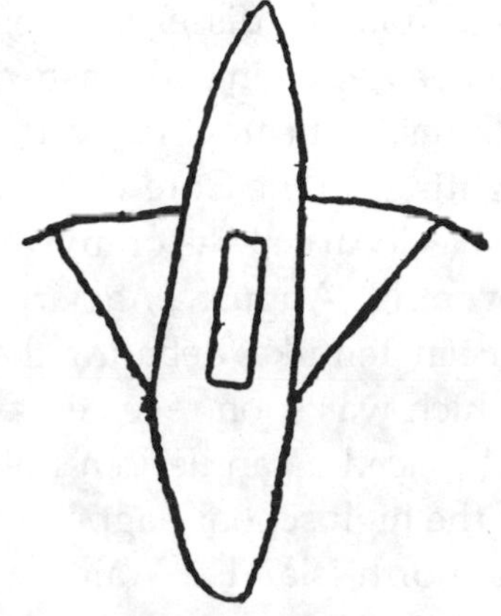

Bottom view of the object as described by pupil Thomas Jenkins, consisting of a long cigar-shaped body, a suspended gondola underneath, and two large sail-like wings.

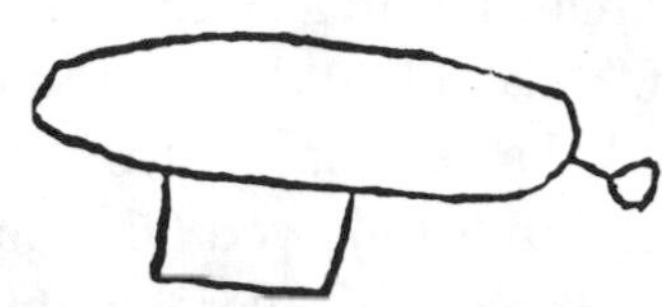

Side view of the object also seen by Thomas Jenkins. He said the propeller-like wheel at the back was revolving rapidly.

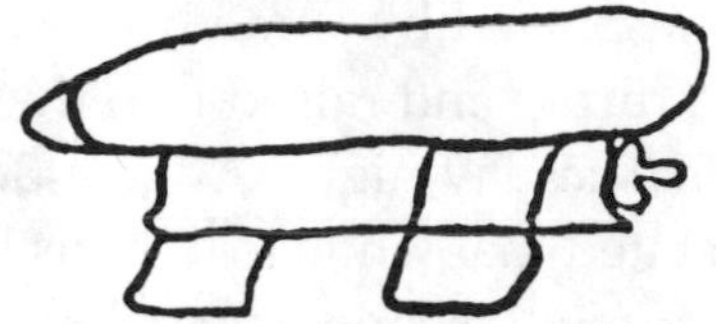

At about 5 P.M. on the next day (Saturday, July 24), another student at the Kelso school, George McDuff, saw the vessel near his home. When interviewed by an *Otago Daily Times* reporter in 1968, sixty years after the incident, McDuff was a farmer living in North Otago. He attributed the sightings to overactive imaginations and claimed he did not see anything.

Shortly after the sighting a party of young men from Kelso trekked into the nearby Blue Mountains in a vain attempt to locate the vessel,[17] and local police also searched.[18] The incident received heavy press coverage, and a deluge of reports followed over the next ten days. On the following evening, July 24, just a few miles away at Kaka Point, another dramatic account was recorded of an airship flying over the beach. A Mr. Bates and several boys observed "a huge illuminated object moving about in the air." The vessel seemed like it was going to land, and in apparent fear that it was a German Zeppelin, thinking it had been attracted by their lantern, the boys ran off, leaving it behind.[19] If the vessel flew within close range again, some of the boys said they would "try to 'prick the bubble' with a bullet."[20]

Near Gore on July 30, two mining dredge hands working the night shift claimed to see an airship at 5 A.M. descend in the fog and circle the area, with "two figures . . . plainly discernible on board."[21] Later that day a rumor began that a Zeppelin had crashed at Waikaka, killing two or three Germans.[22] The report by the dredge hands followed other airship sightings in the Gore vicinity over the previous several nights[23] as well as local reports of mysterious luminous lights.[24] On Sunday evening, August 1, a large crowd gathered in front of the post office at Temuka, debating the origin of a mysterious luminous orb, which was soon revealed as a prank played by some boys who had placed a candle in a hollowed turnip and raised it to the top of the high school flagpole.[25]

On Tuesday night, August 3, on the north island, a Waipawa man stated that while riding his horse near the racecourse, a large, gray, torpedo-shaped vessel with lights at the prow and stern passed overhead, and one of three visible passengers "shouted out to him in an unknown tongue." The ship rose to a great height, circled and disappeared behind a hill.[26] By early August the New Zealand reports began to wane, with the last known sighting of the month near the gold mining community of Waihi on the ninth.[27]

Once the Zeppelin's existence was widely accepted, various past and present events and situations that would have ordinarily received prosaic interpretations were redefined as airship-related. On the night of July 14, Mary Guinan of Kelso watched a gradually dimming "star," but after hearing of subsequent airship sightings, "she at once concluded that it was this she had seen."[28] A mysterious "swaying light" observed by several Christchurch residents for three weeks "excited little comment" until the airship reports, and one witness said that it "seemed to be attached to some object moving gently across the line of sight."[29] When a farmer in the Black Hills found two gas cans on a remote slope inaccessible by car, it was suggested that the oil was used to fuel an airship motor.[30] In the Otama district, another farmer thought an airship may have landed for repairs after he found several screw wrenches in his field.[31] W. S. McIntosh of Hedgehope reported that when he and two friends were trapping near Glenham during the previous winter, they had seen a mysterious aerial illumination "resembling a searchlight" hovering about thirty-five feet off the ground three hundred yards away from them. McIntosh said, "At the time . . . I did not say much about it, as I knew people would not credit it."[32]

While a Zeppelin was the prominent explanation for these sightings, alternative folk theories included a local inventor's secret airship trial flights,[33] a luminous cloth attached to a carrier pigeon or sea gull,[34] "a visitation from another world,"[35] and myriad atmospheric and meteorological phenomena.[36]

Many press accounts described the airship's presence factually, especially at the beginning of the episode, when ambiguous aerial "lights" were often depicted as "airships."[37] However, as the episode continued, the press generally grew more incredulous. One editorial associated the reports to alcohol consumption, noting that airship sightings "may mean development of the keg business."[38] In accordance with prevailing psychological theories of the period, namely Gustave LeBon's view of crowd contagion as a form of mental disorder, psychopathological explanations were often advanced. One press columnist compared sightings to religious revivals, implying that LeBon's concept of primitive instinct was aroused and rationality was lost.

> Revival excitements, like airship excitements, are matter for public comment; in neither case is it sacrilege to suggest natural causes. . . . Natural causes?—given a crowd, speaker that can play upon its emotions, with a singer that teaches it to express them in voluptuous dance rhythms, and you have for your revival excitement some very obvious natural causes.[39]

Some witnesses were characterized as suffering from "aerialitis."[40] A letter published in the *Otago Daily Times* described the sightings as a "craze," warning of the danger of lost self-control. The author classifies the reports as a "popular delusion" in reference to Charles Mackay's classic book on the subject.[41]

> Sir.—The airship craze is getting beyond a joke. There is a danger of our level-headed community becoming the laughing stock . . .

> [of] the greater world. We do not want to be advertised in that way. . . . The world has had a great many examples of "extraordinary popular delusions," such as the South Sea Bubble, the tulip mania in Holland . . . the persecution of witches. . . . These phenomena arise in times of public excitement, when every whisper and shrug is taken as evidence, and the capacity to weigh matters is for the time submerged by some human passion, such as fear or greed.[42]

The author concluded by noting that the "German scare, the Dreadnought episode, and the conquest of the air" had combined to create an improbable yet plausible threat that culminated in a popular delusion. One resident wrote to express surprise at the public's gullibility, facetiously noting that a Zeppelin invasion by the Germans or Japanese was remote, but the episode was almost certainly an attack by octopuslike Martians: "The presence of a dead squid on the beach at Burkes a few days ago is fairly conclusive evidence."[43] It was widely noted in many newspapers from late July that sales of fire balloons[44] had increased dramatically,[45] and their remains were often found in the vicinity of sightings. Press accounts became increasingly skeptical in early August,[46] as numerous reports of mysterious aerial lights were increasingly described as stars[47] or fire balloons.[48]

On July 29, the *New Zealand Herald* editor described them as "flights of fancy," while commentary in the *Evening Post* referred to them as "hot-air" ships, remarking that a combination of hoaxes and misperceptions of heavenly bodies composed "the nucleus of an aerial German invasion."[49] After residents reported seeing what appeared to be a searchlight circling above the town of Nelson, a reporter quipped: "It has come at last. We have been expecting the dread news for weeks. . . ."[50] By early August, press accounts became still more incredulous, even despite vivid descriptions:

> Nelson took more interest in astronomy last evening than it has ever done before. People in all directions stood and stared upwards at the sky. An airship had come to Nelson.
>
> There it was, plain enough. Some people could even tell that it had an acetylene lamp at the front of the car [gondola] which was shining so brightly. Others declared that there were lights shining, just as is the case with a motor car.

> Attempts, fortunately unsuccessful, were made to break into the Atkinson Observatory and Mr. F. G. Gibbs was literally besieged by telephone and callers. The fact that the light was seen to move was what particularly gave rise to the opinion that the "airship" which was making those night attacks down south, had at last arrived in Nelson, and was skimming about in the air above the town.[51]

The *Timaru Post* described this account as a case of "airship fever."[52] On August 4, the *Otago Witness* reported that their offices had been "inundated with various cartoons mostly depicting a person under the influence of 'John Barleycorn,' gazing with drunken gravity at a street lamp or the town clock or some kind of light which no sober individual would ever mistake for an airship."[53] Another newspaper attributed the sightings to "the silly season," a term used to describe the tendency of reporters to print articles on trivial topics for lack of more worthy news.[54] When the sightings reached the capital, the *Southland Times* sarcastically announced: "Wellington Bitten at Last."[55]

Advertisers capitalized on the airship sightings, with one proclaiming: "The latest news by air ship sent to Kelso was that Anderson's selling out sale is still booming."[56] Mr. G. Whealer of Bluff, an agent for a local liquor manufacturer, wrote that a message was dropped from the airship by Martians on Bluff Hill, requesting ten thousand more cases of Gilmour and Thompson's Scotch Whisky.[57]

During August, there was a brief spate of sightings over Australia, almost exclusively confined to the east coast between August 9 and 14. The Australian press discussion of the perceived German invasion threat was much lower key, and the number of subsequent airship sightings over Australia was much lower, confined to just a few days and almost universally described as the work of a local, nonthreatening airship inventor. All of the press reports describe the airship with different degrees of skepticism, most attributing the observations to overactive imaginations.[58] One reporter used the headline "Aerial Hysteria," cautioning that the reports were not to be taken seriously.[59] The Australian episode occurred as the New Zealand reports were waning, and since no invasion had occurred, a popular view among some Australians was that a local inventor had perfected the world's first practical airship and was making secret trial flights. Correspondingly, the Australian reports were exclusively described as mysterious lights or airships, not Zeppelins, and citizens were enthusiastic during sightings, not anxious as they were in New Zealand.[60]

After a three-week absence of reports in New Zealand, a final flurry of sightings took place at Gore, as hundreds reported a dark cigar-shaped object near the Tapanui Hills between 4:30 and 6 P.M. on September 1 and 2.[61] The reports abruptly ended when a press correspondent visited the site and found that the sensation was caused by "repeated flights of thousands of starlings, which, prior to nesting season, were making their temporary homes in a clump of pine trees."

> About 5:00 P.M. movements from the pine trees commenced. The birds would rise up in one thick black mass and circle round in the sky. Their evolutions were wonderful to behold. At first they would look like a dark cloud; then they would assume the shape of a very long strip, darting up into the air and then descending with very great rapidity towards earth, at one minute compressed formation, and at another in extended line. . . . As they ascended into the air their numbers were so great that their wings make a great noise, just as if it was the whirl of machinery in motion.

The reporter quipped that " 'birds; only birds!' soon became the general cry."[62] With the Gore sightings, the New Zealand airship scare had come to a close.

Notes

1. Discussion of the phantom Zeppelin sightings has been almost exclusively confined to several contemporary books on unidentified flying objects, with suggestions that they represent extraterrestrial spaceships. See M. Stott, *Aliens Over Antipodes* (Sydney: Space-Time Press, 1984), pp. 9–54; M. Dykes, *Strangers in Our Skies*: *UFOs Over New Zealand* (Lower Hutt, 1981), pp. 16–31; H. Fulton, "Mysterious Objects Haunt

Skies of 1909, Many Strange Sights Witnessed Some 40 Years Ago," *Official Quarterly Journal of Civilian Saucer Investigation* (New Zealand) 4, no. 4 (1957): 23–26.

2. *Wellington Dominion*, May 1, 1909, p. 3.

3. *Wellington Dominion*, May 8, 1909, p. 5.

4. *Wellington Dominion*, May 12, 1909, p. 5.

5. *Wellington Dominion*, May 14, 1909, p. 5.

6. C. Gibbs-Smith, *Aviation: An Historical Survey from Its Origins to the End of World War II* (London: Her Majesty's Stationery Office, 1985), pp. 145–46.

7. The following headline typified press reaction: "Military Airship Preferred to Dreadnoughts. . . . A Remarkable Agitation Is Going on in Germany to Build a Huge Aerial Fleet, Instead of Many Dreadnoughts," *Wellington Dominion*, May 19, 1909, p. 7.

8. *Wellington Dominion*, May 19, 1909, p. 8.

9. *The New Zealand Herald*, May 1, 1909.

10. I. F. Clarke, "American Anticipations: The First of the Futurists," *Futures* 18 (1986): 584–96.

11. J. Clute, *Science Fiction: The Illustrated Encyclopedia* (New York: Dorling Kindersley, 1995), pp. 44–45.

12. It is notable that just prior to and encompassing the New Zealand sightings, a spate of phantom airships, typically described as Zeppelins, were observed across England, accounts of which appeared widely in the New Zealand press. See "Airships and Scareships," *Evening Star*, July 7, 1909, and numerous other New Zealand newspapers. The following is an excerpt from this account: "The people who are always discovering German spies in England disguised as waiters or tourists have found a new occupation of apparently absorbing interest. They are writing to the papers to report having seen mysterious airships making midnight voyages over various parts of England. The ghostly vessels have been seen at spots as distant from each other as Belfast and East Ham, but the most numerous reports are from the eastern counties. The 'Daily Express' is full of dark tales of a long, cigar-shaped craft dimly visible through the night air, passing overhead with a whirring noise. Those watchers who are particularly lucky espy searchlights and hear 'foreign sounding' voices." For similar accounts in the New Zealand press, see "Mysterious Airships," *Timaru Herald*, July 23, 1909; "Real Scareship," *Timaru Herald*, August 14, 1909.

13. *Otago Daily Times*, July 16, 1909, p. 10; "A Mysterious Light. Was It an Airship? Excitement in the South," *The New Zealand Herald*, July 27, 1909.

14. The following account appeared in "Was It Made in Germany?" *Evening Star*, July 27, 1909: "The explanation that is finding favor with those who have put two and two together is that the fact that German vessels are in New Zealand waters is responsible for it. They aver that the German Government yacht Seestern, for which the German warship Condor, which left Auckland on Sunday, is 'supposed' to search for (the Seestern being said to be considerably overdue at the Island from Brisbane), is, they state, in reality off the New Zealand coast. They are not backward in advancing the theory that the Seestern set the airship free somewhere in the neighborhood of the Nuggets, where it was first observed. . . . A thorough elucidation of the whole mystery is awaited with keen interest." For similar discussions of the German origin of the mysterious lights, refer to: "The 'German' Theory," *Evening Star*, July 29, 1909; "The German Scare," *Timaru Post*, July 28, 1909; "Airship Mysteries," *The New Zealand Herald*, July 27, 1909. In a letter to the editor of the *Otago Daily Times*, August 3, 1909, one resident proclaimed: "Now, with regard to the origin of this airship, I pinned my faith at the start to the German cruiser theory, and I will stick to that. . . . Where is this cruiser Seestern and where is the Condor? One or both of these boats may have dirigibles of this type stowed away on board. Deflated, 'the thing' may be quite compact, and the gas generator—of course, a more unwieldy piece of goods—remains on board when 'the bird' flies away."

15. A. Brunt, "The New Zealand UFO Wave of 1909," *Xenolog* 101 (1975): 2.

16. "The Airship Mystery. Stories of Mysterious Lights," *Otago Witness*, August 4, 1909.

17. "The Mysterious Lights. Seen in Widely Separated Districts," *Otago Daily Times*, July 30, 1909.

18. "Searching at Kelso," *Evening Star*, July 29, 1909.

19. *Clutha Leader*, July 27, 1909.

20. Ibid.

21. "Two Miners See the 'Ship,' " *Dominion*, July 31, 1909; "Airship Seen by Two Dredge Hands. At Close Quarters. Two Persons on Board," *Evening Star*, July 30, 1909; "Close View of the Craft," *The Auckland Star*, July 31, 1909. The time and location of this sighting suggests that they misidentified the moon.

22. "Testimony by School Children. A Black Object," *Evening Star*, July 31, 1909.

23. "With a Headlight Attached," *Dominion*, July 31, 1909; "More Airship Stories," *The Auckland Star*, July 30, 1909. This included a report in

early August of a Gore man who observed an airship that appeared to sport two large fans. Refer to *Waikato Argus*, August 3, 1909.

24. "In the Gore District," *Evening Star*, July 29, 1909.

25. *Geraldine Guardian*, August 3, 1909.

26. *Hawkes Bay Herald*, August 6, 1909.

27. Brunt, "The New Zealand UFO Wave," p. 7, quoting a New Zealand Broadcasting Service documentary from 1961; "The Mysterious Lights," *Geraldine Guardian*, August 12, 1909.

28. "The Mysterious Lights," *Otago Witness*, August 4, 1909.

29. "A Strange Light in Canterbury," *Evening Star*, July 29, 1909.

30. *Timaru Post*, August 11, 1909.

31. Ibid.

32. "Seen Last Winter," *Otago Witness*, August 4, 1909.

33. "Was It an Airship?" *Timaru Post*, July 14, 1909; "One Man Sees an Airship," *Dominion*, July 31, 1909.

34. "Observed at Wide Intervals," *Otago Witness*, August 4, 1909.

35. *Cluth Leader*, July 30, 1909.

36. "Oamaru Opinions," *Otago Witness*, August 4, 1909; "A Possible Explanation," *Dominion*, August 3, 1909. One man suggested the possibility of "a luminous haze or cloud." See *Otago Daily Times*, July 30, 1909. For a suggestion that some reports were ignis fatuus, or "will-o'-the wisp" (phosphorescent light generated from decaying organic material), or electrical discharges common on ships at sea during foggy weather (corposant or St. Elmo's Fire), see "Jack in the Lantern," *Evening Star*, July 30, 1909; "Seen at Temuka," *Geraldine Guardian*, July 31, 1909; "Atmospheric Luminosity" (letter), *Southland Times*, July 31, 1909; "The Mysterious Light. Supposed Airship," *Timaru Post*, July 30, 1909.

37. "The Airship Mystery Seen at Dunedin," *Evening Star*, July 28, 1909, p. 4; "Clear Evidence," *Evening Star*, July 29, 1909, p. 4; "The Kelso Airship. Cumulative Evidence," *Otago Daily Times*, July 29, 1909, p. 7; "The Airship, Seen in North Otago," *Otago Daily Times*, July 30, 1909, p. 8; "What the Dredge-Men Saw," *Auckland Weekly News*, August 5, 1909, p. 21; "The Airship. Further Evidence from Kelso. Statements by Eye-witnesses," *Otago Daily Times*, August 6, 1909, p. 5.

38. *Wellington Dominion*, July 28, 1909, p. 6.

39. *Otago Daily Times*, August 7, 1909, p. 6.

40. *Dunedin Evening Star*, August 4, 1909, p. 5; *Wellington Dominion*, August 11, 1909, p. 8.

41. C. Mackay, *Memoirs of Extraordinary Popular Delusions and the Madness of Crowds*, vol. 2 (London: Office of the National Illustrated

Library, 1852). In the preface to his book, Mackay remarked that, "We find that whole communities suddenly fix their minds on one object, and go mad in its pursuit. . . . Men, it has been well said, think in herds, it will be seen that they go mad in herds, while they only recover their senses slowly, and one by one" (pp. vii–viii).

42. Letter to *The Otago Daily Times*, August 3, 1909, p. 10.

43. "That Flying Machine" (letter), *Evening Star*, August 3, 1909.

44. Fire balloons were available in New Zealand during this period and typically sold at shops selling pyrotechnics. They consisted of paper balloons with candles attached near the mouth and were made buoyant by the generation of heat. The stimulus for artificial devices sent aloft during the Zeppelin sightings was more likely to have been kites, which were more popular and cheaper.

45. "Possible Explanations," *Otago Daily Times*, August 30, 1909; "Fire Balloons Suggested," *Evening Star*, July 29, 1909; "A Fire Balloon Found in Dunedin," *Geraldine Guardian*, July 31, 1909.

46. For instance, on the evening of August 10, four reports of mysterious lights were recorded in the *Southland Times*, August 11, 1909. The first two were from Goulburn and Moss Vale in Australia, the other two from Waihi and Stony Creek in New Zealand. The reports were limited to no more than four sentences and appeared as follows: "In the Air. Glimmers at Goulburn," "Visions in Victoria," Wonder at Waihi," and "Stony Creek Stratagem."

47. "A Remarkable Sight. Strange Movements of a Star," *Dominion*, August 7, 1909.

48. "A Fire Balloon. Found in York Place," *Otago Daily Times*, July 30, 1909; "Fire Balloons," *Tapanui Courier*, August 4, 1909.

49. "Hot-air Ships," *Evening Post*, August 2, 1909.

50. *Thames Star*, July 31, 1909.

51. *The Nelson Mail*, August 3, 1909.

52. "The Supposed Airship. Nelson People Hoaxed," *Timaru Post*, August 3, 1909.

53. "The Mysterious Lights. Seen in Widely Separated Districts," *Otago Witness*, August 4, 1909.

54. "The 'Airship,' " *Tapanui Courier*, August 4, 1909.

55. *Southland Times*, August 4, 1909.

56. *Tapanui Courier*, July 28, 1909.

57. *Southland Times*, August 2, 1909, p. 5.

58. "Another Aerial Mystery. Mysterious Light in Victoria," *Sydney Morning Herald*, August 9, 1909, p. 7; "Lights in the Air," *Melbourne Argus*,

August 9, 1909, p. 7; "Is It an Airship?" *Sydney Morning Herald*, August 10, 1909, p. 7; "The Goldburn 'Airship.' Lights Reported for a Week," *Sydney Morning Herald*, August 11, 1909, p. 10; "Mysterious Lights Seen in New South Wales," *Melbourne Argus*, August 11, 1909, p. 6; "Venus and Jupiter. Planets in Conjunction," *Melbourne Argus*, August 13, 1909, p. 7; "Stars in Conjunction," *The Mercury* (Hobart), August 13, 1909; "Mysterious Lights," *The Mercury* (Hobart), August 14, 1909, p. 4; "Celestial Phenomenon Lights Visible in Sydney," *Sydney Morning Herald*, August 14, 1909, p. 14; "Mysterious Lights. Astronomical Lights. . . . A Feasible Explanation," *Sydney Morning Herald*, August 14, 1909, p. 10. Consider the following characteristic report filed from Zeehan, Tasmania, on August 13, appearing in *The Mercury* [Hobart], August 14, 1909, under the headline: "Phenomenon in the Sky": "A number of residents of Zeehan report today having seen mysterious lights in the sky shortly after 7 o'clock last night. There were two lights, white and brilliant, which seemed to be travelling rapidly in a north-westerly direction against the wind, and soon disappeared behind a cloud. As the lights travelled, one appeared to grow smaller and the other larger.

This phenomenon was, doubtless, the conjunction of the stars, Venus and Jupiter."

59. *Sydney Morning Herald*, August 7, 1909, p. 13; "Venus and Jupiter," *The Mercury* (Hobart), August 16, 1909.

60. The following report is typical:

"Moss Vale, Monday—A good deal of excitement was occasioned to-night by the appearance of a mysterious light or an illuminated body to the south-east of the town. Quite a number of people gathered in the main street, and speculation was rife as to the meaning of the strange illumination. Above the large light some large body was distinctly visible, as the rays of light were reflected upon its surface. The supposition generally held is that the mysterious floating light is either a large balloon or airship. . . .

"Passengers on to-night's Melbourne express were afforded a view of the mysterious night-light which has been observed floating above the southern highlands and coast between Mittagong and Wollongong during the last two nights. When the express reached Hilltop quite a score of passengers crowded on the platform at each end of the corridor carriages on the lookout for the 'airship,' as it was called. Their vigilance was soon rewarded, for as soon as the express hauled out from the deep cuttings, a large, bright light became visible a few miles away towards the coast. Apparently it was in motion, and could be plainly distinguished from the stars, but the distance was too great to detect the nature of the floating body. Its elevation appeared to be about 2000 ft" (*Goulburn Evening Penny Post*, August 10, 1909).

61. "More Seeing at Gore," *The Southland Times*, September 2, 1909; *The Southland Times*, August 3, 1909.

62. *The Southland Times*, September 4, 1909.

5

The New England Airship Hoax of 1909–10

Between December 13, 1909, and January 23, 1910, residents of the New England seaboard region of the northeastern United States were convinced that a local businessman had invented the world's first practical heavier-than-air flying machine. This long-anticipated invention would revolutionize aviation. While large portions of entire states believed the rumors, tens of thousands of seemingly stolid, responsible citizens actually reported sighting the vessel sailing through the frosty night sky. The rumors and subsequent sightings triggered an extensive search to uncover the vessel's whereabouts. No abandoned farmhouse or local eccentric escaped inquiry from the determined army of inquisitive reporters. Journalists from across the United States and from as far away as Europe soon converged on Boston and Worcester, Massachusetts, where most observations were reported. It was hailed as the story of the century, perhaps even the millennium. At the height of the episode, even representatives of foreign governments arrived in order to assess the potential commercial and military applications of such a vessel.

Following intense press scrutiny and an investigation of the reports, it soon became evident that the ship's existence was a colossal hoax. Yet before the deception was realized, scores of eyewitnesses, including businessmen, police officers, prominent politicians, and judges, believed that they had actually seen the vessel. Many were certain that they could discern the roar of its powerful engine churning in the distance, while a few even emphatically claimed to distinguish the outline of the pilot maneuvering through the night-time sky.

The highest concentration of sightings was over Massachusetts (sixty-one), with other sightings in Rhode Island (ten), Connecticut (seven), Vermont (six), New York (one), and Maine (one). Sightings often involved large portions of towns and cities. The predominant folk theory held that prominent local entrepreneur, inventor, and businessman Wallace E. Tillinghast was making secret nocturnal flights of his newly perfected airship.

Prelude to the Delusion

In the years immediately preceding the episode, intense excitement swept across Europe and North America in anticipation of the first practical, mechanically powered heavier-than-air flight. Enthusiasm waxed and waned with each of the five attempts at piloted powered flight between 1874 and 1899. These crude, modest successes were interspersed with numerous failures. From the first known attempt in 1874 until 1899, there were just five successful documented flights. Each was erratic, brief, and mundane by contemporary standards. However, with the dawn of the twentieth century there were rapid, dramatic advances coupled with heavy newspaper coverage of powered flight attempts, leading to a spectacular climax just prior to the airship delusion.

> The years 1908-9, brought wide publicity and belated acclaim. Orville's tests for the War Department . . . and Wilbur's flights in Europe before enthralled crowds, including the kings of Spain and England, became . . . front-page news. Meanwhile, the flights of other pioneers, like Glenn Curtiss, stirred additional interest in aviation.[1]

It was during 1909 that British aviation historian Charles H. Gibbs-Smith noted that "the aeroplane came of age" and was accepted as a practical vehicle for two reasons: Louis Bleriot's flight across the English Channel on July 25 and the world's first aviation meeting in France, from August 22 to 29:

> If the Channel crossing made the greatest impact on the public, it was the Reims aviation week which provided the greatest technical and governmental stimulus to aviation, and proved to officialdom and the public alike that the airplane had indeed "arrived." . . .
>
> Reims marked the true acceptance of the airplane as a practical vehicle, and as such was a major milestone in the world's history.[2]

Gibbs-Smith has compiled a chronological list of all known piloted powered flight between 1874 and 1908. Rapid progress in powered flight was especially dramatic in the two years immediately preceding the episode. In 1907 there were an unprecedented fourteen such flights, climaxing in forty-seven in 1908.[3] Another measure of intense public exposure to aviation feats immediately prior to the 1909 episode can be obtained by examining the *New York Times Index* for the years 1900–1909. In 1900, under the listing of "aeronautics," one article appeared. By 1905, this figure had reached 58; and it rose quickly to 138 in 1907, 466 in 1908, and 964 in 1909, the year of the hoax.

Chronology of Events

It is within this historical setting that the *Boston Herald* of December 13, 1909, published a lengthy newspaper interview with prominent local businessman Wallace Tillinghast, a credible and creative figure,[4] in which he confidently proclaimed to have perfected and flown the world's first sophisticated airship, far exceeding any devices of the period. Tillinghast also asserted that his experimental flights were continuing. This fantastic account appeared in spectacular front-page headlines:

TELLS OF FLIGHT 30 MILES IN THE AIR
Engineer says he sailed from Worcester to New York
to New York Harbor at Night in
Aeroplane of his Own Invention
CLAIMS CIRCLING STATUE WHEN 4000 FEET UP
Wallace E. Tillinghast says He Invented Machine Under Cover
and is Going to Smash International Records

WORCESTER, Dec. 12—Wallace E. Tillinghast of this city, vice-president of a manufacturing company here, made public a story today . . . [that] he invented, built, and tested an aeroplane capable of carrying three passengers with a weight limit of six hundred pounds, a distance of about three hundred miles with a stop to replenish the supply of petrol, at a rate of 120 miles an hour.

He refuses to say where his flying machine is . . . as he wants to enter into Boston contests next year as a sure winner. He says that on Sept. 8 he made a night trip to New York and return, at which time the machine was thoroughly tested. . . .

In describing his machine, Mr. Tillinghast says: "It is one of the monoplane type, with a spread of 72 feet, a weight of 1550 pounds, and furnished with a 120-horsepower gasoline engine made under my own directions and specifications. It differs from others in the spread of the canvas, the spread of the plane and in stability features. Special attention is given in making it adaptable for high speed. All the important parts are covered by patents.

"Other distinguishing features are that it cannot be capsized, is easily controlled and the occupants ride on the body of the machine instead of having the body of the machine behind them. The headlight is made by the use of acetylene gas generated on the machine. I decline to say where the machine was built or is stationed, because it is the business of no one but myself and my mechanics.

"I also decline to say what is the limit of speed of the aeroplane or the highest altitude that I can reach, because I wish to enter the international races in a fair trial and without rivals knowing what speed reported at the recent meeting at Reims that I feel sure the result will be that the Tillinghast aeroplane is more than an 'also ran.' . . .

"The machine is no experiment, as it has been thoroughly tested. All of the tests have been under the cover of night and have been considered successful."

Tillinghast stated that he had made trial flights on four different machines in recent years, including eighteen in the most highly perfected vessel, and claimed that his secret workshop and testing area were unknown "to everyone except himself and his workmen, and even the inhabitants of that district do not know what is going on." He was also cunning, aware at the time of his *Boston Herald* interview that a lifeguard on Fire Island claimed to have heard a noise like an aeroplane engine in the distance on an evening in early December. Ever the opportunist, Tillinghast revealed in his interview that on the evening of December 8, he and two mechanics had flown from the vicinity of Worcester to New York City, where he circled the Statue of Liberty in New York harbor before returning to his secret airstrip and shop. He claimed that when passing Fire Island, one of the cylinders began making an irregular noise and he was forced to fly near the beach. Before giving his interview, he would have almost certainly been aware of press reports appearing several days earlier, in which lifeguard William Leach reported hearing the sound of "an aeroplane pass high above him while he was doing patrol duty."[5]

While Tillinghast's story was a hoax, it seemed plausible in the wake of his reputation as an inventor, coupled with recent rapid progress in aerial flight technology and the expectant social climate. Within two days of the published interview, news of Tillinghast's purported feats made headlines in virtually every New England newspaper and many others throughout the world. The heavy press coverage included conflicting opinions regarding the legitimacy of his claims by aviation experts, local authorities, and newspaper editors. Wilbur Wright scoffed at the notion, while aviationist Glenn Curtiss declared it to be "extraordinary if facts can be improved."[6] The ensuing newspaper debate provided a degree of legitimacy to the initial hoax interview. It was at this point that many locals believing claims to be true, began rethinking various past events in light of this new worldview.

The day following Tillinghast's hoax interview, December 14, E. B. Hanna of Willimantic reported that on the same night that Tillinghast claimed to circle the Statue of Liberty, he saw a "bright light" crossing the nighttime sky for about an hour.[7] Upon reading the Tillinghast interview, Mr. Hanna concluded that it was likely his flying machine. Despite the ambiguous nature of the sighting, the *Willimantic Chronicle* printed the speculative headlines "What Mr. Hanna Saw May Have Been the Worcester Airship! . . . Now Thinks That It May Have Been the Aeroplane in Which Wallace E. Tillinghast Claims to Have Made a Flight from Boston to New York and Return."[8]

The next sighting occurred over Boston Harbor early on December 20, and it received sensational front-page headlines. Immigration inspector Arthur Hoe reported seeing an airship flying rapidly through the clear night-time sky,[9] but it was later determined that Hoe had mistaken the masts of the steamship *Whitney* for the circling airship.[10] Despite the vagueness of Hoe's observation, in light of widespread recent press publicity given to Tillinghast's spectacular claims, the *Globe* published Hoe's account, reporting as fact that an airship, most likely belonging to Wallace Tillinghast, was seen.[11] The combination of widespread press coverage of Tillinghast's interview, Hoe's sighting, and press accounts of the earlier sightings by Hanna and lifeguard William Leach lent plausibility to the vessel's existence. New England residents began reinterpreting recent events as airship-related and scrutinized the skies for evidence of the mysterious vessel.

Cyril Herrick wrote in a letter to the *Boston Globe* that the most likely explanation for his sighting of a "double meteor" during the previous year was the Tillinghast airship:

> I [would like to] recount the following, seen while in camp on the shores of Lake Winnipesankee last August. Shortly after dark one evening we saw approaching from Meredith way, two bright lights in the sky a fixed distance apart, high in the air and drawing near with lightning speed. Passing our camp, whatever it was, disappeared over toward the Ossipee hills. Only the great speed of the lights marred our belief that it was an aircraft. All doubt was dispelled the next morning by news received from two vacation people a half-mile distant—Dr. Frank Chapman of Grovetown, N.H., and Dr. Walter Westwood of Beachmont, but saw them returning about an hour later. Thus the meteor theory is disposed of, and this news from Worcester as to Tillinghast offers itself as a refreshing possible hypothesis in explanation of the strange sight we saw that night.[12]

Meanwhile, several Willimantic, Connecticut, residents told a reporter from the *Hartford Daily Times* that one night in early September they had spotted an unusual aerial object that, in light of recent events, must have been the airship.[13]

The first mass observations in the vicinity of Worcester took place on the evening of December 22, as an airship was reported by over two thousand people, "circling" Boston several times and remaining visible for some three hours and twenty minutes. The incident began at about 5:40 P.M., when a squad of police officers noticed an unusual aerial light.[14] By about 6:30, a crowd of Christmas shoppers and several policemen reported an unusual light estimated to be one thousand feet aloft in the southeast, steadily growing in size. By seven o'clock the "airship" had "sailed over the city," remaining stationary for several minutes over the State Mutual Life Insurance building.[15] An "airship" was also sighted at about six the same evening in nearby Marlboro, heading northwest.[16] There were hundreds of reports in nearby Worcester, Marlboro, Cambridge, Revere, Greendale, Nahant, Maynard, Fitchburg, Leominster, and Westboro, which spread over the telephone. As with previous press coverage, the airship's existence was typically reported as factual, although the *Berkshire Evening Eagle* described it as a "fire balloon."[17] One report said that Tillinghast "was seen by fully a thousand residents here tonight repeatedly circling the city in a huge airship."[18] Another account stated that "there is no doubt that some person was navigating a heavier-than-air machine here."[19]

The mass sightings continued for several days and were concentrated in the vicinity of Boston and Worcester. On December 23, the vessel reappeared above Worcester and several nearby communities between 6:00 and 7:30 P.M. In Worcester an estimated fifty thousand residents poured into the streets and nearly brought the city to a standstill:[20] "In the main thoroughfares people with bundles stood agape. . . . Men and boys poured from the clubrooms and women rushed from the houses to view this phenomenon. The streets were thronged."[21] While the *Boston Globe* reported that the Worcester sightings were of Venus, mass observations in Boston, Revere, Cambridge, and Willimantic were described with less skepticism.[22] Other press accounts continued to lend plausibility to the airship stories, such as the *Boston Herald's* headline "Mysterious Air Craft Circles About Boston for Nearly Six Hours."[23] Alex Randell of Revere even claimed to see "the frame quite plainly,"[24] while Baltic resident P. D. Donahue stated that he could make out two men in the vessel as it passed overhead.[25] When the strange light was seen by many residents above Willimantic, even its mayor, Daniel Dunn, said that "there was no doubt but that it was an airship."[26]

The episode peaked on Christmas Eve, with thirty-three separate reports from Massachusetts, Rhode Island, and Connecticut to Vermont, New York, and Maine. In Boston, on December 24 "thousands upon thousands of people . . . stood on sidewalks, street corners and squares from soon after dark till well on toward midnight" hoping for a glimpse of the airship. Most were rewarded.

> Lower Washington st, Dock sq, Scolay sq, Tremont row, Court st, Bowdoin sq, Court sq, Tremont st and the Common were haunted by large groups of more or less excited and awe-struck belated Christmas shoppers, many of them laden with bundles, all gazing well up into the zenith at the gleaming lights. . . .
>
> At the corner of Washington and Summer sts the elevated roads starter had the hardest job he had since the last big fire in his district, all owing to the crowd of sky gazers that would persist in obstructing the car track.
>
> On the Common a policeman got extremely angry at a bystander who undertook to argue against the genuineness of the airship and to suggest that the signal lanterns might be stars. "Haven't I seen the airship standing here?" demanded the bluecoat with an asperity that discouraged argument to the point. . . .
>
> Another man plainly distinguished that one of the twin lights was green, the other red, as they should be to conform to the rules of navigation, and he flatly told an observer at his elbow that he must be blind not to be able to see the difference in the color of the lights.
>
> Another man expressed doubt whether the airship was really moving but he was assured in gentle but firm tones by another that undoubtedly the operator had temporarily shut off his power, but that the machine had been moving unmistakably a few minutes before.

> A large majority of observers commented on the frequent ascent or descent of one end of the airship. Now it appeared to be gliding higher in space, then taking a chute downward in a gradual and graceful plane.
>
> A large group at the corner of Bromfield and Tremont sts showed the most marked agitation seen during the evening, for at one time, from that point, the airship appeared to be a few feet lower than the top of Park-st church steeple and so near that everybody felt sure that it was certain to crash into the steeple.
>
> Just when the nervous tension had reached its most critical stage, apparently, the operator appeared to see his danger, for the machine approached no nearer and appeared to be at a standstill as the crowd uttered a concerted sigh of relief and dispersed, to be succeeded by another a moment later.[27]

Many of Tillinghast's actions were deliberately ambiguous in an obvious effort to bask in the notoriety as well as to solidify the rapidly emerging consensus that he was the airship inventor. While he continually noted that he had never sought the initial publicity for his invention, and in fact had been hounded by an industrious journalist to obtain the initial interview, a reporter for a rival newspaper, the *Boston Globe*, subsequently learned that the reporter who obtained the original interview "with the great inventor, didn't have to spend any sleepless nights running down Mr. Tillinghast." The day before the interview Tillinghast had telephoned the *Boston Herald* and requested to meet with a journalist the following day, "as he had an item to get out."[28]

Tillinghast was the perceived inventor and pilot, and his movements were closely monitored.

> [P]eople who saw the airship took it for granted that Tillinghast was the aviator, and a Journal reporter, with others, at once made inquiries and learned that Mr. Tillinghast was away from home and that he telephoned his house from his office at four o'clock in the afternoon that he would not be home tonight. Further, [he] usually goes to where he says his aeroplane is hidden in [an] automobile but his auto is now out of repair, and he was seen taking a train shortly after four o'clock this afternoon. At eleven o'clock tonight he had not returned to his home and he was not

> expected until morning. All this taken into consideration, together with the . . . thin black form of the airship hovering about the city from almost every point . . . leaves no doubt in the minds of all who witnessed it that Mr. Tillinghast was the operator and the airship was his own invention.[29]

On December 24, when numerous sightings were reported across New England, the *Boston Journal* reported that when Tillinghast returned home in the morning, "his eyes were terribly bloodshot and his face was cut and wind tanned, showing every evidence of having been out in a strong high and cold wind for a long while." On the basis of this description, the reporter concluded that it was "almost certain Mr. Tillinghast is the mysterious aviator of the marvelous airship."[30]

Tillinghast's silence about his airship during this time served only to enhance the claims made during his hoax newspaper interview and was interpreted as affirming the evidence. He was characterized as secretive, a common stereotype of inventors of the period. As the search for the secret location of Tillinghast's airship broadened, scores of sheds and buildings in remote locations were scrutinized as possible hiding places. One reporter was arrested for trespassing on private property while checking a shed owned by a business associate of Tillinghast. While not actually seeing the vessel, the reporter concluded that it must be the secret machine shop, for why else would they have arrested him?[31]

The reports tailed off dramatically from Christmas to the end of the month with the exception of six sightings on December 27. Newspaper editors and citizens were increasingly skeptical. People began evoking the popular ideas of French psychologist Gustave LeBon, which attributed the sightings to individual, "primitive" impulses activated within emotional situations that produced a form of temporary irrationality or madness.[32] While a *Boston Globe* reporter described the city of Marlboro, Massachusetts, as "airship crazy,"[33] a reporter in nearby Rhode Island depicted it as "airship mad," implicitly comparing it to LeBon's contagious mental disease model, which was well known during this period.

> The epidemic of infected vision that has turned Massachusetts upside down struck town with a bang late yesterday afternoon. From the time that the sun went down until the last shopper had found his way home this morning all kinds of aerial craft circled over the city. . . . On the streets the greeting wasn't "Merry Christmas." It was "Did you see it?"[34]

One newspaper editor commented that "these must, indeed, be times sorely troublesome to the human imagination." He concluded that rapid progress in knowledge and technology "have no doubt brought the popular mind under no little strain and made it more susceptible than common to seeing phantoms in the air if not ghosts on the earth."[35]

By December 26, a deluge of skeptical press accounts began to appear. The *Boston Globe* expressed concern that residents of Worcester and its environs would soon become the laughingstocks of the world, since reporters representing newspapers from around the globe were wiring information that there was apparently little basis for the "fantastic stories."[36] That same day C. D. Rawson of Worcester confessed to sending up large owls with lanterns and a reflector attached to their legs.[37] A letter to the editor noted that most observations were consistent with misidentifications of Venus, which was prominent in the western sky in the early evening.[38] One press correspondent wired back to his West Virginia office, noting the growing doubts of the remarkable claims: "Go where you will in New England today and you will hear them talk about Tillinghast and his mysterious airship. The majority of New Englanders don't believe in Tillinghast."[39] By December 27, several correspondents with a vested interest in keeping the sensational story alive were criticized by their colleagues. One editor commented that while the mysterious light was seen on three consecutive evenings in the same position of the sky between 6 and 7 P.M. and corresponded exactly with Venus, "one ambitious news writer . . . sent long dispatches to two New York papers, telling how hundreds had stood out and watched the airship maneuver, and the metropolitan papers printed the story along with the story of Tillinghast's ship, giving the impression that it was the Worcester man." The editor concluded that the brilliant light "without doubt, is Venus."[40]

The steadily increasing skepticism soon turned to embarrassment and then hostility, as residents in Boston and especially Worcester were becoming the butt of jokes and ridicule by the national press, and there were fears that the publicity would have a negative impact on business investment in the region. This led to demands that Tillinghast either prove his assertions or refrain from making such claims.

> The rather ridiculous advertising which is coming to Worcester in this way annoys the staid folks who are proud of the commercial reputation of their city. They have awakened to the fact that the weird stories of flying marvels are not simply local in their effect and therefore are planning to take action.
>
> Several members of the Worcester Automobile Club, who are affiliated with the Worcester Board of Trade, propose to ask that body to take steps either to justify the stories that have gone all over the world or to ask for some reasonable explanation.
>
> They feel that the Board of Trade should ask Wallace E. Tillinghast to corroborate the wonderful tales of his aeroplane. It is their intention . . . that he must back up his statements with some reasonable proof or deny that he is responsible for the stories.
>
> It is their purpose to prove to the world either that there is a wonderful airship in the vicinity of Worcester or that the whole thing is a hoax and that the city does not sanction the peculiar brand of notoriety in which it has basked. . . . They want to settle the thing once and for all time. . . .
>
> Tillinghast will be asked to show his machine to a reputable delegation of citizens and some newspapermen. If he really says that he has some kind of ship and wishes to protect it provision will be made to insure him profound secrecy as to his plans.
>
> The main point is that the citizens who are interested in the move believe they should protect the reputation of their city. . . . If there be absolutely no basis for all the airship worries which have descended upon New England, they want to publish the fact to the world and close the incident.
>
> It is planned to put this "proposition" before Secretary Davidson of the Board of Trade on Monday.[41]

While such attempts failed, Tillinghast and his family were overwhelmed by the media spotlight. He was a virtual prisoner in his home and was constantly followed wherever he went. This seemed to accomplish what the business community could not achieve—to silence Tillinghast.

> Tillinghast . . . is absolutely incommunicado. The notoriety that has followed him since the mysterious lights were seen has seriously interfered with his business and with his home life. He has not been permitted an hour's peace. At his office there are constantly two or three persons who want to know something. At the door of his place of business and at his home he is closely watched by mysterious men. When he is at home his telephone rings constantly. . . . [T]he constant clangor is not conducive to his good nature.[42]

Only four sightings were reported during January, and these were met with great incredulity. When several Willimantic residents, including a police officer, noted an unusual nocturnal light in early January, the press descriptions were restricted to just two small paragraphs. There was no credible suggestion that an airship was actually sighted, and one newspaper proclaimed: "Willimantic people have been 'seeing things' again."[43] When the airship was sighted by R. W. Tyler of East Poultney, Vermont, on the evening of January 6, a local press account began sarcastically: "The expected has occurred, the inevitable has come to pass. Rutland county has seen the airship."[44] On the evening of January 19, several Fair Haven Heights, Connecticut, residents reported observing the airship, at which time the local newspaper prominently published the opinion of a local astronomer who had studied the object through a telescope and was certain that it was the star Sirus.[45] It was at this point that the reports ceased, ending the remarkable and strange sequence of events.

Notes

1. R. E. Bilstein, *Flight in America 1900–1983: From the Wrights to the Astronauts* (London: John Hopkins University Press, 1984), p. 15.

2. C. H. Gibbs-Smith, *Aviation: An Historical Survey from Its Origins to the End of World War II* (London: her Majesty's Stationery Office, 1985), pp. 145–46.

3. Ibid., pp. 231–36.

4. "Tillinghast to His Story Clings," *Berkshire Evening Eagle*, December 14, 1909.

5. "Noise Like an Aeroplane. Fire Island Surfman Heard It in Air; Sure It Was Not Geese," *Boston Herald*, December 13, 1909, p. 1.

6. "Tillinghast to His Story Clings," *Berkshire Evening Eagle*, December 14, 1909.

7. "What Mr. Hanna Saw May Have Been the Worcester Airship!" *Willimantic Chronicle*, December 14, 1909, p. 8.

8. "What Mr. Hanna Saw . . . ," *Willimantic Chronicle*, December 14, 1909, p. 8.

9. "Sailed Over the Harbor. Unknown Airship Makes a Flight in Night. . . . Immigration Inspector Hoe Able to Distinguish Part of Framework of Craft," *Boston Globe* evening edition, December 20, 1909, p. 1.

10. "Boston Airship a Boat's Masts. Inspector Hoe Mistook Towering Sticks of the *James S. Whitney* for Framework of Mysterious Night Flier," *Boston Herald*, December 21, 1909, p. 12.

11. "Sailed Over the Harbor . . . ," *Boston Globe* evening edition, December 20, 1909, p. 1.

12. "Air Ships Seen at Night," *Boston Globe*, December 23, 1909, p. 6.

13. "Light Seen in Hartford, Also," *Hartford Daily Times*, December 24, 1909, p. 3.

14. "Worcester Agape at Airship Lights. Wallace E. Tillinghast May Have Been Flying Above City. Business at Standstill While People Watch . . . ," *Boston Herald*, December 23, 1909, p. 1.

15. "Worcester Palpitating. All Excitement Today Over That Airship. Tillinghast Generally Given Credit for Being the Man. So Many People Saw It That No Question Is Raised of Some Craft Making Flight," *Boston Globe* evening edition, December 3, 1909, p. 1.

16. *Boston Herald*, December 23, 1909, p. 1.

17. "Light Caused by a Toy Balloon," *Berkshire Evening Eagle*, December 23, 1909, p. 1.

18. "Thousands See Big Airship Over Worcester . . . Machine Circles City Several Times at Height of Two Thousand Feet," *Boston Journal*, December 23, 1909, p. 1.

19. "Worcester Palpitating . . . ," *Boston Globe* evening edition, December 23, 1909, p. 1.

20. "Mysterious Air Craft Circles about Boston for Nearly Six Hours. Some Declare They Discern Outlines of Monoplane Bearing Two Men . . . ," *Boston Herald*, December 24, 1909, p. 1.

21. "Airship Is Just Venus," *Boston Globe*, December 24, 1909, p. 1.

22. Refer to the following press accounts appearing in the *Boston Globe*, December 24, 1909, p. 1: "Seen in Boston. Many Persons Positive They Saw the Light of Some Mysterious Navigator of the Air"; "Revere Sees Its Wings. Several Observers Say They Were Able to Make Out Outlines of the Airship"; "Cambridge Also Sees It. Airship Described as Moving from West to East and Then in Opposite Direction"; "Again the Searchlight."

23. "Mysterious Air Craft Circles about Boston . . . ," *Boston Herald*, December 24, 1909, p. 1.

24. "Skyship of Mystery Flies above Boston. Revere Man Gets Close Enough to See Framework and Hears the Engine . . . ," *Boston Journal*, December 24, 1909, p. 1.

25. "Mystery Airship Just Like Venus. Machine Hovers Over Willimantic," *Daily Times*, December 24, 1909, p. 3.

26. Ibid.

27. "Certain as the Stars. Airship Again on Route. Even Skeptics See Its Changing Lights," *Boston Globe*, December 25, 1909, p. 1.

28. "Tillinghast Very Modest," *Boston Globe*, December 20, 1909, p. 14.

29. "Mr. Tillinghast Absent," *Boston Journal*, December 23, 1909, p. 1.

30. "Skyship of Mystery Flies above Boston . . . Worcester Man Again Absent from Home All the Evening," *Boston Herald*, December 24, 1909, p. 1.

31. "Craft of Mystery Finally Tracked to Its Lair—Perhaps! Home of the Worcester Aeroplane Located in West Boyleson, Massachusetts, It Is Believed . . . ," *Willimantic Daily Chronicle*, December 24, 1909, p. 1.

32. G. LeBon, *Psychologie des foules*, 2d ed. (Paris: Felix Alcan, 1896).

33. "Marlboro Has It, Too," *Boston Globe* evening edition, December 23, 1909, p. 1.

34. "City Is Airship Mad. All Kinds of Aeroplanes Flying About, According to Reports," *Providence Journal*, December 25, 1909, p. 2.

35. *Springfield Republican* (editorial), January 2, 1910, p. 6.

36. "Airship Story Worries Them . . . ," *Boston Globe*, December 26, 1909, p. 14.

37. "Airship Owl Is Worcester Tale. C. D. Rawson Says He Hitched Lights to Birds and Let Them Fly on Nights Skycraft Was Seen," *Boston Sunday Herald*, December 26, 1909, p. 15.

38. "Venus and the Public Rye," *Providence Sunday Journal*, December 26, 1909, sec. 2, p. 5.

39. "Tillinghast in His Shop, Not in His Airship. New Englanders

Probably Mistake Venus for a Soaring Flying Machine and Get Excited," *Wheeling Register*, December 26, 1909.

40. "Willimantic Laughs at the Airship Faking," *Hartford Daily Times*, December 27, 1909, p. 11.

41. "Worcester Angry Over Airship. City, Tired of Notoriety, Wants Tillinghast Asked to Prove Assertions," *Providence Journal*, December 27, 1909, p. 11.

42. Ibid.

43. "The Inky Sky, and Not a Star in Sight," *Willimantic Daily Chronicle*, January 7, 1910, p. 1; "Willimantic Men See Things Again," *Hartford Courant*, January 8, 1910, p. 1.

44. "The Inevitable Airship," *Rutland Daily Herald* (Vermont), January 10, 1910, p. 4.

45. "Fair Haven Sees Phantom Airship . . . Astronomer Has Solution," *Hartford Daily Times*, January 19, 1910, p. 9.

6

The British UFO Panic of 1912–13

> It was realized, though certainly not universally, that as soon as an efficient flying machine made its appearance England lay open to an invasion from the air, that her traditional reliance upon the Navy and seapower was no longer so valid as it had been in what was looked upon as the dawn of a new age, the air age. As one contemporary expressed it . . . "England is no longer an island."
>
> —Alfred Gollin[1]

This chapter describes the context of a collective delusion that occurred in Great Britain over a five-month period during 1912–13, involving the mass sightings of imaginary Zeppelins. This episode was precipitated, as were many of them, by rumors exacerbated by widespread press speculation concerning a possible aerial invasion and the tendency of newspapers to present many claims as factual. The rumors were rendered plausible in the wake of rapid aeronautical advancements coupled with the German armament buildup. The phantom Zeppelins symbolized prevailing xenophobic sentiments that typified the period.

The War Scare Context

Between October 14, 1912, and March 1, 1913, tens of thousands of people across Great Britain reported seeing Zeppelins that far exceeded the technological capability of the period. The popular folk theory held that the sightings were of hostile German Zeppelins on aerial reconnaissance missions as a prelude to invasion. In the years immediately preceding the episode, anti-German sentiments rose steadily. The period between 1907 and the start of World War I was characterized by extraordinary public fear over the growing strength of the German military, especially relative to Zeppelin airships and dreadnought naval vessels, and the perceived weakening of the British navy.

In 1909 Britain's vulnerability to aerial attack was recognized and its long-standing rule as the unrivaled sea power suddenly questioned.[2] "Hysteria germanica" began to grow[3] and continued to wax and wane until the beginning of World War I.[4] Here is a summary of Anglo-German relations in 1909:

> The Admiralty in these circumstances feared that Germany might, by a sudden spurt in shipbuilding, overtake the British superiority in Dreadnoughts. Technical experts in every Navy in the world believed that victory or defeat in the next war at sea would turn upon . . . ships of this class or type.
>
> These anxieties were intensified by the novelty of the situation. No one in authority had any genuine experience of this kind of arms race. When the idea of German acceleration found its way into the German popular press a national panic was the result. There were no sane limits to the fears expressed in Britain in March and April 1909. Liberal Ministers were roundly condemned as traitors who had abused the trust placed in them by the nation. Some sections of the Press proclaimed that Britain's centuries-long . . . superiority at sea was . . . about to be lost to the Germans. It was widely believed that deadly balances were being altered and that Britain, owing to the lack of vigilance of the Liberal Government, was in mortal peril of a naval defeat and a consequent German invasion.[5]

Despite a general acknowledgment of Germany's naval challenge and increasing military strength between October 1906 and 1909, there had been no great concern over Britain's immediate security relative to hostile German intentions.[6] In 1906 Sir C. Hardinge foresaw no immediate German naval threat, concluding that "it is not likely to be made for some years to come."[7] From this period until 1909, although Anglo-German relations were unfriendly, most major British political figures believed that a German challenge to Britain's long-held naval superiority was in the distant future.[8]

Anglo-German tensions and mistrust had been steadily growing from 1907 to the start of World War I in 1914, but in 1912 "the naval race" between the two powers was especially daunting, and by late April "London and Berlin were as far apart as possible."[9] With news of a German plan to construct three additional battleships, the British Admiralty became concerned with the large increase of German battleships on active service. This led to a vigorous debate in which the Admiralty considered ordering its remaining large ships home from the Mediterranean,[10] provoking "a furious row throughout the rest of the year over whether Britain was still an 'imperial' power or merely a North Sea one."[11]

Through the first half of 1912, there were several well-publicized attempts by the British to achieve a German arms agreement, but all efforts failed to reach a compromise. Tensions escalated further in October 1912 with the outbreak of the first of three Balkan wars, which had a negative impact on Anglo-German relations. During November 1912, the month of the first documented Zeppelin sighting, so concerned were Britain and France by the possibility of a war with Germany, that they implemented the Grey-Cambon exchange, which morally obligated Britain to aid France in the event of a Franco-German altercation.[12] This agreement heightened Belgian distrust of Britain and fueled concerns that Belgium, a French neighbor, might side with Germany. Between February 1909 until the German invasion to Belgium on August 2, 1914, fears of a secret German-Belgian agreement were reported in Britain.[13] During the period of the Zeppelin sightings through 1914, the distance between England and Germany was "as wide as ever," and the political mood in Britain prior to World War I was filled with anxiety:

> The country was, to be sure, unusually turbulent in the years 1911–1914; the constitutional crisis, the industrial unrest, most dangerous of all, the Ulster question were producing bitterness, intransigence and a willingness to contemplate the use of violence which had rarely been seen in Britain for seventy or eighty years.[14]

During a naval crisis symposium in June and July 1912, Prime Minister Arthur Balfour also voiced concern that Germany would soon overtake Britain's long-held stranglehold as the world's superior naval power.

The Ascendancy of Aerial Technology

Rapid advancements in German aerial technology, making Germany the unquestioned world leader with its Zeppelin airships, further heightened invasion fears and lent plausibility to rumors of a potential invasion of Britain. The British preoccupation with such an invasion was expressed in various science-fiction novels during the latter nineteenth and early twentieth centuries.[15] The main theme of these books was arguing for "higher budgets and a stronger war machine."[16] Yet many other magazines and nonfiction books expressed concern over Britain's poor standing in the field of aerial technology, and discussed instead the potential of such technology to result in unprecedented destruction, including books like H. G. Wells's novel *The War in the Air* (1908).[17]

> In factual articles the danger that Britain was lagging behind the aeronautical developments of Russia, Germany and France were constantly brought to our attention. One good example of this type of warning appeared in The Strand Magazine of July 1911. The article by a well-known and respected aviator, Claude Grahame-White, was titled "The Aerial Menace. Why There Is Danger In England's Apathy." Accompanying it is an aerial view of London at night. The sky is full of aeroplanes and the caption informs us that they are, "A Fleet of Two Thousand Aeroplanes Dropping Bombs on London." Grahame-White sums-up the situation by noting that:

> As each year goes by this peril of the destructive potentialities of the aeroplane will increase. Its scouting powers will improve also. The longer we delay in England in this regard to placing ourselves abreast of other nations in aerial armaments the worse our position will be.[18]

It is within this environment that the "Zeppelin" sightings occurred.

The Zeppelin Sightings

The waves of claims and public discourse about Zeppelin incursions over Britain began at Sheerness on October 14, 1912, when several residents including Lieutenant Raymond Fitzmaurice, claimed to hear an aircraft at about 6:45 P.M., and some saw a distant aerial light which they assumed emanated from an airship. The incident did not receive widespread publicity until November 21, when Member of Parliament Mr. Joynson-Nicks inquired about the rumored Zeppelin sighting, which was to become popularly known as "the Sheerness Incident," asking Winston Churchill if Britain had airships "equivalent in size and power . . . capable of travelling at the rate of sixty miles an hour, and Mr. Churchill replied in the negative."[19] An examination of the minutes of the meeting of the Committee of Imperial Defence held on December 6, 1912, revealed that despite public denials, Churchill privately believed the sighting was of a Zeppelin.[20] Several days later the editors of *The Aeroplane* concluded that the "Sheerness incident" was almost certainly a Zeppelin, warning that "never was the 'Wake up England' spirit more immediately of importance."[21] This story prompted intense British press speculation that Zeppelins were flying over England, and on December 3 an airship was reported near Portsmouth.[22] With continued press coverage of the issue, a deluge of reports soon began to pour in from across the country.

Just before daybreak on January 4, 1913, road inspector John Hobbs reported a bright light over Dover, which he assumed to be an airship and which several newspapers described as fact.[23] At dusk on January 18, the Glamorgan chief constable Captain Lionel Lindsay claimed to see an airship emitting a trail of black smoke, although conditions were so foggy and poor "that one could not define it."[24] While the *Yorkshire Post* cautiously stated that Captain Lindsay saw "what he believes to have been a large aircraft,"[25] many press accounts described this fleeting observation as an airship.[26] Over the next several days many people came forward claiming that they too had seen the airship light that evening[27] or in the days prior to Captain Lindsay's report.[28] In the wake of these reports, Mr. Joynson-Hicks told a reporter of his belief that "foreign dirigibles are crossing the English Channel at will," displaying his alarm at the state of British defenses.[29] The sightings continued virtually unabated, with reports of airships almost nightly until March 7, when they suddenly stopped. The following press account summarizes the reports over a one-week period in late February:

> Everyday new reports arrive of more airships. . . .
>
> FRIDAY. Scarborough (searchlight seen and engine heard). Bridlington (lights and dim shape seen). Selby (long cigar-shaped body, searchlight . . . other lights . . . noise of motor heard). Hunstanton (rapidly moving lights seen).
>
> SATURDAY. Scarborough (lights and dim shape seen). Corbridge-on-Tyne (lights seen). MONDAY. Sanday, Orkney Isles (airship seen). Witherness (lights and . . . body of the vessel seen).
>
> Portsmouth (lights seen). Ipswich (ordinary lights, powerful searchlight, and body of the vessel seen; throb of engine heard).
>
> TUESDAY. Horsea (white and red lights and cone of airship seen). Hull (lights seen). Grimsby (lights and dim shape seen). Leeds (bright light and dim shape seen). Seaforth, Liverpool (bright light and outline of vessel . . . whirring of propeller and throb of the engine heard). Portishead, Somerset (lights and outlines of airship seen). Castle Dommington, Derbyshire (lights seen; engine heard). Dover (lights seen; engine heard). Hunstanton (bright lights seen).
>
> WEDNESDAY. Portland Harbour (dazzling searchlight and clear outline of airship seen; sound of propeller heard). Hyde (flashing lights and long, dark moving object seen). Romiley (. . . vivid searchlight seen). Avonmouth, Bristol (two lights seen).

THURSDAY. Hucknall, Nottinghamshire (airship and powerful searchlight seen). Kirkcaldy and Rosyth (brilliant light and dimly outlined airship seen). Liverpool and New Brighton (bright lights and dim shape seen). Ardwick, Manchester (two head lights and a tail light seen).[30]

The sightings in South Wales were mystifying, as the Zeppelin would have had to have crossed the English Channel in daylight, yet there were no corresponding sightings in England.[31] This prompted speculation in some quarters that the mysterious vessel was actually an airship that was being secretly developed by a local inventor,[32] or more likely by the War Office in response to the Zeppelin threat.[33]

As the sightings continued, what had earlier been described as a possible or actual airship of unknown origin was increasingly referred to as a hostile Zeppelin. Cardiff aeronaut E. T. Willows made headlines when he suggested that it could have been one of several Zeppelins that were capable of making the journey.[34] On January 23 a Knowle resident expressed fear that a man-o-war airship was recently seen over Bristol.[35] A Manchester man described his displeasure with the government for allowing Britain's lack of aerial preparedness: "The country will not be satisfied with a reassurance that the Admiralty has the matter in hand."[36] A former naval officer noted the enormous advantages of a foreign power's knowing the nocturnal geography and suggested bolstering coastal defense.[37] A British press correspondent in Germany warned of the German superiority in airship technology, remarking ominously that "England's maritime superiority [had] lost its whole significance, as superiority in the air [now] brings mastery of the world."[38] A technical editor of the leading aviation journal *Flight*, A. F. Berriman expressed his conviction that Zeppelins were capable of making long-distance voyages over England.[39]

Skeptical press reports grew more common, especially from February 6 onward. One common explanation for the sightings was the misidentification of Venus,[40] which was prominent in the evening sky during the episode. Fire balloons were found near some sites and were suspected as the stimulus for several sightings.[41] More novel explanations included the theory that a local aeronautical expert had anchored a small model airship to a moving motor car,[42] and rubber balloons with an attached battery and light were used to determine wind direction.[43] Some hypothesized that the noise often associated with the aerial light may have been "flocks of wild geese."[44] Unusual atmospheric illusions[45] were also suspects.

Actions by the British government only reinforced the belief in Zeppelin aerial incursions. During the second week of February, Parliament passed a bill giving officers the right to fire at any mysterious aircraft. The bill was approved with virtually no discussion, so people assumed that "naval and military authorities had received confidential reports which assured them that the airships of foreign powers [Germany] were making reconnaissances."[46] At a meeting of the Aeronautical Society, Major Sykes of the Royal Flying Corps declared, "Great Britain is no longer an island. Since Nelson defeated the united fleet at Trafalgar, Great Britain has held the mastery of the sea . . . [and] invasion was always improbable, if not even impossible. But the aeroplane has destroyed the inviolability of the English air."[47] Major B. Baden-Powell warned of the possibility of German airships carrying bombs that could be dropped on London, drawing parallels to H. G. Wells's *War in the Air,* in which London was destroyed by an aerial attack.[48]

Near the end of the sighting reports, many Britons ridiculed the witnesses, something that the German press had done since the start of the episode. A Penarth resident wrote: "The German airship Flying Venus, showing bright headlight, with no body discernible, was plainly seen between eight and ten o'clock this evening," signing his name "SCARED ONE."[49] German newspapers typically referred to the "airship ghost."[50] Psychopathological explanations were also discussed in the press, especially in the waning two weeks. The editors of the *London Daily Mirror* suggested that England was in the midst of an epidemic of "airshipitis" and quoted a prominent mental doctor who claimed that mass hallucinations were responsible.[51] A psychologist was quoted as saying that "the idea of a wandering ship . . . is so firmly fixed . . . that these mind impressions succeed in rendering it visible."[52] When a couple in Kilmarnock, Scotland, attributed a distant light to the vessel, a local newspaper proclaimed: "The Airship Epidemic . . . Breaks Out."[53] Many German newspapers described the reports in pathological terms. One press headline stated: "The Airship Psychosis in England."[54] The *Germania*, Berlin organ of the Centre Party, said the reports were laughable, the result of "iniquitous influencing of the masses,"[55] while another account referred to it as "the new English sickness."[56]

The phantom Zeppelin sightings reflected the prevailing sociopolitical climate in Britain just prior to World War I. The skies reflected the collective psyche, and a variety of ambiguous, prosaic, almost exclusively nocturnal aerial stimuli, circumstances, and events were widely redefined. For over a century prior to the episode, Britain's status as the world's naval leader was never seriously challenged, but this long-held rule was suddenly shattered with the advent of rapid aeronautical advancements.

Notes

1. A. Gollin, *No Longer an Island: Britain and the Wright Brothers, 1902–1909* (London: Heinemann, 1984), p. 2.
2. Ibid., p. 433.
3. Ibid., p. 437.
4. P. M. Kennedy, *The Rise of the Anglo-German Antagonism 1860–1914* (London: George Allen and Unwin, 1980), pp. 441–63.
5. Gollin, *No Longer an Island*, p. 437.
6. Ibid., pp. 1–2.
7. K. M. Wilson, *The Policy of the Entente: Essays on the Determinants of the British Foreign Policy 1904–1914* (Cambridge: Cambridge University Press, 1985), p. 106.
8. Ibid. Wilson documents this complacency: "Admiral Sir A. K. Wilson . . . [stated] in May 1907 on current Admiralty War Plans . . . of the case of a purely Anglo-German conflict, that 'it was difficult to see how such a way could arise,' . . . Grey himself noted in November 1907 that the Germans were 'a long way behind' in dreadnoughts: 'We shall have 7 Dreadnoughts afloat, before they have one, without our laying down anymore. In 1910 they will have 4 to our 7, but between now and then there is plenty of time to lay down new ones if they do so. . . . The Foreign Office know that the German Navy posed no insurmountable threat to British Superiority at sea; that the risk of invasion, as distinct from raids, was minute; that the Germany were more afraid of attack by Britain . . . than vice versa.' "

9. Kennedy, *Rise of Anglo-German Antagonism*, p. 451.

10. S. R. Williamson, *The Politics of Grand Strategy: Britain and France Prepare for War, 1904–1914* (Cambridge, Mass., 1969), pp. 227–99; P. G. Halpern, *The Mediterranean Naval Situation 1908–1914* (Cambridge, Mass., 1971), pp. 1–110.

11. Kennedy, *Rise of Anglo-German Antagonism*, p. 451.

12. Ibid., p. 452.

13. B. J. Weiss, "The Evolution of Britain's Military and Diplomatic Commitment to France, 1904–1914" (Ph.D. diss., History Department, University of Illinois at Urbana, 1967).

14. Kennedy, *Rise of Anglo-German Antagonism*, p. 454.

15. N. Watson, G. Oldroyd, and D. Clarke, *The 1912–1913 British Phantom Airship Scare* (Mount Rainier, Md.: Fund for UFO Research, 1988).

16. D. Suvin, "The Extraordinary Voyage, the Future War, and Bulwer's 'The Coming Race': Three Sub-Genres in British Science Fiction, 1871–1885," *Literature and History* 10 (1984).

17. Watson, *British Phantom Airship Scare*, p. 3.

18. Ibid.

19. "The Alleged Visit of a Foreign Airship," *London Times*, November 22, 1912, p. 8.

20. Watson, *British Phantom Airship Scare*, p. 10.

21. *The Aeroplane*, November 28, 1912, p. 497.

22. "Airship over Portsmouth," *London Times*, December 4, 1912, p. 6.

23. "Unknown Aircraft over Dover. Reported Night Visits of a Lighted Machine," *The Times of London*, January 6, 1913, p. 6; "Aircraft from the Sea. Mysterious Flight Before Daybreak," *London Daily Express*, January 6, 1913, p. 7; "Mysterious Airship. Flight over Dover," *London Daily Telegraph*, January 6, 1913, p. 10; "Dover Airship Mystery," *Bristol Evening News*, January 7, 1913, p. 4; "Mystery Airships," *London Daily Times*, January 7, 1913, p. 5; "Airship Mystery. Was It a Zeppelin? The Hansa at Sheerness," *Bradford Daily Telegraph*, January 14, 1913.

24. "An Airship over Cardiff," *Times of London*, January 21, 1913, p. 10.

25. "A Mystery of the Sky. Chief Constable's Vision of an Airship," *Yorkshire Post* (Leeds), January 21, 1913. For another cautious press description, see: "Airship Mystery. Cardiff Story of Unknown Vessel's Night Flight," *Nottingham Daily Express*, January 21, 1913.

26. "Mysteries of the Air. Unknown Craft Seen over Cardiff. Third in a Month," *South Wales Daily Post*, January 21, 1913, p. 6.

27. "The Airship at Cardiff," *Times of London*, January 22, 1913, p. 10;

"Cardiff Airship Mystery. Chief Constable's Story Supported by Other Eye-Witnesses," *Nottingham Daily Express*, January 22, 1913; "Airship Mystery," *Western Mail* (Cardiff), January 22, 1913, p. 6; "The Mysterious Airship," *Yorkshire Post*, (Leeds), January 22, 1913. "Seemed to Carry a Searchlight" (letter), *Western Mail*, January 25, 1913; "That Mysterious Airship. Seen at Foxwood, Rogerstone, near Newport, Jan. 23" (letter), *Monmouthshire Evening Post* (Newport), January 25, 1913, p. 5.

28. "Two Mysterious Aircraft," *London Daily Express*, January 22, 1913, p. 5.

29. "Is There Secret Garage in This Country? War Time Danger. M.P. Alarmed at Country's Lack of Preparation," *Daily Dispatch* (Manchester edition), January 22, 1913.

30. "Seeing Airships. Everybody's Doing It," *Manchester Guardian*, March 1, 1913, p. 9.

31. "Airship Mystery. Sighted by Many People," *South Wales Daily Post* (Swansea), January 22, 1913, p. 3.

32. "Mysterious Airship. Seen for a Seventh Time," *Liverpool Courier*, February 3, 1913.

33. "The Mysterious Airship. Seen over Bristol," *Bristol Evening News*, February 7, 1913, p. 3; "That All!" *The Wiltshire Telegraph* (Devizes, Wiltshire), February 15, 1913, p. 2; "Fly-by-Night. Another Cruise by the Mysterious Airship," *Bath and Wilts Chronicle* (Bath, Somerset), February 8, 1913, p. 3.

34. "Welsh Airship Mystery," *London Daily Express*, January 23, 1913, p. 5; "Is It a German? The Mystery of the Airship. Mr. E. T. Willows' Opinion," *South Wales Daily Post*, January 23, 1913, p. 6; "The Mystery Airship. Track of Craft Through Glamorgan. Is It a German Vessel? Suggestion by Mr. E. T. Willows," *Western Mail* (Cardiff), January 23, 1913, p. 5.

35. "Correspondence. Airships over Bristol?" (letter), *Bristol Times and Mirror*, January 25, 1913.

36. "Germany's Aerial Fleet . . . 'Menace' to Our Navy," *Manchester Guardian*, February 27, 1913, p. 8.

37. "Airships or Scareships," *The Aeroplane*, January 30, 1913, p. 111.

38. "The English Phantom Airship," *Berliner Tageblatt* (Berlin) February 25, 1913.

39. "Long-Distance Journeys. Great Possibilities of the German Airships," *London Daily Express*, February 25, 1913, p. 1.

40. "The Planet Venus Responsible," *Manchester Guardian*, February 27, 1913, p. 8; "Mystery Airship. Excitement at Newport," *The South Wales*

Argus, February 6, 1913, p. 6; "Did You See It? Some Reflections on the 'Light' in the Sky. Venus the Beautiful," *The Cambria Daily Leader*, February 6, 1913, p. 7; "The Mysterious Airship. Seen Over Wells and Shepton Mallet," *The Western Gazette* (Yeovil, Somerset), February 7, 1913, p. 2; "Day by Day," *Bath Herald*, February 8, 1913, p. 3; "Notes & Comments," *The Blackburn Times*, February 8, 1913, p. 7; "Venus of an Airship? Attempt to Explain the Mysterious Lights," *The Evening News* (London), February 8, 1913, p. 2.

41. "Airship Hoax," *London Daily Telegraph*, March 1, 1913, p. 9; "Airship Mystery. A Gamekeeper's Find. Fire Balloon in a Moor," *Manchester Guardian*, February 28, 1913, p. 7; "Swansea's 'Airship.' An Explanation," *South Wales Daily Post*, January 22, 1913, p. 5; "Mysterious Airships," *Neath and County Standard* (Neath, Glamorganshire), January 25, 1913, p. 4; "The Airship Rumors. Fire Balloon Found in Yorkshire," *London Times*, February 28, 1913, p. 5; "Strange Lights in the Sky. Fire Balloon Discovered," *Manchester Guardian*, February 28, 1913, p. 7.

42. "A Mysterious Airship," *The Bath Herald*, March 11, 1913, p. 4; "Mysterious Light. What a Newport Man Saw," *The South Wales Argus*, March 10, 1913, p. 4.

43. "The Explanation of the Phantom Airship (Ghost Balloon). Glowing in a Rubber Balloon," *Berliner Tageblatt* (Berlin), February 28, 1913.

44. "Airship or Geese? Midnight Mystery . . . ," *London Daily Express*, January 27, 1913, p. 7.

45. "E. J. P. Writes" (letter), *Manchester Guardian*, February 27, 1913, p. 8; "Is It Auroral Light?" *Manchester Guardian*, March 1, 1913, p. 9.

46. "Night Raids by Air. German Dirigibles Flights over England. The New Peril. Wanted, 1,000,000 to Meet It," *London Daily Express*, February 25, 1913, p. 1.

47. "A Propaganda Campaign Over Mastery of the Air," *Berliner Tageblatt* (Berlin), February 27, 1913.

48. "The Reported Lights," *London Times*, February 27, 1913, p. 6.

49. "Flying Venus" (letter), *South Wales Daily News*, March 3, 1913, p. 5. For similar examples of sarcasm, see: "Correspondence. The Airship Again," *The Bury Times*, March 8, 1913, p. 4; "Fly-by-Night. Another Cruise by the Mysterious Airship. Star-Gazing in Bath," *Bath and Wilts Chronicle* (Bath, Somerset), February 8, 1913, p. 3.

50. "About the Airship Ghost," *Neue Preussische Zeitune* (Berlin), March 8, 1913, Sunday evening edition, p. 2. For other German examples, see "German Ridicule," *London Daily Telegraph*, February 26, 1913, p. 11;

"The German Airship Scare. Incredulity in Berlin. John Bull's Powers of Seeing Visions," *Manchester Guardian*, February 26, 1913, p. 6.

51. *London Daily Mirror*, February 26, 1913.

52. *London Daily Chronicle*, February 27, 1913.

53. "Local Notes. Kilmarnock. The Airship Epidemic. Breaks Out in Kilmarnock," *Ardrossan & Saltcoats Herald* (Ardrossan, Ayrshire, Scotland), March 7, 1913, p. 8.

54. "The Airship Psychosis in England," *Berliner Tageblatt* (Berlin), February 26, 1913.

55. *Morning Post*, February 28, 1913.

56. "Seeing Airships. Everybody's Doing It," *Manchester Guardian*, March 1, 1913, p. 9.

7

Phantom German Air Raids and Spy Missions over Canada, America, and South Africa during World War I

> [U]nder certain conditions men respond as powerfully to fictions as they do to realities, and . . . in many cases they help to create the very fictions to which they respond. Let him cast the first stone who . . . did not accept any tail of atrocities without direct proof, and never saw a plot, a traitor, or a spy where there was none. Let him cast the first stone who never passed on as the real inside truth what he had heard someone say who knew no more than he did.
>
> —Walter Lippman[1]

War Hysteria in Quebec and Ontario during "The Great War"

In late August of 1914, Canada entered World War I following the unanimous vote of a special session of Parliament. This event occurred amid great exuberance and unanimity and was marked by "parades, decorations, cheering crowds and patriotic speeches."[2] Canada was far from the European front lines, and its distant, vast land mass and cold climate also contributed to a feeling of invulnerability to attack or invasion. However, despite an initial enthusiasm to enter the war and a general feeling of distance from its unfolding events, there was a rapidly growing realization that German sympathizers and enemy agents might pose a more immediate threat.

During World War I a series of espionage dramas unfolded. Canada and the United States had their share of actual spy scandals, acts of subversion and sabotage, and there was considerable concern among Canadians that German-Americans and sympathizers acting on orders from Berlin or independently might cross the border and cripple Canada's war efforts. In reality, the acts of espionage, sabotage, and subversion that took place had relatively little impact on everyday life in the United States or Canada, or on the war's outcome. The few successful incidents that did occur only heightened fears and suspicions surrounding the intentions of German sympathizers in Canada and especially in the United States. It is difficult to give an exact figure for the number of enemy acts in Canada, since during the war "there was hardly a major fire, explosion, or industrial accident which was not attributed to enemy sabotage," and by the time an incident had been thoroughly investigated, it "invariably led elsewhere."[3] Beginning in 1914, anti-German hysteria steadily rose in North America and did not subside until well after the armistice agreement that ended the war on November 11, 1918.

During the Great War vivid imaginations and wild rumors were the order of the day, and politicians did little to ease fears. For instance, U.S. President Woodrow Wilson told Congress that Germans "filled our unsuspecting communities with spies and conspirators."[4] The German scare in America reached such proportions that foods, streets, schools, businesses, and cities with Germanic names were renamed; communities prohibited German music or theater performances; and suspected traitors were occasionally assaulted, tarred and feathered, or hanged by vigilantes.[5] Similar social paranoia swept across Canada as schools and universities stopped teaching German, the city of Berlin was renamed Kitchener, and the Anti-German League was formed to rid Canada of all German influence, including products and immigrants.[6] In August 1915, miners in Fernie, British Columbia, refused to work until immigrant employees at the Crow's Nest Pass Coal Company were dismissed, after which they were promptly placed in a makeshift internment camp.[7] As in the United States, politicians further stoked the fires of public hysteria. For instance, the former Saskatchewan lieutenant governor made the sensational claim that 30 percent of Canada's newer provinces were composed of "alien enemies, who made little secret of their desire to see the flag of Germany waving over the Canadian West."[8] Between 1914 and 1918, 8,579 men of German and Austro-Hungarian background were placed in internment camps.[9] But Canadians clearly viewed the greater threat as coming from the United States, where in 1910 there were nearly ten million German-Americans.[10] The German scare was initially more intense in Canada, who entered the war in 1914, while the United States remained neutral until April 1917.

Of the many rumors circulating across Canada during the war, one was particularly persistent and widespread. From the very onset of hostilities it was widely rumored that German-Americans sympathetic to the kaiser had been secretly training for large-scale military raids or an invasion into Canada.[11] During January 1915 the British consul in Los Angeles warned Canadian authorities that German sympathizers were planning attacks on Port Arthur, Fort William, and Winnipeg.[12] Meanwhile,

> the consul general in New York, growing increasingly agitated, claimed that a raid on Canada was imminent and that the Germans had mustered five thousand men in Chicago and up to four thousand in Buffalo. The foreign office in London [claimed] . . . that a "reliable source" had reported that a group of eight thousand men had been formed in Boston and that bombing raids on Halifax and St. John's could be expected.[13]

As "imaginations ran wild, and on the flimsiest of what passed as evidence," there were scores of false accusations about scheming Germans on both sides of the border.[14] British consul-general Sir Courtney Bennett, stationed in New York, held top honors for being the worst offender.[15] In the early months of 1915 Bennett made several sensational claims about a plan in which as many as eighty thousand well-armed, highly trained Germans who had been drilling in Niagara Falls and Buffalo, New York, were planning to invade Canada from New York State. Despite the incredulity of his assertions, Prime Minister Sir Robert Borden requested a report on the invasion stories, a testament to the deep anxiety and suspicion of the period. Canadian Police Commissioner Sherwood assessed the rumors to be without foundation.[16]

In conjunction with the German scare, Canadians were also worried that they could be vulnerable to an aerial attack. Amid these concerns, rumors circulated that German sympathizers from Canada or the United States (almost exclusively the latter) were planning to launch surprise bombing raids or espionage missions using aeroplanes flown from secret airstrips.[17]

It was within this setting that a series of phantom aeroplane scares swept across Ontario and Quebec between 1914 and 1916. Aeroplanes of the period were crude affairs, very limited in maneuverability, and night flying held its own risks, with the first nocturnal flight occurring not until 1910 and lasting just twenty kilometers,[18] yet sightings over Canada during the war took place almost exclusively at night.

The first reports were confined to southeastern Ontario and began in the village of Sweaburg, six miles south of Woodstock, on Wednesday evening, August 13, 1914, when High County constable Hobson and many others reported seeing "two large aeroplanes" pass from east to west.[19] Sporadic sightings of mysterious aeroplanes continued over the next two weeks in such places as Aylmer, Tillsonburg, and Port Stanley.[20] As a result, a special guard was installed at the radio station in Port Burwell on Lake Erie.[21] The next major incident occurred at about 9 P.M. on September 3, when three aeroplanes, with powerful searchlights sweeping the countryside, were spotted in the oil town of Petrolea.[22] Scores of residents watched for hours as "every field glass in Petrolea was brought into requisition."[23] The "aeroplanes" were widely thought "to have some connection with Great Britain's war against Germany."[24] One "plane" flew in the direction of Oil Springs, while a second hovered near Kingscourt and a third appeared to travel eastward toward London along the Grand Trunk, "evidently scanning the line carefully."[25] Petrolea police chief Fletcher was in communication with nearby towns and immediately began interviewing witnesses.[26] Meanwhile, military authorities attempted to allay fears by suggesting the possibility that the planes were merely privately owned aircraft.[27] There were also reports that the planes were owned by an American pilot who crossed the border at night.[28]

Several "mysterious aeroplane[s]" were reported near Hamilton during early September, prompting military personnel to investigate.[29] After a spate of sightings between September 8 and 10 at Springbank, residents were "greatly stirred."[30] One witness was Fred Bridge, who urged Canadian authorities to take the reports seriously.

> With my neighbor, I have seen the flashlights which swept the countryside and have heard the roar of the motors. Last night three of them came down over Springbank....
>
> The people of London [Ontario] are not taking this matter seriously enough. Some of those fellows will drop something in the reservoir and cause no end of trouble. I am a time-expired man of the British army ... [and if] the call is urgent I am prepared to respond.... [E]very farmer in the community should be given a rifle and service ammunition by the department of militia, that these spy aviators might be brought down.[31]

By mid-September the military had issued orders to fire on aeroplanes seen within fourteen miles of any radio stations,[32] and one American plane was even shot at near the border.[33] As the tension grew, a short-lived panic took place in Toronto. On Saturday morning, October 10, a large fluttering kite flown in the city center caused a traffic jam as anxious crowds gathered to try to identify the object, and some even dove for cover. The incident exemplified the "nervous state into which even Toronto is thrown by the talk of war and of raiding aeroplanes."[34] During mid-October, several people on the outskirts of Sault Sainte Marie claimed to have watched an illuminated aeroplane rise into the sky from the American side of the border near Soo Locks and sail over the river above the Canadian locks, which were under close guard by militiamen.[35]

The city of London was greatly alarmed on the morning of October 21, when several soldiers reported that an aeroplane carrying a powerful spotlight flew directly over the Welseley Barracks and nearby ordnance stores early in the morning. Sergeant Joseph, who was on guard duty, stated:

> It was an aeroplane all right . . . I and three members of the guard were sitting around the camp fire when we heard the purr of engines and looking up saw the aeroplane coming from the northeast of the barracks. It had a bright light and was traveling rapidly. It came practically over us and the ordnance stores and then turned to the east and south. There was no use firing at it for it flew too high and at too rapid a rate. It was an aeroplane, of that we are sure.[36]

This incident followed a series of aeroplane sightings and reports of aerial motor sounds in the London vicinity over the previous several weeks, which investigations had traced to causes such as toy balloons or boat engines.[37] Meanwhile, shortly after the barracks sighting at London, Canadian military authorities once again reiterated the implausibility of a spy or war plane flying overhead, since, it was argued, spies could travel in the city unmolested in broad daylight and achieve similar results. They also wondered why planes on a secret mission would use brilliant searchlights that would surely attract attention.[38]

Scattered sightings continued during November. Guards watching over the Toronto power plant reported seeing what appeared to be signal lights flashing from the American side of the border across Lake Ontario. The red, yellow, and green lights appeared during the early morning hours. The militiamen believed the lights were flashed in order "to form different combinations. A close watch is being kept for spies."[39] During this period there were also rumors of sightings in numerous Canadian villages, including Forestville, Quebec.[40]

In the early morning hours of December 3 another major scare in Toronto took place. A series of ambiguous rumbling noises was widely thought to be an aeroplane raid, but it was later suggested that the city's cyclone dredge, in conjunction with war jitters, was responsible for the scare. The *Toronto Daily Star* described the episode somewhat sarcastically:

Aeroplane Raid Robs Citizens of Slumber

Ominous Rumbling, Apparently . . . from Sky, Caused Widespread Uneasiness

> Half of Toronto sat up in bed last night and held its breath, listening to the Germans in aeroplanes flying about over the roof. Towards five o'clock . . . the Star office was deluged with reports that included window and picture rattling, purring noises and everything but bombs. From their reports it was learned that the Germans had investigated Bleecker street at 12 P.M., Indian road and Clinton street at 4 A.M., and had stood directly over 45 St. George street at 4:30 A.M.[41]

Sightings were sporadic until mid-February, with reports of aeroplanes near Niagara Falls on December 10[42] and Montreal during the early morning hours of January 11.[43]

The biggest scare began on Sunday night, February 14, at Brockville, a town on the U.S. border nestled along the St. Lawrence River. Constables Storey, Thompson, and Glacier, and several townspeople were convinced that three or four aeroplanes had passed by the city to the northeast, heading in the direction of Ottawa, about sixty miles due north. The actual sightings were vague, with the exception of "light balls" falling from the sky:[44] "The first machine was flying very rapidly and very high. Very little could be seen, but the unmistakable sounds of the whirring motor made the presence of the aircraft known."[45] Five minutes later a second machine was heard, then suddenly three balls of light fell from the sky, plunging several hundred feet and extinguishing as they hit the river. A few minutes thereafter two more aeroplanes passed over the city.[46]

As word of the sightings spread throughout Brockville, its inhabitants became "wildly excited."[47] At 10:30 P.M., the Brockville police chief sent an urgent telegram to Premier Sir Robert Borden, who summoned Colonel Percy Sherwood, chief of dominion police, and after consultation with military authorities, all lights in the Parliament buildings were extinguished and every blind drawn.[48] Marksmen were posted at several vantage points on Parliament Hill, while the premier and cabinet ministers kept in close communication in the event of an attack during the night. News of the possible attack spread rapidly, and several members of Parliament rushed to the roof of the main building to see if they could spot any aircraft.

The scare in Canada was intensified the following morning, when the *Toronto Globe* implied that the incident had actually happened. Its front-page headline stated: "Ottawa in Darkness Awaits Aeroplane Raid. Several Aeroplanes Make a Raid into the Dominion of Canada. Entire City of Ottawa in Darkness, Fearing Bomb-Droppers. Machines Crossed St. Lawrence River . . . Seen by Many Citizens Heading for the Capital—One Was Equipped with Powerful Searchlights—Fire Balls Dropped." On the American side, the *New York Times*'s description of the incident the next morning was much more cautious, with its headlines stating in part: "Scare in Ottawa over Air Raid . . . but Police Chief's Report is Vague." The same paper also noted that the police chief in Ogdensburg, New York, just twelve miles down the St. Lawrence River from Brockville, stated that no one had reported seeing or hearing anything at the time the aeroplanes were said to have passed near Brockville. In addition, flying machines were also sighted at Gananoque, in Ontario,[49] and earlier sightings of unusual aerial objects were subsequently rethought. For instance, once the news of the sightings spread, an Ogdensburg farmer told police that he had seen an aeroplane on February 12 flying toward Canada.[50]

Within the context of the outbreak of World War I and Canada's involvement, the aeroplane raid appeared plausible. One press account stated, "The fact that the country is at war and the Germans and pro-Germans abound across the border renders it quite within the bounds of possibility, if not probability, that such a raid might occur."[51]

On the following night, February 15, and the early morning hours of the sixteenth, the Parliament buildings again remained dark, and marksmen were posted at strategic locations.[52] This was both a precautionary and a face-saving measure, for information was rapidly coming to light, indicating that a series of toy balloons had been sent aloft the previous night on the American side and was mistaken for enemy aeroplanes. Premier Robert Borden was defensive, and when asked for information on the "invasion," he replied that when told of the reports, he had left the matter to the judgment of the chief of staff and chief of dominion police.[53] The *Toronto Globe* was also embarrassed, since it had reported the aerial incursion as fact in its previous edition. However, in its next edition it blamed the affair on "hysterical" residents in Brockville.[54] Meanwhile, the charred remains of two large toy balloons had been found near Brockville, which local residents, in turn, blamed on boys from nearby Morristown.[55] A number of toy balloons in other locations had also been sent aloft by Americans on February 14 and 15, in commemoration of the centenary of peace.[56] An adviser for the Canadian Aviation Corps, J. D. McCurdy, stated that a mission by German sympathizers from northern New York was highly improbable, especially given the difficulty in night flying.[57]

The last major sighting wave during World War I occurred during mid-July. In the first week of the month, an aeroplane reportedly landed in a field near Nolan Junction, Quebec. Two men carrying plans and papers supposedly disembarked, then shortly after flew off toward Montreal.[58] On July 16, an illuminated aeroplane was seen by Silvanus Edworthy in London,[59] while on the morning of the seventeenth a craft was seen near Massena, Ontario.[60] During midmonth, aeroplanes were widely reported by many people in the vicinity of Quebec City[61] and Montreal.[62] When the craft was spotted near a factory in Rigaud, the lights were extinguished and precautions "taken to protect the place from possible attack."[63] On Sunday night, the eighteenth, a military guard at the Point Edward radio station fired five shots at what he took to be aeroplanes, and two large paper balloons plummeted to the ground.[64]

At 11 P.M. on July 20, a mysterious aircraft was seen by several citizens of Chateauguay, near Montreal, who speculated that a German man who had lived in town for the past five years had secretly flown across the border to the United States. The man had been watched closely since the outbreak of hostilities and disappeared the night the plane was sighted.[65]

Widely scattered nighttime airplane sightings continued from the latter half of 1915 until July 1916, including sightings at Tillsonburg on July 22[66] and at London on August 8 of 1915.[67] On February 5, 1916, a railway worker spotted two aeroplanes near Montreal. There was thought to be a connection between this sighting and a suspicious man who was seen at about the same time under the Victoria Bridge. Fearing an attempt to blow up the bridge, guards on the structure opened fire on the figure, who fled.[68] Several days later on February 13, a rare configuration of Venus and Jupiter resulted in a brilliant light in the western sky that was mistaken by hundreds of residents of London as an aeroplane about to attack.[69] The last known scare during the war occurred at Windsor on July 6, when a biplane was sighted by hundreds of anxious people for about thirty minutes. Several people using binoculars actually claimed "to distinguish the figure of the aviator.[70]

Two War Scares in the United States

As spy and subversion fears increased steadily in the United States with the outbreak of the First World War, numerous books, pamphlets, and newspaper articles, such as Frederic Wile's *The German-American Plot*, and William Skaggs's *German-American Conspiracies in America*,[71] warned of the national security dangers posed by German-Americans. Within this climate of social and political paranoia, the most outlandish rumors about German spies, traitors, and subversives spread like wildfire across the country. These included claims that German submarine captains would disembark from their vessels in secret coastal locations and attend the theater in order to spread influenza and that "a new species of pigeon, thought to be German, was shot"[72] in Michigan. By 1916 fear over the allegiance of German-Americans reached a fever pitch, and there was growing anxiety that America might soon be drawn into the war. Further fueling anxieties was an emotional debate over who to support in the event America entered the war, as many German-Americans publicly pledged their allegiance to the German motherland.[73] German undersecretary Arthur Zimmermann only exacerbated American fears by claiming that in the event the United States decided to enter the war against Germany, "five hundred thousand trained Germans in America . . . [would] start a revolution."[74] The eastern seaboard was particularly tense, since if war was declared it was closest to Europe and situated along the vital Atlantic Ocean shipping lanes.

Thus, military installations along the coast would be prime targets. It was within this setting of war anxiety that a spate of mysterious aeroplane sightings occurred in Delaware and along its borders with neighboring states.

The Delaware Region during 1916

The scare began on Monday evening, January 31, 1916, when a mysterious "aeroplane" was spotted flying near the large gunpowder plants owned by the duPont Company at both Carney's Point and Deep Water Point, just across the Delaware border in New Jersey. Company employees, including guard Captain Albert J. Parsons, reported seeing the craft. Parsons told an excited press corps that the aeroplane was flying at about fifteen hundred feet and was visible for some fifteen minutes before disappearing to the southeast.[75] "The light and the blurred object about it hovered about the powder plant . . . [moving] at times and then appeared to be still and then it seemed to be going up and down or moving in a semi-circle."[76] There was considerable press speculation that the plane was going to drop bombs or was reconnoitering the area for a future attack.[77] A few days later an illuminated aeroplane was seen by several people near Fenton Beach, where "one man declared that his wife started praying that a bomb would not be dropped close by."[78] When an astronomer correlated their sighting with the positions of Jupiter and Venus, the Fenton Beach witnesses steadfastly refused to believe it.[79]

On Saturday night, February 12, the aeroplane was seen over Dover, Delaware, by two people,[80] while on the evening of the fifteenth, at least two dozen residents of Middletown reported seeing the aeroplane in the eastern sky, shining three lights—one red, one white, the other bluish green. It was first spotted by Mr. and Mrs. Norman Beale, hovering above the Delaware River in the direction of Odessa. Mr. Norman called the telephone switchboard with the news, and word quickly spread. One of those who was alerted, town druggist Ernest A. Truitt, claimed that he could not only see the object from his Cochrane Street home, but was "positive he heard a whirring noise, like the noise of a gasoline engine."[81]

A major scare took place in Wilmington on Sunday evening, February 13. People were greatly excited by what was thought to have been a German aeroplane between 8 and 9 P.M. During the sighting, the *Wilmington Morning News* alone received over one hundred telephone calls from anxious citizens who gathered in crowds across the city to gain a better vantage point.

> The first report received at this office stated that the airship was . . . hovering . . . over Ninth and Broome streets, and it was "just floating, with practically no motion." Roofward went the entire office force. . . .
>
> [I]n a few minutes . . . [it] was reported as having circled the Baltimore and Ohio railroad station at Delaware avenue and duPont streets, flying low, and then had sheered off toward the Rockford water tower. . . .
>
> But there was no time for speculation before, according to the next call . . . which came from the Pennsylvania station, the mysterious aircraft was seen slowly circling over the center of the city. . . .
>
> Another caller said it was floating, apparently only a few hundred feet in the air, over Richardson Park.[82]

On the same evening, shortly after the eight o'clock services began at the Lyon Tabernacle, several people inside thought they heard an aeroplane, and police officers and ushers promptly left the building to look for the flying machine.[83] Witnesses said it appeared to drift along Brandywine Creek, then hovered over the Washington Street Bridge before slowly turning and flying out of sight to the southwest.[84] It was also spotted by groups at Queens Anne in Maryland, and Clayton and Dover in Delaware.[85]

The sightings quickly died down when several regional newspapers reported that, after examining the reports, their times of appearance and location in the nighttime sky, it was evident that Venus and Jupiter, being in near conjunction, had created an unusually brilliant light on the horizon—a light that was interpreted according to the predominate concerns of the day.

New Hampshire's War Scare Hysteria of 1917

On April 6, 1917, the United States Congress voted to enter World War I against Germany. There was much debate in the press over the possibility that Germany might launch small raids on U.S. territory in order to disrupt the American war effort, or that sympathizers residing within the United States might mount their own subversion campaign. As with the incident in the Delaware region, the prime target for such activities was assumed to be military installations along the Atlantic coast. Further, on January 31, 1917, Germany announced a renewal of its policy on unrestricted submarine warfare, and there were fears that a German victory would result in their control of the Atlantic Ocean and vital American shipping routes.[86]

During the early morning hours of Friday, April 13, 1917, two national guardsmen from Company L of the Sixth Massachusetts Infantry were stationed on the bridge linking Portsmouth, New Hampshire, and Kittery, Maine, when they thought they heard an aeroplane. After catching sight of it, one of the guards panicked, thinking that the plane was starting to descend to make a pass over the bridge. He immediately fired his rifle at the object, at which point it moved off and soon disappeared in the distance.[87] On the same night, two soldiers guarding a railway bridge at Penacook reported that two mysterious intruders fired four shots in their direction before fleeing into the night. Not a single clue as to these "attackers" was found,[88] and it may have been a backfiring motor or firecrackers in combination with war jitters. That a hostile aeroplane was secretly operating in the skies above New Hampshire, taking off and landing under cover of darkness from a secret air base in the mountains, performing sophisticated maneuvers and remaining aloft for several hours at a time, as was reported, was simply impossible.

Despite the vagueness of these two reports, they fostered considerable anxiety across the state. While the Penacook incident was dismissed for lack of evidence, the aeroplane reports still "caused alarm in military and naval circles, as well as exciting the public."[89] While the possibility that the aeroplane had been launched from an enemy vessel situated off the coast was discussed, it was widely believed that it had taken off from a secret, remote airstrip nestled in the nearby mountains, and circled the area before returning to its point of departure. Naval authorities ordered an investigation into the sightings and issued an urgent appeal to the public in an attempt to determine the identity of the pilot, whom they hoped was a local aviator. In the wake of the Portsmouth publicity, a police officer on duty at Rochester, New Hampshire, claimed that while on patrol he had also heard a noise, which he assumed to have been the "Portsmouth aeroplane" as it passed overhead.[90] Another report on the same night was from James Walker, a motorman on the Dover, Rochester, and Somersworth railway. He stated that the craft was "plainly visible" over Gonic and was "flying high and headed north."[91] By Tuesday, April 17, in the wake of much press publicity, several residents in the East Manchester vicinity reported that they, too, had observed the aeroplane or had heard the whirring of its propeller on Saturday night as it traveled in a northeasterly direction.[92]

The phantom aeroplane sightings abated until the night of April 23, when several residents of North Conway, New Hampshire, saw mysterious lights near Kearsarge Mountain and speculated that "an aviator was maneuvering about the summit."[93] Immediately prior to the sightings rumors had been circulating in the vicinity of North Conway that "a small party of strangers" were recently seen east of Kearsarge, and rumor had it that they were involved with the aeroplane.[94] On April 30 prominent local horseman Charles Churchill of Deerfield was awakened by a peculiar noise, only to discover an aeroplane hovering in the distance and apparently flashing signals toward Portsmouth.[95] About an hour earlier Mrs. Edson Roberts of Wolfeboro had heard the craft above her house, near the East Alton line.

By May 2, however, the aeroplane hysteria subsided in the wake of there being not a single shred of tangible evidence to support the rumors that German sympathizers were engaged in secret reconnaissance missions over the Portsmouth naval base. Another reason for the decline in reports was an embarrassing disclosure about the aeroplane sightings of the previous night. The press reported that the aeroplane heard whirring above Deerfield was actually a large truck rumbling through town in the middle of the night. There is little doubt that the press skepticism following this incident and its ridicule of witnesses discouraged further reports of enemy aeroplanes flying above New Hampshire.[96] The account appeared as follows:

> The still, cool air at Deerfield was rent, late Monday night, by a sound unfamiliar to the ear of residents, and in the distance, an uncertain light was seen to flicker higher and yawn—no, yon.
>
> Numerous night-capped heads poked sleepily through bedroom windows of several farmhouses, spotted the light and located the unusual noises.
>
> "Airships," said one resident, and at once the farmers' phone lines became active. All agreed, as they say in the country press, that Deerfield was menaced by hostile aircraft. All still agree, perchance, and would doubtless continue to agree, except for the fact that somebody always has to take the joy out of life.
>
> In this case it is E. E. Holmes, Manchester truckman, who comes to bat as the *Union* goes to press, and announces that the strange Zeppelin was his big motor truck, which went through Deerfield with a heavy load in the dead of the night.[97]

South Africa's Mystery Monoplanes

> Whether it is a British or German aeroplane nobody knows. Where it comes from is equally a mystery. Where it goes to we cannot guess. How it lands for re-petrolling and where the pilot gets his food are insoluble mysteries.... Why it should carry headlights is hard to say.... Why, too, should it fly by night? Much more useful and interesting observations could be made by daylight.... And why, if it dare not appear by day, does it advertise its whereabouts... after dark?... There is a baffling mystery about it all.[98]

Aeroplane scares during World War I were not confined to North America. Thousands of residents of British South Africa claimed to observe a sinister German monoplane between August 11 and September 9, 1914. It appeared almost exclusively at night and at a distance, and coincided with the war's outbreak in Europe. But there were no aeroplanes in British South Africa during this period.[99] Although three German monoplanes were known to be in adjacent German South-West Africa during this period, none was capable of the sophisticated maneuvers performed, such as remaining in flight for many hours and traveling great distances without refueling.[100] Only after the wave had ceased was it revealed that two of these three German planes had been disabled during this time, while the third was for show purposes and of little practical use.[101]

War had broken out in Europe, but not in British South Africa. However, rumors began circulating across the country that a German monoplane was conducting spy missions for an eventual attack that would involve bombing various targets. In conjunction with these rumors, during the first week of August there were scattered sightings of a mystery plane in the Cape Peninsula region. In discussing the reports, one prominent newspaper stated that "there is no reason to suppose that their information is incorrect, as wholly independent reports seem to establish the fact."[102] From this point on, the floodgates opened, and phantom monoplanes were frightening people in widely spaced areas.

On the evening of August 16, an aeroplane with "a very strong headlight" was seen by fifteen people near Worcester.[103] There were also many sightings near Cape Town and the western districts of the province, prompting appeals to the public to look for the plane so that "its movements could be communicated to the military authorities or the police without delay."[104] When residents near Vryburg reported seeing a mysterious aerial light the previous week,[105] one newspaper heightened concern by proclaiming: "Aerial Scouts! German Aeroplane Near Vryburg."[106]

Press coverage was instrumental in the spread of the aeroplane scare and gave credence to the initial rumors of a German attack. By August 22 six prominent newspapers had all published accounts—described as fact—that one or more potentially hostile German monoplanes were traversing the skies.[107] As is typical with war scares, once the situation was legitimized as real, various mundane events and circumstances were redefined as monoplane-related. For instance, in the Durban district a quantity of sugar that was burned under ambiguous circumstances was blamed on the plane:

> Reports as to the passage of aeroplanes over the Natal coast districts persist, and one statement, with apparently some authenticity behind it, is that soon after the appearance over his plantation of this supposed object, a considerable quantity of a planter's growing sugar had been found to have been burned during the night.[108]

Once the episode was under way, many vague aerial objects that had been casually noted in the previous weeks and months were often recategorized as having been a German plane. In the following incident from Germiston, what was originally thought to have been a shooting star over Pretoria becomes an aeroplane, presumably of German origin.

> Yesterday I received the following interesting communication from a former resident of Pretoria, now of Benoni, which is not without some piquant interest: In regard to the presumed German aeroplane said to have been seen over Pretoria, I should like to relate to you a little experience of my own while in that town. One evening in January, between 9 and 10 P.M., the children called me to the verandah to see a shooting star. We all went to the gate and watched. The supposed star proved to be a powerful light or lamp attached to what appeared to be an aeroplane in shape. For some time the machine circled over the town and then descended about 11:30 P.M. as far as I could guess on to the roof of the Law Courts, not far from where we were. As the machine circled in the air it made a loud swishing kind of noise. I spoke of the matter next day, yet, strange to say, the only one who had noticed it was an old native man.[109]

On August 27 large numbers of people in Durban had become alarmed that falling bombs from German aeroplanes were "about to deal death and destruction from on high," and they began fleeing to their *kraals* (villages) during the crisis.[110] In some cases extra guards were posted at companies employing workers to prevent them from deserting. One whaling company alone reported losing "as many as sixty [men]."[111] The sightings peaked during the last week of August with nighttime observations across South Africa.[112]

By the end of August, the press had grown increasingly skeptical, and sighting reports began to rapidly tail off to a trickle in early September, until ceasing altogether after the second week.[113] The editor of the *Natal Advertiser* told readers of his growing impatience, noting that the topic was surfacing "with nauseating frequency." He continued: "A man comes up to you and says, with all the solemnity of a judge, that he has seen what he calls 'the aeroplane.' You know that he has not, but you cannot very well tell him that he is a blithering idiot."[114] Astronomers noted a remarkable coincidence about most sightings—they took place during the evening and involved a strong headlight—suggesting that they were misidentifications of Venus.[115] Other authorities, including meteorologists[116] and journalists,[117] concurred that people were mistaking stars and planets. One incredulous editor sarcastically described an incident over East London:

> East London, and particularly Oxford-street, was agog with excitement on Saturday evening. At every corner . . . were . . . groups of men, women and children, with eyes goggling, fingers pointing heavenward, and tongues going twenty-four to the dozen as they gaze at an alleged aeroplane in the western heavens. There it was sure enough, visible to all but the blind: at least, a very brilliant light was visible. An aeroplane it was, and of that there was no doubt, for according to various observers it went through all the tricks in an up-to-date airman's repertoire. It looped the loop, squared the circle, spiralled up and spiralled down, volplaned, tangoed to the right and one-stepped to the left, advanced, retired, set to partners, hands down the middle, did everything except . . . descend in the Recreation Ground of the Market Square. And that searchlight, what did that not do? It waxed and waned, appeared and disappeared, twinkled, winked the other eye, and signalled in the Morse code in English, French, Dutch, German . . . and Pitman's shorthand. And all the time it was getting further and further away, though never diminishing in brightness, so that it must have been carried in the tail of the machine.
>
> And oh, the theories that were advanced. Men laid down the law. . . . Ladies became alarmed and wanted to go home and protect their babies from bombs. . . . And it was not until it disap-

peared behind a heavy bank of clouds in the west that East Londoners breathed a sigh of relief at another happy escape, and went home to dip their pens in the candle and write to the "Daily Dispatch" to describe in letters of fire and words of flames the dastardly attempt to blow up an undefended city.

Judge of the general surprise when the same aeroplane appeared yesterday in about the same place. However, it is safe to predict that it may be looked for again to-night and for several following nights. As a matter of fact what was seen was the evening star, Venus, which happened to be particularly brilliant. A heavy bank of clouds fringed with flying scud and aided by vivid imaginations accounted for all the evolutions and manoeuvres, and we have to hesitate in assuring everyone that they may sleep in peace, for if it depends upon this particular aeroplane, no bombs will be dropped on East London.[118]

Notes

1. W. Lippman, *Public Opinion* (New York: Harcourt, Brace, 1922), cited in F. MacDonnell, *Insidious Foes* (New York: Oxford University Press, 1995), p. 2.

2. D. Creighton, *Dominion of the North: A History of Canada* (London: Macmillan & Company, 1958), p. 437.

3. D. Morton, "Sir William Otter and Internment Operations in Canada During the First World War," *Canadian Historical Review* 55, no. 1 (1974): 32–58. See p. 36.

4. MacDonnell, *Insidious Foes*, p. 23.

5. Ibid., pp. 25–26.

6. Morton, "Sir William Otter."

7. Ibid., p. 46.

8. Ibid., pp. 48–49.

9. Ibid., p. 33; R. H. Keyserlingk, " 'Agents within the Gates': The Search for Nazi Subversives in Canada During World War II," *Canadian Historical Review* 66, no. 2 (1985): 211–39.

10. MacDonnell, *Insidious Foes*, p. 21.

11. M. Kitchen, "The German Invasion of Canada in the First World War," *The International History Review* 7, no. 2 (1985): 245–60.

12. Ibid., p. 246.

13. Ibid., p. 246.

14. Ibid.

15. G. S. Mount, *Canada's Enemies: Spies and Spying in the Peaceable Kingdom* (Toronto: Dundurn Press, 1993), p. 40.

16. Ibid.

17. Throughout this chapter we will refer to aircraft of the period as "aeroplanes" instead of the present spelling "airplane," as the former spelling was the standard usage at the time.

18. C. Gibbs-Smith, *Aviation: An Historical Survey from Its Origins to the End of World War II* (London: Her Majesty's Stationery Office, 1985), p. 152.

19. "Reports Aeroplanes Over Oxford Village," *London Free Press* (Ontario), August 13, 1914, p. 2.

20. "Airship in Western Ontario," *Toronto Star*, August 31, 1914, p. 5.

21. Ibid.

22. Presently spelled "Petrolia."

23. "Three Aeroplanes Scan Topography of the Province," *London Free Press*, September 5, 1914, p. 8.

24. Ibid.

25. Ibid.

26. "Petrolea Planes. . . . Military Men Say, 'We Shouldn't Worry,' " *London Free Press*, September 5, 1914, p. 2.

27. "Why Get Excited?" *London Free Press*, September 5, 1914, p. 16.

28. "Believe 'Aeroplane' Is an American One," *London Free Press*, September 5, 1914, p. 16.

29. "Mysterious Flyer Now at Hamilton," *London Free Press*, September 12, 1914, p. 5.

30. "Pipe Line Road Saw Three Aeroplanes. Mr. Fred Bridge . . . and Other People Say They Saw Spies," *London Free Press*, September 11, 1914, p. 9.

31. Ibid.

32. "Airships Restricted in Flights in Canada," *Toronto Globe*, September 18, 1914, p. 7; "Asks Permission to Fly over Ontario," *London Free Press*, September 28, 1914, p. 3.

33. *Niagara Falls Gazette*, September 17, 1914, p. 1.

34. "Had an Aeroplane Scare," *Toronto Star*, October 10, 1914, p. 10.

35. "Aeroplane Reported Hovering Over Soo Locks. Residents Claim to Have Seen Craft Rise from South of American Canal," *Toronto Globe*, October 20, 1914, p. 9.

36. "Soldiers Claim They Saw Airship Over Barracks. . . . Flew Directly Over the Ordnance Stores Department. Men Are Emphatic There

Was No Mistake," *London Evening Free Press* (Ontario), October 21, 1914, p. 1.

37. "Many Reports," *London Evening Free Press*, October 21, 1914, p. 1.

38. "Still See Them, But Military Authorities Are Not Worrying," *London Free Press*, October 23, 1914, p. 2.

39. "Signal Across River?" *Buffalo Express*, November 19, 1914, p. 7.

40. "Seeing Things in Air. Forestville Man Says Two Aeroplanes Went Over Town in Dark," *Buffalo Express*, November 21, 1914, p. 7.

41. "Aeroplane Raid," *Toronto Daily Star*, December 4, 1914, p. 6.

42. "Saw an Aeroplane," *Niagara Falls Gazette*, December 12, 1914, p. 9.

43. "Strange Aeroplane Appears Six Miles from Montreal. Ottawa Officials . . . Will Investigate Matter Immediately," *London Evening Free Press*, January 11, 1915, p. 2.

44. "Brockville's Story of the Air Craft. Dropped Fireballs as They Crossed River," *Toronto Globe*, February 15, 1915.

45. Ibid.

46. Ibid.

47. Ibid.

48. "Scare in Ottawa Over Air Raid. Parliament Buildings Darkened on Report That Three Aeroplanes Crossed the Border," *New York Times*, February 15, 1915, p. 1.

49. "Were Also Seen at Gananoque," *New York Times*, February 15, 1915, p. 1; "Brockville's Story of the Air Craft," *Toronto Globe*, February 15, 1915.

50. "Ogdensburg Heard of This Friday," *New York Times*, February 15, 1915, p. 1.

51. "Police Force Augmented," *London Evening Free Press*, February 15, 1915, p. 1.

52. "Ottawa Again Dark," *New York Times*, February 16, 1915, p. 4.

53. "Parliament Hill in Darkness," *Toronto Globe*, February 16, 1915, p. 2.

54. "Were Toy Balloons and Not Aeroplanes! Brockville's Latest on Sunday Night's Scare," *Toronto Globe*, February 16, 1915, p. 1.

55. Ibid.

56. "Ottawa Again Dark," *New York Times*, February 16, 1915, p. 4; "Were Toy Balloons," *Toronto Globe*, February 16, 1915, pp. 1–2.

57. "Air Raid from the States Improbable," *Toronto Globe*, February 16, 1915, p. 7.

58. "Saw Aeroplane . . . After Landing, Took Flight Towards Montreal," *London Free Press* (Ontario), July 6, 1915, p. 1.

59. "Saw an Aeroplane . . . Passed Over the Southern Part of City," *London Evening Free Press*, July 17, 1915, p. 3.

60. "People Near Massena, Ont., Spy Strange Lights in Heavens," *London Evening Free Press*, July 20, 1915, p. 9.

61. "Saw Aeroplanes Hovering Over City of Quebec. Fully Creditable Persons Reported to Have Noticed Mysterious Aircraft," *London Evening Free Press*, July 21, 1915, p. 1.

62. "Strange Airships Seen Hovering Near Montreal," *London Evening Free Press*, July 19, 1915, p. 7.

63. Ibid.

64. "Point Edward Guard Brings Down Balloons. Were at First Thought to Be Aeroplanes," *London Evening Free Press*, July 21, 1915, p. 7.

65. "French Believe German Officer 'Flew the Loop,'" *London Evening Free Press*, July 22, 1915, p. 1.

66. "Mysterious Light Passes Tillsonburg," *London Daily Free Press*, July 23, 1915, p. 2.

67. "Another Aeroplane Seen Over the City," *London Free Press* (Ontario), August 9, 1915, p. 2.

68. "Two Aeroplanes Reported Close to Montreal," *London Evening Free Press*, February 7, 1916, p. 1.

69. "Display in Sky Mistaken for an Aerial Invasion," *London Evening Free Press*, February 14, 1916, p. 12.

70. "Unknown Aviator Surveys Windsor," *London Evening Free Press*, July 7, 1916, p. 14.

71. MacDonnell, *Insidious Foes*, p. 20.

72. W. Chafee, *Freedom of Speech in War Time* (New York: Cambridge University Press, 1954), p. 70.

73. L. Shores, ed., "World War I," in *Collier's Encyclopedia*, vol. 23 (New York: Crowell-Collier Publishing, 1965), p. 599.

74. MacDonnell, *Insidious Foes*, p. 21.

75. "Mystery Airship Hovering Over Powder Plants . . . Mission Unknown; Rouses Suspicion," *Every Evening* (Wilmington, Delaware), February 3, 1916, pp. 1, 6.

76. "Powder Guard Says He Saw Airship," *The Wilmington News*, February 4, 1916, p. 1.

77. Ibid.

78. "Still Sky Gazing at Fenton Beach," *Delmarvia Star* (Wilmington, Delaware), February 13, 1916.

79. "Studying Astronomy with a Searchlight," *Sunday Morning Magazine* (Wilmington, Delaware), February 20, 1916, part 3, p. 1.

80. "Air Ship," *Every Evening*, February 19, 1916.

81. "Are Sure They Saw an Aeroplane," *Every Evening*, February 16, 1916.

82. "Citizens Declare They Saw Airship," *Wilmington Morning News*, February 14, 1916, pp. 1–2.

83. "They Heard Something," *Every Evening*, February 14, 1916, p. 7.

84. "Honest, Now, Did You Yourself See That Aeroplane?" *Every Evening*, February 14, 1916, p. 7.

85. "Kent County Reports Seeing an Airship," *Every Evening*, February 14, 1916, p. 7.

86. Shores, "World War I," p. 600.

87. "Hunt for Aircraft Base. Fire at Aircraft Near Portsmouth. Effort Now to Trace Its Course—Shots Aimed at Penacook Sentries," "Portsmouth Guards Fire at Plane—Course Is Changed at Once," *Manchester Union*, April 14, 1917, pp. 1, 3.

88. "Hunt for Aircraft," *Manchester Union*, April 14, 1917, pp. 1, 3.

89. "Portsmouth Guards," *Manchester Union*, April 14, 1917, pp. 1, 3.

90. "Strange Aeroplane Heard and Seen by Rochester People," *Manchester Union*, April 14, 1917, pp. 1, 3.

91. Ibid.

92. "Aeroplane Heard Over East Side. Darkness Prevents Clear View of It," *Manchester Union*, April 17, 1917, p. 14.

93. "Lights Hover Over Kearsarge. Movements Suggest Airplane—Close Watch Kept on Mountain," *Manchester Union*, April 26, 1917, p. 1.

94. Ibid.

95. "Aeroplane Seen at Deerfield. Awakened Resident Observes Flashing of Lights—Report from Wolfeboro," *Manchester Union*, May 1, 1917, p. 1.

96. For instance, the next report of a phantom aeroplane over New Hampshire occurred on May 20 and consisted of a tiny article three short sentences in length, on page 2 of the *Manchester Union*. The account simply described the report of Dover resident Mrs. Arabella R. Mason, who claimed to see an aeroplane fly over her farm on Middle Road. See "Airship Seen above Dover," *Manchester Union*, May 21, 1917, p. 2.

97. "Deerfield Zeppelin Has Domestic Tinge," *Manchester Union*, May 2, 1917, p. 5.

98. *Natal Advertiser* (Durban), August 29, 1914, p. 7.

99. "Defense Department and Aeroplanes. No Union Machines,"

Cape Times, August 29, 1914, p. 8; "Those Aeroplanes," *Rand Daily Mail* (Johannesburg), August 29, 1914, p. 5.

100. "Once a Week," *Natal Advertiser* (Durban), August 29, 1914, p. 7; "Our Aeroplanes," *Pretoria News*, September 2, 1914, p. 5; "Aviator Discusses Air Visitors. John Weston's Views," *Cape Times*, September 5, 1914, p. 5.

101. "Aeroplanes in German South-West. Only One Efficient," *Cape Times*, September 21, 1914, p. 8.

102. "Cape Town and Peninsula. Mysterious Airplane Flight," *Cape Times*, August 15, 1914, p. 7.

103. "Aeroplane Sighted," *Cape Times*, August 18, 1914, p. 3.

104. "News of the Day," *Cape Times*, August 18, 1914, p. 5.

105. "Aeroplane Seen at Vryburg," *Cape Times*, August 19, 1914, p. 5.

106. "Aerial Scouts!" *Rand Daily Mail* (Johannesburg), August 19, 1914, p. 5.

107. "The Aeroplane . . . On Table Mountain," *Cape Times*, August 20, 1914, p. 5; "The Aeroplane. Seen at Porterville," *Cape Argus*, August 21, 1914, p. 5; "At Ashton," *Johannesburg Star*, August 21, 1914, p. 4; "That Aeroplane," *Rand Daily Mail* (Johannesburg), August 21, 1914, p. 5; "The Mysterious Aeroplane," *Natal Advertiser* (Durban), August 22, 1914, p. 1; "The Mysterious Aeroplane," *Rand Daily Mail* (Johannesburg), August 22, 1914, p. 5.

108. "Mysterious Aeroplanes. A Natal Report," *Cape Argus*, September 9, 1914, second edition, p. 5.

109. "Something Seen in January," *Johannesburg Star*, August 26, 1914, second edition, p. 4.

110. "Native Restlessness. The Folly of Wild Rumors," *Natal Advertiser* (Durban), August 27, 1914, p. 8.

111. "Alleged Native Restlessness. What the Officials Have Done," *Natal Advertiser* (Durban), August 2, 1914, p. 14.

112. "The Aeroplane Again," *Cape Argus*, August 25, 1914, p. 3; "That Aeroplane! Return Visit to the East," *Cape Times*, August 25, 1914, p. 5; "Seen at Hoetjes Bay," *Cape Argus*, August 26, 1914, second edition, p. 5; "Aeroplane Reports," *Cape Times*, August 26, 1914, p. 5; "Sea Point Aeroplane," *Cape Argus*, August 28, 1914, p. 4; "Day by Day," *Pretoria News*, August 29, 1914, p. 5; " 'Aeroplanes' in Natal," *Rand Daily Mail*, August 29, 1914, p. 5; "Headlight," *Cape Argus*, August 31, 1914, p. 3; "The Mysterious Aeroplane," *Natal Advertiser*, September 31, 1914, p. 1; "Cape Argus. The Aeroplane Again." *Natal Advertiser*, August 31, 1914, p. 5; "Aeroplane at Skinner's Court," *Pretoria News*, August 31, 1914, p. 5.

113. "That Aeroplane. Natal Reports," *Cape Argus*, September 5, 1914, p. 7; "That Aeroplane!" *Natal Advertiser*, September 7, 1914; "That Aeroplane Seen at Warmbaths," *Rand Daily Mail* (Johannesburg), September 10, 1914, p. 2.

114. *Natal Advertiser* (Durban), September 5, 1914, p. 7.

115. "Aeroplane or Planet?" *Johannesburg Star*, August 28, 1914, second edition, p. 5.

116. "Aeroplane Problem. Maritzburg Optician's Solution," *Cape Times*, September 10, 1914, p. 5.

117. "Coloured Planet," *Johannesburg Star*, August 31, 1914, p. 3.

118. "The Mysterious Aeroplane. What East London Saw," *Cape Argus*, August 27, 1914, second edition, p. 5.

8

Sweden's Ghost Rocket Delusion of 1946

in collaboration with Anders Liljegren and Clas Svahn

Between early May and September 30, 1946, a panic swept like wildfire across Sweden as tens of thousands of people reported seeing missiles.[1] This led to the widespread folk theory that remote-controlled German V-rockets confiscated by the Soviets at the close of World War II were being test fired as a form of political intimidation or as a prelude to an invasion. Despite the widely publicized views of Swedish and foreign politicians, military officials, newspaper editors, and scientists supporting the rocket's existence, and voluminous press reports often treating the rockets as fact, no concrete physical evidence was ever found. By the episode's end, Swedish military investigators concluded that most observations were of meteors and related celestial phenomena, and of those that were unexplained, none were V-rockets. This phantom rocket hysteria was one in a long history of Soviet invasion fears that have preoccupied Swedes for centuries.

Historical Sociopolitical Context

The Soviet relationship with northern Europe was characterized by two hundred years of ideological conflict and distrust, exchanges of political rhetoric, spy accusations, border disputes, wars, and fears of invasion.[2] From 1899 to 1914, itinerant Russian workmen traveled the Swedish countryside. They were called "saw-filers" (*sagfilare*), as they were renowned for sharpening various tools, especially saws. Most were Russian farmers from the Novgorod region who traveled to Sweden in the autumn and remained through the winter. Between fifty and three hundred saw-filers came to Sweden each winter to earn good wages.[3] The term eventually became synonymous in Sweden with Russian spies, although the saw-filers' intention of spying was never confirmed.[4] Speculations as to their possible clandestine purpose were particularly intense between 1899 and 1902 and from 1910 to 1914.[5] Swedish police maintained a close surveillance on them and even masqueraded as saw-filers, but none was ever caught in the act of spying. Newspaper editorials were primarily responsible for portraying saw-filers as possible spies.[6]

During the 1930s, mysterious "ghost planes" were seen across northern Sweden. Also popularly known as "ghost fliers" or "flier x," they were typically described as gray monoplanes with no identifying insignias or markings. They were sometimes seen or heard during fierce blizzard conditions, occasionally landing and taking off, and always in remote areas. Sightings of the phantom plane were almost exclusively nocturnal, and there was typically a searchlight beam coming from the craft. Despite a pervasive folk belief in the flier's existence, no plane or secret airfield was ever found. The flier possessed quasi-supernatural qualities, because period aircraft were incapable of operating under treacherous blizzard conditions for hours at a time, performing the daring maneuvers described by witnesses, and eluding the massive military search that ensued during the heaviest concentration of sightings, between December 1933 and February 1934. Many thought the fliers may have been liquor smugglers avoiding customs,[7] or possibly weapons smugglers.[8] The most prominent and more sinister theory held that they were potentially hostile reconnaissance missions from Russia,[9] Germany,[10] or Japan.[11]

Since the early 1980s there have been thousands of reports of phantom submarines in Swedish territorial waters, which are popularly assumed to be Soviet spy missions. The Swedish government's Submarine Commission was given the task of assessing over six thousand reports of suspected underwater incursions between 1981 and 1994.[12] While the Commission's report focuses on a few major incidents that were concluded to have involved Soviet vessels, most cases were ambiguous visual sightings that could not be accurately evaluated, including reports of wave movements,

Den stora gåtan

Vad år det för ena
maskiner som far
i kvallarna sena
och skrämmer envar?

Det blixtrar som vore
det fyrverkeri.
Det lyser som fore
det stjarnskott forbi.

I slott och i kåtor,
på land och i stad
nu tager man gåtor
på entreprenad.

"Det kan val ej vara
raketbomber, tro?
Då måste jag fata
till moster i Hjo!"

Raketernas bågar
i mörknande luft
med skräckstämning plågar
vårt lilla fornuft.

Det vore ej alla
om allt—eller hur?—
var enbart en villa
av optisk natur. DANUS

This poem appeared in a regular column called "This Day's Melody." Entitled "The Big Street," it begins with: "What kinds of machines are those, traveling late in the evenings and frightening each and everyone?" Source: The *Stockholms-Tidningen*, August 18, 1946.

marine lights and sounds, and possible divers. The Commission stated that "many different objects and conditions . . . can be interpreted as being connected to underwater activity," noting that natural explanations had been found for a "great number of reports." It also remarked on the influx of cases in proportion to media publicity.[13] Waves of claims and public discourse about Soviet submarines routinely violating Swedish territory have occurred intermittently throughout this century, becoming particularly intense after 1981, when a Soviet Whiskey Class U137 probably carrying nuclear weapons ran aground during a reconnaissance mission, which resulted in an international incident that engendered Swedish political protests and intense media publicity.[14]

Near the end of World War II, German V-rockets devastated parts of the United Kingdom. Occasionally the rockets strayed into Scandinavia, causing no damage but raising concerns. One V-2 fell near Backebo in southeastern Sweden, leaving a crater sixteen feet wide and nine feet deep. Fears of a destruction like that in England were rekindled in Sweden during 1946, since Russian forces occupied Peenemunde, the former center of German rocket science. Soviet troops controlled much of northern Europe during this time, and it was unclear as to how much Scandinavian territory they might claim in the political uncertainty following the war.[15]

There was speculation as early as March 19 that the Soviets would soon begin test firing rocket bombs. A newswire from the Swedish newspaper agency *Tidningarnas Telegrambyra* appeared in numerous newspapers on March 19, including *Sydostra Sveriges Dagblad*, *Umebladet*, and *Norra Vasterbotten*, and served as a prelude of what was to come in the spring and summer. It quotes the London *Daily Mirror's* Berlin correspondent as stating that "German scientists and technicians who work under Russian supervision will shortly release a number of V-2 bombs from secret research stations on the Baltic." Xenophobia resurfaced between April 23 and 26, 1946, as a series of earth tremors were reported in the Swedish counties of Blekinge, Skane, and Kalmar, and in the vicinity of the Danish island of Bornholm in the southern Baltic. One newspaper suggested that they were Russian tests of nuclear weapons.[16] On April 28 Swedish foreign affairs minister Osten Unden met privately with his Norwegian counterpart Halvard

Lange, who warned that there was great consternation in American political circles that the Soviets would soon possess atomic weapons. Lange stated "that there was an imminent danger of war" and that a group aligned with General Dwight Eisenhower felt that "differences between the U.S. and the Soviets had taken on such a nature that the U.S. ought to strike with a preventative war. President Truman, however, was opposed to this. The rumours came from the U.S."[17]

The Genesis of the Episode

Astronomer Louis Winkler correlates the rocket sightings to a rare confluence of astronomical and meteorological events: geomagnetic comets and the occasional disbursement of their orbital streams in conjunction with exceptionally high solar activity,[18] which generated spectacular auroras, meteors, and cometary spray streaking through the atmosphere.[19] Unusual aerial phenomena were first noted in January of 1946, with reports of meteors and strange glowing clouds. On the morning of January 4, observers across southern Sweden reported that luminous clouds cast eerie red, green, and purple hues on the snowy landscape. At the Revingehed military training field, "army watch-dogs crawled into their kennels," while a horse "lowered his head towards his legs," remaining so for the duration of the twenty-five-minute display.[20] These luminous phenomena were interpreted as extraordinary and intense, but auroral in nature. There were also reports of meteors at Fransborg, northwest of Stockholm, on January 9,[21] above Ljungdalen in Jamtland later that same afternoon,[22] as well as a bright fireball with a long glowing tail seen by many across Dalarna County on January 17.[23] Intermittent reports of fireballs and mysterious auroral activity continued through early May and were almost exclusively defined as natural phenomena.[24] Various other strange celestial activity was reported between January and May of 1946, including a mirage at Gagnef involving a lake, a hill, and several buildings,[25] a mirage of an aerial cargo ship at Visby on Gotland Island,[26] an eerie nocturnal light in Dalarna County,[27] a rainbow-colored halo near the sun at Helsingfors,[28] sun-dogs above

Fagerhult that appeared "like two suns had risen," [29] and unusual spheres of electricity (ball lightning) at Vaderobod[30] and Svaneke.[31]

On the evening of May 3, a "mysterious light" was seen over Stockholm,[32] and on May 21 a yellowish fireball was observed in Halsingborg.[33] While some residents were "disturbed,"[34] there remained little indication of any potential hostility. However, by May 24, earlier reports of celestial phenomena were being reinterpreted as missiles, starting with the early morning sighting of an object over Landskrona. While night watchmen had reported seeing a "fireball with a tail," another observer now described it as a "wingless cigar-shaped body" spurting exhaust sparks.[35] While most press reports were skeptical that it was a missile, newspapers began using such descriptions as "rocket bomb,"[36] "remote-directed bombs,"[37] "projectile,"[38] "V-bomb,"[39] and "V-1-bomb."[40] Media speculation that some sightings were of guided missiles provided a label with which to classify unfamiliar stimuli. As the

Etterkrigs-V'er

—Skulle inte vi kunne komma inn i FN., vi som er det enda landet der det fins krig för ögonblicket!

Sketch entitled "Postwar V-weapons," the caption reads: "Shouldn't we be able to join the UN, we who is the only nation with a war going on!" It appeared in one of Norway's largest newspapers, *Verdens Gang*, August 16, 1946.

sightings continued, the Swedish and foreign press began claiming that the rockets really existed, and the burgeoning reports of meteors, luminous phenomena, and fireballs were increasingly depicted as being Soviet weapons. As Swedish reports of ghost rockets declined dramatically in September, during September and October most Swedish and Scandinavian press reports dealt with non-Swedish sightings.[41]

By May 27, following sightings of fireballs and wingless planes near Karlskrona, Halsingborg, Huddinge, and Hagalund, some newspapers suggested that secret foreign experiments with "new remotely controlled bombs"[42] were the culprit. Sporadic observations of aerial objects occurred through early June in such places as Eskilstuna, Gavle, Kroksjo, Trehorningen, and southern Finland, with descriptions vacillating between a meteor or a missile.[43] On May 28 a metallic object emitting engine sounds passed over Kvicksund and crashed into Lake Malaren.[44] In Katrineholm on May 31 an object resembling "a silver glistening rocket" and traveling at a speed greater than "the fastest fighter plane" was seen at 11:43 A.M.[45] On a road between Uppsala and Rasbo, a driver claimed to have chased a wingless, noiseless, metallic object for three miles.[46] On June 8 an ex-pilot in Eskilstuna reported seeing "a rocket with intermittent exhausts."[47] On June 9 a spectacular "ghost rocket" with a tail streaked across southern Finland, igniting public debate in Finland as to its origin while further heightening concern in Sweden.[48] Just three days earlier Swedish Supreme Commander General Helge Jung warned of the perils of a possible confrontation between the United States and Soviets, as "the flight tracks between Russian and American bases go close by, and over, our country. . . . We must, therefore, count on that a super power is willing to occupy the whole, or parts of, our country before or after such a big conflict."[49] In the wake of the sightings and growing concern over the nature of the mysterious objects, the Swedish Defense Staff sent a memo to national and regional staffs and units in the army, navy, and air force, requesting them to fill out a detailed questionnaire on sightings of mysterious aerial phenomena. The memo stated that "it cannot be ruled out that these [recent sightings] could be connected to tests, by a foreign power, of types of remotely-piloted weapons." The memo also gave guidelines for interviewing civilians who report sightings to military personnel.[50]

As intermittent reports of fireballs and missiles continued through the rest of June and early July, a widespread consensus emerged in Sweden that the Soviets were indeed testing V-rockets. On June 16 an engineer with the railroad stated that he saw a glistening, wingless object emitting a sound like "a two-stroke engine" in Bohuslan.[51] On the night of July 1, "a torpedo-shaped object" was seen two miles south of Tossene at about twelve hundred feet, emitting a loud "humming noise" that gradually faded. "The object was fully visible, had small wings and a tube [pipe] on its stern."[52] A "swallow-like object" resembling a V-2 was spotted over Malmo, in the Skane province, on July 6 by *Sydsvenska Dagbladet* draughtsman Torsten Frykmar.[53]

At 2:30 P.M. on July 9, a spectacular luminous object that was

This cartoon shows a Russian face on the rockets, reflecting the popular folk belief that they were of Soviet origin. The caption read: "The Ghost Rocket: More and more people state that they have seen the ghost rocket." Source: The Norwegian daily paper *Friheten*, August 18, 1946.

later identified as a bolide[54] entered the atmosphere and was seen across the Swedish eastern coast, marking the beginning of massive, widespread missile reports and intensifying press coverage of sightings through September. The bolide was widely thought to be a "radio bomb,"[55] and a Sundsvall newspaper described it as a radio-guided projectile.[56] By July 10, the Defense Staff exhorted the public to report any mysterious aerial sights or sounds to their nearest troop unit,[57] an action that demonstrated concern and the potential seriousness of the situation to the public. The military's involvement in and high-profile inspections of numerous "crash" sites also reinforced the plausible belief that the Soviets were test firing V-rockets. Military officials conducted field investigations of at least twenty-eight cases,[58] and thirty "ghost bomb" fragments were obtained and examined by the military from about one hundred "crash sites."[59] While the existence of even a single rocket was never verified, interviews and press descriptions of these "crashes" reinforced the prevailing mindset.[60] By early August, the chief of Sweden's air defense division, Major Nils Ahlgren, reported that while investigations into the sightings had uncovered no definitive evidence, he was convinced that some were rocket experiments.[61]

Once the rockets' existence was widely accepted, people began rethinking past sightings and redefining them in light of the current rocket mania. Two fires that had no obvious cause were attributed to bombs. On a farmstead in Somlingbacken, Jamtland, Mrs. Maria Vastfeldt heard a loud noise right before her henhouse was consumed by flames,[62] but a subsequent investigation determined the cause as a blasting cap and nitrolite cartridge.[63] Another fire of undetermined origin in the Svartvik sulfite factory's timber store located five miles south of Sundsvall was also attributed to a "ghost bomb fall," despite the police's finding no specific evidence to support the theory.[64] The Institute of Criminology Research subsequently identified the probable cause as an overheated bearing in an engine transmission.[65] On Sunday afternoon, August 11, a barn in a mid-Norrland village collapsed without apparent cause.[66] The incident was "connected to the appearance of the ghost rockets" which had been seen the same day. A police inquiry later concluded that a tornado was responsible.[67] In Jamtland, the mysterious death of three cows belonging to farmer Andera Edsasen was blamed on a rocket projectile containing poisonous material.[68] In mid-July, when an infestation of metal fly caterpillar occurred in the southern Swedish provinces of Skane, Blekinge, and Oland, one citizen wrote to the Defense Staff theorizing a connection with ghost bombs, arguing that they were designed to drop caterpillar eggs. There were also rumors of leaflets falling from flying bombs.[69] The crash of a Swedish B-18 bomber at Valdshult on Monday, August 12, at 10 A.M. prompted intense speculation that it had collided with a space rocket, since witnesses noted that it suddenly plunged almost vertically to the ground,[70] but an inquiry commission later dismissed the theory.[71] On August 12 at 3 P.M., eight concerned citizens telephoned the offices of the *Varmlands Folkblad*, exclaiming

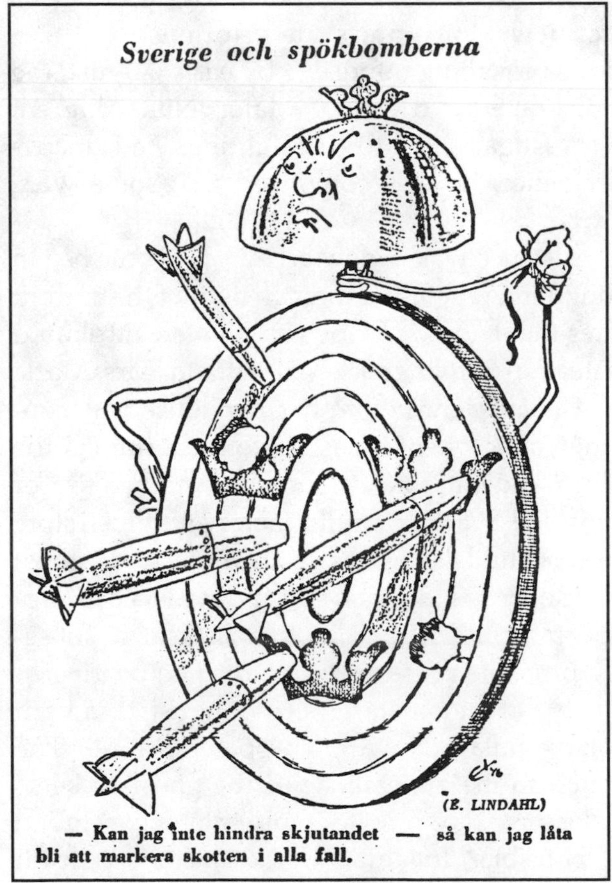

"Sweden and the Ghost Rockets." This cartoon depicts Sweden as a dart board. It says: "If I cannot stop the shooting—then at least I can avoid marking the hits." Source: *Expressen*, August 1, 1946.

that several small, luminous ghost bombs were traveling north over Karlstad just a few hundred feet above the ground. A later investigation determined that "the ghost projectiles were soap bubbles made by a little boy who sat on a sofa . . . with a newly bought bubble apparatus and a can of soap-water."[72]

Throughout the phantom rocket episode, various ordinary ground markings and objects located near recent sightings were intensely scrutinized for their potential association with the rockets. In central Sweden a "pit in the ground" was examined by defense personnel as a possible "ghost bomb mark."[73] A certain deposit of slag and coal-like material was assumed to have fallen from the sky, and people demanded an investigation.[74] One typical "projectile find" in the vicinity of a "crash" site was identified as a steam valve spindle.[75] On August 5, a farmer in southern Sweden told of discovering a "missile" embedded up to a foot into the ground in a remote area of Blekinge.[76] Authorities later identified it as a dislodged airplane antenna.[77]

Skeptical opinions were common from newspaper editors, defense people, and scientists. On July 25 Defense Staff officials noted that many reports were the result of overactive imaginations, warning that sightings were becoming "something of a psychosis." One authority said that "clouds, stars and even boat engines" were precipitating reports.[78] A spurt of sightings over Stockholm was caused by fireworks accompanying the city's "frenzied crab-eating parties."[79] A "mysterious projectile" that exploded on the night of July 13 in Bjorklinge was the subject of police and military investigations and was finally identified as fireworks.[80] One "ghost bomb" sighting in the northern Stockholm suburbs was dismissed after a municipal worker found a radiosonde balloon in the vicinity,[81] while observations of a luminous object over Ulvsundasjon and Stocksund were caused by the same type of balloon from the Bromma weather station.[82] An uproar occurred in Nyhem on the evening of August 20 when residents were convinced that a ghost rocket was being tested after they saw "a dark object which, with moderate speed, steep-dived towards the upper part of the village," soon exploding in a flash of light. The next morning the mystery was solved when the remains of a magpie "which had met its fate in the high voltage lines"[83] were found. On September 16, Swedish Nobel Prize-winning nuclear physicist Manne Siegbahn (1886–1978) dismissed the rocket speculation, noting the absence of "clear evidence that any guided missiles have been flying over Sweden," and instead suggested "hysteria" as a factor.[84] The head of the Rosersberg artillery school, Colonel Sven Ramstrom, asserted that the "bombs" were simply meteorites and pleaded for a reduction in "the bomb psychosis."[85] In late July several newspaper editors expressed this opinion, describing the prevailing mindset in such terms as "rocket psychosis"[86] and "war psychosis."[87] Even a bulletin issued on August 7 by the commanding officer of Sweden's Air Defense Department used the term "rocket psychosis."[88] It is evident from the content of these accounts that such descriptions were not intended to suggest

Irriterande flygfä!

Dessa svärmar av spökraketer
kan tyvärr inte visas hem.
Kommer dom från andra planeter?
Eller är det ett närmare hot?
—Var tusan finns själva getingbot?,
frågar generalstaben och vi med dem.

The words beneath the man say "Defense Staff," and the woman is "Mother Svea," the traditional name for Sweden depicted as a giant woman. The poem says: "The swarms of rockets unfortunately cannot be expelled. Do they come from other planets? Or are they a closer threat?—Damned, where's the wasp's nest? asks the (Defense) General Staff, and we agree." Source: *Morgon Tidningen*, August 13, 1946.

that witnesses were mentally disturbed, but only that they were acting irrationally and had overactive imaginations.

The Swedes and the Soviets traded political accusations about the rockets' origins. The Soviet journal *Novoie Vremia* denounced the test-firing claims as anti-Soviet "slander which is poisoning the international atmosphere."[89] The same publication quoted by a Swedish source characterized the allegations as "Swedish lies" precipitated by mass panic.[90] When the Swedish Defense Department issued its August 6 communique vindicating foreign-power involvement in the "rocket" sightings, *Ny Dag*, a Communist newspaper published in Stockholm, chided the "meddlesome" Swedish press for blaming the Russians and made disparaging references to the truth content of their reports in noting that "the nose is lengthened . . . among the Swedish newspaper family."[91] One editor commented that the Russians were using Sweden "as a shooting range and as a guinea pig at trials with new weapons."[92] Some circles speculated that the missiles were being guided over Sweden as a tactic of intimidation either to "scare us somehow"[93] or as a Soviet response to the well-publicized atomic detonations on Pacific atolls.[94]

Many authorities discussed their most dreaded fear: that the Soviet's newly captured missile technology would soon bear atomic weapons. Political writer Marquis Childs warned in the *New York Post* that the rocket intrusions were an omen of how the next war would be fought. "If the arms race ends in a new and more terrible war, Sweden's advanced civilization will be torn asunder along with nearly any other. . . . It is this which makes the use of Sweden as a suitable military laboratory so serious."[95] The *Svenska Dagbladet's* New York editor, Per Persson, concurred with this assessment and the peril of Sweden: "If these projectiles carried explosive charges of atomic bomb character and if they were directed against industrial centers . . . Sweden would be destroyed and the war would be over."[96] Swedish magazine *Se* described the rocket episode as "a premonition of 'push-button war.' "[97] A press editor confidently asserted: "Now we know what it's all about—trial shootings. And Sweden is the target, or a part of it."[98] One press columnist suggested that the United States should drop "atom bombs on Moscow, before . . . the ghost rockets become palpable,"[99] and other commentators expressed their fear in poems.[100]

American assistance to Sweden during the ghost bomb crisis reflected their concern over the Soviet's long-range missile deployment capacity, given the widespread conviction that they would soon develop atomic weaponry. American aerial warfare expert General James Doolittle flew to Sweden and discussed the sightings with Swedish air force commanders on August 21,[101] the same day that Swedish officials approached Great Britain about buying radar equipment to track the "rockets,"[102] since British radar experts had reportedly visited Sweden to provide firsthand evaluations of radar investigations.[103] Curiously, a British intelligence report ("Investigation of missile activity in Scandinavia," dated September 9) bears no evidence of such a visit. Most of the data in this report are from Norway, and nothing is said about radar sightings or analysis thereof. The radar cases that have been documented in the Swedish Defense Staff archives are unimpressive and are judged as such by competent Swedish air force personnel. Meanwhile, phantom rockets were occasionally sighted during this time in other Scandinavian countries,[104] and to a lesser extent in Europe,[105] but none matched the Swedish reports in terms of volume and social reaction.

In regard to foreign reactions, a London *Daily Mail* journalist, Alexander Clifford, who flew to Sweden to report on the crisis, remarked that the Swedes were acutely "aware of their position as the 'filling in the sandwich' between East and West, and they are a very good and tasty filling too."[106] A British editorial accusing the Russians of testing German missiles warned that the projectile's estimated range of six hundred miles was the approximate distance from Peenemunde to London.[107] The Berlin correspondent for the *New York Herald Tribune* alleged that the Russian war industry in the German occupation zone included one thousand German specialists overseen by Russian officers who were manufacturing V-4 rocket bombs.[108] A German socialist party official claimed that Soviet occupying forces were using secret underground German rocket workshops and captured scientists to conduct aerial experiments.[109]

The End of the Phantom-Rocket Episode

On October 10 the Defense Staff announced the results of its four-month investigation. It concluded that 80 percent of approximately one thousand reports were attributable to "celestial phenomena," and of the 20 percent that were unexplainable, there was no conclusive evidence that any were V-type rockets or other objects of foreign-government origin.[110] It read in part:

> The majority of sightings with certainty result from celestial phenomena . . . [which] often occur but usually do not attract any special attention. Since the interest of the general public was awoken . . . [they] started to take a closer note of them . . . therefore the large number of reports.
>
> Some sightings cannot, however, be explained but this should not be attributed to some sort of object of a different kind. Not enough information is in hand . . . to be able to draw firm conclusions with any certainty concerning their nature, origin and appearance. . . .
>
> Through a collaboration with astronomers it was clear that the two "peaks" in July and August probably were caused by meteors or meteorites.
>
> Even at an early date measures were taken through which the military authorities tried to maintain a certain watch over the aerial territory, seeking to clarify the origin of the phenomena. . . . [Radar tracking] proved impossible to establish . . . what kind of object it was. . . .
>
> [Of the many alleged crashes] . . . remains mainly consist of coke or slag-like formations. . . . In no case has anything come forth that can be considered as if the material came from any kind of space projectile. In certain lakes very thorough investigations have been made because of supposed crashes. So far, however, no find has turned up which can be presumed to originate from a V-type weapon.

During 1947, the year after the rocket crisis had passed, there were more reports of mysterious aerial objects over Sweden, with most observations being described as "flying saucers,"[111] reflecting heavy Swedish press coverage of the massive flying-disk sightings in the United States during that summer. There were also many reports of objects thought to be meteors,[112] but just a few scattered ghost rocket sightings.[113]

The Swedish ghost rocket episode of 1946 is prominent in its lengthy history of security scares involving the Soviet Union as the primary alleged antagonist. There were many major exaggerated security concerns, from the saw-filers to the ghost flier to phantom rockets and mystery submarines. There is no reason to doubt that future episodes will continue—instigated by social and political fears and a relatively small number of perhaps legitimate espionage attempts. Only the form these sightings take will change to reflect the changing political and technological circumstances.

Notes

1. While a small percentage of overall "rocket" observations were reported across Scandinavia and the rest of Europe, the overwhelming majority of cases emanated from Sweden.

2. R. Vayrynen, *Conflicts in Finnish-Soviet Relations: Three Comparative Case Studies* (Tampere: Tampere University, 1972); N. Orvik, *Europe's Northern Cap and the Soviet Union* (New York: AMS, 1973).

3. F. Lindberg, "Var Sagfilarna Ryska Spioner?" (Were the Saw-Filers Russian Spies?) *Horde ni*, 1953: 341–47; F. Lindberg, *Den Svenska Utrikespolitikens Historia* (History of Swedish Foreign Policy) (Stockholm: P. A. Norstedt & Soner, 1958), pp. 117–19, 123–24, 282–83.

4. *National Encyclopedia* [of Sweden], vol. 18, p. 11 (Bokforlaget Bra Bocker: Hoganas, 1995); "Saw Filers and Ghost Fliers," an editorial in the right-wing *Norrbottens-Kuriren*, January 20, 1934.

5. Ibid.

6. Ibid.

7. "The Mysterious Light Still Haunts. Airplanes Seen in Norway and in the North. What's the Truth? Liquor Traders Attend Their Customers in a Modern Way?" *Vasterbottens Folkblad*, December 27, 1933, p. 1; "Liquor by Air from a Depot Outside Norway. The Mysterious Airplane in the Mountains Receives Its Explanation," *Svenska Dagbladet*, December 28, 1933, p. 6; "The Giant Airplane Goes with Liquor over Norrland. A Regular Smuggler's Line between Vasa and Mo in Northern Norway," *Stockholm-Tidningen*, December 28, 1933, p. 1; "Liquor Smugglers Use the

Air for Their Own Purposes," *Vasterbottens Folkblad*, December 28, 1933, p. 1; "Finnish Customs Convinced That Smugglers Fly the Atlantic—the Gulf of Bothnia. Transport Cost Would Be Almost Three Crowns per Liter Through the Air," *Norrlandska Social-Demokraten*, December 28, 1933, p. 1.

8. "Weapons Smuggling by the Mysterious Flights? The Guverte Plateau a Possible Depot," *Nya Dagligt Allehanda*, December 31, 1933, p. 1.

9. "The 'Sawfilers' of the Air Guilty of the Disorder by Mountains and Coasts?" *Vasterbottens Folkblad*, January 10, 1934, p. 1; "The Ghost Fliers of Norrland Soviet-Russian Military Experts!" *Nya Dagligt Allehanda*, January 10, 1934, p. 1; "Soviet Machines That Haunt Us," *Umebladet*, January 11, 1934, p. 1; "Systematic Military Espionage Is the Mission of the Ghost Flier in Norrland," *Aftonbladet*, January 13, 1934, p. 1; "Soviet Machines That Cross Over Swedish Areas? The Boden Fort a Taboo for Strangers. Both Swedish and Norwegian Government Take On Special Measures," *Umebladet*, January 15, 1934, p. 1; "The Flying X's Soviet-Russian Planes in Spite of Denials," *Norrbottens-Kuriren*, January 16, 1934, p. 4; "The Night Fliers Soviet-Russian," *Umebladet*, January 18, 1934, p. 1; "The Ghost Flier Over Kemi Was a Russian. Finnish Authorities Confirm," *Norrbottens-Kuriren*, January 27, 1934, p. 15; "The Ghost Fliers . . . Base and Depot in the Vicinity of Boris Gleb," *Aftonbladet*, January 27, 1934, p. 18; "Do Finnish Authorities Have a Solution? Mysterious Light on the Ice Outside Kemi. Is the Flier of Russian Nationality?" *Svenska Dagbladet*, January 28, 1934, pp. 3, 6; "Is Weapons Transport the Ghost Flier's Main Purpose . . . Russian Base, Thinks Finnish Expert," *Svenska Dagbladet*, January 30, 1934; "Do the Russians Want to Intimidate Scandinavia? The Ghost Raids Russian War Plans, Says Finnish Air Expert," *Aftonbladet*, January 30, 1934, p. 1; "Base of the Ghost Flier," *Nya Dagligt Allehanda*, February 12, 1934, p. 8; "The Secretary of Defense, 'the Ghost Fliers' and the Mysterious Radio Signals," *Nya Dagligt Allehanda*, April 17, 1934.

10. "The Fliers German Front Pilots," *Stockholms-Tidningen*, December 29, 1933, p. 20; "The Hauntings Arranged to Motivate the Demand for New Bombers. Has the Nazi Junker Works and Air Administration Arranged the Matter Together," *Ny Dag* (Communist daily), January 17, 1934, p. 1; "New Theory on the Ghost. German Rockets," *Hufvudstadsbladet* (Helsinki, Finland), February 9, 1934, p. 3; "Crossmarked Airplane Seen at Low Level Over Jokkmokk. . . . Only German Machines Carry Crossmarks," *Social-Demokraten*, March 16, 1937.

11. "The Ghost Flier a Japanese Machine," *Umebladet*, January 23, 1934, p. 3; "The Japanese Warship Near Lofoten?" *Umebladet*, January 24,

1934, p. 1; "The Ghost Flights Now Directed from the White Sea Coasts?" *Vasterbottens-Kuriren*, January 25, 1934; "Japanese Help Cruiser Confirmed Off the Coast of Northern Norway," *Norrbottens-Kuriren*, January 31, 1934, p. 7.

12. *Statens Offentliga Utredningar* (Official Swedish committee reports). *Forsvarsdepartementet* (Ministry of Defense), 1995, p. 135; *Ubatsfragan 1981–1994* (The submarine question, 1981–1994). Report from the Submarine Commission: Stockholm.

13. For a discussion on the submarine debate in the Swedish media, refer to M. Leitenberg, *Soviet Submarine Operations in Swedish Waters 1980–1986* (Washington, D.C.: The Center for Strategic and International Studies; New York: Praeger, 1987); A. Hasselbohm, *Ubatshotet. En Kritisk Granskning av Harsfjardenincidenten och Ubatsskyddskommissionens Rapport* (Stockholm: Prisma, 1984); Q. Agrell, *Bakom Ubatskrisen. Militar Verksamhet, Krigsplanlaggning och Diplomati i Ostersjoomradet* (Stockholm: Liber, 1986); H. von Hofsten, *I Kamp mot Overheten* (Stockholm: T. Fischer & Co., 1993).

14. It was never conclusively proven that the vessel carried nuclear weapons, although analysts from the Research Institute of National Defense found traces suggestive of nuclear activity.

15. B. Sundelius, ed., *Foreign Policies of Northern Europe* (Boulder, Colo.: Westview, 1982).

16. "Nuclear Tests or Settling on the Bottom of the Baltic?" *Helsingborgs Dagblad*, April 27, 1946.

17. Y. Moller, *Osten Unden: A Biography* (Stockholm: Norstedts, 1986), p. 291.

18. "A New Aurora—the Most Beautiful for Ages," *Sydostra Sveriges Dagblad*, March 29, 1946; "The Magnetic Storm the Most Powerful Ever," *Sydostra Sveriges Dagblad*, March 30, 1946.

19. L. Winkler, *Catalogue of UFO-Like Data Before 1947* (Mt. Ranier, Md.: Fund for UFO Research, 1984), p. 4, states that "the uniqueness of the ghost rocket activity is emphasized by additional and accompanying phenomena. Scandinavian newspapers gave accounts of spectacular auroras occurring over Helsinki on Feb 26 and Stockholm on July 26. The preliminary aurora correlates well with the spray date of Encke on February 25, whereas the July 26 aurora corresponds to the onset of the main ghost rocket activity."

20. "Luminous Morning Clouds Frightened Horses and Dogs," newswire report from the Swedish newspaper agency *Tidningarnas Telegrambyra* appearing in various newspapers on January 8. The atypical nature of the

phenomena was noted by weather observers in Horby and Uppsala, according to the 1946 edition of *The Swedish Weather Bureau Yearbook.*

21. Letter from Defense Staff archives from Alice Ahlsen, Fransborg, Barkarby, July 11, 1946.

22. *The Swedish Weather Bureau Yearbook,* 1946.

23. *Borlange Tidning,* January 18, 19, 24, 26, and February 2, 1946; *Dala-Demokraten,* January 19, 1946; *Saters Tidning,* January 19, 1946.

24. There were also numerous reports of meteoric and auroral activity between February and early May 1946. Among the most prominent was a fireball in Vasterbotten County, parts of Vasternorrland and Norrbotten, and in western Finland on February 17, and a possible train of meteors on February 21 in the counties of Vasterbotten, Vasternorrland, Kopparberg, Gavleborg, Uppsala, Ostergotland, and Skaraborg, while an unprecedented aurora borealis was reported for several days in late March. For descriptions of these and other reports, see *Norra Vasterbotten,* February 19–21; *Vasterbottens-Kuriren,* February 21–23; *Ornskoldsviks-Posten,* February 18; *Hufvudstadsbladet,* Helsinki, Finland, February 22, 24, 26, 28, and March 3, 7, 10; *Borlange Tidning,* February 22; *Sundsvalls Tidning,* February 23; *Falu-Kuriren,* February 22; *Smalands Dagblad,* February 22; *Mora Tidning,* February 25; "Northern Lights Continue," *Norra Vasterbotten,* March 26; "Fireball Flew Over the Town Yesterday," *Sundsvalls Tidning,* April 25.

25. *Mora Tidning,* January 14, 1946.

26. "Ship Among the Clouds," *Sydostra Sveriges Dagblad,* May 27, 1946.

27. *Saters Tidning,* January 15, 1946; *Mora Tidning,* January 18, 1946.

28. *Hufvudstadsbladet,* February 22, 1946.

29. *The Swedish Weather Bureau Yearbook,* 1946.

30. *Smalands Dagblad,* April 6, 1946.

31. "Ball Lightning Knocked Down Pedestrians in the Streets," *Sydostra Sveriges Dagblad,* May 4, 1946.

32. "Does a Mysterious Light Betoken Clearer May Weather?" *Morgon-Tidningen,* May 4, 1946, p. 1.

33. "Mysterious Fireball Also Observed in Halsingborg," *Helsingborgs Dagblad,* May 29, 1946.

34. J. Vallee, *Anatomy of a Phenomenon: UFOs in Space* (New York: Ballantine, 1965), p. 43.

35. "Mystery in the Sky in Skane: 'Wingless, Cigar-Shaped Body' Amazes Landskrona Inhabitants," *Morgon-Tidningen,* May 28, 1946, p. 12. A sighting at about the same time by a Danish border guard near the

parish of Rudbbl described a rapidly moving "bright light, followed by a tail." See "The Danes See a Mysterious Fireball Too," *Morgon-Tidningen*, May 29, 1946, p. 7.

36. "Night Workers Took Shelter from the Rocket Bomb in Landskrona," *Aftonbladet*, May 25, 1946; "Rocket Bomb or What? Strange Aerial Body over Landskrona," *Landskrona-Posten*, May 25, 1946.

37. "Remote-Directed Bombs Haunt Both Here and There," *Morgon-Tidningen*, May 27, 1946; "Ghost Flier or Remote-Controlled Bombs?" *Aftontidningen*, May 27, 1946.

38. "Fire-Spewing 'Log'—Meteor or Projectile?" *Expressen*, May 25, 1946.

39. "The V-Bomb Over Landskrona a Piece of Fireworks?" *Goteborgs-Tidningen*, May 25, 1946.

40. "The Wingless Airplane Could Be a V-Bomb," *Dagens Nyheter*, May 26, 1946.

41. For a sighting in Greece during this period see "Rocket Bomb Over Saloniki," *Nationen* (Oslo, Norway), September 6, 1946; for reports in Denmark: "Unknown Airplanes or Ghost Rockets Over Denmark," *Nationen*, September 12, 1946; "Ghost Rocket Explodes Over Sjalland," *Stockholms-Tidningen*, September 15, 1946; for the Netherlands: "Flying Fireballs Over the Netherlands," *Stockholms-Tidningen*, September 15, 1946; "Ghost Bombs Over Holland," *Helsingborgs Dagblad*, September 29, 1946. For sightings in other regions, see: "Ghost Bomb Over Italy," *Helsingborgs Dagblad*, September 23, 1946; "Mysterious Fireballs Over Northern Africa," *Stockholms-Tidningen*, September 21, 1946; "Strange Heavenly Sights Over Portugal," *Sydostra Sveriges Dagblad*, September 19, 1946.

42. "The Meteor Over Karlskrona—Remote Directed Experiment Bomb," May 27, 1946, *Sydostra Sveriges Dagblad*, May 27, 1946; "New Mysterious 'Fireball' over Naval Yard. Experiment with Secret Weapon?" *Expressen*, May 27, 1946; "Mysterious Sky Appearance Also in Stockholm," *Morgon-Tidningen*, May 28, 1946, p. 12.

43. "Sky Phenomenon in Eskilstuna," *Morgon-Tidningen*, June 13, 1946, p. 5; "Flaming Red Meteor in Southern Finland," *Morgon-Tidningen*, June 22, 1946, p. 6; "Mysterious Plane Over Gavle. Long Grey Object Disappears in Smoke Cloud," *Svenska Dagbladet*, July 2, 1946, p. 3; "Mysterious Object Crossed Through the Sky Over Flurkmark," *Vasterbottens-Kuriren*, June 5, 1946, and police reports from investigation in Trehorningen, September 20 in Defense Staff files; Kroksjo information taken from Defense Staff files, War Archives, Stockholm.

44. Defense Staff files.

45. "A 'Silver Cigar' Flies as Rapidly as a Fighter Plane," *Morgon-Tidningen*, June 1, 1946, p. 11.

46. "Ghost Rocket Hunted by Car in Roslagen," *Aftonbladet*, May 28, 1946; Defense Staff files.

47. "V-Bomb Seen Over Hugelsta on Whitsun Eve," *Eskilstuna-Kuriren*, June 11, 1946; *Dagens Nyheter*, June 11, 1946; *Svenska Dagbladet*, June 12, 1946; Notes in Defense Staff files.

48. "Ghost Rocket Also Over Our Country. Sightings in Several Places," *Hufvudstadsbladet*, June 11, 1946; *Helsingin Sanomat*, June 11, 1946; "Ghost Rocket an Ordinary Meteor," *Dagens Nyheter*, June 12, 1946; "Flying Bomb or Meteor, One Asks in Finland," *Helsingborgs Dagblad*, June 12, 1946; *Tidningarnas Telegrambyra* newswire reports on June 10–11, 1946; reports number 68/3:43/1946, 69/3:43/1946 and 82/3:55/1946 from the military attache from the Defense Staff files.

49. *Sydostra Sveriges Dagblad*, June 7, 1946.

50. Memo entitled "Headquarters, Defence Staff Department L [Air Defense] nr 7:49. June 12, 1946. Reports Concerning Light Phenomena." The memo was issued "On Order of the Supreme Commander" and signed by T. Bonde (acting chief of the Defense Staff) and cosigned by Nils Ahlgren (head of the Air Defense department of the Defense Staff).

51. Letter in Defense Staff files, from S. H. Liljhage, chief of staff of the western airbase, Gothenburg, describing a telephone report to the local base by engineer Berglund.

52. Report filled in on July 5, 1946, at 6 P.M. to the research officer on duty at the Defense Staff from the duty officer at the 117 infantry regiment at Uddevalla filed in the Defense Staff archives.

53. Report to the Malmo regional defense area staff to the Defense Staff on July 11, 1946.

54. Astronomer Yngve Ohman of the Stockholm Observatory studied the sightings and concluded that the most likely explanation was a bolide.

55. "Meteor or Radio Bomb," *Svenska Dagbladet*, July 10, 1946, p. 3.

56. "A Radio-Controlled Projectile Over Medepad Yesterday," *Sundsvalls Tidning*, July 10, 1946; "Rocket Projectiles Have Taken Over the Ghost Flier's Role. Vaxholm and Sundsvall Saw Mysterious Space Rockets," *Morgon-Tidningen*, July 10, 1946, p. 1; "The Rocket-Projectile Crashed on Bjorkon," *Sundsvalls Tidning*, July 11, 1946; "The Light Phenomena Continue. No Solution Yet to the Findings at Nolvikssand," *Sundsvalls Tidning*, July 12, 1946

57. "Enigmatical Paper Find from 'Ghost Bomb.' Dalarma-Varm-

land Also Has Had Visits," *Morgon-Tidningen*, July 11, 1946, p. 1; "The Military Has a Bomb Fragment," *Svenska Dagbladet*, July 11, 1946, p. 9.

58. Based on a large number of former secret documents from Defense Staff archives examined by Anders Liljegren and Clas Svahn. In numerous other cases, local police were ordered to conduct investigations.

59. A. Liljegren and C. Svahn, "Ghost Rockets and Phantom Aircraft," in J. Spencer and H. Evans, eds., *Phenomenon: Forty Years of Flying Saucers* (New York: Avon, 1989), pp. 53–60.

60. For descriptions of "ghost bomb" crashes in which "missile" fragments were initially believed to have been found, refer to "The Space Projectile," *Sundsvalls Tidning*, July 13, 1946; "The Njurunda Findings Not Meteorite Stones Declares Research Institute," *Sundsvalls Tidning*, July 14, 1946, p. 1; "Distinct and Good Reports About Bomb and Light Phenomena," *Goteborgs Handels-och Sjofarts Tidning*, July 13, 1946, p. 22; "Space Projectile in Nederkalix," *Svenska Dagbladet*, July 19, 1946, p. 3; "Two Rockets Down in Lake Mjosa? Seen by Several People," *Aftenposten* (Oslo), July 19, 1946; "Rocket Bomb Falls in Mjosa," *Svenska Dagbladet*, July 20, 1946, p. 9; "Ghost Rocket Down in Norrbotten Lake. Two-Meter-Long Projectile—Huge Pillar of Water," *Norrbottens-Kuriren*, July 20, 1946; "Ghost Projectile Delved for in Norrland Lake," *Svenska Dagbladet*, July 21, 1946, p. 3; "Another Space Projectile Down in Norrbotten Lake," *Norrbottens-Kuriren*, July 22, 1946; "Projectile Crash Also in Njutanger," *Sundsvalls Tidning*, July 23, 1946; "Lake Bottom in the 'Bomb Lake' Searched Through," *Morgon-Tidningen*, July 23, 1946, p. 5; "The Bomb Disappeared into the Water and the Swedes Will Now Empty the Lake," *Arbeiderbladet* (Oslo), July 30, 1946; "Mysterious Object Has Been Found in Bleklinge," *Sydostra Sveriges Dagblad*, August 5, 1946, p. 1; "Mysterious Fireball Over Stockholm, Crash Seen," *Dagens Nyheter*, August 10, 1946, p. 1; "Cyclist Nearly Struck by Fist-Sized 'Ghost Rocket,' " *Morgon-Tidningen*, August 10, 1946, p. 10; "Danes Find Metal Piece of a Ghost Bomb," *Morgon-Tidningen*, August 22, 1946, p. 1.

61. "Three Hundred Reports So Far of Luminous Phenomena in the Air. No Definite Results Yet," *Svenska Dagbladet*, August 7, 1946, p. 4; "A Projectile Steers Back Southward?" *Svenska Dagbladet*, August 8, 1946, p. 7.

62. *Tidningarnas Telegrambyra* newswire of July 27, 1946; "Ghost Rocket in the Hen House?" *Stockholms-Tidningen*, July 28, 1946; "Space Projectile Causes a Fire?" *Svenska Dagbladet*, July 28, 1946, p. 5.

63. "MT Continues to Say There Have Been Many Fires . . . in the Dry Weather, Some Probably Started By Arson. Sparks Not Ghost Bomb, the True Cause . . . a Blasting Cap," *Morgon-Tidningen*, August 1, 1946, p. 3.

64. "Ghost Rocket Caused the Svartvik Fire?" *Sundsvalls Tidning*, July 31, 1946; "Ghost Bomb Was Not the Cause of the Svartvik Fire," *Svenska Dagbladet*, August 1, 1946, p. 1.

65. "Over-Heating Thought to Have Caused the Svartvik Fire," *Sundsvalls Tidning*, August 16, 1946.

66. "Ghost Rocket Crashed a Barn in a Norrland Village," *Goteborgs-Tidningen*, August 12, 1946.

67. "A Tornado Demolished the Barn," *Stockholms-Tidningen*, August 13, 1946.

68. "Poisonous Material from Rocket Bombs?" *Morgon-Tidningen*, August 13, 1946, p. 7.

69. Letter from Jan Flinta, Stockholm, August 9, 1946 to the Defense Staff; *Varmlands Folkblad*, July 19, 1946; *Sundsvalls Tidning*, July 20, 1946; *Nya Wermlands-Tidningen*, August 1, 1946.

70. "Did the Accident Plane Collide with a Returning Ghost Rocket?" *Expressen*, August 13, 1946.

71. "Space Rocket Not the Cause for the Valdshult Accident," *Jonkopings-Posten*, July 15, 1946; "Investigation of the B18 Accident: The Pilot Lost Control," *Expressen*, August 16, 1946; "Fatal Accident: The . . . Crash Not Because of Space Rocket," *Morgon Tidningen*, August 16, 1946, p. 11.

72. "Ghost Bomb Theory Fell Apart Like a Soap-Bubble," *Varmlands Folkblad*, August 13, 1946; *Expressen*, August 13, 1946.

73. "Pit in the Ground a Ghost Bomb Mark?" *Svenska Dagbladet*, August 3, 1946, p. 3.

74. "Mysterious Projectile Falls from the Air," *Svenska Dagbladet*, August 9, 1946, p. 3.

75. "The 'Projectile' Is a Steam Valve Part. Experts Agree," *Svenska Dagbladet*, August 16, 1946, p. 3; "Ghost Bomb Screw a Steam Valve," *Morgon-Tidningen*, August 16, 1946, p. 7.

76. "Ghost Phenomenon Hidden in a Moss in a Blekinge Wood," *Dagens Nyheter*, August 4, 1946.

77. "Airplane Antenna Taken for a Ghost Bomb," *Morgon-Tidningen*, August 6, 1946, p. 7; "The Mysterious Find Was an Airplane Antenna," *Sydostra Sveriges Dagblad*, August 6, 1946.

78. "Clouds, Stars and Engines: Ghost Flights Starting to Become a Psychosis, Air Defense Thinks," *Expressen*, July 25, 1946.

79. "Ghost Phenomenon Was Crab Party Rocket?" *Morgon-Tidningen*, August 9, 1946, p. 8.

80. "Space Projectile Was Boys' Fireworks," *Morgon-Tidningen*, July 21, 1946; " 'Radio Bomb' Exploded," *Svenska Dagbladet*, July 16, 1946.

81. "The 'Ghost Bomb' Found," *Svenska Dagbladet*, August 24, 1946, p. 20.

82. "Ghost Bomb Was a Wind Balloon. Observatory Saw an Exploding Star," *Svenska Dagbladet*, August 23, 1946, p. 3.

83. "Steep-Diving Magpie in Nyhem Causes Ghost Rocket Fever," *Ostersunds-Posten*, August 22, 1946.

84. " 'Missile' Is a Meteorite. Swedish Physicist Is Skeptical About Reports of Firing," *New York Times*, September 17, 1946, p. 8.

85. "Bomb Crash at Sigtuna Exposed as Meteorite," *Stockholms-Tidningen*, July 24, 1946.

86. "The Reality Behind the 'Ghost Bombs,' " *Stockholms Tidningen*, July 26, 1946.

87. "The Ghost Bombing," *Halsingborgs Dagblad*, July 27, 1946.

88. "The Ghost Rockets," *Expressen*, August 7, 1946.

89. "Russians Cry 'Slander' to Rocket-Firing Charge," *New York Times*, September 4, 1946, p. 10.

90. "The Russians Talk About Lies and Panic," *Svenska Dagbladet*, September 4, 1946, p. 3.

91. "Sic Transit," *Ny Dag*, August 6, 1946.

92. "Sweden Used as a Shooting Range," *Halsingborgs Dagblad*, July 26, 1946.

93. "Rocket, Meteor or Phantom?" *Aftonbladet*, August 7, 1946.

94. *Smalands Folkblad*, July 27, 1946.

95. "The Ghost Bomb a Serious Threat. 'Monster in Miniature for the Next War,' " *Svenska Dagbladet*, August 7, 1946, p. 7.

96. Ibid.

97. Advertisement for *Se* magazine appearing in *Svenska Dagbladet*, August 16, 1946, p. 9.

98. "The Ghost Bombs," *Vasternorrlands Folkblad*, July 26, 1946.

99. "Around" (column), *Svenska Dagbladet*, August 18, 1946, p. 4.

100. The following appeared in the *Morgon-Tidningen*, July 12, 1946, p. 8: "Trembling people walk about wondering what will happen. . . . Limitless is our wonder, no one knows what it will bring, just now upon the sky, here the horned beast was seen. . . . Terrible is a summer's night, listen to the laughter of the ghosts, when on the wheels of the atom bombs, they play tag in the heavens." A poem in Copenhagen's *Berlingske Tidende*, July 31, 1946, on the last page, made reference to a recent sensational ghost rocket sighting over Byen, expressing relief that the "rocket" was actually a meteor: "People breathed a little scared in Hong. . . . It was like a great meteor in and arc over the region below. People thought at

once of this rocket which travels so mysteriously. . . . But surely people can be at ease in Hong. It was not a great power on an expedition of war." On July 12, a poem titled "Anxiety on the Air" appeared in the *Vasterbottens Folkblad*, stating in part: "What is it that's flying here and there. . . . That man can never rest in peace, of atoms and other troublesome things, in a calmer world some may believe—but I, I believe in nothing." Other poems on the ghost rockets include: "The Great Riddle," *Stockholms-Tidningen*, August 18, 1946; "The Ghost Rocket in Denmark," *Dagens Nyheter*, August 19, 1946.

101. "Doolittle Consulted by Swedes in Bombs," *New York Times*, August 22, 1946, p. 2.

102. "Special to the *New York Times*," *New York Times*, August 22, 1946, p. 2.

103. "Inquiry into Arms in Germany Seen," *New York Times*, August 23, 1946, p. 6.

104. "Ghost Rocket Explodes in Denmark," *Svenska Dagbladet*, August 14, 1946, last page; "Space Projectile Over Helsinki," *Svenska Dagbladet*, August 15, 1946, last page; "Another Danish Sighting," *Svenska Dagbladet*, August 15, 1946, p. 3; "Many Ghost Rockets Over Denmark," *Svenska Dagbladet*, August 17, 1946, p. 13; "Danes Find Metal Piece of a Ghost Bomb," *Morgon-Tidningen*, August 22, 1946. p. 1; "Twelve 'Ghost Bombs' Up Till Now Over Denmark," *Svenska Dagbladet*, August 22, 1946, p. 13; "Ghost Rockets Over Norway," *Svenska Dagbladet*, July 19, 1946, last page.

105. "Ghost Rockets Over France Too," *Svenska Dagbladet*, August 21, 1946, last page; "Carrier Cancels Athens Air Show," *New York Times*, September 6, 1946, pp. 1, 11; "Ghost Bomb Over Austria," *Svenska Dagbladet*, September 13, 1946, last page. A survey of fourteen Italian daily newspapers between July and October 1946 yielded seventy articles primarily describing sightings of mysterious aerial objects over Italy. Edoardo Russo of Torino, Italy (personal communication, 16 January 1997), summarizes these: " 'strange bolides' at Imola and 'rocket projectiles' in Bologna of September 17, 'flying bombs' over Vercelli and a 'fire bolide' again at Imola on the 18th, 'luminous bolides' at Turin on the 19th, at Florence on the 21st and on the 22nd, 'bright signals' over Rome on the 20th, more 'rocket projectiles' at Livorno on September 20 and in Bari on October 5, 'flying bolides' in Trieste on October 12 and even a 'fire disc' at Varazze on October 4." Russo remarks that most reports described rapidly moving luminous objects with tails, which, although initially connected to the Scandinavian phenomena in the press, were subsequently explained as meteorological events by astronomers. For details

on these sightings, refer to the following Italian press reports: "Bombe Volanti Anche a Vercelli?" *Il Giornale Di Torino*, September 20, 1946; "Il Bolide Luminoso. Chi l'ha Visto?" *Gazzetta d'Italia*, September 21, 1946; "Un Bolide Luminoso Nel Cielo di Firenze, *Nazione Del Popolo*, September 22, 1946; "I Bolidi Misteriosi. L'opinione di un Astronomo sull Natura," *Nazione Del Popolo*, September 24, 1946; "I Proiettili Razzo sull'Italia Sono Fenomeni Cosmici," *Corriere Di Sicilia*, September 25, 1946; "Proiettile Razzo Nel Cielo di Livorno," *Corriere Tridentino*, October 1, 1946; "Un Corpo Luminoso Nel Cielo di Bari, *Giornale Alleato*, October 6, 1946; "Un Bolide Volante Avvistato a Bari," *La Prealpina*, October 6, 1946; "Anche Nel Cielo di Trieste i Misteriosi Razzi," *Voce Libera*, October 10, 1946; "I Razzi Luminosi di Trieste Sono Frammenti di una Cometa," *La Prealpina*, October 13, 1946.

106. "Ghost Bomb Awakens Interest in England. Star Reporter Sent to Sweden," *Svenska Dagbladet*, September 4, 1946, p. 3.

107. "Sweden's Bomb," *Manchester Guardian*, August 13, 1946, p. 4.

108. "Rocket Bomb Made in the Hars," *Svenska Dagbladet*, September 8, 1946, last page.

109. "The Russians Experiment with New Rocket Weapon," *Svenska Dagbladet*, August 13, 1946, p. 3.

110. Press release from the Defense Staff published by the *Tidningaras Telegrambyra* news agency, October 10, 1946.

111. "Flying Saucer Over Stockholm," *Stockholms-Tidningen*, July 12, 1947; " 'Flying Saucer' Over Ostersund," *Stockholms-Tidningen*, July 25, 1947; "Flying Saucer Over Haparanda," *Norrlandska Social-Demokraten*, August 6, 1947; "Flying Saucer Over Finspang," *Ostergotlands Dagblad*, August 18, 1947; "Flying Saucer or Meteor Over Helsingborg," *Helsingborgs Dagblad*, October 19, 1947.

112. "Fireball with Tail Appeared Before Lulea Inhabitants," *Norrlandska Social-Demokraten*, August 5, 1947; "Fireball Over Stockholm," *Ostergotlands Dagblad*, December 22, 1947; Letter in the Defense Staff Archives from G. Pettersson, warrant officer with Gota Artilleriregemente, Gothenburg, submitted to the Stockholm Defense Department on November 20, 1947, describing a luminous ball over Gothenburg, November 17, 1947 at 1740 hours.

113. "Ghost Rockets Over Hudiksvall," *Aftonbladet*, October 7, 1947; " 'Space Projectile' Over Appelviken," *Dagens Nyheter*, October 23, 1947, and Ministry of Foreign Affairs Archive.

9

Flying Saucers Come of Age

> [T]he airship . . . the flying saucer are images that carry the same functional load. . . . [T]hey are not real, but symbolic. The differences in the imaginative expression of this symbol are due to the "set" of the individual (the "eye-witness"): level of social development, situation, beliefs. . . . Differences in subjective perceptions of UFOs are conspicuous today. . . . The task of specialists remains to explain this symbol's meaning.
>
> —Varerii Sanarov[1]

While there are a few scattered and often vague historical references to disc or saucer-shaped objects—and a variety of other shapes, for that matter—being sighted in the sky, no consistent pattern emerged until 1947. Prior to this time there is not a single recorded episode involving mass sightings of saucerlike objects. The genesis of the flying-saucer wave of 1947 and numerous sighting clusters that have followed can be traced to the western United States during the summer of 1947. On June 24, Boise, Idaho, businessman Kenneth Arnold was flying his private plane over the Cascade Mountains of Washington State when he saw near Mount Rainer what appeared to be nine glittering objects flying like geese in formation. He kept the rapidly moving objects in sight for about three minutes. His subsequent use of the word "saucer" when he later reported the event received intense media coverage and is generally credited with providing the impetus for the massive wave of worldwide flying saucer sightings that almost immediately followed during that year,[2] and the many other waves since.[3] Despite this deluge of saucer reports, a review of Arnold's original news conference reveals that he described the objects as crescent-shaped, and said only that they moved "like a saucer would if you skipped it across the water."[4] Unlike previous sighting waves, there were no mass reports of phantom airships or ghost rockets.[5] Conditioned by the media, scores of individuals with a saucer mindset saw flying saucers around the globe.

The Associated Press story describing Arnold's "saucers" appeared in over 150 newspapers, encouraging others who had witnessed mysterious aerial phenomena to report their sightings, which numbered in the tens of thousands.[6] The descriptive phrase "flying saucer" allowed people "to place seemingly inexplicable observations in a new category."[7] The text of the original Associated Press dispatch describing the existence of the "saucers" appeared as follows:

> Nine bright saucer-like objects flying at "incredible speed" at 10,000 feet altitude were reported here today by Kenneth Arnold, Boise, Idaho, pilot who said he could not hazard a guess as to what they were.
>
> Arnold, a United States Forest Service employee engaged in searching for a missing plane, said he sighted the mysterious objects yesterday at three P.M. They were flying between Mount Rainier and Mount Adams, in Washington State, he said, and appeared to weave in and out of formation. Arnold said that he clocked and estimated their speed at 1200 miles an hour.
>
> Enquiries at Yakima last night brought only blank stares, he said, but he added he talked today with an unidentified man from Utah, south of here, who said he had seen similar objects over the mountains near Ukiah yesterday.
>
> "It seems impossible," Arnold said, "but there it is."

Sightings of flying saucers are a social construction unique to the twentieth century, a manufactured concept propagated by the mass media.[8] As with the airship episode, there were widely differing views on the stimulus for the saucer reports. While some media reporters ridiculed the sightings,[9] others considered claims plausible,[10] as did numerous scientists[11] and authorities reporting sightings.[12] Further, the official military investigation of the reports fostered public belief in their existence.[13]

The Unique Context of the 1947 Saucer Scare

The post-World War II cold war fostered considerable tension between East and West, beginning with the U.S. foreign policy of intervention to halt the spread of communism, which first occurred in Greece during 1947. Fighting was limited, and most of the conflict was waged through ideological, economic, and political maneuvering, but this fostered a fear of communism that resulted in numerous witch-hunts spearheaded by U.S. Senator Joseph McCarthy. Of even greater concern than ideological communist infiltration of the United States was the possibility that for the first time in history, a devastating atomic war could ensue. Soon atomic fallout shelters were constructed in every American community, and public schools were required to conduct mock attack drills. It is within this setting that the 1947 flying saucer sightings took place.

For the past fifty years or so the most common folk theory about UFO reports involves the existence of extraterrestrials. However, given Americans' cold war mindset, this view was not expressed at the time of Kenneth Arnold's highly publicized "saucer" sighting. The American obsession with the cold war and possible atomic conflict was reflected in the explanations for the sightings. On August 15, 1947, a Gallup poll revealed that 90 percent of Americans surveyed were aware of the flying-saucer sightings and that most believed that U.S. or foreign secret weapons, hoaxes, and balloons were responsible.[14] "Nothing [in the poll] was said about 'alien visitors,' not even a measurable 1 percent toyed with the concept."[15] In fact, Kenneth Arnold made his now-famous sighting public, despite possible ridicule, "for patriotic reasons,"[16] telling the

Associated Press on June 26, 1947, that he believed they may have been "guided missiles." For several weeks following Arnold's sighting, the Federal Bureau of Investigation seriously entertained the possibility that many reports were emanating from Soviet agents who were attempting to promote fear and panic by spreading disinformation. As a result, according to *FBI Bulletin Number 42*, as of late July, local bureau offices were asked to conduct background checks on saucer witnesses.[17] These concerns reflect American preoccupation with the spread of communism during this time. These concerns and a belief that many of the flying objects were remote-controlled rockets reflect a transition from the Scandinavian "ghost rocket" sightings of the previous year, which received considerable U.S. and foreign press coverage. However, with the great number of sightings during mid- and late 1947, it soon became obvious that no communist saucer conspiracy existed.

Once flying saucers became part of taken-for-granted reality, people began to act within a different frame of meaning. Such retrospective interpretation was applied to observations occurring long before the 1947 saucer wave. For instance, in 1910 a minister claimed to see three rapidly moving objects at night, which he believed were meteors, until decades later when flying saucers gained notoriety.[18] On July 15, 1947, a flaming, twenty-eight-inch "saucer" was discovered on a Seattle, Washington, rooftop. After firefighters extinguished the turpentine-soaked object, one observer claimed to see a hammer and sickle on the disc, which, although unfounded, resulted in FBI personnel and military bomb experts rushing to the site.[19] Eight days later, the four-hundred-foot wooden Salmon River Bridge in Oregon was destroyed by a fire of undetermined origin. The FBI investigated the possibility of communist sabotage, but it was also mysterious that the bridge's steel suspension cables had melted in several places, since heat from a wood fire would not ordinarily reach the melting point of steel (2800° F). The ambiguous nature of the fire and its occurrence near the peak of a UFO wave led to speculation that flying saucers were responsible.[20]

The common notion that flying saucers represented a U.S. or foreign secret weapon continued to dominate popular opinion through May 1950, when a *Public Opinion Quarterly* poll appeared.[21] Of the 94 percent of Americans surveyed who had heard of "flying saucers," most (23 percent) believed them to be secret military devices. Only 5 percent placed them in the category of "comets, shooting stars; something from another planet." Later in 1950 the secret-weapon explanation dramatically shifted to an extraterrestrial explanation, and has remained so ever since. The primary reason for this attitude change was the publication of several popular books and magazine articles advocating the extraterrestrial hypothesis. A bestselling book, *The Flying Saucers Are Real* (1950), by retired Marine Major Donald Keyhoe, is one example. Frank Scully's *Behind the Flying Saucers* (1950) claimed that extraterrestrials from a crashed saucer were being kept at a secret U.S. military installation.[22] The book sold sixty thousand copies and was later revealed as a hoax.[23] In *The Riddle of the Flying Saucers: Is Another World Watching?* (1950), science writer Gerald Heard claimed that extraterrestrial "bees" were responsible for the sighting reports.[24] As a result of these books and continued press accounts of sightings, numerous popular articles soon appeared in such magazines as *Life, Look, Time, Newsweek,* and *Popular Science,* typically emphasizing the extraterrestrial hypothesis. From the standpoint of popular literature, it is interesting that between 1947 and January 9, 1950, *The Reader's Guide to Periodical Literature* lists eight magazine articles on flying saucers. However, reflecting the period's popular belief, these articles were listed under the headings of "Illusions and Hallucinations," "Aeronautics," "Aeroplanes," and "Balloons—Use in Research."[25] Beginning in 1952, and continuing to the present, the extraterrestrial theory was solidified as the dominant motif in UFO movie and television portrayals.[26]

The most significant aspect of the transition from the belief that flying saucers were weapons to the idea that they are extraterrestrials' spacecraft is found in the explanation put forth by the writers of these popular articles: concern over A-bomb development and the aliens' desire to help earthlings survive a dangerous period. This belief continues to be the most favored explanation for the persistence of contemporary UFO reports.

Stereotypes of UFO Witnesses

Ever since worldwide sightings of flying saucers were triggered by Kenneth Arnold's report in 1947, individuals reporting saucerlike objects in the sky have been typically branded as irrational or psychologically disturbed, due to the fantastic nature of their claims and stereotypes of such witnesses, and not firsthand psychiatric evaluation. This stigma has continued despite repeated scientific findings demonstrating the highly unreliable nature of human perception, as discussed in chapter 1. The vast majority of flying-saucer reports involve distant lights at night, which is strongly suggestive of misinterpretations of mundane natural or human-made stimuli such as stars, planets, airplanes, satellites and so on. But clearly, in all but a small percentage of cases, mainstream theories of social psychology can explain clusters of mass flying-saucer sightings as normal behavior. Various atmospheric effects can also engender misidentifications. Under certain conditions that are not infrequent, stars and planets can appear to jump, flicker, pulsate, or change colors. It does not matter whether witnesses are well educated in other fields. Former U.S. president Jimmy Carter even appeared to have mistaken Venus for a UFO.[27] Sociologist Ron Westrum recounts a cautionary tale:

> I have had a witness of high education point to the star Arcturus as an anomalous object in the sky. I myself once watched a strange light bobbing on the horizon. This turned out to be a porch light, as I determined by training a telescope on it; but someone unfamiliar with the autokinetic effect might well have believed that they were witnessing a genuine anomaly. (In fact, the persons who were with me were not entirely convinced even after I trained the telescope on the object.)[28]

American sociologist David Swift documents how the popular Western assumption that UFO enthusiasts are socially deprived or are believers in occult philosophy and as such encompass only a small portion of the population is an underlying theme in literature on the subject.[29] Sociologist Marcello Truzzi has placed UFO beliefs in a "waste basket" category of the occult that encompasses such "esoteric" items as belief in the "prophet" Edgar Cayce, sea serpents, werewolves, Sasquatch, and vampires. In placing UFOs in this category, Truzzi claims that belief in these items "either have small scope and influence or are in an actual state of decline."[30] The very fact that Truzzi, a prominent scholar of the supernatural and the sociology of knowledge, can make such comments underscores the extent to which social scientists misjudge the appeal of secularized magic in modern times. Religious scholar Robert Ellwood also places the UFO movement within the context of various occult groups, contending that the number of UFO believers is small, with little promise of future growth:

> Only an ignorance of history could lead to the feeling that spirituality of the alternative reality type is really more widespread in America today than at many other points in European and American History. Regardless of publicity, the total number of people affected by all the movements in this book do not represent more than a few percent of the population of America, and the percentage is not likely to grow much in the future.[31]

The assumption that UFO believers represent a small, albeit deviant, irrational or psychopathological portion of the population is strongly disputed in the results of Gallup polls of 1966, 1973, and 1978.[32] In 1966 46 percent surveyed believed that UFOs "are something real," and 29 percent responded that they were "imaginary." By 1978, the figures had increased to 57 percent believing they were real and 27 percent thinking they were imaginary.

Flying saucer witnesses and nonwitnesses who simply believe in the existence of such objects have often been called hysterical and irrational. Sociologist Neil J. Smelser's classic book on collective behavior views the etiology of "saucer" sightings within this category, depicting witnesses as emotionally unbalanced.[33] Writing in the *Journal of Popular Culture*, popular UFO author John Keel applies a psychoanalytic perspective to members of the flying-saucer subculture and classifies many members of flying-saucer clubs as "neurotic and paranoid personalities."[34] He offers the following typical personality profile of a person interested in the study of UFOs or involved with the UFO social world:

> The teen-aged ufologist [UFO researcher] is most often isolated on a farm, or separated from his peers because of his eccentric personality. The housewives are often suffering from marital problems (the divorce rate among female ufologists is high), or are the type of personality who busies herself with all kinds of community and social affairs, merely adding UFOlogy to her list of escapist activities. . . . The hardcore believer has an extremely suspicious nature, perhaps because he/she has created an imaginary self-image and constructed the necessary lies to maintain it. Thus they tend to believe that everyone else shares these personality flaws. They often project or transfer their own problems to the UFO witnesses they interview, . . . [who] have been branded liars by UFO enthusiasts who thought they detected their own behavioral problems in them. . . . The two types of distinguishable personalities present at UFO conventions and club meetings are the obsessive-compulsive and the paranoid-schizophrenic.[35]

While famous psychoanalyst Carl Jung and physician J. A. Meerloo relate the phenomena to the need for the existence of a higher power, they also suggest the likelihood that many experiences result from repressed, infantile, sexually oriented conflicts.[36] In his witty exposé of pseudoscientific eccentrics and their followers, science writer Martin Gardner assumes that most saucer "cults" are composed of "neurotic middle-aged ladies."[37] Smelser contends that participants in all UFO "cults," and for that matter *any* norm or value-oriented social movement, are engaging in irrational, "hysterical" behavior. Canadian sociologist H. Taylor Buckner has characterized members of flying-saucer "cults" as mentally ill and unbalanced, based on his observations at numerous meetings.[38] Buckner writes that "by any conventional definition the mental health . . . is quite low. Hallucinations are quite common. . . . If one were to attend a meeting and watch the action without knowing in advance whether the audience was in a mental hospital or not, it would be very difficult to tell, because many symptoms of serious illness are displayed."[39] This interpretation is not unlike medical historian Gregory Zilboorg's portrayal of people alleged to be witches during the sixteenth and seventeenth centuries as typically suffering mental illness,[40] a contention which has received much recent criticism.[41]

Religious cult author Christopher Evans views many of those who believe in flying saucers as partaking in a "cult of unreason,"[42] while D. W. Swift notes that several skeptics have erroneously branded anyone who thinks UFOs are extraterrestrial spacecraft as belonging to "the lunatic fringe."[43] Scientist and writer Arthur C. Clarke takes this position, describing flying saucer witnesses as typically exhibiting "irrationality" and "nuttiness."[44] Other scholars have labeled many witnesses as mentally ill or hallucinating. Psychiatrist Berthold Schwarz notes that until recently, the mass media have attributed UFO sightings to mental disturbances in observers despite contrary evidence.[45] Dr. Herbert Strentz analyzed 511 UFO news items selected from U.S. Air Force and civilian files. Of these, ninety-four (18.4 percent) included references to witnesses who refused to be identified or who said they would never again publicly make another report or who suggested that people who see or report UFOs "could be considered gullible, untrustworthy, drunk, unstable or have other characteristics that may make them fit subjects for ridicule . . . [or] mentioned physical, personal or property damage a person suffered after making public a report of a UFO."[46]

The Symbolic Significance of Modern Flying Saucer Waves

The persistent, widespread beliefs in extraterrestrials and the reports that supposedly confirm the presence of alien craft coincide with and reflect the secularization of American society and Western societies in general. It is as if many people are attempting to resurrect the power and function of God within a plausible rationalistic framework. In other words, UFOs seem to be a substitute for God. Hundreds of UFO organizations have been formed since 1947. Members meet regularly to reinforce their beliefs in UFOs and often hear "testimony" from witnesses or pseudoscientific lectures purporting to provide proof of alien visitations. Since these "proofs" are vague and cannot be verified by the general scientific community, the people in these "congregations" are forced to rely on faith. Prophets throughout history have gone on wilderness vision quests and zealously described how they were rewarded for their pure character. Correspondingly, the classic UFO close-encounter witness is almost always alone in a remote location and purports to be chosen as an intermediary between otherworldly beings and humanity to deliver a vital message that must be heeded, which is frequently so ecstatic as to be indescribable.

In the transition from the era of airships and phantom rockets to flying saucers, the full transcendent meaning of sightings is resurrected, free of the rationalistic limitations that previously muted their power, having been removed by the exaggerated hope and optimism from the very technology in which they are clothed. Soon after the extraterrestrial hypothesis became widely accepted during the early 1950s, many people claimed to have conversed with otherworldly beings. While the airship "inventors" espoused the virtues of imminent technological advancements, extraterrestrials perform a more overtly divine function and are often described in fantastic terms. These beings commonly possess the ability to float, walk through walls, communicate telepathically, heal, and foresee future events.

A central theme in alien encounters is that the extraterrestrials are visiting Earth to save humanity from nuclear destruction.[47] Apocalyptic portents are also common, such as nuclear or natural disasters destroying large portions of civilization if humans do not recant their sinister ways, as well as other evil outcomes.[48] Warnings primarily center on technological misuse, such as genetic engineering, the depletion of natural resources,[49] and the hole in the ozone layer.[50] Sometimes the aliens perform benevolent deeds, such as offering gifts[51] or special knowledge about their utopian otherworld, or provide trips to this otherworld.[52] These accounts of otherworldly contact have more in common with biblical revelation than with mundane airship inventors. While the images are different from contact stories in the recent past, they are similar to events described in mythology. Ancient narratives describe angels carrying mortals to heaven and providing visions of a future new world order that all humanity can share if they conform to certain truths. Today spaceships transport beings of superior technology and intelligence—so advanced that they possess magical qualities that offer the promise of conquering humanity's most daunting problems.[53] Taken to its logical extreme, if aliens do make contact, perhaps their "magical" technology can perform transcendent functions other than saving Earth from nuclear disaster, such as curing various ailments. Extraterrestrials have reportedly cured cancer,[54] chronic pain,[55] healed injured legs[56] and arms,[57] allowed an infertile woman to bear children,[58] cured a kidney ailment,[59] earache,[60] myopia, and rheumatism.[61] Further, since such beings are often described as immortal or having lengthy lifespans in comparison to humans,[62] they could share their technology and transform humans to the immortal realm of gods.

Scientists have dismissed reports of fairies, religious encounters, and other such unprovable phenomena as implausible and in so doing have transferred people's belief in the spiritual realm and its powers to aliens. In noting the parallels between fairy lore and UFO lore, many UFO researchers have reinterpreted the thousands of documented fairy sightings, conversations, and abductions before the twentieth century[63] as encounters with extraterrestrials by people preconditioned to see fairies.[64] The power and function of the UFO symbol has increased exponentially over the past one hundred years to the point where modern alien encounters resemble accounts of early religious prophets and tales of witches and fairies. In the last fifty years we have evolved from the descriptions of antiquated flying saucers of the 1940s and 1950s, complete with clumsy exhaust systems and clunky ladders, cumbersome Buck Rogers-style helmets and human appearance, to descriptions of diminutive beings with large heads who float from their vessels, often materialize or vanish in an instant, and communicate telepathically.

It is important that scientists not dismiss UFOs simply as the product of deviance, irrationality, or mental disturbance. The emphasis on scientific approaches to understanding the social sciences is primarily responsible for the present pseudoscientific status of UFOs, as is the failure to recognize or take as problematic the notion of rationality as a cultural category. Consequently, the symbolic significance of UFOs has been obscured. Contemporary interpretations of UFOs serve the unconscious longing for omnipotent beings in a secular age. Folklorist Thomas Bullard observes that the seemingly limitless possibilities of extraterrestrial science border on the magical. Science may have evicted ghosts and witches from our beliefs, but it just as quickly filled the vacancy with aliens having the same qualities. Only the outer trappings are new.[65]

To obscure the meaning of UFOs is to risk viewing diversity as eccentricity or creativity as abnormality. To do so is to deprive the Western world of its own cultural heritage and censor the ethnographic record. The answer to the UFO mystery is not likely to be found by scrutinizing the skies, but instead by looking to ourselves and understanding the human mind and why the flying saucer symbol has captivated the imagination of the world. Perhaps it is a reflection of ourselves and the times we live in.

The Roswell "Crashed" Saucer

History is a valuable tool in the arsenal of scientists because it distances participants from the events they participated in, allowing them to obtain a less emotional, more contextual perspective in understanding and assessing extraordinary claims. For instance, in past centuries, a popular folk belief in witches and fairies with magical powers was prevalent in Western societies. So pervasive was this belief in everyday life during the seventeenth century that such acclaimed scientists as Robert Boyle, Francis Bacon, Sir Isaac Newton, and Thomas Hobbes could not liberate their writings from the superstitions of their milieu.[66] Boyle suggested interviewing British miners to determine if any had encountered subterranean demons, while Bacon believed "malign spirits" may have been be responsible for witchcraft. In John Locke's celebrated *Essay Concerning Human Understanding*, he wrote that "spirits can assume bodies of different bulk, figure or configuration."[67] Virtually all modern-day scientists would dismiss claims of real witches or fairies as ridiculous, yet many of these same academics are likely to believe in the existence of alien visitors and abductions, or that satanic cults kidnap thousands of children for ritual sacrifices. Such is the power of our social environment.

Between 1900 and 1950, humanlike aliens typically landed in

crude saucers that rested on large metal legs, climbed down ladders brandishing ray guns that were attached to Batman-style utility belts around the waist, and claimed to hail from Mars. This caricature is laughable in comparison to present-day aliens with large heads and bulbous eyes who instantly materialize or vanish and usually claim to have traveled from outside our solar system. The same comparative historical approach can be fruitfully applied to crashed-saucer claims in order to show that they are part of a broader myth.

In July 1947 a flying saucer supposedly crashed during a thunderstorm in the desert near Roswell, New Mexico, killing or critically injuring its crew. It is claimed that the U.S. military sealed off the area, carted away the evidence, and has engaged in a cover-up ever since to protect the public from mass panic. The best evidence to verify these claims is of the "soft" variety—verbal accounts by alleged eyewitnesses. Most of these narratives are secondhand and hearsay, commonly referred to in folklore literature as "friend of a friend stories." There is overwhelming evidence that the "saucer" was actually debris from a top secret experiment being conducted at Alamogordo, New Mexico, called Project Mogul. New York University scientists were involved in a project that flew balloons into the atmosphere with instrument packages attached to detect pressure waves emitted from Soviet nuclear-weapons tests.[68] Claims that the U.S. government had a crashed saucer in its possession were originally made by the military itself during the initial stages of the investigation on July 8.[69] By the following day, it correctly announced that the object was instead part of a balloon launch.[70]

In evaluating the accuracy of the Roswell incident, it is interesting to note that there have been several other claims of crashed saucers in various parts of the world since 1947, including other crash claims in the southwestern United States. But is it really credible to believe that it would be possible to keep such a secret from the public? Even the atomic bomb secrets were leaked to the Soviets. Further, why spend hundreds of millions of dollars on radio telescopes for the SETI program (Search for Extraterrestrial Intelligence) if the government already knows what's out there? Important pieces of evidence for understanding what lies behind these crashed saucer stories can be garnered from history, folklore, and psychology, for accounts of crashed UFOs and dead aliens have circulated since the nineteenth century.

The following letter appeared in the Sunday morning edition of the *Houston Post*, May 2, 1897, page 4, signed by a Mr. John Leander.

> There is an old sailor living now in El Campo [Texas] with his daughter who has proclaimed that he . . . had actually seen people from another world. His immediate relatives have known of the circumstances for some years, but he says the story has never been published. The name of the old gentleman is Mr. Oleson, and for many years he was a boatswain in the Danish navy, but at the time he saw the airship he was a mate on the Danish brig Christine.
>
> In September 1862, the Christine was wrecked [during a fierce storm] in the Indian ocean on a desert rock or island several miles in size. This rock is set down on charts of the ocean, but is not mentioned in geographies. . . .
>
> [The survivors] had given up all hope and had clustered at the base of a cliff waiting for the awful end, while the wind howled and the furious waves dashed against the rock.
>
> Suddenly another terror was added to the horrors of the scene, for high in the air they saw what seemed to be an immense ship driven, uncontrolled in the elements . . . and it crashed against the cliff a few hundred yards from the miserable sailors.
>
> Speechless with fear, they crept toward the wreck. It seemed a vessel as large as a modern battleship, but the machinery was so crushed that they could form no idea as to how the power was applied to the wings or sails, for they could plainly discern the fact that it was propelled by four huge wings. Strange implements and articles of furniture could be seen jumbled in an almost shapeless mass. They found in metal boxes covered with strange characters what they afterward discovered to be very wholesome and palatable food which, with the water in the rocks, saved them from immediate death.
>
> But their horror was intensified when they found the bodies of more than a dozen men dressed in garments of strange fashion and texture. The bodies were a dark bronze color. But the strangest feature of all was the immense size of the men. They had no means of measuring the bodies, but estimated them to be

> more than twelve feet high. Their hair and beard were also long and as soft and silky as the hair of an infant.
>
> They found tools of almost every kind but they were so large that few of them could be used. They were stupefied with fright and one man, driven insane, jumped from the cliff into the boiling waves and was seen no more.
>
> The others fled in horror from the fearful sight, and it was two days before hunger could drive them back to the wreck. After eating heartily of the strange food, they summoned courage to drag the gigantic bodies to the cliff and tumble them over.
>
> Then with feverish haste they built a raft of the wreck, erected sails and gladly quit the horrible island. . . . They tried as best they could to steer for Vergulen island, but fortunately in about sixty hours fell in with a Russian vessel headed for Australia. Three more of the old man's companions succumbed to their injuries and the awful mental strain and died before reaching port.
>
> Fortunately as a partial confirmation of the truth of his story, Mr. Oleson took from one of the bodies a finger ring of immense size. It is made of a compound of metals unknown to any jeweler who has seen it, and is set with two reddish stones, the name of which are unknown to anyone who has ever examined it. The ring was taken from a thumb of the owner and measures 2¼ inches in diameter.

Several elements of this story bear a strong resemblance to the Roswell incident: A secondhand narrative of alien creatures in a space vessel that crashes in a remote, barren location. The craft is destroyed and foreign writing is found inside. Their bodies are disposed of and the debris lost. A piece of confirming evidence is salvaged.

Compare this narrative with one purported to have occurred in Aurora, Texas, near the turn of the twentieth century, filed by journalist S. E. Haydon. Remember that our interest in these accounts is their narrative content and not their truth or falsity per se.

> About six o'clock this morning the early risers of Aurora were astonished at the sudden appearance of the airship which has been sailing through the country.
>
> It was traveling due north, and much nearer the earth than ever before. Evidently some of the machinery was out of order

> for it was making a speed of only ten or twelve miles an hour and gradually settling toward the earth. It sailed directly over the public square, and when it reached the north part of town collided with the tower of Judge Proctor's windmill and went to pieces with a terrific explosion, scattering debris over several acres of ground, wrecking the windmill and water tank and destroying the judge's flower garden.
>
> The pilot of the ship is supposed to have been the only one on board, and while his remains are badly disfigured, enough of the original has been picked up to show that he was not an inhabitant of this world.
>
> Mr. T. J. Weems, the United States signal service officer at this place and an authority on astronomy, gives it as his opinion that he was a native of the planet Mars.
>
> Papers found on his person—evidently the records of his travels—are written in some unknown hieroglyphics, and can not be deciphered.
>
> The ship was too badly wrecked to form any conclusion as to its construction or motive power. It was built of an unknown metal, resembling somewhat a mixture of aluminum and silver, and it must have weighed several tons.
>
> The town is full of people to-day who are viewing the wreck and gathering specimens of the strange metal from the debris. The pilot's funeral will take place at noon to-morrow.[71]

In his book *UFOs—Explained*, the former senior editor of the respected publication *Aviation Week and Space Technology*, Philip Klass, meticulously investigated this case and pronounced it to be a hoax.[72] Despite these conclusions, some UFO researchers continue to travel to the tiny community of Aurora, armed with cameras, Geiger counters, metal detectors, pickaxes, and shovels in hopes of locating the purported grave of the unfortunate alien.

There were other alleged UFO crashes in America during the nineteenth century, most coinciding with the 1896–97 wave of imaginary airship sightings. Like contemporary saucer conspiracy theories, there were even claims of a government cover-up during the airship wave. According to one account, the airship sightings were secret military experiments: "A profound secrecy has been maintained as to what has been accomplished, even army officers themselves only getting vague inklings of what is going on."[73] There were also claims that airships were being constructed and hidden in U.S. military installations, including Fort Sheridan near Chicago and Fort Logan in Colorado.[74]

On the night of December 3, 1896, a wrecked airship was found in the gully of a cow pasture in a San Francisco suburb after dairy farmers heard a loud bang followed by cries for help. Rushing to the scene, they found two dazed occupants staggering near a forty-foot cone-shaped tube of galvanized iron with broken wings and propellers. After causing a local sensation, and under cross-examination by those inspecting the "wreckage," the alleged pilot, J. D. deGear, eventually confessed that the "ship" had been pulled to the top of the hill in a wagon and pushed over.[75] The spot had been chosen for its strategic location behind a clump of trees less than one hundred feet from the road and a nearby saloon (which, incidentally, enjoyed a boom in business during the spectacle).[76]

On the evening of April 4, 1897, an airship supposedly crashed on the J. Sims farm near Bethany, Missouri, killing its pilot.[77] Less than a week later, a flying machine reportedly plunged into a reservoir near Rhodes, Iowa.[78] A search proved fruitless. On April 16 another vessel allegedly crash landed outside Waterloo, Iowa.[79] In Tennessee, it was rumored that an aircraft had plunged to earth in the middle of the night, sinking without a trace into Sycamore Creek in Cheathma County,[80] while, according to another account, the airship had met with an accident in the Tennessee mountains, where it was being repaired by the inventor.[81]

Claims of pre-Roswell UFO crashes were not limited to the United States. For instance, during the Second World War, the British government allegedly obtained the wreckage of a downed saucer containing tiny aliens.[82] And there have been numerous claims of crashed UFOs around the world since the Roswell incident.[83]

The Psychology of Crashed UFO Narratives

The solution to the crashed UFO accounts is not likely to be obtained by examining some remote desert locale in hopes of finding a piece of alien spacecraft or by watching the heavens, but instead by asking ourselves what hidden psychological needs are being satisfied. Folklorist Jan Brunvand contends that for legends to persist in modern society "as living narrative folklore" they must contain three key elements: "a strong basic story-appeal, a foundation in actual belief, and a meaningful message or 'moral.' "[84] Accounts of crashed saucers and government cover-ups easily meet each of these criteria. They make for fascinating reading and discussion and are made believable in scores of popular books and films. These narratives contain a poignant message about our secular age, in which science and reason have expelled gods, ghosts, and demons from our minds, quickly replacing their absence with more plausible and equally compelling contemporary themes to stimulate our imaginations: complex government conspiracies and alien creatures. That many people envisage such an exciting and wondrous universe over a godless, alienless, mechanistic existence should come as no surprise.

Notes

1. V. Sanarov, "On the Nature and Origin of Flying Saucers and Little Green Men," *Current Anthropology* 22 (1981): 165.

2. D. B. Johnson, "Flying Saucers—Fact or Fiction?" (Ph.D. diss., University of California journalism department, 1950).

3. R. Sheaffer, *The UFO Verdict* (Amherst, N.Y.: Prometheus Books, 1981); T. E. Bullard, "Mysteries in the Eye of the Beholder: UFOs and Their Correlates as a Folklore Theme Past and Present" (Ph.D. diss., Indiana University folklore department, 1982).

4. M. Gardner, *Fads and Fallacies in the Name of Science* (New York: Dover, 1957), p. 56; R. D. Story, *The Encyclopedia of UFOs* (New York: Doubleday, 1980), p. 25; M. Sachs, *The UFO Encyclopedia* (New York: Perigee, 1980), pp. 207–208.

5. From the time of Arnold's sighting until 1950, there were numerous reports of missilelike aerial objects, reflecting the popular notion that the mysterious sightings represented a domestic or foreign secret weapon. While there were several missile reports, from the very beginning of the 1947 wave, and subsequently, most objects were saucer-shaped. For instance, T. Bloecher's 1967 *Report on the UFO Wave of 1947*

catalogs a minimum of eight hundred sightings during this wave alone. Of these, approximately two-thirds were saucer-shaped (Bullard, "Mysteries," p. 259). Accounts of missile sightings include: "Glowing Missile Seen in Sky—by Five Persons," *San Francisco News*, October 14, 1947; "Cavalry to Aid Mexico Mystery Bomb Search," *San Francisco Examiner*, October 14, 1947.

6. T. Bloecher, *Report on the UFO Wave of 1947* (Washington D.C.: self-published, 1967).

7. D. Jacobs, *The UFO Controversy in America* (New York: Signet, 1975), p. 37.

8. H. Hackett, "The Flying Saucer: A Manufactured Concept," *Sociology and Social Research* 32 (1948): 869–73.

9. "Just Seeing Things, Scientists Assert," *St. Louis Star Times*, July 9, 1947, p. 1; H. W. Blakeslee, "Optical Laws May Explain Flying Saucers," *St. Louis Post-Dispatch*, July 7, 1947, p. 7.

10. Jacobs, *UFO Controversy*, pp. 35–62.

11. "Flying Saucer Mystery. . . . Science Observer Believes Objects Radio-Controlled," *Medford Mail Tribune* (Medford, Ore.), July 6, 1947; "Flying Saucers Are Real Space Ships, Navy Rocket Aide Says," *Oakland Post-Enquirer*, February 23, 1950; F. Brutto, "Nazis Pioneered 'Saucers': Scientist Says They're Real," *Oakland Post-Enquirer*, March 24, 1950; "UC Scientist Admits He's Baffled by Saucer Reports," *Berkeley Daily Gazette*, July 28, 1952.

12. "Pilots Report Seeing Discs," *Boise Statesman* (Idaho), August 20, 1947; "More Flying Saucers: Air Force Boys Saw 'Em," *Oakland Post-Enquirer*, March 23, 1950; "AF Reports 'Saucers' on Radar," *Berkeley Daily Gazette*, July 22, 1952; "Fighter Pilot Chases Disc 37,000 Feet," *Oakland Post-Enquirer*, March 8, 1950; "Noted Astronomer Admits He Was 'Flying Disc' Viewer," *Berkeley Daily Gazette*, July 8, 1952.

13. A. J. Snider, "Radar Crews Keep Watch for Saucers," *San Francisco Chronicle*, August 11, 1952; "Flying Saucer Radar, Spotter Posts Are Urged," *Richmond Independent*, February 26, 1951, p. 16; "Fourth Air Force Drops Disc Inquiry; Search Held Futile," *San Francisco Examiner*, August 9, 1947.

14. G. Gallup, "Nine Out of Ten Heard of Flying Saucers," *Public Opinion News Service*, Princeton, N.J., August 15, 1947.

15. L. Gross, *UFOs: A History, Volume 1, July 1947–December 1948* (Scotia, N.Y.: Arcturus Books, 1982), p. 30.

16. Ibid., p. 11.

17. B. Maccabee, "UFO Related Information from FBI File: Part 1,"

The UFO Investigator (November 1977), p. 3 (official publication of the National Investigations Committee on Aerial Phenomena); Gross, *UFOs: A History,* p. 16.

18. C. Lorenzen and J. Lorenzen, *UFOs Over the Americas* (London: N.E.L. [Signet], 1968).

19. Gross, *UFOs: A History,* p. 37.

20. K. Arnold and R. Palmer, *The Coming of the Saucers* (Wisconsin: Amherst, 1952), pp. 188–89; Gross, *UFOs: A History,* p. 29.

21. *Public Opinion Quarterly* (1950), pp. 597–98.

22. F. Scully, *Behind the Flying Saucers* (New York: Henry Holt, 1950).

23. Bullard, "Mysteries," p. 251; G. Little, *The Archetype Experience* (Moore Haven, Fla.: Rainbow, 1984), p. 52

24. G. Heard, *The Riddle of the Flying Saucers* (London: Carroll & Nicholson, 1950).

25. J. A. Blake, "Ufology: The Intellectual Development and Social Context of the Study of Unidentified Flying Objects," in R. Wallis, ed., *Sociological Review Monographs* 27 (1979), pp. 315–37, *On the Margins of Science: The Social Construction of Rejected Knowledge.*

26. A. Simon, "The Zeitgeist and the UFO Phenomenon," in R. Haines, ed., *UFO Phenomenon and the Behavioral Scientist* (Metuchen, N.J.: Scarecrow, 1979), pp. 43–59; J. Keel, "The Flying Saucer Subculture," *Journal of Popular Culture* 8, no. 4 (1975): 871–96, see p. 877.

27. Sheaffer, *UFO Verdict.*

28. R. M. Westrum, "Witnesses of UFOs and Other Anomalies," in R. Haines, ed., *UFO Phenomena and the Behavioral Scientist* (Metuchen, N.J.: Scarecrow, 1979), p. 96.

29. H. T. Buckner, "The Flying Saucerians: An Open Door Cult," in M. Truzzi, ed., *Sociology in Everyday Life* (Englewood Cliffs, N.J.: Prentice-Hall, 1968); D. I. Warren, "Status Inconsistency Theory and Flying Saucer Sightings," *Science* 170 (1970): 559–603; D. H. Menzel, "UFOs—the Modern Myth," in C. Sagan and T. Page, eds., *UFOs—A Scientific Debate* (New York: W. W. Norton, 1972); R. Ellwood, *Religious and Spiritual Groups in Modern America* (Englewood Cliffs, N.J.: Prentice-Hall, 1973).

30. M. Truzzi, "The Occult Revival as Popular Culture: Some Random Observations on the Old and Nouveau Witch," in M. Truzzi, ed., *Sociology for Pleasure* (Englewood Cliffs, N.J.: Prentice-Hall, 1974), p. 399.

31. Ellwood, *Religious and Spiritual Groups,* p. 298.

32. D. W. Swift, "Who Believes in UFOs?" *Journal of UFO Studies* 2 (1980): 7–12.

33. N. Smelser, *Theory of Collective Behavior* (Englewood Cliffs, N.J.: Prentice-Hall, 1962).

34. J. Keel, "The Flying Saucer Subculture," *Journal of Popular Culture* 8 (1975): 871–96.

35. Ibid., pp. 873–74.

36. C. G. Jung, *Flying Saucers: A Modern Myth of Things Seen in the Sky* (New York: Harcourt, Brace and World, 1959); J. A. M. Meerloo, "The Flying Saucer Syndrome and the Need for Miracles," *Journal of the American Medical Association* 203, no. 12 (1968): 170; J. A. M. Meerloo, "Le Syndrome des Soucoupes Volantes," *Medecine et Hygiene* 25 (1967): 992–96.

37. Gardner, *Fads and Fallacies*, p. 329.

38. However, these qualitative impressions have failed to be substantiated by sociologists George Kirkpatrick and Diana Tumminia, who conducted demographic surveys of a California flying-saucer cult. See Kirkpatrick and Tumminia, "A Case Study of a Southern California Flying Saucer Cult," a paper presented at the eighty-fourth annual meeting of the American Sociological Association, August 9–13, 1989, in San Francisco, California. A minority of researchers do not share Buckner's typification of UFO "cults." These include religious scholar J. Gordon Melton, who contends that typical members are "ordinary people with some extraordinary beliefs" (p. 38). See R. Westrum, D. Swift, and D. Stupple, "Little Green Men and All That," *Society* 21, no. 148 (1984): 37–44. R. Balch and D. Taylor, ("Seekers and Saucers: The Role of the Cultic Milieu in Joining a UFO Cult," in J. Richardson, ed., *Conversion careers: In and Out of the New Religions* [London: Sage, 1978]) emphasize "the importance of studying religious cults in their social and cultural context" (p. 62). Thus, a belief in the prophecies of two people calling themselves "Bo" and Peep" and claiming that during an impending apocalypse their followers would be safely transported to heaven in a UFO may sound bizarre to outsider observers and prompt abnormal or psychopathological labels of members. However, Balch and Taylor note that the message "was firmly grounded in the metaphysical world-view. Bo and Peep put together an eclectic mixture of metaphysics and Christianity that many seekers found appealing because it integrated a variety of taken-for-granted beliefs, including flying saucers, reincarnation, Biblical revelations, and the physical resurrection of Jesus" (p. 56).

39. H. Buckner, "The Flying Saucerians," pp. 226, 228. Buckner (personal communication, 1989) writes that, regarding the attribution of mental illness to flying-saucer clubs, "I would not write now as I did in the 1960s." He goes on to emphasize the importance of "part-time alternate reality" in shaping UFO-related mind outlooks.

40. G. Zilboorg, *The Medical Man and the Witch during the Renaissance*

(Baltimore: Johns Hopkins University Press, 1935). He states: "No doubt is left in our mind that the millions of witches, sorcerers, possessed and obsessed were an enormous mass of severe neurotics, psychotics, and considerable deteriorated organic deliria . . . for many years the world looked like a veritable insane asylum without a proper mental hospital" (p. 73).

41. See T. Szasz, *The Manufacture of Madness* (New York: Harper & Row, 1970); R. Neugebauer, "Treatment of the Mentally Ill in Medieval and Early Modern England: A Reappraisal," *Journal of the History of the Behavioral Sciences* 14 (1978): 158–69; T. J. Schoeneman, "Criticisms of the Psychopathological Interpretation of Witch Hunts: A Review," *American Journal of Psychiatry* 139, no. 8 (1982): 1028–32; T. J. Schoeneman, "The Mentally Ill Witch in Textbooks of Abnormal Psychology: Current Status and Implications of a Fallacy," *Professional Psychology: Research and Practice* 15, no. 3 (1984): 299–314.

42. C. R. Evans, *Cults of Unreason* (London: Harrap, 1973).

43. Swift, "Who Believes in UFOs?" p. 11.

44. A. C. Clarke, *Voices from the Sky* (New York: Pocket, 1980), pp. 197–202.

45. B. E. Schwarz, "Psychiatric and Parapsychiatric Dimensions of UFOs," in R. F. Haines, ed., *UFO Phenomena and the Behavioral Scientist* (Metuchen, N.J.: Scarecrow Press, 1979); B. E. Schwarz, "Saucers, Psi and Psychiatry," in *Proceedings of the 1974 MUFON Symposium*, sponsored by the Mutual UFO Network, Akron, Ohio, June 22, 1974; B. E. Schwarz, "Psychiatric Aspects of UFOlogy," in *Proceedings of the Eastern UFO Symposium*, sponsored by the Aerial Phenomena Research Organization, Baltimore, Maryland, January 23, 1971; B. E. Schwarz, "UFOs in New Jersey," *Journal of the Medical Society of New Jersey* 66, no. 8 (1969): 460–64; D. C. Overlade, "Psychological Evaluation of Mr. Ed," *Mutual UFO Network Journal* (December 1988): 7–8.

46. H. J. Strentz, "A Survey of Press Coverage of Unidentified Flying Objects, 1947–1966" (Ph.D. diss., Northwestern University department of journalism), p. 125.

47. For typical accounts, refer to W. Ferguson, *My Trip to Mars* (Potomac, Md.: Cosmic Study Center, 1954); G. Adamski, *Inside the Spaceships* (New York: Alelard-Schuman, 1955); O. Angelucci, *The Secret of the Saucers* (Wisconsin: Amherst, 1955); H. Menger, *From Outer Space to You* (Clarksburg, W.Va.: Saucerian Press, 1959); Lorenzen and Lorenzen, *UFOs Over the Americas*; T. Bethurum, *People of Planet Clarion* (Clarksburg, W. Va.: Saucerian Press, 1970); J. Spencer, *The UFO Yearbook* (Springfield,

Mass.: Phillips, 1976), pp. 65–69; G. Creighton, "The Humanoids in Latin America," in C. Bowen, ed., *The Humanoids* (Great Britain: Futura, 1977), pp. 84–129; R. L. Sprinkle, ed., *Proceedings of the Rocky Mountain Conference on UFO Investigation* (Laramie: University of Wyoming, 1981). Of primary importance is the narrative content of these fantastic reports. Thomas Bullard amplifies the contention that such reports are a valid subject of study in his article "UFO Abduction Reports: The Supernatural Kidnap Narrative Returns in Technological Guise," *Journal of American Folklore* 102 (1989): 148: "What matters here is not the ultimate nature of the reports but their status as narratives, their form, content, and relationship to comparable accounts of the supernatural encounter."

48. D. Kraspedon, *My Contact with Flying Saucers* (London: Neville Spearman, 1959); P. M. H. Edwards, "MIB Activity Reported from Victoria, B.C.," *Flying Saucer Review* (London) 27, no. 4 (1981): 7–12; N. Blundell and R. Boar, *The World's Greatest UFO Mysteries* (New York: Exeter, 1983), p. 189; B. Hopkins, *The Haunting of Kitley Woods*, Mutual UFO Network 1982 UFO Symposium Proceedings, 1984, pp. 168–84; J. Rimmer, *The Evidence for Alien Abductions* (Wellingborough: Aquarian, 1984); D. S. Rogo, *UFO Abductions* (New York: Signet, 1980).

49. E. Macer-Story, "Pennsylvania Woman Healed by Alien Practitioner," *Pursuit: Journal of the Society for the Investigation of the Unexplained* 13 (1980): 146–49.

50. W. Strieber, *Transformation* (New York: Beach Tree Books/Morrow, 1988).

51. J. G. Fuller, *The Interrupted Journey* (New York: Dial, 1966); T. Bullard, *UFO Abduction Reports: The Measure of a Mystery, Volume 1: Comparative Study of UFO Abductions* (Mt. Rainier, Md.: Fund for UFO Studies, 1987), p. 141.

52. A. Berlot, *Discos Voadores da Utopia a Realidade* (Rio de Janeiro: Arturo Berlet, 1967); R. Fowler, *The Andreasson Affair* (Englewood Cliffs, N.J.: Prentice-Hall, 1979); L. Sprinkle, "Investigation of the Alleged UFO Experience of Carl Higdon," in R. Haines, ed., *UFO Phenomena and the Behavioral Scientist* (Metuchen, N.J.: Scarecrow, 1979), pp. 225–357; *Proceedings of the Rocky Mountain Conference*, pp. 81–83; F. Whiting, "The Abduction of Harry Joe Turner," *Mutual UFO Journal* 145 (1980): 3–7; R. Marshland, "Two Claimed Abductions in Brazil," *Aerial Phenomena Research Organization Bulletin* 31, no. 10 (1983): 1–2.

53. My thanks to Thomas Bullard for this observation.

54. R. Bartholomew, *UFOlore: A Social Psychological Study of a Modern Myth in the Making* (Stone Mt., Ga.: Arcturus, 1989). pp. 179, 235.

55. H. Holzer, *The UFOnauts* (New York: Fawcett, 1976), pp. 58–68.

56. G. Creighton, "Healing from UFOs," *Flying Saucer Review* 15, no. 5 (1969): 21–22; R. Sigismond, "CE IIIs: New Dimensions in Investigations," *The International UFO Reporter* 7, no. 5 (1982): 9–15.

57. T. A. Hartman, "Another Abduction by Extraterrestrials," *Mutual UFO Network Journal* 141 (1979): 3-4.

58. Macer-Story, "Pennsylvania Woman Healed."

59. I. Granchi, "An Encounter with 'Rat Faces' in Brazil," *Flying Saucer Review* (London) 29, no. 1 (1983): 6–13.

60. L. Willis, "Mother and Child Texas Abduction Case," *Mutual UFO Network Journal* 167 (1982): 3–7.

61. R. Blum and J. Blum, *Beyond Earth: Man's Contact with UFOs* (New York: Bantam, 1974), p. 147.

62. T. Bethurum, *Aboard a Flying Saucer* (Los Angeles: De Vorss, 1954); J. Keel, *Our Haunted Planet* (Connecticut: Fawcell Books, 1971), pp. 183–84.

63. T. Keightley, *The Fairy Mythology* (London: Longman, 1882); R. Kirk, *The Secret Commonwealth of Elves, Fauns and Fairies* (London: Longman, 1815); W. Y. Evans-Wentz, *The Fairy-Faith in Celtic Countries, Its Psychological Origin and Nature* (Rennes, France: Oberthur, 1909).

64. J. Michell, *The Flying Saucer Vision* (New York: Ace, 1974), pp. 57–58; G. Creighton, Postscript to the Most Amazing Case of All," *Flying Saucer Review* (London) 11, no. 4 (1965): 24–25; J. Vallee, *Passport to Magonia: From Folklore to Flying Saucers* (Chicago: Henry Regnery, 1969).

65. Bullard, "UFO Abudction Reports," p. 168.

66. P. Hughes, *Witchcraft* (Baltimore: Penguin, 1952); E. Goode and N. Ben-Yehuda, *Moral Panics: The Social Construction of Deviance* (Cambridge, Mass.: Blackwell, 1994).

67. M. Wolf, "Witchcraft and Mass Hysteria in Terms of Current Psychological Theories," *Journal of Practical Nursing and Mental Health Services* (March 1976): 23–28.

68. R. L. Weaver, "Air Force Report on the Roswell Incident," in K. Frazier, B. Karr, and J. Nickell, eds., *The UFO Invasion* (Amherst, N.Y.: Prometheus Books, 1997), pp. 98–112; D. E. Thomas, "The Roswell Incident and Project Mogul," in ibid., pp. 113–22.

69. "RAAF Captures Flying Saucer on Ranch in Roswell Region. No Details of Flying Disk Are Revealed," *Roswell Daily Record*, July 8, 1947, p. 1; "Army Announces Finding 'Saucer,' " *Rapid City Daily Journal* (South Dakota), July 8, 1947; "Disk Lands on Ranch in N.M.—Is Held by Army," *Seattle Times*, July 8, 1947; "U.S. Army to Examine a 'Flying Disk,' " *London Times*, July 9, 1947.

70. "Flying Disk Part of Weather Balloon," *St. Louis Post-Dispatch*, July 9, 1947, p. 1; " 'Disk' Found in New Mexico Declared Weather Balloon," *The Oregonian*, July 9, 1947; "Airmen End Excitement Over Object," *The Oregonian*, July 9, 1947; "Report of Finding Disc Explodes; It's a Weather Balloon," *St. Louis Star Times*, July 9, 1947.

71. "A Windmill Demolishes It," *Dallas Morning News*, April 19, 1897, p. 5.

72. P. Klass, *UFOs—Explained* (New York: Random House, 1976).

73. "Airships May Be Uncle Sam's," *The Galveston Daily News*, April 29, 1897, p. 10.

74. Ibid.

75. "An Airship which Rode in a Wagon. Was Planted in a Gulch," *San Francisco Chronicle*, December 4, 1896, p. 5.

76. "Plunged from a Dizzy Height. . . . It Landed Suddenly in a Ditch," *The Call* (San Francisco), December 4, 1896, p. 1; "An Airship in the Mud. Night of Weird Whirrings, Cries and Crashes behind Twin Peaks," *San Francisco Examiner*, December 5, 1896, p. 1.

77. "An Inquest Now in Order. Air Ship Falls Near Bethany and One Man Said to Be Killed," *St. Joseph Daily Herald*, April 6, 1897, p. 5.

78. "Stranger Than Fiction," *Iowa State Register*, April 13, 1897, p. 1.

79. "Is a Clever Fake. Airship Comes Down at Waterloo with One Passenger," *Cedar Rapids Evening Gazette*, April 16, 1897, p. 1.

80. "Hypothetical Fate of the Wonderful Airship," *Nashville Banner*, April 17, 1897, p. 1.

81. "That Airship. It Is Out of Order and Is Now Resting for Repairs in the Tennessee Mountains," *St. Louis Post-Dispatch*, April 25, 1897, p. 10.

82. T. Good, *Beyond Top Secret* (London: Pan, 1997), p. 21.

83. S. Friedman and D. Berliner, *Crash at Corona* (New York: Paragon House, 1992); K. Randle, *A History of UFO Crashes* (New York: Avon, 1995).

84. J. H. Brunvand, *The Vanishing Hitchhiker* (New York: W. W. Norton, 1981).

10

UFOs as a Collective Delusion

The word "delusion" is used by psychiatrists to describe a persistent pathological belief associated with serious mental disturbance, usually psychosis. Sociologists and social psychologists use the term "collective delusion" or "mass delusion" in a different sense, to describe the spontaneous, temporary spread of false beliefs within a given population. Excluded from this definition are mistaken beliefs that occur in an organized or ritualistic manner. This term is also a common source of confusion since it is often used as a catch-all category to describe a variety of different behaviors under one convenient heading. There are several types of mass delusions, four of which have some association with UFOs: immediate community threats, community flight panics, wish-fulfillment, and small-group scares. Mass delusions differ from prominent religious myths and popular folk beliefs in that the former occur in an unorganized, spontaneous fashion, although they may become institutionalized. Examples of such institutionalization include forming organizations intended to confirm the existence of alien visitors.

History is replete with examples of group delusion, many of which may seem humorous to those outside the historical or cultural setting. For instance, in 1806 near Leeds, England, people became terror-stricken, believing that the end of the world was imminent after a hen began laying eggs with the inscription "Christ Is Coming." Masses of people thronged to glimpse the miraculous bird until it was discovered that the eggs had been inscribed with a corrosive ink and forced back into its body. This is one of many examples from Charles Mackay's 1852 classic, *Memoirs of Extraordinary Popular Delusions and the Madness of Crowds*.[1] Unfortunately, the outcomes of group delusions are often more sinister: Nazism, mass suicide, moral witch-hunts, hunts for real witches, Communist infiltration scares, the Crusades, and unfounded fears about the casual transmission of AIDS, to name but a few.

While some historical episodes of collective delusions are legendary, modern occurrences are remarkably similar. The four types of delusion mentioned above all involve a rapid spread of false—but plausible—exaggerated beliefs that gain credibility within a particular social and cultural context. They can be positive and take the form of wish-fulfillment, but are more often negative and spread by fear. Rumors are an essential ingredient common to each category of delusion. As people attempt to confirm or dismiss the accuracy of these unsubstantiated stories, everyday objects, events, and circumstances that would ordinarily receive scant attention become the subject of extraordinary scrutiny. Ambiguous happenings are soon redefined according to the new definition, resulting in a self-fulfilling prophecy. Many factors contribute to the spread of delusional episodes: the mass media, low education levels, the fallibility of human perception, cultural superstitions and stereotypes, group conformity, and reinforcing actions by authority figures, such as politicians, or institutions of social control, such as police or the military.

Immediate Community Threats

The first type of mass delusion involves exaggerated feelings of danger within communities, where members of the affected population are concerned about what is believed to be an immediate personal threat. Episodes usually persist for a few weeks to several months and often recur periodically. Participants may express excitement and concern, but not panic and take flight. The underlying process of fantasy creation involves the flaws of human perception and the tendency for people in group settings who share similar beliefs to yield to the majority consensus.

Examples of immediate community threats include each of the war-scare UFO waves discussed previously. But there are many similar examples of community threats that have nothing to do with UFOs. For instance, occasionally the feared agent is a mysterious attacker believed to be terrorizing an area. During a two-week period in 1956, newspapers in a Taiwan community reported that a maniacal figure was randomly slashing victims with a razor or some such weapon.[2] At least twenty-one people reported attacks. N. Jacobs, who studied the events concluded that affected persons, mainly women and children of low income and education, reinterpreted ordinary scratches and slash marks to a crazed slasher. The social delusion was amplified by sensational press coverage that treated the enigmatic figure's existence as reality. In the wake of plausible newspaper accounts that manipulated people's perceptions to include the existence of a daring slasher, police eventually determined that various ordinary lacerations were erroneously attributed to the phantom. In one case, a middle-aged man described to police in vivid detail how he was slashed by a cavorting figure who was carrying a mysterious black bag. After a physician determined that the wound could not have resulted from a razor, but came instead from a blunt object, the "victim" admitted to being unable to recall the circumstances surrounding the wound's appearance, assuming he was slashed "because of all the talk going around." Another incident involved an elderly man who sought medical treatment for a wrist laceration. The man's doctor reported the incident to the police after the man casually described being touched by a stranger and then noticed he was bleeding. It was subsequently determined that the "slash" was actually an old wound that had been reopened by inadvertent scratching.

There are other historical examples of imaginary attackers. In Paris, near the turn of the twentieth century, many people mistakenly reported being "pricked with a long hat pin or the like,"[3] while several communities in Yorkshire, England, between 1938 and 1939 recounted attacks by "a razor-welding maniac," until police determined that the episode was entirely imaginary.[4]

A different twist on slasher-related social delusions involves rumors of cattle mutilations reported across the midwestern United States between 1969 and 1980.[5] Hundreds of dead cattle were found with one or more parts missing, most commonly the sex organs, ears, and mouth. Rumors flew that Satan worshippers or extraterrestrials were responsible. The belief in extraterrestrial visitors was common in the United States during this period, with several popular books[6] and television programs[7] suggesting an association between the mutilations and either cultists or extraterrestrials. Hundreds of circumstantial UFO and cult-related newspaper articles appeared during this time in ordinarily credible media,[8] which lent further plausibility to the rumors. As mutilation stories gained widespread media attention, the number of cases rose dramatically. While dead cattle often have their organs consumed by various natural predators, many ranchers who would not ordinarily pay close attention to their animal carcasses began examining the cadavers for evidence of alleged alien or cultic surgical removal of body parts. According to sociologist James Stewart, the "mutilations" were caused by small nocturnal predators that are unable to easily penetrate cattle hides and gravitate to the most exposed and softest parts, their sharp side teeth giving the impression of surgical incisions.[9] And the lack of blood in many of the animals still gave credence to the blood-cult rumors, despite veterinarians who cautioned that the blood in dead animals coagulates after several days, making it look as if the carcass were drained.[10]

Sometimes the imaginary threat is from an agent that is believed to cause illness, such as the series of phantom attacks in Mattoon, Illinois, during two weeks in 1944, involving a "mad gasser."[11] In Auckland, New Zealand, in 1973, fifty drums of the compound merphos were being unloaded at a wharf when it was suddenly noticed that several barrels were leaking, and a chemical-like smell began permeating the air. After immediate requests for information on its toxicity, authorities were wrongly informed that it was extremely toxic, after which at least four hundred dock workers and nearby residents received treatment for a variety of psychosomatic complaints, such as headache, difficulty breathing, and eye irritation.[12]

In non-Western societies, immediate community threats are often closely associated with cultural traditions, as in the case of head-hunting panics that have occurred for centuries in remote parts of Malaysia and Indonesia.[13] These episodes represent fears by "primitive" peoples of losing political control to a distant central government. Head-hunting scares are characterized by sightings of head-takers and finding their alleged paraphernalia. Just as the vast, ambiguous nighttime sky is an excellent catalyst for spawning UFO sightings, and lakes are conducive to sea-serpent reports, the thickly vegetated southeast Asian jungle is ideal for imagining head-hunters lurking in the dense foliage. Villages are often paralyzed with fear, travel is severely restricted, sentries are posted, and schools commonly closed for months. Most head-hunting scares coincide with the nearby construction of a government bridge or building, during which it is widely believed that one or more human heads are required to produce a strong, enduring foundation. These fears are a projection of the status of tribal-state relations and reflect "ideological warfare between the administrators and the administrated."[14]

Community Flight Panics

A second type of collective delusion is the community flight panic, where people attempt to flee from an imaginary threat. This category is rarely associated with UFOs, but when they do occur in conjunction, the results can be spectacular. Episodes may last a few hours to several days or weeks, subsiding only when it is realized that the harmful agent did not materialize. Perhaps the best-known example is the panic that ensued in the United States on Halloween eve, 1938, following the radio reenactment of H. G. Wells's book *War of the Worlds* by the CBS Mercury Theater.[15] Author H. Cantril noted that in general those who panicked failed to exercise critical thinking, such as calling the police or checking other media sources. There remains a great potential for similar hoaxes to recur if they are presented with plausibility and a degree of realism. A similar broadcast in South America nearly a decade later had disastrous consequences. During 1949, near Quito,

Ecuador, a radio play based on *War of the Worlds* resulted in tens of thousands of frantic residents pouring into the streets and running for their lives, preparing to defend themselves against Martian gas raids. Broadcast in Spanish, the program was highly realistic and used the name of a local community, Cotocallo, as the Martian landing site. The play included impersonations of politicians, vivid eyewitness descriptions, and was so convincing that police rushed to the nearby town to repel the invaders. Quito was left with a skeleton police force that was unable to prevent an angry mob from burning down the radio station that broadcast the drama, killing fifteen people, including the event's mastermind.[16]

Spontaneous mass flights from the city of London have occurred over the centuries in response to prophesies of its destruction by a great flood in 1524, the day of judgment in 1736, and an earthquake in 1761.[17] One of many contemporary examples involving apocalyptic prophesies and mass panic occurred in Adelaide, Australia, in the month leading up to January 19, 1976. Many people fled the city and some even sold their homes after "psychic" John Nash predicted that an earthquake and tidal wave would strike at midday. In examining the circumstances of the event, many of those who sold their homes or ran to the hills for the day were first-generation Greeks and Italians. Both countries have a long history of devastating earthquakes, and the belief in clairvoyants is generally taken very seriously there.[18]

Collective Wish-Fulfillment

Mass wish-fulfillment involves processes similar to those that cause community threats, except the object of interest is esteemed and satisfies psychological needs. Cases typically last for a few weeks or months and recur periodically in clusters. Episodes involve a subconscious wish that is related to human mortality in conjunction with a plausible belief, fostering a collective quest for transcendence. Examples include Virgin Mary "appearances,"[19] "moving" religious statues in Ireland,[20] waves of claims and public discourse surrounding reports of fairies in England before the twentieth century,[21] and flying-saucer sightings.[22]

On May 25, 1953, more than 150,000 people converged on a ten-acre site surrounding a well at Rincorn, Puerto Rico, awaiting the appearance of the Virgin Mary predicted by seven local children. As the purported hour approached, many miracles were reported: colored rings around the sun, the Virgin silhouetted among the clouds, healings, and a general sense of well-being.[23] By 5 P.M., when most of the crowd had dispersed, many had seen or experienced nothing extraordinary. Intense media publicity had preceded the event, and a local politician had enthusiastically endorsed the prediction, organizing the children to lead throngs of pilgrims in mass prayers and processions prior to the event.[24] During the "miracle" a team of sociologists who mingled with the crowd and conducted interviews found that the majority of pilgrims believed in the authenticity of the children's claim and were seeking cures for either themselves or friends and relatives.[25] A variety of ambiguous objects in the immediate surroundings mirrored the hopeful and expectant religious state of mind of many participants.[26]

On the night of July 29, 1992, beginning at about 11 P.M., nearly two hundred students and a female instructor at the Hishamuddin Secondary Islamic School in Klang, Malaysia, observed a variety of seemingly miraculous sights in the sky during a five-hour period, including the word "Allah" (God) in Arabic. A total of twenty-six images were reported. The following evening, July 30, the words "Allah" and "Muhammad" reportedly appeared while the students were praying in a school field. Unlike the first episode, this time the script was much larger. The images in both instances were reportedly formed in, on, or by clouds. Twenty-six drawings of the images were made by students,[27] yet they appear to have misperceived clouds in the night sky reflective of their religious background.[28]

Mass wish-fulfillments fill the spiritual void left by the ascendancy of rationalism and secular humanism. Within this context, and fostered by sensationalized documentaries, movies, and books, contemporary people have been conditioned to scan the heavens for "UFOs" representing "technological angels."[29] These sightings serve as a projected Rorschach inkblot test of the collective psyche, underscoring the promise of rapid technological advancement during a period of spiritual decline.

Accounts of UFO occupants and fairies depict godlike beings

capable of transcending natural laws and thus potentially elevating humans to their immortal realm. They reflect similar themes found in religion, mythology, and folklore throughout the world, camouflaged for contemporary acceptance.[30] Transcendence and magical or supernatural powers are an underlying theme in most wish-fulfillments. Even observations of imaginary or extinct creatures such as Bigfoot and the Tasmanian tiger, once considered the sole domains of zoology, have undergone recent transformations with the emergence of a new motif among paranormal researchers that links extraterrestrial or paranormal themes with phantom animals.[31] The existence of such animals can be viewed as antiscientific symbols undermining secularism. Like claims of contact with UFOs or the Virgin Mary, evidence for the existence of Bigfoot and Tasmanian tigers ultimately rests with eyewitness testimony which is usually unreliable.

Small Group Scares

Small group scares is another category of collective delusion that has yet to be discussed in scientific literature. These involve individuals in close physical proximity, within temporarily close settings, where escape routes are limited. Incidents occur in isolated, ambiguous geographical surroundings, when participants panic after seeing something unusual that is assumed to pose an immediate threat. Thus, an aerial light source is transformed into a flying saucer, or bushes rustling or an unfamiliar noise becomes Bigfoot. Table 1 lists fourteen cases of small-group pursuits, sieges, or attacks. Most involve sightings of UFOs and mysterious creatures. While the factual quality of such reports varies, and there are numerous historical reports, only episodes that were thoroughly investigated by reputable authorities are included. In all cases investigators possess doctorates, are police officers, or are personally known to the authors. Small group scares often occur during UFO waves and can contribute significantly to an escalation of community excitement and interest, since they tend to receive widespread and spectacular press coverage.

Table 1. Descriptions of Small Group Scares Published Between 1973 & 1993

Source	*Setting*	*Time/Date*	*Trigger*	*No. of Witnesses*	*Exacerbating & Relationship Events*
Rogo 1980	Car, remote road, Utah, USA	12 A.M. summer 1969	Aerial lights; assumed pursuit by extraterrestrials	3 (Married couple & child)	Driver fatigue (36 hours with no sleep); car mishap; driver hallucination
Hind 1982	Car, remote road, Fort Victoria, Zimbabwe	2 A.M. June 1, 1974	Aerial lights; assumed pursuit by extraterrestrials	2 (Married couple)	Driver fatigue; anxiety-induced dissociation as driver reports car operated autonomously
Schwarz 1983	Car, remote road, Norway, Massachusetts, USA	3 A.M. October 27, 1975	Aerial lights; assumed pursuit by extraterrestrials	2 (Friends & co-workers)	Driver fatigue; anxiety-induced dissociation as driver reports car operated autonomously
Story 1980	Car, remote road, Houstonville, Kentucky, USA	11:15 P.M. January 6, 1974	Aerial lights; assumed pursuit by extraterrestrials	3 (Close friends)	Anxiety-induced dissociation as driver reports car operated autonomously
Johnson 1978	Car, remote road, Brockworth, UK	10:15 P.M. June 19, 1978	Aerial lights; assumed pursuit by extraterrestrials	5 (Same family)	Anxiety-induced dissociation as driver reports car operated autonomously
Sheaffer 1981	Car, remote road, Indian Head, New Hampshire, USA	12 A.M. September 20, 1961	Aerial lights; assumed pursuit by extraterrestrials	2 (Married couple)	Fatigue; misidentification of an ambiguous aerial light
Evans 1979; Story 1980	Car, remote road, Aveley, UK	10:10 P.M. October 27, 1974	Aerial lights; assumed pursuit by extraterrestrials	5 (Same family)	Car trouble; bumpy road; heavy fog

Baster-field	Car, remote road, 100 km from Esperance, Australia	7:45 P.M. March 27, 1982	Aerial lights; assumed pursuit by extraterrestrials	2 (Friends)	Fatigue; traveling non-stop on long journey; unusual sleep routine alternating between sleeping and driving each hour; misidentification of Venus
Baster-field	Car, remote road, Nullarbor, Australia	5 A.M. January 20, 1988	Aerial lights; assumed pursuit by extraterrestrials	4 (Same family)	Fatigue; traveling non-stop from Western Australia following family dispute; dust
Schwarz 1983	Isolated field, Uniontown, Pennsylvania, USA	9 P.M. October 25, 1973	Aerial light, ambiguous noises, shadows; assumed pursuit by ETs	13 (Local UFO network members & same family)	Firing rifle at shadows; anxiety-induced dissociation in main percipient
Davis & Bloecher 1979; Story 1980	Isolated house, Kelly, Kentucky, USA	8 P.M. August 21, 1955	Aerial light, misidentification of shadows & noises; assumed ET pursuit	11 (Same family) plus friend	Shooting star, barking dog
Barthol-omew et al. 1992	Isolated house Kinderhook, New York, USA	10:30 P.M. September 24, 1980	Unfamiliar animal noise; panic; assumed "Monster" threat	5 (Same family)	Local Bigfoot folklore; firing shotgun
Westrum 1985	House in sparsely inhabited area of Lowell, Michigan, USA	Night, September 7, 1978	Quasi-paranoia; assumed pursuit by intruders	5 (Same family)	Quasi-paranoia
Westrum 1985	House in sparse area of Shelbyville, Michigan, USA[32]	Night November 1978	Assumed pursuit by drug police	2 (Unmarried couple)	Quasi-paranoia; drug police folklore; uninhabited area

UFO Examples

On the evening of August 21, 1955, members of the Sutton family reported being terrorized by space creatures on their remote farm near the tiny community of Kelly, Kentucky.[33] Ten family members (seven adults, three children) were inside the farmhouse with landlord William Taylor. Taylor told police that while drawing water from a backyard well at about 7 P.M., he saw a luminous "flying saucer" land in a nearby gully. The family was incredulous to Taylor's account, believing it to be an embellishment of a falling meteor. By 7:30, after a pet dog started barking uncontrollably, Taylor and Sutton reported seeing a faint glow in a distant field, which appeared to be slowly approaching the house. They soon saw what looked like a three-and-a-half-foot-tall creature with an oversized head, elongated arms, and elephantlike ears. Panicking, they grabbed their guns, withdrew to just inside the house, and began firing. During the next three and a half hours, the creatures peered into windows on several occasions and were shot at. By 11 P.M., with the children in hysterics, everyone crammed into two cars to summon the police. A search of the house and surroundings revealed nothing extraordinary, and the last officer departed by 2:15 A.M. Soon after, the family's mother, who was lying in bed staring at a window, became convinced that a creature was peering in. After alerting the household, more sightings and intermittent shooting continued until 5:15 A.M., just prior to sunrise. All eleven people reported seeing the creatures at some point. A subsequent investigation by police revealed no unusual physical evidence, only a house riddled with bullets and frightened occupants.

Perhaps the most well-publicized phantom scare involves the purported contact with extraterrestrials by Betty and Barney Hill of Portsmouth, New Hampshire. The couple was driving on a remote section of the Daniel Webster Highway in September of 1961 when Betty noticed a bright "star" in the sky. They became increasingly excited after watching the object for thirty miles along the highway. Barney stopped the car several times so his wife could get a better view with the binoculars. Betty was convinced that the object was a spaceship. Finally Barney stopped the car and stepped out for a closer look. Peering through binoculars, he thought he saw humanoid figures and bands of light around a spacecraft. He panicked, began laughing and crying hysterically while repeating, "They're going to capture us." He ran back to the car, and they hastily sped off.

They arrived home two and a half hours behind schedule, so they eventually underwent regressive hypnosis to account for the "missing time" and their recurring nightmares. The therapy revealed an apparent kidnapping by aliens.

In retrospect, however, the couple almost certainly misinterpreted Jupiter for a spaceship. Betty reported that she saw two objects near the moon, a star below it, and a more brilliant starlike object above it, which she thought was a spacecraft. On the night in question, Saturn was the bright star below the moon, "with Jupiter a more illuminated star-like object above it. Thus, Mrs. Hill's description of the initial sighting of the supposed UFO strongly suggests that she mistook the planet Jupiter for a UFO."[34]

Australian UFO Scares

On the afternoon of January 19, 1988, in Perth, western Australia, a domestic dispute broke out between members of the Knowles family, resulting in Faye Knowles and her three sons, Wayne, eighteen, Sean, twenty-one, and Patrick, twenty-four, piling into their car and setting out to visit relatives in Melbourne, several thousand miles away. After thirteen hours of virtual nonstop traveling, the exhausted group passed between the tiny towns of Madura and Mundrabilla, in remote western Australia, before dawn. Sean, the driver, was the first to notice a strange light on the road that he thought was a spaceship. The object was brilliant white and soon disappeared. Shortly afterward a similar light appeared behind their car. Sean panicked and accelerated quickly to get away from the light.

The group reported that their car was raised into the air and then dropped, at which point the rear tire blew out. After changing the tire, they traveled on to Mundrabilla, where two truck drivers saw the family and noted that they looked very disturbed. One of the truck drivers said there was an unusual "black ash" on the family's car, whereas the other noted only normal road grime. The episode made world headlines when the family was interviewed by police and claimed that their car had literally been picked up by a UFO and was covered in black ash. However, when a policeman inspected their car, he reported only normal road dirt. UFO researcher Keith Basterfield conducted a thorough investigation of the incident and obtained a copy of the police record interview, police photos of the car, and even tracked down the two truckers. One truck driver had been driving behind the family and reported that she had not seen anything unusual, despite clear skies and a flat horizon. The Australian Mineral Development Laboratory examined the car and its flat tire, finding nothing out of the ordinary. After the lab obtained a sample of the "ash" from the police department, analysis of the sample revealed that it was composed entirely of clay and salt particles—just what would be expected on a vehicle traveling across the sandy Nullarbor Plains near the Great Southern Ocean.

In a separate incident in western Australia at 7:45 P.M. on March 27, 1982, Francis Collins, a thirty-four-year-old shop owner, and Maggie Yeend, a forty-two-year-old potter and weaver, left Merredin in the evening for a lengthy journey to their home town of Esperance, four hundred miles southeast of Perth. The two friends were tired even before setting out and decided to take turns driving for one hour, then sleeping the next. By 3 A.M. they were fifty miles west of their destination when Maggie noticed a light in the sky near the horizon, watched it for several moments, then woke Francis, saying, "There's a UFO in front of us." Both women described a large ball of white light ahead to their left, which seemed to be on a collision course with them. Frances's first thoughts were "that it was coming for us, would explode the van and I could not get home to my children and no one would know what happened." At one point, Maggie shouted, "Frances, look behind us. Is it another one?" This light turned out to be a truck. They decided that their van was having engine trouble, as it would not go faster than forty-five miles per hour. Convinced that they had had a close encounter with a UFO, which had affected the van's performance, they reported the incident to police upon arriving in Esperance. An investigation by Keith Basterfield revealed that they almost certainly mistook Venus for a spacecraft and convinced themselves that it was affecting their van. At 2:27 on the morning in question, Venus rose as azimuth 105 degrees; at 3 A.M. it was at 7 degrees elevation and azimuth 101 degrees; and at 3:45 was at 17 degrees elevation and azimuth 94 degrees. Its astronomical magnitude was 4.1, the brightest object in the sky. Basterfield examined a detailed map of the road they were on at 3 A.M., noting that it ran azimuth 135 degrees for 15 miles, then 070 degrees for the next 20 miles, and 20 miles at roughly 090 degrees before turning 160 degrees for the final 7 miles. Thus, the positions they reported their UFO had been in matched the positions of Venus. Their descriptions fit that of Venus, and they did not report seeing both Venus and the UFO in the morning sky.

In another incident, a phantom overnight siege was reported by people in a sparsely inhabited area near Lowell, Michigan, in 1978. According to sociologist Ron Westrum,[35] who interviewed the people a month after the episode, Masters, a twenty-four-year-old suspected drug dealer, and Cordell, twenty-nine (not their real names), became increasingly suspicious of mundane events near the house, such as finding half of a grape bubble-gum wrapper on the roof and the other half near a wood pile. They also thought there were people peering in the windows at night.

By the afternoon of November 7, both men suspected the house was being watched and so were "on the lookout." They saw several fleeting figures lurking outside during the day. Near dusk, the two thought they saw a "kid" in a camouflage suit. Cordell pursued the figure unsuccessfully, then warned "the people he felt were hiding but could not see that if the nonsense did not stop somebody was going to get shot." Shortly thereafter, both men thought they heard people near the back door. Cordell fired a warning shot. Masters telephoned a friend to bring over some more guns. A third companion, Hamby, twenty-three, soon joined them. Keeping a watchful vigil, at about 1:30 A.M., they fired ten shots at "figures" near the house. When Hamby insisted that he did not see or hear anyone, they thought they may have imagined it. However, they continued to hear and see intermittent noises and figures throughout the morning. Near 5 A.M., they panicked, after believing they were under attack, and began firing indiscriminately. Cordell was certain that he shot someone hanging from the roof in front of the bedroom window.

> Hamby fired a .44 magnum through a refrigerator—I saw the hole myself—at a person in the kitchen, whom he heard slam against the sink, fall on the floor, and make gurgling noises, as if critically wounded. . . . All three were extremely scared; Masters to the point where he was re-loading spent cartridges into the revolver. At 5:30 A.M., they called the sheriff's department. Because one of them was on parole, and had a real interest in not being associated with firearms or drugs, it demonstrates the degree of their desperation.[36]

After Hamby fired a shotgun blast that was intended to draw the attention of a police car, but struck its windshield instead, the three were charged with assault with intent to commit murder, which was later reduced to firearm misuse. A police search yielded no evidence of intruders or of bullets fired by anyone but the three.

Common Features

All fourteen episodes listed in Table 1 took place at night in dark, isolated environments, with the group "leader" often remarking that he or she was physically or mentally fatigued, which enhances suggestibility and reduces critical thinking ability. In popular folklore dark, isolated environments are populated with nefarious creatures or agents, which correspond to the phantom attack scenarios. All such cases involve relatives or close friends. The primary witness (the first to draw attention to the unusual agent, to initiate detailed discussion as to its origin, or to panic) almost always holds an influential social position (is the oldest in the group, household head, vehicle driver, or group leader) and is the one who interprets the stimulus as a potential threat. In each case, the group soon reaches a bogus consensus that the object or agent is pursuing them. The ambiguous stimulus is then rapidly defined within popular cultural labels (Bigfoot, extraterrestrial spacecraft, drug dealers or drug police).

From a psychiatric standpoint, there is no evidence of "generalized anxiety disorder," or "specific" or "social phobia." However, in five instances, the dominant social figure exhibited characteristic features of acute stress disorder, as defined in the *Diagnostic and Statistical Manual of Mental Disorders*.[37] In four such cases, a panic ensued when the driver of a car, after believing the vehicle was being pursued by an alien spaceship, suddenly exhibited dissociative symptoms, became unresponsive and accelerated the motor vehicle, heightening fear and panic among the other passengers.[38] A fifth case, involved a boy who seemed to be possessed shortly after he and a group of onlookers claimed to see a UFO and strange creatures in a wooded area of Uniontown, Pennsylvania.[39]

Many people begin to have breathing problems, nausea, dizziness, blurred vision, rashes, and headache as a result of the incident, all of which are common psychogenic features of anxiety-generated conversion reactions. Similar psychogenic symptoms are especially common in cases involving a purported pursuit by extraterrestrials.[40]

Once the episode ends, people often cannot account for "lost" time and have difficulty recalling the event. However, time estimates are very poor when one is under extreme stress, and are subject to wide variability,[41] while, as discussed in chapter 1, the accuracy of eyewitness recall and memory reconstruction are also notoriously unreliable. This effect is especially pronounced when one is under great stress, such as a perceived threat to self and family or friends. Further, various astronomical,[42] meteorological,[43] and geophysical phenomena[44] are commonly misidentified as UFOs. Each episode in Table 1 is characterized by a conspicuous absence of confirming physical evidence. For example, the media made much of the mysterious black dust in the Mundrabilla case, but on examination, it was found to be entirely mundane. All that remains is eyewitness testimony from a small, socially cohesive unit, with no independent observers from outside of the particular social dynamic.

Non-Western Social Delusions

Human gullibility is limited only by plausibility. This is especially apparent in non-Western countries where superstitions are often rampant. For example, in some cultures it is believed that eating certain foods or having contact with "ghosts" can cause one's sex organs to rapidly shrivel. It is a remarkable example of the power of self-delusion that men in parts of Asia continue to experience "koro" epidemics, convinced that they are the victims of a contagious disease that causes their penises to shrink.[45] Episodes are triggered by rumors and last from a few days to several months and often affect thousands. Victims suffer intense anxiety, sweating, palpitations, insomnia, and often take the extreme measure of placing clamps or strings onto the penis or having family members hold it in relays until treatment is obtained, usually from native healers. Occasionally women are affected, believing that their breasts and vagina are being pulled into their bodies. During an episode on the tiny island nation of Singapore in 1967, thousands of citizens, both male and female, were affected, forcing the government to declare an emergency.[46] Pandemonium reigned during another outbreak in northeast India in 1982. So widespread was the panic that medical authorities took the drastic measure of touring the region with loudspeakers to reassure anxious residents and measuring penises at intervals to demonstrate that no shrinkage was taking place.[47]

The Lure of UFOs

UFOs have a special place in the history of social delusions. It is ironic that religious themes increasingly dominate the symbolic imagery of mysterious aerial objects. Imaginary sightings of Andree's balloon over Canada during the late nineteenth century coincided with intense interest in his attempt to reach the North Pole and a feeling that this age-old dream was finally possible. During the American airship waves of 1896–97 and 1909 there were widespread rumors that a scientist was about to conquer the heavens and an exaggerated optimism that an American would be the first person to perfect a heavier-than-air flying machine. Observations of Thomas Edison's "electric star" further reflected the boundless optimism that Americans placed in science and inventive ingenuity. All of these episodes served as a projection of the collective psyche, underscoring the promise of rapid technological advancement during a period of spiritual decline.

Since 1947 and the dawn of the flying saucer era, we have been confronted with "magical" machines that carry the functional equivalent of "technological angels."[48] UFOs possess a powerful, seductive lure that continuously changes to confirm our deepest fears or realize our greatest desires. Only the form changes to reflect the social and cultural context. To marginalize or pathologize these beliefs based on the fantastic nature of the reports per se is to obscure their symbolic significance and underestimate the innovative human capacity to adapt to change and find meaning in myriad ways. As technology continues to advance and the human imagination becomes increasingly transfixed on the vast possibilities that await us in space, what new symbols will emerge?

Notes

1. C. Mackay, *Memoirs of Extraordinary Popular Delusions and the Madness of Crowds* (London: Office of the National Illustrated Library, 1852).

2. N. Jacobs, "The Phantom Slasher of Taipei: Mass Hysteria in a Non-Western Society," *Social Problems* 12 (1965): 318–28.

3. W. H. Burnham, *The Normal Mind* (New York: D. Appleton-Century, 1924), pp. 337–38.

4. P. Sieveking, "Fear and Loathing in France," *Fortean Times* 67 (1993): 47.

5. J. R. Stewart, "Cattle Mutilations: An Episode of Collective Delusion," *Zetetic* (presently the *Skeptical Inquirer*) 1, no. 2 (1977): 55–66; T. Hines, *Pseudoscience and the Paranormal* (Amherst, N.Y.: Prometheus Books, 1988), pp. 278–80.

6. F. Smith, *Cattle Mutilations: The Unthinkable Truth* (Cedar Mesa, Colo.: Freeland Publishers, 1976); J. J. Dalton, *The Cattle Mutilators* (New York: Manor, 1980).

7. See, for example, L. Howe, "A Strange Harvest," TV documentary, KMGH, channel 7, Denver, Colorado, May 25, 1980.

8. See for example: "Cattle Mutilations Remain a Mystery," *Eagle River News Review* (Wisconsin), January 26, 1978; "Mystery Still Surrounds Animal Mutilations," *Springdale News* (Arizona), November 26, 1978; "Tracking the Cattle Mutilators: Satanic Groups Suspected," *Newsweek*, 95, p. 16 (January 21, 1980); "Did Horse Mutilator Come from Outer Space?" *Gastonia Gazette* (North Carolina), May 24, 1980; "Cattle

Ripper Returns," *The Sun* (Edmonton, Canada), September 17, 1981; "Dluce Rancher Loses Another Cow to Mysterious Mutilation," *Albuquerque Journal* (New Mexico), May 31, 1982.

9. Stewart, "Cattle Mutilations," pp. 64–65.

10. In terms of legitimation by institutions of social control and authority figures, during April of 1979, the federal government approved a $44,170 grant to investigate a series of mutilations in New Mexico. Despite finding only prosaic explanations—predators, scavengers, decomposition—U.S. Senator and former astronaut Harrison Schmitt continued to focus national attention on the issue by urging the Justice Department to initiate a separate probe (See G. Olson, "Schmitt Urges Federal Mutilation Probe," *Rio Grande Sun*, April 17, 1980). For an examination of the apparent genesis of the cattle mutilation myth, refer to R. E. Bartholomew, "Mutilation Mania—The Witch Craze Revisited: An Essay Review of *An Alien Harvest*," *The Anthropology of Consciousness* 3, nos. 1–2 (1992): 34–35.

11. D. Johnson, "The 'Phantom Anesthetist' of Mattoon: A Field Study of Mass Hysteria," *Journal of Abnormal Psychology* 40 (1945): 175–86.

12. W. R. McLeod, "Merphos Poisoning or Mass Panic?" *Australian and New Zealand Journal of Psychiatry* 9 (1975): 225–29.

13. G. Forth, "Construction Sacrifice and Head-Hunting Rumours in Central Flores (Eastern Indonesia): A Comparative Note," *Oceania* 61 (1991): 257–66; R. H. Barnes, "Construction Sacrifice, Kidnapping and Head-Hunting Rumours on Flores and Elsewhere in Indonesia," *Oceania* 64 (1993): 146–58.

14. R. A. Drake, "Construction Sacrifice and Kidnapping: Rumour Panics in Borneo," *Oceania* 59 (1989): 269–78.

15. H. Cantril, *The Invasion from Mars: A Study in the Psychology of Panic* (Princeton, N.J.: Princeton University Press, 1940).

16. "Mars Raiders Caused Quito Panic; Mob Burns Radio Plant, Kills 15," *New York Times*, February 14, 1949, pp. 1, 7.

17. Mackay, *Memoirs of Extraordinary Popular Delusions.*

18. R. E. Bartholomew, "A Brief History of Mass Hysteria in Australia," *Skeptic* 12 (1992): 23–26.

19. M. Persinger and J. Derr, "Geophysical Variables and Behavior: LIV. Zeitoun (Egypt) Apparitions of the Virgin Mary as Tectonic Strain-induced Luminosities," *Perceptual and Motor Skills* 68 (1989): 123–28; R. Yassa, "A Sociopsychiatric Study of an Egyptian Phenomenon," *American Journal of Psychotherapy* 34 (1980): 246–51.

20. C. Toibin, *Moving Statues in Ireland: Seeing Is Believing* (County Laois, Ireland: Pilgrim Press, 1985).

21. R. Kirk, *The Secret Commonwealth of Elves, Fauns and Fairies* (London: Longman, 1812); W. Evans-Wentz, *The Fairy-Faith in Celtic Countries* (Rennes, France, 1909).

22. R. Sheaffer, *The UFO Verdict* (Amherst, N.Y.: Prometheus Books, 1981).

23. M. Tumin and A. S. Feldman, "The Miracle at Sabana Grande," *Public Opinion Quarterly* 19 (1955): 124–39.

24. E. Goode, *Collective Behavior* (New York: Harcourt Brace, Jovanovich, 1992).

25. Tumin and Feldman, "Miracle at Sabana Grande."

26. There are numerous similar reports among religious faithful claiming to observe miraculous events or objects. In 1986 a devout Catholic grandmother, Rita Ratchen, who lived in a tiny Ohio town, was driving along a road when she saw what appeared to be a miraculous image on the side of a soybean oil tank. The yellowish-orange tank had rust spots that resembled an image of a man dressed in robes with outstretched arms. A child appeared next to the man. The figure was thought to be that of Jesus Christ. Once the media reported the story, hundreds of people began flocking to the tower, many of whom agreed that on it was a miraculous image. It is noteworthy that the tower "image" was highly ambiguous. The perceived figures were so faint that when a local newspaper published a picture of the tower, the editor had to get an artist to enhance the photos!

In 1988 a somewhat similar incident occurred at a church in Lubbock, Texas. The pastor had recently returned from a pilgrimage to Yugoslavia, where visions of the Virgin Mary had been reported for years. Several reportedly miraculous occurrences were witnessed by church members, including the smelling of an odor resembling roses, and visions. In August, about 12,000 people were attending a celebration of the Virgin Mary's alleged ascension into heaven when several extraordinary events happened. One man said that he could see a flock of doves flying over the church. Sociologist Erich Goode remarks that during a mass at the church conducted near dusk, shrieks could be heard from some crowd members as the sun began to shine through the clouds. In response, "some prayed, and some pointed toward the clouds. Others said they saw Jesus in the clouds, some saw Mary, and some saw heaven's gates. Church deacons took testimony from individuals who had seen visions and apparitions. . . ." For a discussion of these two cases, refer to Goode, *Collective Behavior*, p. 171, citing G. Jaynes, "In Ohio: A Vision West of Town," *Time*, September 29, 1986, pp. 8, 14; L. Belkin, "Reports of Miracles Draw Throngs," *New York Times*, August 17, 1988.

27. J. Abdullah, *A Report of the Interview with the Female Teacher and Students at the Hishamuddin Secondary Islamic School, Klang* (Confidential report, n.d.).

28. R.E. Bartholomew, *Miracle or Mass Delusion?: What Happened in Klang, Malaysia*? Study compiled for Pusat Islam (Islamic Center), the Prime Minister's Department, Kuala Lumpur, Malaysia. A similar incident was reported on June 12, 1990, in Algeria, when the Islamic Salvation Front Party won an upset election victory. While the party leader was speaking to a crowd of supporters who were standing and shouting, "*Allah Akhbar*" ("God is Great!"), a cloud reportedly formed the shape of the word *Allah* (God) in the direction of the Muslim holy city of Mecca, (refer to *The Daily Telegraph*, London, June 16, 1990). Since 1990, there have been numerous reports of Muslims reporting the appearance of Islamic symbols, most typically Arabic script, in a variety of countries and settings.

29. C. Jung, *Flying Saucers: A Modern Myth of Things Seen in the Sky* (New York: Harcourt, Brace and World, 1959).

30. T. Bullard, "UFO Abduction Reports," *Journal of American Folklore* 102 (1989).

31. J. Clark and L. Coleman, *Creatures of the Outer Edge* (New York: Warner, 1978); T. Healy and P. Cropper, *Out of the Shadows: Mystery Animals of Australia* (Chippendale, New South Wales, Australia: Ironbark, 1994).

32. For a list of the sources for cases cited in Table 1, see, in order of appearance: D. Rogo, *UFO Abductions* (New York: Signet, 1980); C. Hind, *UFOs: Close Encounters of an African Kind* (Salisbury, Zimbabwe: Gemini, 1982); B. Schwarz, *UFO Dynamics: Psychiatric and Psychic Aspects of the UFO Syndrome*, vols. 1 and 2 (Florida: Rainbow Books, 1983); Story, *The Encyclopedia of UFOs* (1980); F. Johnson, *The Janos People* (London: Spearman, 1980); R. Sheaffer, *UFO Verdict*; H. Evans, *UFOs: The Greatest Mystery* (London: Albany, 1979); Keith Basterfield, personal communication (1997); I. Davis and T. Bloecher, *Close Encounter at Kelly and Others of 1955* (Evanston, Ill.: Center for UFO Studies, 1978); P. Bartholomew, R. E. Bartholomew, B. Brann, and B. Hallenbeck, *Monsters of the Northwoods: An Investigation of Bigfoot Sightings in New York and Vermont* (Utica, N.Y.: Northcountry, 1992); R. Westrum, "Phantom Attackers," *Fortean Times* (Winter 1985): 54–58.

33. Davis and Bloecher, *Close Encounter at Kelly*; J. A. Hynek and J. Vallee, *The Edge of Reality: A Progress Report on Unidentified Flying Objects* (Chicago: Henry Regnery, 1975); R. J. M. Rickard, "More Phantom Sieges," *Fortean Times* (Winter 1985): 58–61; Story, *The Encyclopedia of UFOs*.

34. Sheaffer in Story, *The Encyclopedia of UFOs*, p. 176.

35. Westrum, "Phantom Attackers."

36. Ibid., p. 55.

37. American Psychiatric Association, *Diagnostic and Statistical Manual of Mental Disorders*, 4th ed. (Washington, D.C.: American Psychiatric Association, 1994).

38. R. Story, *The Encyclopedia of UFOs*; Johnson, *Janos People*; Hind, *UFOs: Close Encounters*; Schwarz, *UFO Dynamics*.

39. Schwarz, *UFO Dynamics*.

40. R. E. Bartholomew, K. Basterfield, and G. S. Howard, "UFO Abductees and Contactees: Psychopathology or Fantasy-Proneness?" *Professional Psychology: Research and Practice* 22 (1991): 215–22.

41. R. Buckhout, "Eyewitness Testimony," *Scientific American* 231 (1974): 23–31. See p. 25.

42. W. R. Corliss, *Handbook of Unusual Natural Phenomena* (Glen Arm, Md.: The Sourcebook Project, 1977).

43. E. Condon, *Scientific Study of Unidentified Flying Objects* (New York: Bantam, 1969).

44. M. Persinger and J. S. Derr, "Geophysical Variables and Human Behavior: XIX. Strong Temporal Relationships between Inclusive Seismic Measures and UFO Reports within Washington State," *Perceptual and Motor Skills* 59 (1984): 551–56; M. Persinger and J. Derr, "Geophysical Variables and Behavior: XXIII. Relations between UFO Reports within the Uinta Basin and Local Seismicity," *Perceptual and Motor Skills* 60 (1985): 143–52.

45. Collective koro is unlike sporadic individual cases without social or cultural beliefs related to sexual organ shrinkage. There have only been about 40 documented cases of individual koro in the scientific literature, and in virtually all of these subjects their condition was associated with major psychiatric conditions, organic disease, or drug intake. Victims of group koro appear psychologically and physically normal, their symptoms are brief and they are most appropriately described as experiencing a social delusion related to sociocultural convictions. See R. E. Bartholomew, "The Social Psychology of 'Epidemic' Koro," *International Journal of Social Psychiatry* 40, no. 1 (1994): 46–60.

46. A. L. Gwee, "Koro—Its Origin and Nature as a Disease Entity," *Singapore Medical Journal* 9, no. 1 (1968): 3–6; C. I. Mun, "Epidemic Koro in Singapore," letter, *British Medical Journal* (March 9, 1968): 640–41.

47. A. Chakraborty, S. Das, and A. Mukherji, "Koro Epidemic in India," *Transcultural Psychiatric Research Review* 20 (1983): 150–51.

48. Jung, *Flying Saucers*.

Part II

Strange Experiences: Real or Fantasized?

Part I clearly demonstrates that any one of us could misinterpret things seen in the sky. This tendency is especially pronounced during times of stress or great anticipation. To experience such an event really has little to do with a person's mental health or rationality. A claim that someone saw something that looked like a UFO is not grounds for doubting that person's sanity or judgment. Recent Gallup polls show that millions of people around the world claim to have seen UFOs.

A claim that one has been contacted or abducted by aliens is much more serious. Such phenomena will be considered separately. Part I presented the data on which we based our analysis of UFO sightings and the conclusions drawn from the data. The picture that emerges from examining the cases of alien contact or abduction in part II is more tentative due to the nature of the data. There is a certain amount of overlap between the data used in parts I and II. Recall, for example, that a few people reported having conversed with space beings who emerged from UFOs. However, the overwhelming majority of reports in part I were of people who claimed to have seen strange things in the sky.

The fundamental assumption of part II is that we have *not* been contacted by aliens. Every scientific investigation must rest on basic assumptions in order to proceed, and this is, by far, our most important presupposition. Readers who are convinced of alien contact might be thinking, *Bartholomew and Howard are typical scientists—they have made their minds up ahead of time, and this study is just a rubber stamp of their personal prejudices.* Science is based on evidence, reason, and logic, not on emotions and wishful thinking. Does this mean we are certain aliens have not contacted Earth? No. But based on the evidence to date there is no clear evidence of alien contact that is acceptable to the general scientific community; hence, it seems a prudent assumption.

Some readers may now be saying to themselves, *How can you say that there's no good evidence? What about scientists like John Mack at Harvard, who has concluded that there is enough evidence to prove the existence of aliens?* While Mack has made such assertions, he is certainly in a small minority of scientists. The same is also true of evidence for ESP or Bigfoot. Rupert Sheldrake, a former researcher in biochemistry in Cambridge, England, believes in ESP. Grover Krantz at Washington State University is convinced that Bigfoot exists. There are a small number of scientists who claim to have proof or believe the evidence favors the existence of aliens, but we are referring to the majority of the scientific community. This is not to suggest that Mack is crazy or incompetent, but just that scientists are human too. Perhaps Mack is right and aliens are here. In his opinion there is enough evidence, but this conclusion has yet to be established for the majority in the scientific community.

11

In Praise of Foresight and Fantasy

> I've seen many tragedies in my life—fortunately, most of them never occurred.
>
> —Mark Twain

The humor in Mark Twain's quip comes from our almost unassailable belief in the phrase "seeing is believing." If one actually *sees* something occur, then one has excellent grounds for believing. While we know there can be enormous discrepancies in interpreting the meaning of a certain event (as the research on eyewitness testimony amply demonstrates[1]), we all accept that *something* did occur if people actually say they saw it happen. For example, while we might get wildly different stories from four eyewitnesses of how a car accident occurred, our sanity would be questioned if we wondered whether *anything* had actually occurred. "Are you out of your mind?" the four eyewitnesses would cry in unison. "Why do you think that ambulance took that person to the hospital? How did those two cars get turned into wrecks? Why is there stalled traffic in every direction as far as the eye can see?"

While corroborating evidence (e.g., bodies, wreckage) is helpful, it is merely circumstantial to the most important evidence—

four competent observers claim to actually have seen the accident occur! In the absence of eyewitnesses, we might suspect that the circumstantial evidence had been produced by a traffic accident, but other explanations are still possible (e.g., a tornado). However, all such speculation melts away the moment a disinterested (i.e., neutral) spectator steps forward and declares that he or she actually *saw* the event occur. The humor in Twain's quip results from his first declaring himself a credible eyewitness ("I've seen many . . .") and then stating an impossibility (". . . that never occurred").

"Excuse me, Mr. Twain!" you might sputter in righteous indignation. "If you *saw* something, then it must have occurred!" The twinkle in the mischievous midwesterner's eye signals that you've been had. There is ambiguity in how one can "see." The mind can see in several ways. In one form of sight, the eyes are used—vision. In another approach to seeing, the intellect is used—foresight. Finally, in a third mode of sight, the imagination is used to see—fantasy. It is clear that Twain was able to "see" more important truths with his intellect and imagination than he saw with his eyes. Perhaps he suspected that his quip might catch us unaware, because he knew that most people are overreliant upon their eyes and underuse their intellect and imagination.

In Praise of Foresight

Foresight works so well, and in so many ways, that some people mistakenly think that foresight and thinking are synonymous. They are not. For example, one can use the intellect to analyze past events, but this does not involve foresight. One uses foresight when one tells a possibly true tale of the future and then mentally examines the outcomes of this possible future in order to determine whether or not it would represent an acceptable outcome.

For example, it is now 2:30, and my sons expect me to pick them up from school at 3:00. Should I first go get another cup of coffee and then pick them up? The ideal time to leave my office is 2:40. (Anything later than a 2:55 departure guarantees that I'll arrive late, and thus I will incur a cash penalty for each son for after-school care.) Getting coffee can take from five to fifteen minutes—depending on who I meet between my office and the coffee lounge. Once back in my office, it takes me from ten to thirty minutes to drink the coffee. Assuming all goes perfectly (five minutes to get the coffee and ten minutes to drink it), I will leave at 2:45, five minutes later than ideal but still early enough. Assuming typical times (ten minutes to get the coffee and twenty minutes to drink it), I leave at 3:00 and am certain to pay afterschool fees—one heck of an expensive cup of coffee!

Or perhaps Twain had the following sort of tragedy in mind as one he foresaw and thus took steps to ensure that it never occurred: "If I attend the party alone, I might be propositioned by someone, but I'm sure I'll be able to decline if my wife is present. If she is not present, then I can still decline unless I am drunk. Here's how I'll avoid a tragedy: I'll invite my wife to attend the party. If she accepts, I can drink if I wish. If she declines, I either go but don't drink or, if I can't be certain that I won't drink, I simply will not go."

I've foreseen many tragedies in my life (e.g., being late when picking up my boys; falling prey to temptations), but fortunately most of them never occurred. In the first case, my foresight actually might have been the cause of the bad luck (e.g., meeting someone interesting on my way to the coffee lounge) not occurring. In the second case my wife's presence at a party might preclude a proposition that would have occurred had she stayed home. Or the proposition might occur in spite of her presence at the party, but under those circumstances I would be able (whether drunk or sober) to respond, "No. That really wouldn't be a good idea."

These are but two of literally millions of examples of how foresight can be an invaluable tool in enriching our lives. In the next chapter we will learn that the meaning of an alien "abduction" or a prolonged "contact" is ambiguous and the interpretation of the event's meaning is up to us. So how ought we to interpret the event? It turns out that foresight provides the crucial tool in helping us to determine the meaning of the "contact" or "abduction" event for ourselves, for potential helpers (e.g., therapists, family members), and for society at large.

In Praise of Fantasy

Someone once said that novelists are the luckiest people, for they live many lives—whereas the rest of us live but one. Since the events in a novel never actually occurred, one is totally dependent on the novelist's imagination to determine not only what can and cannot occur but also what will occur. The novelist's imagination becomes lord over all it surveys in its fantasies. And what of the demands of reality? Are there absolutely no constraints on a novelist's fantasy? Apparently little or none. As Henry James wrote, "The only obligation to which in advance we may hold a novel, without incurring the accusation of being arbitrary, is that it be interesting."[2]

A young infant's attention is drawn by almost anything. As infants grow into young boys and girls their interests become more refined (e.g., they enjoy stories, cartoons, as well as objects, such as toys, which they can use to create their own fantasies). During this stage of development, the fact that many of these fantasies "could not possibly occur" does not bother these youngsters in the slightest.

Children roam freely in the world of unfettered fantasy because it is the most interesting and exciting world they know. However, with time and training young men and women acquire a taste for more realistic stories—some of which actually occurred (i.e., nonfiction stories). The point of interest here is that children originally travel between the world of fantasy and reality quite freely—often not "knowing" that they are crossing a significant divide.

Because life is more interesting on the fantasy side, a child would be crazy not to spend more time there than on the boring, constraining, "real" side of his or her experience. Since a child can create a perfect, imaginary playmate so easily, why wouldn't he or she enjoy spending more time with this ideal companion than with hurtful, frustrating, or noncompliant peers? Young boys and girls relish their hours engaged in rich, satisfying fantasies, and over time they begrudgingly learn to spend greater amounts of time living in the "real world."

One reason that young children can be oblivious to reality for so many years is because we adults protect them from the world's worries and dangers. Many lower organisms like fish, frogs, or insects never see their parents. Not only do adults of many species fail to protect their young, but they are often their offspring's most lethal predators. Why has nature molded human parents into such dedicated protectors of their young? What developmental tasks could possibly have such evolutionary importance that they justify leaving human children virtually defenseless—save for their parents' intercession—for over a decade?

An enormously long period of dependency is required to develop higher mental processes such as language use, the mores of social life, and the creative use of capacities like foresight and fantasy. Humans spend decades puzzling over the question of what is real and what is fantasy. Each of us has come to a very sophisticated answer to the question of what is real and what is fantasy. We all think we know where the line of demarcation between the real and the fanciful is. Fortunately or unfortunately, we don't always agree with one another on the positioning of that line.

For example, is God real? Some people believe that all God-talk lies in the domain of fantasy. For others, God represents the most concrete and important of all realities. Similarly, where do you stand on the reality of black holes, quasars, pulsars, fuzzy attractors, free will, superconductivity, and cold fusion? This book's second author is old enough to remember a time when *all* of these concepts were nothing more than scientists' fantasies. How many of them do you think have now passed into the land of the real? Any? Yes! All? No! Is it simply a matter of time until all of these scientists' fictions make it into the domain of reality? Probably not—in our opinion. We wager that at least one of these concepts—cold fusion—will never make it into the land of the real. If we are correct, it will enter the "nice try but no go" category of failed scientific concepts, where it will join the ether, phrenology, astrology, ESP, Lamarkean evolution, and many other scientific fictions that proved to be less than satisfactory, and therefore have not been demonstrated to be "real."[3]

The point of this discussion—how science transports certain fictions into reality while denying other fictions admittance—is to highlight the fact that enormous changes have occurred in the second half of the twentieth century regarding the relationship among fantasy (creative theorizing), reality (concepts and the theories currently in closest agreement with the epistemic values),[4] and science (the social activity whereby scientific fictions are tested and improved).[5] When something is said to represent a "scientifically proven fact," what that means is now up for grabs (in both the philosophic and the scientific communities) as it never has been before.[6]

Happily, all of the newer understandings of why science progresses as well as it does heighten the importance of the role of scientific creative fantasies. Perhaps we now better appreciate the crucial role that disciplined fantasy plays in the continuing evolution and refinement of modern thought. Nature was prescient in providing humans with long periods where they could refine the creativity and discipline of fantasy. Without this skill, the achievements of modern science would not be possible. As distinguished philosopher of science Carl P. Hempel is reported to have once marveled, "What is the world that it can be known by mind? What is the mind that it can know the world?"

Unfortunately, some people have not kept current with the revolution in the philosophy of science over the last twenty years. Those people are probably still operating with a vision of how science works that has now been discredited. Perhaps you've heard of the realist—antirealist debates in philosophy of science, or the objectivist—constructivist debates in many scientific disciplines.[7] Regardless of how these controversies eventually settle out, they are destroying our old positivistic, objectivistic understandings of how science works. These older views of science were based largely on what philosopher Richard Rorty refers to as "mirror of nature" images.[8] The newer notions of science rely on different construals of "truth" and "reality" in their appreciations of how science progresses.

Reality—What a Concept!

For most people, the reality of God and religion is so strong that they are willing to live their lives according to the dictates of their religious beliefs. But to this book's authors, all of our life experiences appear to have been completely natural (as opposed to supernatural—demanding a religious explanation). Similarly, no experience in my life suggests that aliens have made contact with humans.

Thus my own experiences do not now compel me to be a theist or a believer in aliens. Consequently, I might choose either to believe or not to believe in these possibilities (God or aliens). If it is important to God or to aliens that I believe in them, then they must make themselves better known to me than they have done to date.

I am, however, open to new experiences. Consider the following thought experiment (a research strategy of ever-increasing importance in contemporary science) on what experiences might actually change my mind about the existence of God or aliens. The Saint Paul story furnishes a tale of a dramatic conversion of an anti-Christian (Saul) into the most committed of Christians (Paul). We put a new spin on the Saint Paul story to highlight the kind of evidence (i.e., experiences) that would compel us to alter our present beliefs. This is a humorous thought experiment, in the hope that (with apologies to William Congreve) "humor has charms to soothe the overcommitted breast."

Imagine that in the near future the second author finds himself riding on a horse from Jerusalem to Damascus in order to torture and murder some poor alien abductees if they are unwilling to admit that UFOs do not exist. Suddenly the skies darken, and I say, "Whoa! This don't look so good." A bolt of lightning then knocks me off the horse, and I think, *No big deal! People get struck by lightning all the time—I'm just glad to be alive to interpret the experience.* But when a booming voice from out of the heavens says, "George, George, why doest thou persecute righteous UFO abductees so?" *that's* when it becomes a nonnatural experience for me. The voice orders, "You are no longer to be called George; henceforth you are to be known as 'Stupid.' "

"I've always thought stupidity was an underappreciated trait in humans," I reply. "I'm thrilled to be known as 'Stupid.' By the way, Lord, how do your friends address you?" If the voice says, "Yahweh," I'm suddenly Jewish. If God says, "Allah," then I believe in Islam. If "Buddah," I'm a Buddhist. If "Jesus," a Christian. If the voice says, "Zarathustra," I'm momentarily confused. But so great is my commitment to empiricism[9]—even in the religion domain—that eventually I'd be thrilled to be known as "Stupid the Zoroastrian"!

Or imagine that the lightning bolt had been a laser, and the booming voice replied, "I am Jaopg from the planet Rooze." Suddenly this experience would have nothing to do with God and religion. I would immediately believe completely in the "reality" of alien contact. However, since no experience in my life currently suggests the existence of visitors from another world, I choose not to believe in aliens *for pragmatic reasons*. The next chapter will spell out the pragmatic consequences of belief or nonbelief in aliens in most contemporary societies.

All of this talk of belief (or nonbelief) in God or aliens for pragmatic reasons probably strikes most readers as a bit odd. This is because most people believe in the existence of a free standing, objective reality. Black holes either do or do not exist; aliens either have or have not contacted humans; there either is or is not a God; humans either do or do not possess ESP; and so forth. It is the job of science to go out and get hard, objective evidence of the existence (or nonexistence) of any of these entities or human powers. Then rational humans will believe in aliens, if aliens do exist; we will believe in ESP, if humans possess that power; and so forth. This is the position contained in the "spectator view of science" or "science as the mirror of nature." On this view, one holds the world up to science and the undistorted "Truth" or "Reality" about the world will then pop out at you. Again, this represents an older, less sophisticated understanding of what science is able to achieve.

Instead, think of scientific evidence as a possible truth that is created when the world (or specific entities such as human beings or aliens) are approached from a particular system of beliefs. Might that evidence tell us something of importance about our objects of study? Absolutely! Does science tell us the Truth (the complete truth and the final truth) about our objects of investigation? Absolutely not! Finally, the newer construals of how science works its wonders highlight the importance of disciplined fantasy (creative theories) and accurate foresight (as seen in the predicative accuracy or empirical adequacy of these theories) in the progress of scientific rationality. Because of our newer, more sophisticated understanding of how science works its wonders, fantasy and foresight are two human powers that deserve even greater praise than we had imagined.

Notes

1. E. F. Loftus, "Memory and Its Distortions," in A. G. Kraut, ed., *G. Stanley Hall Lectures* (Washington, D.C.: American Psychological Association, 1982), pp. 119–54; E. F. Loftus and K. Ketcham, *Witness for the Defense* (New York: St. Martin's Press, 1991).

2. Henry James, *The Art of Fiction and Other Essays* (New York: Oxford University Press, 1948).

3. By the way, how many of you chose "free will" as a concept that science wouldn't demonstrate as real? Sorry folks! Free will passed into scientific reality a few years ago. G. S. Howard and C. G. Conway, "Can There Be an Empirical Science of Volitional Action?" *American Psychologist* 41 (1986): 1241–51. D. L. Lazarick, S. S. Fishbein, M. J. Loiello, and G. S. Howard, "Practical Investigations of Volition," *Journal of Counseling Psychology* 35 (1988): 1–26. G. S. Howard, "Some Varieties of Free Will Worth Practicing," *Journal of Theoretical and Philosophical Psychology* 14 (1994): 50–61. Self-determination (or freedom of the will) is now every bit as much a scientific reality as are, for example, black holes and superconductivity.

4. T. Kuhn, *The Essential Tension* (Chicago: University of Chicago Press, 1977).

5. Ibid.; E. McMullin, "Values in Science," in P. D. Asquith and T. Nickles, eds., *Proceedings of the 1982 Philosophy of Science Association*, vol. 2 (East Lansing, Mich.: Philosophy of Science Association, 1983), pp. 3–23; G. S. Howard, "The Role of Values in the Science of Psychology," *American Psychologist* 40 (1988): 255–65.

6. R. Rorty, *Objectivity, Relativism and Truth: Philosophical Papers*, vol. 1 (New York: Cambridge University Press, 1991).

7. H. Putnam, *The Many Faces of Realism* (LaSalle, Ill.: Open Court, 1987); G. S. Howard, "Culture Tales: A Narrative Approach to Thinking, Cross-Cultural Psychology, and Psychotherapy," *American Psychologist* 46 (1991): 187–97.

8. R. Rorty, *Philosophy and the Mirror of Nature* (Princeton, N.J.: Princeton University Press, 1980).

9. Technically, I am now describing the philosophic principle of radical empiricism that was first promulgated by William James, *Essays in Radical Empiricism* (New York: Longmans, Green & Co., 1912).

12

UFO "Abductees" and "Contactees": Psychopathology or Fantasy-Prone?

Whatever these anomalies may or may not be, one thing is certain: they keep on happening. They have survived centuries of misattribution and misunderstanding, of doubt and debunking. Prophets and psychics still perform . . . prodigies, ordinary men and women continue to report extraordinary sights and sounds. If this is all an illusion, then it is high time that the mechanism of such persistent illusion was revealed.

—Hilary Evans[1]

Psychopathological interpretations of individuals claiming contacts with extraterrestrials typify the few psychiatric evaluations of such behavior. This chapter will present biographical analysis performed on 154 subjects reporting temporary abductions or persistent contacts with UFO occupants. The 154 case histories are remarkably devoid of a history of mental illness. However, in 132 cases, identifications were made with one and often several major characteristics of what psychologists S. C. Wilson and T. X. Barber[2] first identified as the fantasy-prone personality (FPP), a set of characteristics not typically found in the general population. While functioning as normal, healthy adults, FPPs experience rich fantasy lives, scoring dramatically higher (relative to control groups) on such characteristics as hypnotic susceptibility, psychic ability, healing, out-of-body experiences, automatic writing, religious visions, and apparitional experiences. In our study, UFO "abductees" and "contactees" evidence a similar pattern of characteristics to FPPs.

Are You Crazy?

Imagine you have a new neighbor whom you meet for the first time. The neighbor calmly describes the following event: "I know you'll find this hard to believe, but last week I was abducted by aliens who held me for about seven hours in their spaceship." After careful questioning, you find that your new neighbor believes that he is also telepathic, has had religious visions in the past, and spent a large part of his childhood conversing with an imaginary playmate. You describe the neighbor to a friend, who asks, "Is there extreme psychopathology here? Do you believe your neighbor is severely disturbed?" What would be your answer?

Ever since mass sightings of flying saucers were first reported, those claiming contact with saucer occupants (or even some claiming to watch such craft at a distance) were often labeled socially deviant or mentally disturbed. Such diagnoses were often based on the fantastic nature of the claims and not on firsthand psychological evaluation. Despite the unreliability of eyewitness testimony[3] and the ambiguous nature of most flying saucer reports (usually misinterpretations of ordinary celestial objects[4]), the media has typically attributed sightings to "psychopathological disturbances in the witness."[5]

While there are few psychological studies of people claiming regular communication with extraterrestrials—contactees—or temporary abductions aboard a spaceship—abductees—virtually all such people have been characterized as mentally disturbed or irrational. Psychologists Lester Grinspoon and Alan D. Persky,[6] for instance, explain many contact claims as psychopathological, the result of *folie á deux* psychosis and psychopathic personalities, yet these authors failed to study witnesses firsthand or cite a single case. Of six patients claiming contacts with extraterrestrials, psychiatrists L. Mavrakis and J. Bocquet[7] diagnosed five as suffering from a paranoid delusional state. In applying a psychoanalytic perspective to members of the "flying saucer subculture," John A. Keel[8] classifies many contactees as "neurotic and paranoid personalities" (p. 871). Both Carl Jung and Joost Meerloo[9] relate the phenomena to the need for the existence of a higher power and the likelihood that many experiences result from repressed, infantile sexually orientated conflicts. Similar interpretations have been made by sociologists who characterize typical members of flying-saucer clubs, particularly those reporting contacts, as mentally ill:

> [In] flying saucer clubs I have had contact with . . . by any conventional definition the mental health . . . is quite low. Hallucinations are quite common. . . . If one were to attend a meeting and watch the action without knowing in advance whether the audience was in a mental hospital or not, it would be very difficult to tell, because many symptoms of serious illness are displayed.[10]

This psychopathological interpretation is not unlike the labels ascribed to people accused of witchcraft during the sixteenth and seventeenth centuries. "Witches" were considered "maniacs or melancholics," "detracted in mind,"[11] or suffering from disorders of "neuropathology," as was believed by Charcot, Esquirol, Janet, and Freud.[12] This classification has held until recent times, with the work of Zilboorg,[13] that most medieval witches were considered mentally ill. The predominant interpretation of witchcraft during the past twenty years, however, has shifted. The contemporary view is predicated on detailed historical and archival research and has shifted toward a culturally relativistic position considering the unique historical sociocultural milieu of individuals and their behavior.[14]

Boston-area psychiatrist Dr. Benjamin Simon's use of hypnotherapy with a couple claiming a UFO abduction,[15] Florida psychiatrist Dr. Bertold Schwarz's in-depth evaluations of abduction and contact victims who were found to be mentally healthy,[16] and Mavrakis and Bocquet's[17] examination of contact and abduction subjects are the only firsthand psychological studies of UFO abductees and contactees known to exist. While such firsthand evaluations are beyond the scope of the present study, we will compare the characteristics of a sample of UFO abductees and contactees from archival data with the "fantasy-prone personality"[18] (FPP). On the basis of this comparison, suggestions for the psychological understanding of such cases will be discussed.

The Fantasy-Prone Personality

There is an entire class of normal, healthy individuals who are prone to experiencing exceptionally vivid and involved fantasies. Such people often have difficulty distinguishing between fantasy and reality and tend to keep their fantasy worlds closely guarded secrets. Based on preliminary research by J. R. Hilgard[19] and subsequent work by Wilson and Barber,[20] approximately 4 percent of the population falls into the FPP category, ranging in degree from mild to intense. Wilson and Barber uncovered this category while administering a battery of tests and interviews to twenty-seven "excellent" and twenty-five "nonexcellent" female hypnotic subjects.[21] Their findings have since received support in studies using more heterogeneous samples.[22] The results of these investigations have implications for understanding an important component in many UFO abduction and contact reports, especially those who persistently report such phenomena and who have typically been considered to be psychopathological.

In providing a brief overview of their findings, Wilson and Barber noted that most fantasy-prone subjects (92 percent) estimated spending half or more of their working day fantasizing, compared to 0 percent in their control group.[23] In discussing the vividness of their subjects' experiences, Wilson and Barber found that the fantasy-prone actually "see," "hear," "smell," and "feel" what is being described in conversations or on television.[24] Sixty-five percent of the FPPs reported that their fantasies were "as real as real" (hallucinatory) in all sense modalities and were experienced in an "automatic" or "involuntary" manner (compared to 0 percent in the control group).

> They see sights equally well with their eyes opened or closed. Also, imagined aromas are sensed, imagined sounds are heard, and imagined tactile sensations are felt as convincingly as those produced by actual stimuli. . . . Almost all of the fantasy-prone subjects have vivid sexual fantasies that they experience "as real as real" with all the sights, sounds, smells, emotions, feelings, and physical sensations . . . [and they] are so realistic that 75 percent of the fantasizers report that they have had orgasms produced solely by sexual fantasies.[25]

Fifty-eight percent of the FPPs (8 percent in the control group) reported spending a "large part" of their childhood playing or interacting with fantasized people or animals (so-called imaginary friends), claiming to have "clearly seen, heard and felt them in the same way that they perceived living people and animals."[26]

As children, all but one of the FPPs lived in a make-believe world much or most of the time. Of those playing with dolls or toy animals, 80 percent believed them to be living, with unique feelings and personalities. While imaginary playmates are common in children, and in recent years have been viewed as a sign of mental health and creativity,[27] there are important differences between the fantasy-prone and control groups on this dimension.

> Many of the twenty-five subjects in the comparison group also pretended their dolls or stuffed animals were alive; however, with three exceptions, they did so only when they were playing with them. Although they made-believe that the dolls and toy animals had personalities and said and did specific things, the make-believe play was always confined to a specific period and the toys did not seem to have an independent life.[28]

While most (perhaps all) children play make-believe games, it is uncommon for them to continue with imaginary companions into adulthood. But the extensiveness and vividness of imaginary companions apparently does not decrease substantially for the fantasy-prone group as adults. Based on their findings, Wilson and Barber hypothesized that many figures from history who claimed psychic or paranormal experiences may have been fantasy-prone.[29]

The Present Study

Extensive personal UFO literature collections provided us with sufficient material to test a parallel hypothesis to that of Wilson and Barber by comparing a sample of abductees and contactees to Wilson and Barber's FPP and control groups. Our sample consisted of 154 UFO abductees and contactees on whom there was biographical information. Biographies ranged from less than a paragraph in a few cases to an entire book or series of books. Data cover reports of alien contacts from the sixteenth century through 1988, with over 90 percent of the reported cases having taken place between 1950 and the present. This study assesses the percentage of subjects who exhibit major FPP symptoms. The analysis represents an extremely conservative estimate of the incidence of FPP symptoms in abductees and contactees, since the symptoms of the FPP were not known until recently, and many abductees and contactees were simply not asked whether they experienced all of the symptoms of the FPP syndrome. All such instances would make the present data set look more like the Wilson and Barber control group and less like their FPP group. Table 2 presents 132 cases out of the 154 (86 percent) where one or more of the major symptoms of the FPP profile were reported.

Table 2*
Summary of 132 Alleged UFO Abductees and Contactees with Major Fantasy-Prone Personality Characteristics Based on a Sample of 154 Subjects

Author	Percipient	Time Frame	Fantasy-Prone Characteristics
(Swedenborg 1758, 1860; Van Dusen 1975; Suares and Siegel 1977)	Emmanuel Swedenborg	Sixteenth century	Astral travel, psychic, repeater
(Smith 1976; Steiger and Whritenour 1969)	William Denton	1866	Telepathy, astral travel, repeater

*See Appendix B for bibliography for Table 2.

(Flournoy 1963; Rawcliffe 1959; Moore 1977)	Catherine Muller	1894	Psychic medium, astral travel, repeater
(Musgrave 1980)	"boy"	1912	Telepathy
(Dickhoff 1964; Drake 1974)	Mrs. H. C. Hutchinson	1924	Psychic, telepathy, repeater
(Musgrave 1984)	Retired Minister	1932	Religious visions, apparitions, astral travel, repeater
(Menger 1959)	Howard Menger	1932	Telepathy, poltergeist, repeater
(Bullard 1987)	Albert Lancashire	1942	Apparitions
(Brownell 1980)	Mark Probert	1947	Trance medium, telepathy, repeater, prophecy
(Ferguson 1954)	William Ferguson	1947	Astral travel, repeater
(Clark and Coleman 1975)	Paul Solem	1948	Telepathy, religious vision, repeater
(Noonan 1967)	Allen Noonan	1940s	Telepathy, astral travel, religious visions, trance medium
(Short 1959-1977; Beckley 1980)	Robert Short	early 1950s	Telepathy, medium, repeater
(Hopkins 1981)	"Virginia Horton"	1950	Excellent hypnotic subject, telepathy, repeater
(Fry 1954; Story 1980)	Daniel Fry	1950	Telepathy, repeater
(Rogo 1980)	Harrison Bailey	1951	Apparitions
(Angelucci 1955; Reeve and Reeve 1957; Jung 1959; Jacobs 1976)	Orfeo Angelucci	1952	Telepathy, astral travel, psychic, religious visions, repeater
(Van Tassel 1952, 1958, 1976)	George Van Tassel	1952	Psychic medium, prophecies, telepathy, repeater
(Girvin 1958)	Calvin Girvin	1952	Astral projection, premonitions, telepathy, religious visions
(Bethurum 1954, 1958, 1970; Girard 1982)	Truman Bethurum	1952	Telepathy, psychic, repeater
(Michael 1955, 1977)	Cecil Michael	1952	Astral travel, psychic, telepathy, repeater
(Adamski 1953, 1955, 1961)	George Adamski	1952	Telepathy, repeater, automatic writing

(Kraspedon 1959)	Dino Kraspedon	1952	Psychic, repeater
(Williamson 1954)	George H. Williamson	1952	Telepathy, automatic writing, repeater
(Lee 1959, 1962)	Gloria Lee	1953	Psychic ability, automatic writing, telepathy, repeater
(Brownell 1980)	Yolanda	circa 1953	Psychic, astral travel, visions, automatic writing, repeater
(Miller 1959; Fuller 1980)	Will Miller	1954	Telepathy
(King 1962; Fuller 1980; Story 1980; Nebel 1961)	George King	1954	Psychic medium, telepathy, apparitions, repeater, healing, visions
(Norman and Miller 1974; Norman 1980)	Ruth Norman	1954	Trance, medium, telepathy, repeater
(Festinger, Riecken and Schacter 1964)	"Marian Keech"	1954	Automatic writing, prophecy, repeater
(Fuller 1980)	Von Cihlar	circa 1954	Telepathy, psychic
(Nelson 1956, 1960; Brownell 1980)	Buck Nelson	1954	Healing, repeater, religious visions
(Gansberg and Gansberg 1980)	Lydia Stalnaker	1955	Telepathy, excellent hypnotic subject, medium, healing ability, precognition, spirit possession
(Mundo 1956, 1964, 1970, 1983; Beckley 1980)	Laura Mundo	1950s	Telepathy, poltergeist, astral travel, repeater
(Martin 1959)	Daniel Martin	1955	Psychic ability, body floating
(Klarer 1980; Hind 1982)	Elizabeth Klarer	1956	Telepathy, repeater
(Anderson 1956; Brownell 1980)	Carl Anderson	1956	Telepathy, healing, voices, automatic writing, psychic, religious visions, repeater
(Brownell 1980; Sachs 1980; Fuller 1980)	Wayne Aho	1957	Telepathy, astral travel, religious visions, prophecy, repeater
(Press 1957a, 1957b; Keel 1970)	Joao de Freitas Guimaraes	1957	Telepathy, repeater
(Bowen 1977b)	Mrs. Cynthia Appleton	1957	Telepathy, repeater
(Bullard 1987)	Shirley McBride	1957	Telepathy

(Gansberg and Gansberg 1980)	"Jessica Rolfe"	1958	Telepathy, precognition, poltergeist, astral travel, repeater
(Fuller 1980)	Brady	circa 1958	Psychic medium, repeater
(Schmidt 1950; Sachs 1980)	Reinhold Schmidt	1958	Telepathy, levitation (of car), repeater
(Fuller 1980)	Stanford	1958	Telepathy, psychic, medium, repeater
(Brownell 1980)	Frank Buckshot	1959	Telepathy, religious visions, repeater
(Beckley 1980)	Helio Aguiar	1959	Automatic writing, prophecy
(Brownell 1980)	Aleuti Francesca	1950s	Prophecy, channeling, telepathy, repeater
(Gansberg and Gansberg, 1980)	Ellicia Gruen	1950s	Poltergeist, precognition, healing, automatic writing
(Bender 1962; Barker 1956, 1983; Fuller 1980)	Albert Bender	1950s	Psychic, prophecy, astral travel, repeater
(Rowe 1958)	Kelvin Rowe	1950s	Telepathy
(Beckley 1980)	Francis Steiger	roughly 1950s	Psychic, religious visions, prophecy, repeater
(Fuller 1966) (Schwarz 1983a)	Betty Hill	1961	Telepathy, excellent hypnotic subject poltergeist, psychic ability
(Bullard 1987)	Mark Brinkerhoff	1964	Psychic, telepathy, precognition, repeater
(Bowen 1977b; Press 1965)	Felipe Martinez	1965	Prophecy, repeater
(Keel 1971)	Anonymous male	1965	Telepathy, repeater
(Owens 1963, 1972; Sachs 1980)	Ted Owens	circa 1965	Psychic medium, telepathy, psychokinesis, precognition, repeater
(Edwards 1967; Binder 1968; Basterfield 1980)	Miss M. Travers	1966	Telepathy
(Fowler 1979, 1982; Rimmer 1984)	Mrs. Betty Andreasson	1967	Telepathy, excellent hypnotic subject, repeater, apparitions, poltergeist, automatic writing

(Steiger 1978)	Anonymous young girl	1967	Telepathy
(Vallee 1969; Tarleton 1967)	Anthony de Polo	1967	Telepathy, repeater
(Smith 1976)	Herbert Schirmer	1967	Telepathy, excellent hypnotic subject
(Bowen 1977a; Press 1969)	Benjamin Solari Parravicini	1968	Telepathy
(Holzer 1976)	Shane Kurz	1968	Clairvoyance
(Maria 1970)	Wilson da Silva	1968	Telepathy, clairvoyance, repeater
(Rogo 1980)	"Bill"	1969	Excellent hypnotic subject, telepathy
(Randles 1976)	Mrs. Hamilton	1969	Apparitions
(Rogo 1980)	Lorri Briggs	1970	Excellent hypnotic subject, religious visions, out-of-body experiences, apparitions, levitation, teleportation, repeater
(Press 1971a)	Anonymous housewife	1970	Psychic, telepathy, repeater
(Brownell 1980)	Brian Scott	1971	Psychic, voices, automatic writing, telepathy, repeater
(Schwarz 1983b)	Stella Lansing	as early as 1971	Psychic, telepathy, precognition, telekinesis, apparitions, religious visions, spirit medium, repeater
(Rogo 1980)	"John Hodges"	1971	Apparitions, psychokinesis, excellent hypnotic subject,
(Roe 1978)	"Luke"	1971	Telepathy, astral travel
(Buhler 1973; Creighton 1971; Press 1971b)	Paulo Caetano Silveira	1971	Telepathy
(Randles 1988)	Sandra and Peter Taylor	1972	Psychic
(Press 1972)	Luis Bracamonte	1972	Telepathy
(Basterfield 1981a, 1981b)	Mrs. Maureen Puddy	1972	Telepathy, apparitions, repeater
(Painter 1973)	Ventura Maceiras	1973	Telepathy, healing, repeater
(Keel 1975)	Anonymous female	1973	Telepathy, prophecy, repeater

(Haisell 1978)	Jerry Armstrong	1973	Apparitions, poltergeist, precognition, automatic religious writing, astral travel
(Bowen 1977a)	Aarno Heinonen	1973	Apparitions, precognition, repeater
(Lorenzen 1977; Sachs 1980)	Charles Hickson	1973	Telepathy, prophecy, excellent hypnotic subject, repeater
(Hopkins 1981)	"Steven Kilburn"	1973	Excellent hypnotic subject
(Vorilhon 1974, 1978, 1986; Vallee 1979; Stevens 1982)	Claude Vorilhon	1973	Telepathy, prophecy, repeater
(Evans 1979; Randles 1988; Bullard 1987)	John Day	1974	Excellent hypnotic subject, prophecy, poltergeist, apparitions
(Randles 1976)	Mr. "L"	1974	Apparitions
(Hind 1982; Rogo 1980; Evans 1984)	"Peter"	1974	Telepathy, astral travel, apparitions
(Gansberg 1980; Tongco 1974; Bullard 1987)	Carl Higdon	1974	Clairvoyance, healing, precognition, out-of-body experiences
(Schwarz 1983a)	David Stephens	1975	Psychic, poltergeist, levitation of object, medium, apparitions
(Press 1975; (Musgrave 1984; Kask 1976)	German Navarrete	1975	Telepathy, prophecy, astral travel
(Lorenzen 1976)	Charles Moody	1975	Apparent telepathy, prophecy
(Press 1979; Stevens 1982; Kinder 1988)	Billy Meier	1975	Telepathy, psychic repeater
(Clark 1976; Bullard 1987)	Sandra Larson	1975	Telepathy, astral travel, poltergeist
(Stringfield 1977)	Mona Stafford, Elaine Thomas, Louise Smith	1976	Apparitions, out-of-body experiences, psychic abilities
(Hartman 1979)	Toni M. and husband	1975	Apparitions, psychic
(Hopkins 1979)	Vincent "L" and John "D"	1975	Clairvoyance
(Schwarz 1983a)	Herbert Hopkins	1976	Psychic, telepathy, healings, dowsing, spirit contact
(Spencer 1976)	John Sands	1976	Prophecy

(Barker 1977)	Francessco Ojeda	1976	Telepathy
(Blundell and Boar 1983)	Mrs. Greta Woodrew	1976	Psychic medium, astral travel, telepathy, prophecy, repeater
(Randles 1988)	"Shelley"	1976	Psychic, levitation, body "floatings," telepathy
(Press 1977)	Luis Sandoval	1977	Telepathy
(Blundell and Boar 1983; Harris 1976)	Mrs. Joyce Bowles	1976	Levitation, repeater
(Dykes 1981)	Female "B"	1977	Telepathy
(Basterfield 1988)	"Rachel Jones"	1977	Telepathy
(Sprinkle 1981)	Marina Torpey	1978	Psychic
(Press 1978a)	Sara	1978	Poltergeist
(Bartholomew 1989)	Ignacio Sanchez Munoz	1978	Telepathy
(Johnson 1980; Blundell and Boar 1983)	John Mann	1978	Excellent hypnotic subject
(Press 1978b)	Miguel Herrero Sierra	1978	Telepathy
(Press 1981)	Francisco Ramon Jimenez	1978	Out-of-body experiences, healing, repeater
(Stevens and Herrmann 1981)	Bill Herrmann	1978	Body floating, repeater, psychic ability, apparent automatic writing
(Hendry 1980)	Patrick	1979	Telepathy, precognition, repeater
(Hind 1982)	Mrs. Meagan Quezet	1979	Excellent hypnotic subject
(Bullard 1987)	"Linda"	1979	Precognition, previous apparition, repeater
(Wiklund 1980)	Lilli-Ann Karlsson	1979	Telepathy
(Whiting 1980; Bullard 1987)	Harold Turner	1979	Psychic, apparitions
(Basterfield 1979; Little 1980)	Mark Allen	1979	Astral travel
(Randles 1983)	Alan Godfrey	1980	Apparition
(Sprinkle 1981)	Gene Gautreau	1980	Psychic
(Randles 1988)	Linda Taylor	1981	Psychic, visions

(Randles 1988)	Hayward, Hawkins, and Walters	1981	All psychic with a history of visions
(Press 1983a)	Sergio Baeza	1983	Telepathy
(Press 1983b)	Alfred Burtoo	1983	Telepathy
(Rogo 1987)	"Sammy Desmond"	1984	Psychic, psychokinesis, repeater
(Strieber 1987)	Whitley Strieber	1985	Astral travel, excellent hypnotic subject, apparitions, repeater
(Randles 1988)	Mrs. "B"	1988	Psychic, repeater
(Beckley 1980)	Barbara Hudson	Unknown	Psychic, medium, repeater
(Beckley 1980)	Jane Allyson	Unknown	Psychic, medium, repeater
(Beckley 1980)	Thelma B. Terrell	Unknown	Psychic, medium, repeater, telepathy
(Beckley 1980)	Lynn Volpe	Unknown	Psychic, medium, prophecy, astral travel, religious visions

UFOs and "Psychic" Phenomena: Results

Wilson and Barber have noted a significant relationship between subjects reporting frequent "psychic" occurrences and FPPs. For example, while 92 percent of the FPPs they studied see themselves as psychic or sensitive and report numerous telepathic and precognitive experiences, just 16 percent of the comparison group reported such experiences.[30] In the present sample, 75 percent were categorized as psychic and/or telepathic or experiencing poltergeist activity. It seems plausible that psychic incidents may have been perceived by a greater number of subjects but were unreported in the biographies, as most of the subjects' accounts typically center on the UFO experience, not their psychic history.

Out-of-Body Experiences

Of Wilson and Barber's fantasy group 88 percent (compared to 8 percent of comparison group subjects) reported "realistic out-of-the-body experiences."[31] By comparison, in our sample 21 percent reported "astral travel," "astral projection," "out-of-body experiences," "bi-location," or body floating. Again, because of the differences in data collection procedures employed with our sample of subjects, this 21 percent estimate could well be a serious underestimate. These experiences typically occur about equally with lone subjects or within a séance with multiple witnesses. During the 1860s, William Denton of Massachusetts was a popular spirit medium and lecturer who claimed to astrally project his body, enabling him to contact beings from Venus and describe to onlookers the content of his experiences.[32]

Automatic Writing, Healing, Apparitions, Religious Visions

While 50 percent of Wilson and Barber's fantasizers (8 percent in the control group) reported automatic writing by a guiding "spirit or a higher intelligence," about 8 percent of our biographies mentioned automatic writing ability. Such writing typically occurred on a daily basis, and after the initial few experiences subjects had the ability to write spontaneously. Twenty-four percent of our sample described themselves as channels for regular written messages but technically could not be classified in this category, as automatic writing was not explicitly mentioned. But if the two categories are combined, it would represent 32 percent of our sample.

Wilson and Barber found that over two-thirds of their subjects labeled as FPPs reported the ability to heal (0 percent in comparison group), while 73 percent of fantasizers reported apparitions (16 percent in the control group). In our sample just over 14 percent reported apparitions, and just under 6 percent claimed healing ability. While six FPPs (none in the comparison group) reported religious visions, 11 percent of our sample mentioned such experiences. Under the category "religious visions" are included only those experiences of a religious or spiritual nature interpreted by subjects as separate from the UFO experience. However, to have included all alleged UFO encounters by aliens claiming to be acting on behalf of a god (almost always Christ), easily half of our sample could be categorized as religious visionaries.[33]

Hypnotic Susceptibility

The hypnotic susceptibility category is difficult to evaluate, since the majority of the UFO abductees and contactees had never been hypnotized. Just 9 percent of our sample were described as excellent hypnotic subjects. There is, however, anecdotal evidence within the UFO contactee and abductee literature supporting a relationship between ease and degree of hypnotic states and the UFO percipient. Consider the following three opinions by UFO researchers who have been involved firsthand with hypnotic regressions. The first is by psychiatrist Berthold Schwarz.

> In my experience UFO contactees, unlike most across-the-board psychiatric patients, or so-called healthy people, have been usually easy to hypnotize or almost always go rapidly into deep somnambulistic trances.[34]

UFO author-investigator Ann Druffel's[35] experience coincides with that of Dr. William McCall, who has regressed numerous UFO abductees and found that reluctance on the part of the other witness or witnesses "seems to be part of a peculiar pattern." Druffel continues,

> Time and time again in various cases, a primary witness will be easily regressed, giving a vivid and full account of the experience; any corroborating witness to the same case will either resist hypnosis altogether or prove a very poor trance subject.[36]

Similar findings have been mentioned by other UFO researchers who have conducted firsthand interviews with alleged abductees or contactees.[37] These general anecdotal findings on hypnotic susceptibility correspond with results by Wilson and Barber and Lynn and Rhue.[38] In each study a strong relationship was found between FPPs and hypnotic susceptibility.

Physiological Effects

Wilson and Barber note that a high proportion of their FPP sample reported physiological effects in conjunction with fantasies. Nineteen FPPs, and only two in the comparison group, reported sickness or physical symptoms corresponding with their fantasy content.

> [M]ost said they had experienced quite frequently throughout their lives something such as the following: becoming physically ill when they thought (incorrectly) that they had eaten spoiled food or developing an uncomfortable and continuous itch when they (incorrectly) believed that they had been contaminated with lice. . . . [One subject] told us about the time she recaptured a neighboring child's pet frog that had escaped, remembered that she had been told that frogs cause warts, and then developed a wart on her hand that was highly resistant to treatment.[39]

Further, fifteen FPPs would become physically ill while watching television violence, and seventeen experienced heat or cold as if it were affecting them directly. One subject told "how she was freezing as she sat bundled in a warm living room while she was watching *Dr. Zhivago* in Siberia on television."[40]

Numerous subjects in our sample reported a variety of physiological symptoms in the wake of their alien contacts. These aftereffects were consistent with and reflective of their contact scenarios. For instance, Barney Hill developed a ring of warts around his genital area corresponding to the position of a cuplike device he said was placed there by his abductors.[41] During subsequent hypnotic regressions the warts became inflamed.[42] Following an alleged abduction near Norway, Maine, in 1975, David Stephens, a twenty-one-year-old poultry processing worker, reported that he had reddish skin, general soreness, burning eyes, swollen hands and feet, breathing difficulty, a sore throat, and chills.[43] Correspondingly, Stephens said that during the abduction there was intense light, blood and body samples were extracted from him, and he was examined by "a type of X-Ray machine" that went "all over him."[44] During a now famous abduction near Sao Francisco de Sales, Brazil, on October 15, 1957, farmer Antonio Villas Boas claimed to have been taken aboard an alien craft and given a medical examination. Boas reported numerous symptoms in conjunction with the incident to gastroenterologist Olavo T. Fontes of the Brazilian National School of Medicine. These included nausea, headache, sudden onset of sleepiness, general fatigue, severe watering of the eyes, appetite loss, and "his body hurt all over."[45]

The most frequently reported symptoms in our sample involved rashlike facial and body marks, itchiness, headache, dizziness, and burning or watery eyes. These symptoms typically occur in cases involving medical examinations by aliens where the subject is often stuck with a needlelike device and blood is extracted, or the subject is exposed to bright lights or X-rays. In a similar manner, psychosomatic reactions reported during mass hysteria outbreaks correspond with the prevailing social norm. According to investigators, psychosomatic symptoms occurring in cases of hysterical conversion and mass hysteria in general include skin rashes, fainting, trance states, dizziness, bad mouth taste, blurred vision, stomach complaints, sleepiness, headache, vomiting, and dry mouth.[46] A variety of similar symptoms were associated with "witches" and their victims during the Salem witch trials of the late seventeenth century.[47]

Within our sample, there are numerous instances of reported copulation and general mischievous sexual encounters with aliens. Sexual encounters can take the form of ongoing contacts or singular events. Brazilian subject Antonio Villas Boas falls into the latter category, claiming to have been taken aboard an oval-shaped craft, undressed, and seduced by an extremely fair-skinned, freckled young female with high cheekbones. Regarding the sex act, he said it was a normal act, and she behaved just as any woman would.[48]

Spiritual Themes

In addition to frequently interacting with imaginary companions, FPPs fantasized a supernatural worldview that typically included the taken-for-granted existence of a variety of mythical guardians and spirit beings.

> When they were children, almost all of the fantasizers believed in fairies, leprechauns, elves, guardian angels, and other such beings. . . . [F]or some, encounters . . . were vivid and "as real as real"; for instance, one told us how as a child she would spend hours watching in fascination the little people who lived in her grandmother's cactus garden that adults kept insisting were not there. With few exceptions, their belief in elves, fairies, guardian angels, tree spirits, and other such creatures did not terminate during childhood; as adults they either still believe in them or are not absolutely sure that they really do not exist.[49]

Several subjects in our sample mentioned their belief in seen or unseen guardians or spirits. These beings almost without exception were viewed in a religious context (guardian angels, Jesus, a famous saint), or the subjects have one or a combination of extraterrestrial guardian contacts or ongoing encounters with mythical beings, such as fairies.

The case of Jessica Rolfe is typical. She claims that at age five, while living with her family in Miami Beach, Florida, she was visited one night in bed by three well-built tall "men" with golden skin. They lifted her from bed, telepathically asking, "Would you like to come with us now?" After refusing the invitation, they returned her to her bed, and comforted her before disappearing. She claims that ever since various alien males from the same race visit her bedside and teach her many things.[50]

Although in our sample we were able to identify only twenty instances where UFO witnesses discussed their interactions with guardian angels, spirits, or unseen beings (and their belief in them as adults), the following statement from a UFO researcher who has interviewed numerous contactees is interesting.

> About eight years ago, as he traveled around the country while lecturing, well-known parapsychologist Brad Steiger noticed that many men and women he met, actually claimed memories of having come to this planet from "somewhere else," or to have experienced an interaction with paranormal entities since their earliest childhood. Steiger came to call these individuals "Star People" and noticed that they had many . . . physiological anomalies which obviously placed them apart from the rest of society. . . .

> [T]he pattern profile of the "Star People" contains the following elements: . . . Had unseen companions as a child. Natural abilities with art, music, healing, or acting. Experienced . . . psychic events. Had an unusual experience . . . [at an early age] which often took the form of . . . a visitation by human-type beings who gave information and comfort. Have since maintained a continuing series of episodes with "angels," "elves," "masters," or openly declared UFO intelligences. . . . [D]espite a seemingly bizarre belief that they are not from here, . . . all appear normal and rational otherwise.[51]

It is important to mention here that about 45 percent of our sample claimed to have undergone multiple experiences. In many other instances it was implied that these were ongoing, yet they were left out, as it was not possible to be certain.[52]

Relating These Results to the Contemporary Social Context

The current social milieu plays a role in the relationship between the fantasy-prone process and the FPPs' worldview. The FPPs living in the twentieth century are heavily exposed to books, television programs, and movies on the subject of extraterrestrial visitation. It is only natural, therefore, to expect their experiences to reflect the science-fiction and popular beliefs of the time. This could explain why prior to the nineteenth century there are virtually no explicit reported contacts with extraterrestrials. Yet, in the United Kingdom and Europe especially, there were thousands of reported sightings, abductions, and contacts with fairies at this time.[53] This relationship between UFO encounters and fairy lore was first mentioned by British investigator Gordon Creighton and later by French astrophysicist Dr. Jacques Vallee, Loren Coleman, Jerome Clark, John Rimmer, and Hilary Evans.[54]

Our preliminary findings suggest that the similarities between characteristics of FPPs and UFO abudctees and contactees is a potentially fruitful avenue of research. While not all UFO abductees and contactees are FPPs, this exploratory study supports the hypothesis that a significant portion of this population falls into the FPP category. Unfortunately, FPPs experiencing UFO-related contacts and abductions may have often been labeled as psychopathological. In this regard, it is appropriate to quote from Wilson and Barber, who hint at the potential for significant others or therapists to enrich the lives of FPPs by helping them understand their syndrome.

> Most of those we saw again later told us that our interviews had made a significant difference in their lives. They typically stated that they had gained greater understanding of themselves and felt less alone—previously they had assumed that no one else was like them. Following participation in our project, some of the fantasizers felt ready to share their "secret" with important people in their lives. One told her husband of twenty years and gave him a copy of our preliminary report of the study[55] so that he could see her as she really was. Another gave a copy . . . to her counselor so that he could understand her.[56]

Finally, it is interesting to note the shifting content of contemporary FPPs. If abductees and contactees are overrepresented as fantasy-prone personalities, instead of romantic visions of fairies of yesteryear, the images of the modern-day FPP reflect the period and culture into which they are born. It is not surprising, then, that the earliest, most common alien messages concerned fear of nuclear destruction. Recently, the messages have warned of the approaching ecological problems that face our planet.

> [A]bduction reports are important. They contain a message about ourselves . . . a message put forward by a growing number of people who have perhaps no other way of expressing the anxieties and crises of their lives. . . . It is a message given to us by the hidden parts of our being, and it is a message we should listen to carefully.[57]

We are all frightened by the possibilities of a catastrophic future for our world. If humans are to take effective actions to forestall such horrors, someone must first identify the horrific possibilities. Our problem is that articulating anticipated catastrophes is a difficult task for many people. Perhaps having God speak through a prophet or an alien speak through an abductee represents a psychologically easier way to address future nuclear or ecological horrors. The messages of modern UFO abductees and contactees mirror the anxieties prevalent in the societies of their times.

Notes

1. H. Evans, *Intrusions—Society and the Paranormal* (London: Routledge and Kegan Paul, 1982).

2. S. C. Wilson and T. X. Barber, "Vivid Fantasy and Hallucinatory Abilities in the Life Histories of Excellent Hypnotic Subjects ('Somnambules'): Preliminary Report with Female Subjects," in E. Klinger, ed., *Imagery, Volume 2, Concepts, Results, and Applications* (New York: Plenum Press, 1981).

3. R. Buckhout, "Eyewitness Testimony," *Scientific American* 231 (1974): 23–31; E. F. Loftus and J. C. Palmer, "Reconstruction of Automobile Destruction: An Example of the Interaction Between Language and Memory," *Journal of Verbal Learning and Verbal Behavior* 13 (1974): 585–89; G. Wells and J. Turtle, "Eyewitness Identification: The Importance of Lineup Models," *Psychological Bulletin* 99 (1968): 320–29.

4. J. A. M. Meerloo, "Le Syndrome des Soucoupes Volantes," *Medecine et Hygiene* 25 (1967): 992–96.

5. B. Schwarz, "Psychiatric and Parapsychiatric Dimensions of UFOs," in R. Haines, ed., *UFO Phenomena and the Behavioral Scientist* (Metuchen, N.J.: Scarecrow Press, 1979).

6. L. Grinspoon and A. D. Persky, "Psychiatry and UFO Reports," in C. Sagan and T. Page, eds., *UFOs: A Scientific Debate* (Ithaca, N.Y.: Cornell University Press, 1973).

7. D. Mavrakis and J. Bocquet, "Psychoses et Objets Volants Non Identifies" [Psychoses and unidentified flying objects], *Canadian Journal of Psychiatry* 28 (1983): 199–201.

8. J. A. Keel, "The Flying Saucer Subculture," *Journal of Popular Culture* 5 (1975): 871–96.

9. C. G. Jung, *Flying Saucers: A Modern Myth of Things Seen in the Sky*, trans. R. F. C. Hull (New York: Harcourt, Brace and World, 1959); Meerloo, "Le Syndrome"; J. A. M. Meerloo, "The Flying Saucer Syndrome and the Need for Miracles," *Journal of the American Medical Association* 203 (1968): 170.

10. H. T. Buckner, "The Flying Saucerians: An Open Door Cult," in M. Truzzi, ed., *Sociology in Everyday Life* (Englewood Cliffs, N.J.: Prentice-Hall, 1968).

11. W. E. H. Lecky, *History of European Morals Volumes I and II* (reprint, New York: Braziller, 1955).

12. T. S. Szasz, *The Manufacture of Madness* (New York: Harper & Row, 1970); T. J. Schoeneman, "Criticisms of the Psychopathological Interpretation of Witch Hunts: A Review," *American Journal of Psychiatry* 139 (1982): 1028–32.

13. G. A. Zilboorg, *The Medical Man and the Witch during the Renaissance*, The Hideyo Nogushi Lecures (Baltimore: Johns Hopkins Press, 1935); G. A. Zilboorg and G. W. Henry, *History of Medical Psychology* (New York: W. W. Norton, 1941).

14. G. Rosen, *Madness in Society: Chapters in the Historical Sociology of Mental Illness* (New York: Harper & Row, 1968); Szasz, *Manufacture of Madness*; J. Kroll, "A Reappraisal of Psychiatry in the Middle Ages," *Archives of General Psychiatry* 29 (1973): 276–83; N. P. Spanos, "Witchcraft in Histories of Psychiatry: A Critical Analysis and an Alternative Conceptualization," *Psychological Bulletin* 85 (1978): 417–39; R. Neugebauer, "Treatment of the Mentally Ill in Medieval and Early Modern England: A Reappraisal," *Journal of the History of the Behavioral Sciences* 14 (1978): 158–69; Schoeneman, "Criticisms of Psychopathological Interpretation."

15. B. Simon, "Hypnosis in the Treatment of Military Neuroses," *Psychiatric Opinion* 4 (1967): 24–29.

16. B. E. Schwarz, "UFOs: Delusion or Dilemma?" *Medical Times* 96 (1968): 967–81; B. E. Schwarz, "UFOs in New Jersey," *Journal of the Medical Society of New Jersey* 68 (1969): 460–64. B. E. Schwarz, "UFO Contactee Stella Lansing: Possible Medical Implications of Her Motion Picture Experiments," paper presented at 1975 annual meeting of the American Society of Psychosomatic Dentistry and Medicine, Montclair, N.J., September 21, 1975. This paper was published the next year in *Journal of the American Society of Psychosomatic Dentistry and the American Society of Psychosomatic Denistry and Medicine* 23 (1976): 60–68; B. E. Schwarz, *UFO Dynamics: Book I* (Florida: Rainbow, 1983a); B. E. Schwarz, *UFO Dynamics: Book II* (Florida: Rainbow, 1983b).

17. Mavrakis and Bocquet, "Psychoses et Objets Volants Non Identifies."

18. Wilson and Barber, "Vivid Fantasy and Hallucinatory Abilities."

19. J. R. Hilgard, *Personality and Hypnosis: A Study of Imaginative Involvement* (Chicago: University of Chicago Press, 1970); J. R. Hilgard, *Per-*

sonality and Hypnosis: *A Study of Imaginative Involvement*, 2d ed. (Chicago: University of Chicago Press, 1979).

20. Wilson and Barber, "Vivid Fantasy and Hallucinatory Abilities"; S. C. Wilson and T. X. Barber, "The Fantasy-Prone Personality: For Understanding Imagery, Hypnosis, and Parapsychological Phenomena," in A. A. Sheikh, ed., *Imagery: Current Theory, Research, and Application* (New York: Wiley, 1983).

21. Wilson and Barber, "Fantasy-Prone Personality."

22. S. Myers and H. Austrin, "Distal Eidetic Technology: Further Characteristics of the Fantasy-Prone Personality," *Journal of Mental Imagery* 9 (1985): 7–66; S. Lynn and J. Rhue, "The Fantasy-Prone Person: Hypnosis, Imagination, and Creativity," *Journal of Personality and Social Psychology* 51 (1986): 404–408; S. Lynn and J. Rhue, "Fantasy-Proneness and Psychopathology," *Personality and Social Psychology* 53 (1987): 327–36; S. Lynn and S. Rhue, "Fantasy Proneness: Developmental Antecedents," *Journal of Personality* 55 (1987): 1.

23. Wilson and Barber, "Fantasy-Prone Personality."

24. Ibid.

25. Ibid., p. 351.

26. Ibid., p. 346.

27. M. Pines, "Invisible Playmates," *Psychology Today* 12 (1978): 38–42.

28. Wilson and Barber, "Fantasy-Prone Personality," p. 346.

29. Ibid.

30. Ibid.

31. Ibid.

32. W. Denton, *The Soul of Things* (Boston: privately published, 1873); J. Hudson, *Those Sexy Saucer People* (San Diego: Greenleaf Classics, 1967); Keel, "Flying Saucer Subculture," pp. 871–96. Of lone percipients reporting astral experiences, a quiet setting, such as meditation or resting in bed prior to sleep, appears to induce the experience. Contactee William Ferguson always began his numerous encounters during meditation. His experiences were consciousness-raising, providing keen insights into his life.

> Upon my return to Earth. . . . I thought I would go into the living room where an old gentleman . . . was staying at my house . . . to see if he would recognize me. As I went into the living room I spoke to him, but there was no response. He couldn't see nor hear me. . . . There were a lot of things I could do and think about and understand, that I never could have understood before. So I went back to the room where I had been relaxing, . . . and I looked for my body, but my body isn't there, . . . I again placed

myself upon the lounge and remained quiet until my being was transformed back into this three-dimensional dense matter projection, and thereupon went into the dining room and told my wife about my experience. (W. Ferguson, *My Trip to Mars* [Potomac, Md.: Cosmic Study Center, 1954]).

33. Between one-quarter and one-third of our sample reported a quasi-religious tone in the content of their alien messages. Buck Nelson, a famous 1950s contactee, was instructed during a trip on a flying saucer to write the "Twelve Laws of God on Venus," paralleling the Ten Commandments (W. Brownell, *UFOs: Key to the Earth's Destiny* [Little Creek, Calif.: Legion of Light Publications, 1980], pp. 68–72), while the multiple abductee claims of Betty Andreasson reflect her fundamentalist Christian background, claiming to have communicated with God and been given a Bible during some encounters (R. Fowler, *The Andreasson Affair* [Englewood Cliffs, N.J.: Prentice-Hall, 1979]). While both abductees and contactees report UFO experiences with religious overtones, contactees generally keep a higher public profile, founding organizations and writing books and pamphlets, most privately published. Brownell, for instance, lists twenty-one different organizations for contactees in the United States alone, and this is far from exhaustive.

34. Schwarz, "Psychiatric and Parapsychiatric Dimensions of UFOs."

35. A. Druffel, "Encounter on Dapple Gray Lane: Part 2," *Flying Saucer Review* 23 (1977): 2.

36. Ibid., p. 21.

37. J. Rimmer, *The Evidence for Alien Abductions* (Wellingborough, Northamptonshire: Aquarian, 1984); A. Lawson, "What Can We Learn from Hypnosis of Imaginary Abductees?" *Mutual UFO Network Journal* 120 (1977): 7–9; M. Moravec, "Psychological Influences on UFO 'Abductee' Testimonies," M. Moravec and J. Prytz, eds., *UFOs over Australia: A Selection of Australian Centre for UFO Studies Research Findings and Debate*, published by the Australian Centre for UFO Studies, 1985.

38. Lynn and Rhue, "Fantasy-Proneness and Psychopathology"; "Fantasy Proneness: Developmental Antecedents."

39. Wilson and Barber, "Fantasy-Prone Personality," p. 358.

40. Ibid.

41. Rimmer, *Evidence for Alien Abductions.*

42. J. Fuller, *The Interrupted Journey* (New York: Dial, 1966).

43. Schwarz, *UFO Dynamics: Book I*; Rimmer, *Evidence for Alien Abductions.*

44. J. Lorenzen and C. Lorenzen, *Abducted! Confrontations with Beings from Outer Space* (New York: Berkeley, 1977).

45. R. Story, *The Encyclopedia of UFOs* (New York: Doubleday, 1980); G. Creighton, "Postscript to the Most Amazing Case of All," *Flying Saucer Review* 11 (1965): 24–25.

46. M. J. Colligan and L. R. Murphy, "A Review of Mass Psychogenic Illness in Work Settings," in *Mass Psychogenic Illness: A Social Psychological Analysis,* ed. M. Colligan, J. Pennebaker, L. Murphy (Hillsdale, N.J.: Lawrence Erlbaum Associates, (1982).

47. C. Hansen, *Witchcraft at Salem* (New York: George Braziller, 1969).

48. Ongoing sexual contacts were more common. Typical is the case of Elizabeth Klarer of Drakensberg, South Africa. A seemingly sincere lady who has come under extreme criticism and ridicule in the press, she has staunchly maintained that since April 7, 1956, she has had sex with and a child by "Akon" from the planet "Menton." Akon contacted her for "breeding" purposes as their race needed "new blood" and she was chosen for one of their "experiments." They fell in love and had a son, "Alying," who she often visits along with Akon on Menton. True to the typical FPP sexual profile, her alien companion was very handsome and ideal, while the planet Menton was a utopian existence, having no war, politics, or disease (C. Hind, "UFOs: African Encounters" [Zimbabwe: Gemini, 1982]; E. Klarer, *Beyond the Light Barrier* [Cape Town, South Africa: Timmons, 1980]).

49. Wilson and Barber, "Fantasy-Prone Personality," p. 346.

50. A. Gansberg and J. Gansberg, *Direct Encounters: The Personal Histories of UFO Abductees* (New York: Walker and Walker, 1980).

51. T. G. Beckley, *Timothy G. Beckley's Book of Space Contacts* (New York: Global Communications, 1980), pp. 33–34.

52. Interestingly, both Wilson and Barber ("Fantasy-Prone Personality") and Lynn and Rhue ("Fantasy Proneness Developmental Antecedents") found greater levels of punishment during childhood among subjects classified as fantasy-prone. Although unable to find data on this category in our biographical analysis, given the sensitive nature of the category and the accompanying social stigma, this is understandable. Further, it would seem unlikely for instances of childhood punishment or abuse to appear in a book where UFO experiences are the primary topic. In this regard, it is worth noting the view of James Lorenzen, the late international director of the Aerial Phenomena Research Organization:

> One thing we have learned when we have gone into the background of persons who claim to have been abducted by UFOs, to

have had contacts with UFOs, or to have received messages from space is that for the most part they have a history of being battered children or have had sad histories in other ways. (C. G. Fuller, comp. and ed., *Proceedings of the First International UFO Congress* [New York: Warner, 1980], p. 325)

53. R. Kirk, *The Secret Commonwealth of Elves, Fauns and Fairies* (London: Longman, 1815); T. Keightley, *The Fairy Mythology* (England, n.p., 1815); W. Y. Evans-Wentz, *The Fairy-Faith in Celtic Countries* (Rennes, France, 1909); K. Briggs, *An Encyclopedia of Fairies* (New York: Pantheon, 1976).

54. Creighton, "Postscript," pp. 24–25; J. Vallee, *Passport to Magonia—From Folklore to Flying Saucers* (Chicago: Henry Regnery, 1969); L. Coleman and J. Clark, *The Unidentified* (New York: Warner, 1975); Rimmer, *Evidence for Alien Abductions*; H. Evans, *The Evidence for UFOs* (Wellingborough: Aquarian, 1983); H. Evans, *Visions, Apparitions, Alien Visitors* (Wellingborough: Aquarian, 1984).

55. Wilson and Barber, "Vivid Fantasy and Hallucinatory Abilities."

56. Wilson and Barber, "Fantasy-Prone Personality," p. 367.

57. Rimmer, *Evidence for Alien Abductions*, p. 153.

13

The Further Reaches of Human Experience

The study presented in chapter 12 suggests that UFO abductees and contactees more closely resemble normal subjects who exhibit the FPP syndrome than they do the non-FPP control group. But this finding does not suggest that the group of percipients exhibits fewer psychopathological symptoms than a control group of normal subjects. The critical issue is not whether one diagnostic categorization (normal/pathological, FPP/non-FPP) is more correct than the other. Recall that all conceptual schemes are human creations that help us to understand phenomena and direct us toward effective practice. The normal/abnormal distinction has often served as the vantage point from which mental health professionals tried to understand the puzzling reports of abduction or contact by aliens. Since these people report an experience that society believes could not possibly have occurred, they possess psychopathological symptoms. Thus, it is definitionally true that they can be categorized as pathological individuals. However, they also are (in all likelihood) fantasy-prone personalities. In putting such individuals in two conceptual groups, we now provide an additional degree of freedom for understanding or therapeutic intervention. Fantasy is an important human characteristic.

Seeing UFO abductees and contactees as otherwise normal people who happen to be overactive fantasizers will be socially and therapeutically beneficial to the UFO witnesses.

William James on Truth and Reality

William James, founder of scientific psychology in America,[1] offers insights that can be applied to UFO witnesses. One of James's most basic philosophical principles is the pragmatic view of truth and reality.

> *In the relative sense,* then, the sense in which we contrast reality with simple unreality, and in which one thing is said to have *more* reality than another, and to be more believed, *reality means simply relation to our emotional and active life.* This is the only sense which the word ever has in the mouths of practical men. *In this sense, whatever excites and stimulates our interest is real*: whenever an object so appeals to us that we turn to it, accept it, fill our mind with it, or practically take account of it, so far it is real for us, and we believe it. Whenever, on the contrary, we ignore it, fail to consider it or act upon it, despise it, reject it, forget it, so far it is unreal for us and disbelieved.[2]

In a little less than two decades, James had refined this perspective into his instrumental (or pragmatic) view of reality and truth:

> Let me now say only this, that truth is *one species of good,* and not, as is usually supposed, a category distinct from good, and coordinate with it. *The true is the name of whatever proves itself to be good in the way of belief, and good, too, for definite, assignable reasons.*[3]

This view of truth or reality as that which is significant or useful clashes with the objectivist notion that truth and reality reside in characteristics of the real world (as envisioned in the mirror-of-nature view of reality presented in chapter 11). Many have claimed that the most profound recent advance in the philosophy of science is in the shift away from this objectivist metaphor for science toward a Jamesian, instrumentalist view that truth lies in what is useful or practical.

Because mental-health professionals have always been confronted with the immediate problem of what to do with the clients sitting before them, they have always been sensitive to the importance of an idea's practicality. But this penchant for seeing value in the utility of an idea, technique, or diagnosis has often clashed with the long-standing Western belief that truth involves something more than what is individually significant or pragmatically useful.

For example, James might have argued that clinicians have used diagnostic categories over the years because diagnostic systems enable them to conceive of clients' problems in ways that lead them to helpful therapeutic interventions. Such utility is the chief argument for the validity of any diagnostic categorization scheme. But scientist-practitioners are committed to periodically testing the utility of various diagnostic practices by comparing their beliefs with possible alternatives. Such periodic testing, with the possibility of revising one's beliefs, lies at the very heart of scientific rationality and clinical wisdom.

The narrative approach to human thought is now sweeping psychology.[4] From a narrative perspective, assigning a particular diagnosis to a certain set of symptoms tells a particular story about the meaning of the symptoms. Doing so is justified to the extent that the story helps to understand the client, the etiology of the problem, the ways in which the symptoms might be ameliorated, and so forth. But the essence of rationality for the scientist-practitioner lies in the periodic testing, honing, refining, and possible revising of modes of thought and action. This involves the scientist or clinician telling another possibly true story about the meaning of the pattern of symptoms in question. To the extent that this changed story makes an important difference (i.e., possesses greater practical utility, represents a more intellectually satisfying understanding, produces additional ethical or professional benefits, suggests novel predictions that are later empirically corroborated, etc.[5]) relative to the initial story, to that extent is its probable superior truth affirmed. This is how contemporary scientists employ James's pragmatic criterion of truth in their work.

This book presents a story that depicts some UFO abductees and contactees as fantasy prone rather than as severely disturbed individuals. In addition to furnishing mental-health professionals with an alternative scheme for diagnosis and treatment of such clients, we hope to demonstrate to scientist-practitioners that the heart of professional rationality rests not in the truth of current beliefs, but in a commitment to improving these beliefs. As philosopher of science Stephen Toulmin put it, "A man demonstrates his rationality not by a commitment to fixed ideas, stereotyped procedures, or immutable concepts, but by the manner in which, and the occasions on which, he changes those ideas, procedures, and concepts."[6]

The emergence of this constructivist metatheory in psychology[7] has moved us away from either/or considerations of the truth value of differing conceptualizations (e.g., psychopathological or fantasy prone). Issues of "truth" often give way to considerations of utility. Because human thought might be understood as instances of storytelling,[8] psychotherapy can be seen as instances of story elaboration, narrative modification and repair.[9] The critical issue, for the diagnosis of UFO abductees and contactees, takes on a different hue in a constructivist perspective. Is it helpful to the course of therapy to identify the client as a person whose rich and absorbing fantasy life can sometimes be harnessed to produce creative and productive personal and professional lives (as was often the case with Wilson and Barber's[10] normal FPP sample), or as one whose runaway fantasies invite derision and potentially risk the diminishment of the quality of life and societal status? Can therapy framed in this manner help UFO witnesses more than therapeutic efforts grounded in the view that such clients' psychopathology is pervasive? We'll never know the answer to these last questions until mental health professionals begin to treat these clients from the FPP perspective.

UFO Clubs

More generally, how might abductees and contactees themselves think of their experiences with aliens? At present, most people who "come out" publicly with their stories risk ridicule, but it is natural for people to talk about such unsettling experiences, despite society's generally unsupportive attitude. Thus, many such people have sought out support groups of like-minded individuals.

While William James would see UFO groups as a healthy way to deal with the experience of UFO contact, these pro-UFO groups often fall into the same mistakes as society in general—they tend to focus on the *reality* of specific aliens and alien contact. In doing so, group members simply take the opposite stance against the objectivist majority in (what James believes to be) a completely wrongheaded conversation. Does anyone really believe that the possibility of the existence of aliens will be settled by people stating their beliefs, and objecting to the beliefs of people who think differently? Of course not! The more important function for UFO groups (from James's perspective) would be to help people think pragmatically about the consequences of their beliefs and how they will act (or refrain from acting) on those beliefs in their everyday lives.

Recall our praise of foresight in chapter 11. UFO clubs could be helpful to the extent that they encourage people to use their foresight to determine and deal with the likely pragmatic consequences of their belief or their decision not to believe that their experiences with aliens: (a) really occurred; (b) reflect their fantasy-proneness; (c) represent pervasive psychopathology; (d) suggest that they should let only their most intimate friends know their beliefs; (e) suggest that they announce their beliefs to the world; and so forth. While UFO clubs often already serve this important function, there is a strong temptation for groups to lapse into an unhelpful fixation on objectivist, ontological concerns, such as "What were your aliens like?" and "Did your abduction include experimentation and questioning?" Further, conversations at clubs could well devolve into conspiracy theories, which are pragmatically unhelpful.

If you are convinced that aliens do not exist and that no contacts or abductions have occurred, you may well believe that UFO percipients are either hoaxers or crazy. From this perspective, any solution, such as seeing the issue as a case of overactive fantasies, is suspect because it gives some degree of credence to either a lie or craziness. Thus, all talk of seeing the abduction as the result of an overactive fantasy that may or may not be pragmatically useful to continue to believe might strike you as ill-advised and potentially dangerous.

But consider the case of Whitley Strieber.

Prior to the night of December 26, 1985, fantasy novelist Whitley Strieber had it all: wealth, fame, a loving wife, a successful career. During the 1970s and early 1980s he attained global notoriety as an author of best-selling novels. *The Wolfen*, *The Hunger*, and *Black Magic* are but a few. Some were even made into movies. But something bizarre happened to him that night.

Strieber was asleep with his wife, Anne, in a picturesque log cabin nestled in upstate New York. Snow fell lightly outside. Sometime during the night he awoke with a bolt. Startled upon hearing an unnerving swirling sound in the downstairs living room, he stiffened with fear, peering intensely at the bedside burglar alarm panel. All was normal according to the reassuring glow of lights. Then, still puzzled but beginning to reassure himself, he was suddenly overcome with disbelief. One of the bedroom doors was opening. A small figure edged around the corner. Strieber lay mute and paralyzed with wonder and fright. It was impossible, yet it was happening. The silhouette of a three-and-a-half-foot-tall creature moved forward. Glaring brightness suddenly flooded the room as the motion-sensitive light went on. Strieber groped for the shotgun by the bed and pursued the creature downstairs, but a search of the premises revealed nothing. Confused, he returned to the bedroom. Without warning the figure jumped out and rushed toward him. Everything went black. He next recalls being paralyzed and floating into what appeared to be an alien spacecraft, where tiny creatures probed his mind. This incident is one of several contacts Strieber has claimed since.

Strieber's 1987 book *Communion: A True Story*[11] is a confession of his belief that he has been visited by aliens over many years, twice abducted and examined by them. That the book sold more than five million copies suggests that many people find the topic worthy of attention. In it Strieber describes his extreme agitation and numerous paranoid symptoms that appeared to be worsening until he "admitted the truth" to himself that the aliens and his abductions were real. The book documents how this decision led to a remission of his symptoms and an improvement in his relationships with family and friends.

Although Strieber's decision to see the aliens as real fits his life nicely, we suspect that few clinicians could feel comfortable in endorsing Strieber's accommodation with reality. But his options were extremely limited: either the aliens did not exist and he was delusional, or the aliens were real and society is struggling mightily to repress that terrifying reality. If you were Whitley Strieber, which option would you choose?

What about a third possibility—that the aliens did not exist and that Strieber is a fantasy-prone personality type? He gave evidence of virtually every FPP symptom in *Communion*. Might Strieber, his family and friends stand a better chance of understanding his experiences from the perspective of an FPP storyline?

Alien Contact and the Search for Truth

Are there aliens out there? Have they already made contact with humans? Appendix A presents over two hundred brief case histories of reported communication between aliens and humans. Far from exhaustive, this compilation represents but the tip of the iceberg of a growing social phenomenon. What cannot be denied is that science is searching for answers to this question with all the intellectual and technological resources in its power. Similarly, the explosion of books, movies, and television programs that posit alien contact proves that the imaginations of the creative and artistic communities are consumed with this idea. Why wouldn't the rest of humanity want to get in on this exciting exploration into the possibility that there might be other forms of intelligent life out there? Don't many scientists in their enthusiasm sometimes overstate their scientific claims? Don't members of the artistic community sometimes go overboard and produce bad books, bad movies, and bad TV? Then why is it a surprise that some ordinary people also get carried away?

Of course, this book cannot be drawn to a close without restating the assumption upon which the entire project rests—that the UFO sightings, contacts, and abductions do not occur. Consider a parallel phenomenon—belief in God. Some have the gift of faith, and others do not. To the believer, proof of the existence of God is unnecessary; to the nonbeliever, proof is impossible. While religious believers attempt to share their "truth" with others they are often scorned and derided by society. But only if the final judgment comes will the prophet have honor in his own country.[12] If aliens arrive among us, who wouldn't be proud to have been the first to have been contacted or abducted?

Since most people probably don't believe that the day of unquestioned alien contact will ever arrive, it is more important to examine the opposite side of the God/alien parallel above. What if God didn't create humans—what if humans created the idea of God?[13] Would we then have to decry all believers in religion as having been "out of touch with reality" all their lives? Of course not! Their belief in God made religion a part of the reality of their lives. On balance, religion seems to be a useful and good influence on humans.[14] One is hard-pressed to come up with an alternative worldview (e.g., liberal democracy, secular humanism, communism, free market capitalism) upon which to stake one's life that produces more positive and fewer negative benefits overall.[15] Religion helps most people to lead happier, healthier, and more charitable lives than they might have lived with alternative worldviews. But even if your summary evaluation on religion is more negative, most of us would still defend theists' right to think, believe, and say whatever they desire, so long as it doesn't infringe on the rights of others.

So what is the pragmatic evaluation of belief in aliens if aliens don't exist? Obviously that will vary from person to person. Suppose belief in aliens leads a young person to pursue a career in astronomy that eventually produces great scientific breakthroughs. Was her belief in an "untrue fiction" a bane upon her existence? What of Whitley Strieber's experience? He got a book, a movie, fame, fortune, relief from noxious psychological symptoms, and more out of his experience. Is this not a blessing overall? Perhaps, perhaps not. There are negative aspects to Strieber's and everyone's choice of belief systems. Every choice of which stories we believe about reality as if they were literally true, involves both gains and losses. Thus it is the utility of the various belief systems available to us that ought to hold the key to our decisions regarding what we ought to believe.

If we someday learn that there is no God, how will we evaluate the history of religious belief? Did we learn anything about our nature as humans from our experiment with religion? What of the good that came from the many billions of people whose lives were enriched by their beliefs of God? Were these not enormous benefits to derive from a "failed" experiment?

Similarly, imagine that someday humanity's great experiment to determine if Earth holds the only intelligent life in our universe is answered negatively. Will all our efforts then have to be counted as wasted? Certainly not! For this end returns us to our beginning—all that will remain are humans seeking meaning in life and companionship in an otherwise cold and lonely universe. Does this not tell us something very important about ourselves? Even this meager reward would be rich indeed, for it would help us to better understand what it means to be human.

Yet what if our spiritual journey leads us to God and our scientific journey leads us to other intelligent beings? Then no honest scientist, theologian, or believer who played any role at all in these journeys would need to justify their part in humankind's great adventures of discovery.

Notes

1. E. G. Boring, *A History of Experimental Psychology* (New York: Century, 1929).

2. W. James, *The Principles of Psychology* (New York: Holt, 1890), p. 924.

3. W. James, *Pragmatism* (New York: Longmans, 1907), pp. 76–77.

4. J. Bruner, *Actual Minds, Possible Worlds* (Cambridge, Mass.: Harvard University Press, 1986); L. Cochran, *Portrait and Story* (Westport, Conn.: Greenwood, 1986); G. S. Howard, *A Tale of Two Stories: Excursions into a Narrative Approach to Psychology* (Notre Dame, Ind.: Academic Publications, 1989); M. Mair, *Between Psychology and Psychotherapy: A Poetics of Experience* (London: Routledge, 1989); D. McAdams, *Power, Intimacy and the Life Story* (Homewood, Ill.: Dorsey, 1985); D. P. Polkinghorne, *Narrative Psychology* (Albany: SUNY Press, 1988); T. R. Sarbin, ed., *Narrative Psychology: The Storied Nature of Human Conduct* (New York: Praeger, 1986); D. Spence, *Narrative Truth and Historical Truth* (New York: Norton, 1982); E. Stone, *Black Sheep and Kissing Cousins* (New York: Penguin, 1988).

5. G. S. Howard, "The Role of Values in the Science of Psychology," *American Psychologist* 40 (1985): 255–65; T. Kuhn, *The Essential Tension* (Chicago: University of Chicago Press, 1977); E. McMullin, "Values in Science," in P. D. Asquith and T. Nickles, eds., *Proceedings of the 1982 Philosophy of Science Association,* vol. 2 (East Lansing, Mich.: Philosophy of Science Association, 1983), pp. 3–23.

6. S. Toulmin, *Human Understanding* (Princeton, N.J.: Princeton University Press, 1972), p. x.

7. J. S. Efran, R. J. Lukens, and M. D. Lukens, "Constructivism: What's In It for You?" *The Family Therapy Networker* 12 (1988): 26–35; K. J. Gergen, "The Social Constructionist Movement in Modern Psychology," *American Psychologist* 40 (1985): 266–75; S. Scarr, "Constructing Psychology: Making Facts and Fables for Our Times," *American Psychologist* 40 (1985): 499–512.

8. Polkinghorne, *Narrative Psychology*; Mair, *Between Psychology and Psychotherapy*; G. S. Howard, (1991). *op. cit.*

9. Howard, *Tale of Two Stories.*

10. S. C. Wilson and T. X. Barber, "Vivid Fantasy and Hallucinatory Abilities in the Life Histories of Excellent Hypnotic Subjects ('Somnambules'): Preliminary Report with Female Subjects," in E. Klinger, ed., *Imagery, Volume 2, Concepts, Results and Applications* (New York: Plenum Press, 1981).

11. W. Strieber, *Communion: A True Story* (New York: Avon, 1987).

12. To paraphrase the Gospel of Matthew 13:57.

13. Social scientists have a long tradition of putting a decidedly negative spin on the role of religion in human lives. For example, Karl Marx considered religion to be the "opiate of the masses," while Sigmund Freud saw all religion as infantile attempts at wish fulfillment (S. Freud, "The Future of an Illusion," in James Strachey, ed., *The Standard Edition of the Complete Psychological Works of Sigmund Freud,* vol. 21 [London: Hogarth Press, 1961], pp. 3–56 [original work published in 1927]). However, from the pragmatic point of view (W. James, *Pragmatism: A New Name for Some Old Ways of Thinking* [New York: Longmans, Green & Co., 1907]; W. James, *The Varieties of Religious Experience: A Study in Human Nature* [New York: Longmans, Green & Co., 1902]; W. James, *A Pluralistic Universe: Hibbert Lectures at Manchester College on the Present Situation in Philosophy* [New York: Longmans, Green & Co., 1909]), such attempts to "explain away" religion miss the point of religion completely. The present authors agree with James's view in this regard.

14. In spite of our overall positive evaluation of religion, the authors

recognize that religious belief is rarely an unqualified good. For example, in spite of the tremendous good that the Catholic Church has produced over the years, it is still is at least partially responsible for the Crusades, the Inquisition, the Hundred Years' War, the current strife in Northern Ireland, and many other regrettable historical events.

15. Recognize that a believer in a particular worldview is the person least likely to be able to list that perspective's drawbacks. Thus, if readers have a difficult time imagining the downside to any of the worldviews noted above, they might need to do some homework. For example, for all the benefits of free-market capitalism, it has been criticized for what it does to the working class (by Karl Marx) and more recently for the ecological destruction it wreaks upon our earth (see G. Hardin, *Living within Limits: Ecology, Economics and Population Taboos* [New York: Oxford University Press, 1993]; G. S. Howard, *Ecological Psychology: Creating a More Earth-Friendly Human Nature* [Notre Dame, Ind.: University of Notre Dame Press, 1997]).

Appendix A

The UFO Contact Catalogue

A Chronological Listing of over Two Hundred Cases of Reported Communication between Aliens and Humans

1. 1906, South Dakota

Watching a craft land near a well, Herbert V. DeMott (age nine) approached it, and "a door rolled back and I was welcomed inside." The occupants, ordinary-looking men, "sat on camp stools." He was told the craft's outer shell contained "helium gas, and when the lever was moved the magnetism from the earth was cut off," which enabled the vessel to rise. The occupants took water from a horse trough for use "in making electricity."

Democrat-Herald (Albany, Oregon), August 27, 1973.

2. Late July 1909, Port Molyneux, New Zealand

An airship landed and the witness reportedly talked with its Japanese-appearing occupants.

The Bruce Herald (Milton, New Zealand), August 2, 1909, citing a 1909 letter sent to and published in *The Free Press* (Clutha, New Zealand).

3. 1912, western Canada, morning

A six-year-old boy living on a farm claims to have been in contact with "space men" in a round craft resembling a helicopter. The short male beings had no knees or elbows and had circular feet; they examined the boy, communicating telepathically.

John B. Musgrave, *UFO Occupants & Critters* (Amherst, Wis.: Amherst Press and Global Communications, 1980), pp. 40, 56, citing a personal phone conversation between John Brent Musgrave and the witness, in addition to a letter at the Center for UFO Studies, Evanston, Illinois.

4. Summer, 1920, Mattawa River, Ontario, Canada

As a teen, Albert Coe claims to have been walking in a rocky area and heard a young blond, blue-eyed boy caught in the rocks, yelling for help. He wore a silvery, leatherlike suit with broken "dials and instruments" on his chest. The boy said he had landed his "plane" nearby, stopping to fish. Helping him back to the "plane," Coe found a silver-colored saucer (about twenty feet in diameter) standing on three legs. The boy made Coe vow secrecy about the incident, and Coe pushed the boy up into the vessel, which flew off.

Coe claims a series of contacts with the being over the years, often fishing together. He was one of one hundred volunteers sent "at the turn of the century" to monitor Earth's technological development and encourage peace. The entity and his companions are from Tau Ceti but now live on Venus. They've placed an "ionized neutralizing screen" around Earth, preventing "any hydrogen chain reaction" which could destroy it. They have life spans of six hundred years, are vegetarians, and have the sole intent "to help their fellow man."

Daily News (Philadelphia, Pennsylvania), July 5–7, 1967, in articles by Jack Helsel.

5. August 20, 1924, Denver, Colorado

Mrs. H. C. Hutchinson claims to have received psychic messages from Elder Brothers on Mars. They said Martians colonized Earth two million years ago—building Atlantis, Lemuria, and Antarctic cities. Martians now live underground on Mars. She was told that Martians don't make love, but healthy, intelligent females have babies via parthenogenesis, which is frustrating to Martian men and one of the reasons they are visiting Earth—to reconquer it. ("Parthenogenesis" is defined in *Webster's* as "reproduction by the development of an unfertilized ovum, seed, or spore, as in certain insects, algae, etc.")

W. Raymond Drake, *Gods and Spacemen in the Ancient West* (New York: New American Library, 1974), p. 15, citing Robert Ernest Dickhoff, *Homecoming of the Martians* (Makelumna Hill, Calif.: Health Research).

6. 1924, Holy Name Convent School, Dade City, Florida, day

Mrs. Evelyn Wendt, beauty salon operator, recalls an incident fifty years earlier, when she was a schoolgirl playing in the yard of the Holy Name Convent School. "The first thing I remember is that this egg-shaped thing was on the ground, and this bright light was shining in my eyes." The light went out, a "hatch" opened, and little robot people emerged. "They were smaller than I and resembled animated flowers with faces where the bud would be. Remember, I was just a bitty thing then, and kids don't fear flowers."

They carried a weaponlike device to the school's science building. "I wanted to help them, but someone said, 'Stop.' I replied that they were so small, I was going to assist. The creatures let me try, but I couldn't even budge the machine. I was told they were going to stop the work that was being done in the science building and they said if the work continued, they would destroy the place." Asked what the "work" was, she said she didn't know. "All I know is later I heard the place was a shambles."

She said, "There seemed to be a man with the little people . . . everything looked real, even though I wasn't so sure. The conversation wasn't real talking," but she understood mentally what was being said. As they were leaving, "they asked if I wanted to go. I said, 'No,' but I could have gone." She adds, "They promised to come back for me in thirty-five years, but that was up a long time ago, and nothing happened that I know of." Then the "saucer" flew straight up, hovered a minute and disappeared.

Timothy G. Beckley, *Timothy G. Beckley's Book of Space Contacts* (New York: Global Communications, 1981), pp. 26–27, quoting from *The Weekday* newspaper (West Palm Beach, Florida).

7. October 15, 1928, Lake Geneva, Wisconsin

Farmer Velma Thayer claims a flying saucer landed and "little fellows" (blond and four feet six inches to five feet three inches tall) emerged and stayed for ten days. One of them, Ramu, said they hailed from Saturn and were part of a scout ship with peaceful intentions. She claims the U.S. military placed a single guard around the saucer and high-ranking officials inspected it. The saucer flew off when the guard fell asleep. Thayer says she occasionally makes contact with the beings.

Enquirer (Cincinnati, Ohio), August 1955.

8. May 4, 1932, 150 miles north of Toronto, Canada

A retired minister claims to have seen bright lights and visions when having to make important decisions about church affairs. "All at once the main street was lit up with the whitest of white lights. It was much brighter than the Sun at noon days . . . the City lights looked like globs of blood in the whiteness. The light came from 'a round Cloud' with an 'etched' or 'scalloped' outer edge . . . a light streamed down like a laser beam, which I've seen since." He then turned and saw "standing beside me . . . a young man with golden hair" and a similar colored suit. "He had radiant blue eyes, [was] about my height—he smiled, oh how beautiful he was. He told me my real work would be training . . . in that City, he said remember the cottage in the rear of the Mansions are as important as those who dwell in the mansions. . . ."

Personal letter from John B. Musgrave, citing a letter written to him by a retired (anonymous) minister, dated March 16, 1976. Musgrave is employed with the Mobile Planetarium Project of the Provincial Museum of Alberta, Edmonton, Canada.

9. 1932, New Jersey

At age ten, sign painter Howard Menger claims to have encountered "the most exquisite woman my young eyes had ever beheld." She had golden hair and eyes and wore a shiny, nylonlike seamless outfit similar to what a skier would wear. "I have come a long way to see you, Howard . . . and to talk with you." She "knew where I had come from and what my purpose would be on Earth." She said "her people" had been watching him for a long time and "we are contacting our own." The woman "answered questions before I could ask them . . . she seemed to know all my thoughts." She was "about my mother's height." She told Howard "of a great change to take place . . . wasteful wars, torture and destruction would be brought on by misunderstandings of people." Before leaving, she told him they would meet again and that "they will always be around—watching out for you . . . guiding you."

In his several subsequent contacts, he described the aliens as looking "just like we do," except for their dress. They "come from Mars, Saturn, Venus and probably Jupiter." Because they are "our brothers" and "love us," their purpose is to create a higher understanding "so we can help ourselves in preventing any future destruction of our planet." They are vegetarians, and have schools, cities, factories, and gardens. During a later contact, Menger says he was flown to the moon in a bell-shaped craft, and he saw many buildings and was able to breathe comfortably in the atmosphere.

Howard Menger, *From Outer Space* (New York: Pyramid, 1967), also published as *From Outer Space to You* (Clarksburg, W.Va.: Saucerian Press, 1959).

10. Winter, 1936, near Port Colborne, Ontario, Canada

At age fifteen, Johann Purchalski observed "a saucer type object" pass over Port Colborne and land in a nearby field. While investigating, he found a "space ship" and was introduced to the occupants. Johann said "they did not wish to cause any harm by killing any of the earth people." After being shown "their machinery, I left." He was given a metal badge which "states that [the ship] was owned by a member of the Planet Mars Police Force in the main city, Marsopolis."

Personal letter from John B. Musgrave, Mobile Planetarium Project at the Provincial Museum of Alberta, Edmonton, Canada, citing *Saucers, Space & Science,* 1965 yearbook, p. 21.

11. January 12, 1947, northeastern USA, 7:30 P.M.

At age forty-six, William Ferguson was heavily into meditation and relaxation techniques, and while in a deep meditation state he traveled at "the speed of consciousness" and reached Mars within ten seconds. A "great Celestial Being" greeted him and said he wanted to discuss "the observations that we have made of your planet . . . and we also want to tell you things that we want you to say to Earthlings." The "Celestial Being," called Khauga, showed him a great canal network and large cities enclosed in an electromagnetic field. Martians moved via levitation. They all had red hair and were about a foot shorter than humans, with broad features (not sharp) and red complexions. Their scientists (called Uniphysicists) dressed in cream-colored gold-trimmed robes and had shoulder-length hair. Ferguson was asked, "Is it true . . . people on your planet go out and kill one another in battle?" Khauga replied, "The very thought . . . to us is abhorrent." Martians "are twenty thousand years ahead of us in all kinds of thinking, consciousness, spiritual development, and scientific development." Knowing Earth has "been passing through a great crisis . . . and that they needed assistance," the Martians told Ferguson, "We are going to release positive energy particles into the Earth's atmosphere . . . to counteract the negative energy particles that man himself has released." Khauga wanted the following message relayed: "To all fellow Earthmen, I can assure you we are now in a wonderful development period in our Earth's history. We have entered the expansion phase of our development, and as a result, all things will become new and finer for the enjoyment and happiness for each and every being."

William Ferguson, *My Trip to Mars,* a 13-page pamphlet published by the Cosmic Study Center, 7405 Masters Drive, Potomac, Maryland 20854 USA, September 1954.

12. July 23, 1947, near Bauru, state of São Paulo, Brazil

Jose C. Higgins heard a high-pitched whistle as he watched a large grayish-white metallic disc land, resting on three legs. After his coworkers fled, he found himself alone with three seven-foot-tall entities in "transparent suits covering head and body, and inflated like rubber bags." They carried "metal boxes" on their backs. Clothing, visible through the suits, resembled brightly colored paper. The beings, all identical, had large bald heads, huge round eyes, no eyebrows, and legs longer in proportion than ours. Higgins found them strangely beautiful.

They surrounded him and apparently tried to lure him into the disc, but, seeing they shunned sunlight, he managed to elude them and hid nearby for half an hour. Watching from thick shrubs, he watched them move with extraordinary agility, frolicking about and tossing huge stones. They then reentered the craft and flew off.

Gordon Creighton, "The Humanoids in Latin America," in C. Bowen, ed., *The Humanoids* (Great Britain: Futura, 1977), pp. 88–89, citing *Diari da Tarde* (Curitiba), Brazil, August 8, 1947; *O Cruzeiro* (Rio de Janeiro), 1954; *La Razon* (Buenos Aires), Argentina, April 13, 1950; *Flying Saucer Review* 7 (November–December 1961), which cites a report from the Aerial Phenomena Research Organization.

13. 1948, Lineville, Alabama

An anonymous woman was drawing water from a well when a bright round object landed in a nearby cornfield. Two men with long hair and beards and wearing long robes emerged. One approached and told her in accented English not to be afraid, assuring her no harm if she would cooperate and answer some questions. After they talked for about thirty minutes, she ran into her house, but the other being stood in the doorway. The two beings then reentered the craft and flew off.

Alabama Times, March 25, 1973.

14. December 4, 1949, Volta Redonda, Brazil

Mario Restier claims to have been taken to an unknown planet in an object similar to a "bathtub" filled with liquid. He passed out during the trip and awoke upon landing to find a planet of handsome beings about five feet ten inches tall. Told to wear their clothing, he put on a toga and electric shoes and was shown a space museum, factories, and "study district." After staying for about three days, he returned to Earth and found four months had passed. Restier also claims a later contact.

SBEDV Bulletin, April 15, 1968; also *SBEDV Special Bulletin of Humanoid Cases*, 1975.

15. March 13, 1950, Penon de los Banos, Mexico

A ship "equipped with a powerful propeller" landed and a pilot emerged speaking Spanish. The Martian told a native that cities on Mars were underground and Venus was very hot, humid, and overrun with flying reptiles. He said Earth will destroy itself in World War III, after which Martians will colonize our planet. A strong sulphur smell filled the air as the ship left.

El Universal (Mexico City), March 14, 1950.

16. July 23, 1950, near Guyancourt Airport, France, 11 P.M.

Claude Blondeau saw two round objects "resembling two enormous folded napkins, one upside down on the other" hovering above the ground. A normal-sized man in a "flying suit" emerged from each craft. They "installed or moved" a "plate that rested on a base similar to rubber." Blondeau approached, asking if they were having trouble. One replied (in French), "Yes, but not for long." The inside was brilliantly lit and contained a chair next to a control console, with a large steering wheel. Asking how the ship was operated, the man replied, "Energy." The being reentered the craft, the portholes glowing as it left. The entire episode lasted two minutes.

Jimmy Guieu, *Flying Saucers Come from Another World* (London: Hutchinson, 1956), pp. 229–31.

17. Summer 1950, Manitoba, Canada

After seeing an NBC-TV documentary in January 1979 on UFO abductions, Virginia Horton (pseudonym) told UFO investigator Budd Hopkins that at age six on her grandfather's Manitoba farm, while going to gather eggs in a barn, she remembered standing in the yard and her leg being wet. Her left leg had a painless one-half-inch-deep by one-inch-long incision, but no tear in her jeans. She requested regressive hypnosis, which was performed by New York psychologist Dr. Aphrodite Clamar in 1979. She told that while walking to the barn, she was suddenly lying on a "couch" and seeing "plenty of light" (soft grayish in tint). She was told that her leg cut wouldn't hurt, "that they need a little bitty piece of you for understanding." An unseen being said, "We're from a long way away" in the sky and that there are many inhabited worlds similar to Earth. The being said his place of origin was "nice" and "he was very happy." He offered to take her at a later time to visit other worlds, but cautioned: "Your Mom would be upset if we went away for a while."

Horton was reminded by her mother (during a 1979 phone conversation) that ten years later, while on a picnic with her parents in a wooded area in France, she emerging from the woods with blood on her blouse and no apparent memory of what happened. Under hypnosis with Dr. Clamar, she recalled hearing her name being called telepathically, and she walked to a grounded UFO, was escorted inside and made to feel happy. Tissue and blood samples from inside her nose were taken. She was told to forget the experience.

Budd Hopkins, *Missing Time: A Documented Study of UFO Abductions* (New York: Richard Marek, 1981), pp. 128–53, 184–215.

18. July 1951, Atlanta, Georgia

Fred Reagan claims that while flying his Piper Cub, a bright "lozenge" collided with him, causing the plane to crash from a height of eight thousand feet. After several seconds he stopped falling and was drawn up into the object. Inside was a trio of three-feet-high beings looking like "stalks of metallic asparagus." Reagan passed out and later regained consciousness, finding himself lying on a soft substance and hearing a mechanical-sounding voice. It said, "We have corrected an abnormality in your body, called cancer . . . we offer this as slight reparation for the loss we have caused you." The beings were on Earth "to observe" our "primitive civilization." He passed out again and awakened in a hospital after being found near his wrecked plane. Reagan reportedly died soon after from brain tissue degeneration due to radiation exposure.

Action Magazine, May 1955.

19. 1951, Spain

Someone named Bordas claims to have met and supplied food to aliens and has since been contacted regularly. They come from "Titan."

Jacques Vallee, *Messengers of Deception* (New York: Bantam, 1980), pp. 59, 90–93, originally published in June 1979, Berkeley, Calif.: And/Or Press.

20. May 23, 1952, Los Angeles, California, 12:45 P.M.

Orfeo Angelucci suffers a prickling sensation in the hands, arms, back, and feet during the approach of thunderstorms, and claims similar "symptoms" just prior to or after alien contact. He claims to have seen a flying saucer in Trenton, New Jersey, August 4, 1946. Contact was allegedly made on May 23, 1952. Driving home from work just outside Los Angeles, he felt a prickling sensation while observing a red, luminous, oval-shaped object in the sky. Angelucci followed it off a side, road where it hovered above a field. Several beings appeared on a luminous screen, communicating telepathically. He was told that friendly, helpful beings were visiting Earth because life on Earth was at a crisis point.

During a later contact (August 2, 1952), he described meeting a spaceman who was taller than he, well-built, wearing a tight-fitting, seamless uniform. The alien was totally solid but wavered like a ghost. He said Earth was called "the home of sorrows" and we face a crisis which in history will be known as "the Great Accident." Space people are here to assist humanity during this critical period.

Bryant Reeve and Helen Reeve, *Flying Saucer Pilgrimage* (Amherst, Wis.: Amherst Press, 1957), pp. 222–32.

21. Late July 1952, near Mormon Mesa, Nevada, about 5 A.M.

Falling asleep in his truck in the Nevada desert, Truman Bethurum awoke surrounded by "eight to ten small men, all about four feet eight inches to five feet high." He said the beings were fully developed men. They spoke English, saying, "We have no trouble with any language." Bethurum was invited aboard a nearby saucer-shaped "space scow" and was introduced to their captain, Aura Rhanes, whose "smooth skin was beautiful olive and roses." The thirty-two-man crew were "Latin types . . . [with complexions] something like Italians." All were neatly dressed in uniforms similar to those "worn by Greyhound bus drivers." All had coal-black hair and dark eyes. Aura Rhanes wore a black skirt and red blouse. She was four and a half feet tall, and she said they hailed from the planet Clarion. They came to Earth to rekindle old values like family and home in order to prevent a nuclear holocaust and bring humanity closer to God. Bethurum wasn't told how old Aura was because, like Earth women, she was cautious about revealing her age, but she assured him she was "under a thousand." Based on conversations with Captain Rhanes, Bethurum predicted that "there will be no atomic or hydrogen warfare, ever," and that "our five-year-old children of today will not marry soldiers. We are on the threshold of a lasting peace and prosperity era."

Truman Bethurum's personal scrapbook (original copy), courtesy of Robert C. Girard, UFO book dealer, Scotia, New York.

22. October 14, 1952, Bakersfield, California, 9:30 A.M.

Auto repair shop owner Cecil Michael observed a flying saucer with two humanlike occupants near Bakersfield in mid-August. He viewed the craft "too closely" and "had been spotted and tagged for a return visit."

At about 9:30 A.M. on October 14, Michael was working alone in his shop when two "big men" (some 220 pounds and about six feet tall) walked in. They had "medium dark" complexions, were "smooth-shaven" and "athletic" appearing. They asked telepathically: "Did we scare you, Red?" "You sure as hell did," he replied. The beings stayed for a couple of months, vanishing whenever customers came.

One day, the beings put Michael in a "trance" state, taking him on a telepathic trip. He was tied up inside a saucer, and the two beings took him to an orange planet that was very hot (about one hundred degrees), where he met the "devil." Suddenly, "In the middle of a light, Christ appeared in plain view. . . . I turned to the old bum [the devil] and, pointing my hand to the light, said, "If you don't let me go, He will send for me." The devil responded: 'Yes, He is always interfering.' " Michael was returned to Earth after spending about two and a half weeks on the planet. Upon returning, the two space beings tried to regain his friendship, asking him to write the story of the incident with the devil for the benefit of humanity. The beings then left, never to return.

Cecil Michael, *Round Trip to Hell in a Flying Saucer* (Auckland, New Zealand: Phoenix, 1971), originally published by Vantage Press, n.p., 1955.

23. November 20, 1952, California desert, afternoon

Prior to his initial contact, George Adamski claims to have taken over five hundred photos of UFOs. After several unsuccessful expeditions to the California desert in hopes of meeting aliens, he reported contact on November 20. A "gigantic cigar-shaped silvery ship without wings or appendages" landed in a flash of light. A man from Venus, shorter than Adamski, but generally human in appearance, with long, beautiful golden hair, emerged. They communicated telepathically for about an hour. "Orthon" said the friendly Venusians "are concerned about the buildup of radioactivity in the

Earth's atmosphere. They feel the radiation from the U.S. and Russian atomic tests is a danger to our planet." On several future occasions Adamski claims contacts with space beings, frequently being invited to board ships from Venus, Mars, Saturn, and Jupiter, often enjoying the company of "beautiful" female inhabitants. The beings were normal enough in appearance that they often made contact with humans in bars and nightclubs before inviting them aboard. An elderly space being, "The Master," told Adamski that the space people came to save Earth from nuclear destruction and that Adamski had been selected to warn humankind.

George Adamski, *Inside the Spaceships* (New York: Abelard-Schuman, 1955).

24. 1952, Angatuba Mountains, state of São Paulo, Brazil

Aladina Felix (alias Dino Kraspedon) claims that a bell-shaped UFO landed in the mountains, and he entered it and made contact. One of the occupants, a man over six feet tall, told him they lived on Io and Ganymede (two moons of Jupiter), where there were races of tall, medium, and small people, including races of black, white, and red-skinned beings. The craft then left.

In March 1954, Felix claims a male Venusian pilot came to his house in a cashmere suit, white shirt, and blue tie. They have met on numerous occasions since, discussing flying saucers, how they fly, and the universe.

In 1965, Felix warned of disasters to hit São Paulo, and in 1968 predicted a wave of violence in the city. He was correct. In 1968 public buildings and police stations were dynamited. When the perpetrators were caught, Felix was named as leader and arrested on August 22, 1968. The group reportedly planned to take over Brazil via a series of assassinations.

Dino Kraspedon, *My Contact with Flying Saucers* (London: Neville Spearman, 1959); John A. Keel, *Why UFOs* (New York: Manor, 1970), pp. 261–63; also published as *UFOs: Operation Trojan Horse* (New York: Putnam's Sons, 1970); Gordon Creighton, "The Humanoids in Latin America," in Charles Bowen, ed., *The Humanoids* (Great Britain: Futura, 1977), p. 90, citing in part, Dino Kraspedon, *Meu Contacto com os Discs Voadores* (Rio de Janeiro, 1958), the original Portuguese edition of *My Contact with Flying Saucers*.

25. 1952, Lomo de Ballena, Peru, 4:30 P.M.

Driving north on the Pan-American Highway, an anonymous male identified only as C.A.V. said he saw a shining metallic, sandy-colored disc hovering just above the ground. He approached it and three "mummylike" figures (five feet tall) emerged. Their legs were "joined together" like "twin bananas" standing on "one large foot." Their "head had no features" except for a transparent jelly-like substance "with a bubble in the middle" where the eyes should be. They were naked, showed "no sign of sex," and had "towely skin." They asked (in English) if they were in North America. Upon being told it was South America, they spoke Spanish. They came from another star, they said, and asked C.A.V. to take them to his leader. "They were frightened that, by playing . . . with atomic explosions . . . we would not only destroy the world but endanger the universe." They never "fought over silly things like flags and lands" and "had no sex problems like us humans." In fact, they "did not practice sex," claiming to be asexual, reproducing by fission. During the encounter, one did so. C.A.V. boarded the craft, was taken on a brief trip and returned. The beings then flew off.

Jim Lorenzen and Coral Lorenzen, *UFOs over the Americas* (London: N.E.L. [Signet Paperback, 1968]), pp. 122–48; *Flying Saucer Review* 16, no. 6 (1970): 12.

26. Between August 17 and 20, 1953, Ciudad Valleys, Mexico, 6 P.M.

Working underneath his broken-down vehicle on the side of a highway, Salvador Villanueva, a Mexican taxicab driver noticed two pairs of legs standing nearby. He discovered two pleasant-looking men, each about four and a half feet tall and clad in one-piece "seamless gray corduroy" garments from neck to toe, with wide shiny boxes on their backs. Under their arms they held "helmets like those worn by pilots or by American football players." As many Mexican Indians are short, their height didn't alarm him.

Only one of the men spoke (in Spanish), "stringing the words together" in a strange accent, while the other apparently understood the conversation but did not speak. At first they discussed trivial matters, including his car. Then, at one point, the man said,

"We are not of this planet. We come from one far distant, but we know much about your world."

At dawn Villanueva went with them to their saucer-shaped craft, located in a clearing by the road. They crossed a swampy area in which Villanueva's legs sank deeply, but the legs of both men remained clean. "When their feet touched the muddy pools, their belts glowed, and the mud sprang away as if repelled by some invisible force."

Villanueva was invited aboard the craft, which stood on three great metal spheres, but he declined and ran away. The craft rose, began glowing intensely, then shot off at fantastic speed.

Gordon Creighton, "The Humanoids in Latin America," in Charles Bowen, ed., *The Humanoids* (Great Britain: Futura), pp. 90–91, citing Desmond Leslie, "Mexican Taxi Driver Meets Saucer Crew?" in *Flying Saucer Review* 5 (March/April 1959): 8.

27. March, 1954, near Santa Maria, state of Rio Grande do Sul, Brazil

Rubem Hellwig claims to have twice contacted aliens. The first encounter (March 1954) occurred as he was driving down a road and saw a melon-shaped craft about the size of a Volkswagon car resting near the road. The crew consisted of two men (about five feet tall) with slim builds and brown faces. Hellwig stopped the car and approached. One man was inside the object and the other was collecting specimens of grass. Hellwig claims he somehow understood what they asked him, which was where could they get some ammonia. After he directed them to a nearby town, the craft emitted bright blue and yellow flames as it vanished silently and instantly.

Early the next day, Hellwig claimed to have contacted a similar machine but with a different crew. The trio said they were scientists, they spoke enthusiastically of Brazil's natural resources, and were surprised that unlike other people they encountered, Hellwig didn't flee in fear.

Gordon Creighton, "The Humanoids in Latin America," in Charles Bowen, ed., *The Humanoids* (Great Britain: Futura, 1977), pp. 91–92, citing *Diario de Noticias* (Rio de Janeiro), August 25, 1965.

28. August 15, 1954, Dewey County, Oklahoma, day

Gladys White Eagle claims to have heard a loud noise and seen a flying saucer land near a riverbank. A tall, thin, dark-skinned male with a long beard emerged and said the United States would be destroyed by an earthquake and a bomb on October 13, then he laughed. He told her to return to the same location on September 17, but she was too frightened.

Daily News (Clinton, Oklahoma), September 17, 1954, p. 1; *Daily News*, September 19, 1954, p. 1.

29. October 4, 1954, Chaleix, Dordogne, France

A cauldron-shaped object about the size of a small truck landed in a Mr. Garreau's field. A door opened and two normal European-looking men in brown coveralls emerged and shook hands with him. They asked, "Paris? North?" The farmer was so shocked he didn't reply. The beings then stroked his dog before they flew off.

Jacques Vallee, *Passport to Magonia* (Chicago: Henry Regnery, 1969), p. 226.

30. October 12, 1954, Montlucon, France, evening

A railroad worker, Mr. M. Laugere, encountered a metallic torpedo-shaped object near a gas-oil tank. A being "covered with hair or wearing a long, hairy overcoat" stood nearby. Laugere asked what he wanted, and the being spoke a word that sounded like "gasoil." As Laugere fled, the craft flew away.

Christian Science Monitor, October 15, 1954. Jacques Vallee, *Passport to Magonia* (Chicago: Henry Regnery, 1969), p. 226.

31. October 12, 1954, Sainte-Marie d'Herblay, France, 10:30 P.M.

Gilbert Lelay was walking and saw a "phosphorescent cigar" in a pasture and a man in a gray suit, boots, and gray hat nearby. The man put his hand on Lelay's shoulder and said in French, "Look, but don't touch." He held a flashing sphere emitting purple rays in his other hand. He then reentered the craft, which had colored lights and what appeared to be a control console. The door shut, the object rose up, made two loops, and flew off while radiating light.

Jacques Vallee, *Passport to Magonia* (Chicago: Henry Regnery, 1969), p. 147.

32. October 14, 1954, island of d'Oleron, Bay of Biscay, France

Jules Martin, a schoolmaster, claims to have encountered two beautiful females from Mars. They wore leather helmets, boots, and gloves. The pair borrowed his pen to write down hieroglyphs, then left—apparently flying off.

Harold T. Wilkins, *Flying Saucers Uncensored* (New York: Pyramid, 1974), p. 245, originally published in 1955 by Citadel Press (New York).

33. 1954, near Lansing, Michigan

Charles A. Laughead, staff medical officer at Michigan State University, Lansing, Michigan, began communicating with beings from "outer space" mainly via trance mediums. After receiving several prophecies that came true, an alien called Ashtar told him the world would end December 21, 1954, when North America would split in two, with the Atlantic coast sinking into the ocean. Also, France, England, and Russia would sink. Ashtar said Laughead and a few select followers would be saved by spaceships. On that day, he and a small group of believers gathered in a garden to be rescued. They were told not to wear metal items and thus discarded their pens, belt buckles, cigarette lighters, etc. Nothing happened.

John A. Keel, *Why UFOs* (New York: Manor, 1970), pp. 260–61.

34. 1954, Raon-l'Etape, Vosges, France, 2:30 A.M.

A Czechoslovakian citizen living in France, Lazlo Ujvari was heading for work starting at 3 A.M. when he met a portly man of medium height a quarter mile from his house. The man wore a gray jacket with shoulder insignias, a motorcycle helmet and was carrying a gun. After the man addressed Ujvari in an unknown language, Ujvari tried speaking Russian, to which the stranger immediately responded, asking in a high-pitched voice, "Where am I? In Italy, in Spain?" He then asked how far he was from the German border, and, "What time is it?" Ujvari replied, "It's 2:30." The being then pulled out a watch and bluntly snapped, "You lie—it is four o'clock." He then inquired how far and in what direction Marseilles was. He had Ujvari walk on the road with him. They soon came upon a grayish saucer-shaped craft (three feet high and five feet in diameter with an antenna on top) on the road. Ujvari approached to within thirty feet when the man told him to move away. The object soon flew off "with the noise of a sewing machine."

Jacques Vallee, *The Invisible College* (New York: E. P. Dutton paperback edition, 1976), pp. 26–27; Jacques Vallee, *Passport to Magonia* (Chicago: Henry Regnery, 1969), pp. 146–47; Allan Hendry, *The UFO Handbook* (New York: Doubleday, 1979), p. 141.

35. August 30, 1955, Mulberry Corners, Ohio, 1:45 A.M.

Driving home, David Ankenbrandt saw a bright yellow light land. He stopped, approached and found a domed craft (thirty feet in diameter). A paralyzing green ray hit him and a man (at least six feet tall) in a one-piece outfit came out and said in a high-pitched voice to tell the government to stop all wars. The being reentered the object and flew off. Two days later, Ankenbrandt went to the spot and encountered the same being, who repeated the earlier message.

Report filed by O. D. Hill, *Project Bluebook.*

36. 1955, Toronto, Canada

An inner circle of twelve people claim to have made "tele-contact" with "saucer people." Their voice carried an unearthly accent which varied depending on which planet a particular speaker was from. They found English difficult to speak and said they had to learn it before being able to communicate with the group. One of the lectures was on vegetarianism.

Personal letter from John B. Musgrave, employee of the Mobile Planetarium Project at the Provincial Museum of Alberta, Edmonton, Canada, citing the publication *Canadian Flying Saucers* by Michael, pp. 3–4.

37. 1955, near Jacksonville, Florida, late afternoon

At age nine, Lydia Stalnaker was with her bother and sister walking on a dirt road to her parents' farm. A bright light suddenly flashed and a man appeared on the road. They panicked, fleeing and "hysterically crying." For several days the three were scared. A search of the area revealed nothing. The children's "fearful dreams" continued. One night in August 1974, Stalnaker (now a divorcée with two daughters) saw a bright light while driving near Jacksonville, Florida. She pulled off the road to get a better view. Another car stopped and a vaguely familiar man sat watching with her, commenting, "Yes, and it's right on time." He was under five feet five inches with a dark complexion. At his suggestion, at about 9 P.M. they drove in his car to the site of what she thought was a crashed plane. She began having breathing difficulties and next recalled returning to Jacksonville with the man, her forehead hurting and stomach nauseated. When she reached her car it was midnight, but it seemed just a few minutes had passed. She felt sick for several days but soon felt better. She then began hearing mysterious voices encouraging her to improve her physical condition. She obeyed, taking vitamins, fasting, taking karate lessons, and finding "religion again." She also experienced nightmares of being operated on by masked people in a brightly illuminated room. After seeking psychiatric aid no mental problems could be detected.

In May 1975, Arizona hypnotist Dr. Art Winkler suggested that she may have seen a UFO during the unaccountable time, something she doubted. Under hypnosis she experienced intense pain (yelling, screaming, gasping for air), and the session was ended. Dr. James Harder later hypnotized her, and in combination with partial-memory conscious recall Stalnaker told of being put on an operating table after boarding a UFO. She saw three types of beings. One was a "large, fearsome-looking creature with no hair, large ears . . . small facial features—small cheekbones and mouth—but large fire-red eyes and ash gray skin." The other types appeared to be subservient. One closely resembled humans but were extremely attractive and had tannish-gold skin. She was stuck with needles while on the table, and the beings tried to reassure her despite the pain. They said she was "chosen . . . because of her chemistry."

Stalnaker also remembered under hypnosis being abducted at age nine, taken aboard a UFO with similar-type creatures, and undergoing a similar experience on an operating table. They "took knowledge out of my head—they know all about me." They said she had been "chosen" and they would return. Stalnaker saw her brother and sister also being examined. The being said they hailed "from a galaxy to the right of our galaxy" and they have a base off the Florida coast under the ocean. She also claims to be able to heal the sick after the encounters. "The aliens told me I was going to get it."

Alan Gansberg and Judith Gansberg, *Direct Encounters: The Personal Histories of UFO Abductees* (New York: Walker & Walker, 1980).

38. April 7, 1956, Drakensberg, South Africa, early morning

After sighting UFOs on several previous occasions, on April 7 Elizabeth Klarer got a feeling to return to her parents' farm. She walked to a nearby hill where she had seen UFOs before, and a huge metallic spacecraft rested there. A man (six feet six inches tall) stood by the saucer. He had longer than normal hair which was white at the temples, a deeply lined face and gray eyes. His cheekbones were high and prominent, his eyes slanting strangely toward the temples. He wore a one-piece cream-colored suit. He took Elizabeth's hand, saying, "Not afraid this time?" Akon said he and another similar-looking man on the ship were from the planet Menton, 4.2 light-years from Earth. The ship had three rooms: a main cabin, a cooking and eating section and a bathroom. Akon had contacted Klarer for breeding purposes, as their race needed new blood. She was chosen for one of their experiments. They fell in love and had a son, Alying, whom she visits often along with Akon on Menton. Elizabeth says Menton has no politics, war, or disease. She communicated both by speech and telepathically.

Natal Witness (South Africa), April 16, 1983. Cynthia Hind, *UFOs: African Encounters* (Zimbabwe: Gemini, 1982), pp. 21–43.

39. July 17, 1956, Van Nuys, California, 4:20 A.M.

Todd Kittredge was awakened by a loud noise and his barking dogs and watched an eight-feet gold-colored sphere land in his yard. Three men about six feet five inches tall with long blond hair and green one-piece outfits came out. Todd shook hands with them, and they said in mechanical-sounding voices that they hailed from Venus and were on a mission to help Earthlings. Todd claimed several later encounters.

C.S.I. Newsletter, no. 6; *Project Bluebook.*

40. April 1957, near Pajas Blancas Airport, Cordoba, Argentina

Riding along a road, a man's motorcycle quit. Dismounting to investigate, he hides in a nearby ditch upon noticing a large disc near the ground just ahead. A man (about five feet eight inches tall) emerges, gently coaxing the motorcyclist out of the ditch then stroking his forehead to calm him. The stranger wore a tight-fitting outfit similar to a diver's suit, apparently made of some kind of plastic.

Entering the craft, the man saw five or six similarly dressed men seated before instrument panels. An intensely bright light filled the cabin, which had several large square portholes. After the man was escorted back to his motorcycle, his companion placed a hand on his shoulder and then reentered the disc, which appeared to be of an iridescent bluish-green metallic composition. It then flew rapidly away.

Gordon Creighton, "The Humanoids in Latin America," in Charles Bowen, ed., *The Humanoids* (Great Britain: Futura, 1977), pp. 98–99, citing *Diario de Cordoba* (Cordoba), Argentina, May 1, 1957, and Charles Bowen, "A South American Trio," *Flying Saucer Review* 11 (January/February 1965): 19.

41. July 1957, Croara Ridge, near Rome, Italy, day

After eating lunch, Luciano Galli left home and was headed back to work when a black car pulled up and a man he had met once on a Rome street asked him to take a ride. He agreed, and a third man drove them to a saucer by Croara Ridge. Galli followed the tall, dark-complexioned, black-eyed man into the craft. Suddenly, two lights flashed and he was told, "We have just taken your picture." He was taken for a ride to a nearby two-thousand-foot-long cigar-shaped space station, which several saucers were entering and leaving. They went into a chamber with "four or five hundred people there . . . standing and walking around." After touring the complex, Galli was returned to Croara Ridge. The whole episode lasted less than four hours.

John A. Keel, *Why UFOs* (New York: Manor, 1970), pp. 186–87, also published as *UFOs: Operation Trojan Horse* (New York: Putnum's Sons, 1970).

42. July 1957, Bela Island, Brazil, evening

Brazillian lawyer Joao de Freitas Guimaraes was walking alone on a beach when a pot-bellied object surfaced and came ashore. Two men, about five feet ten inches tall wearing tight green uniforms, emerged. He tried Portuguese, Italian, English, and French, but they didn't understand anything. The pair helped him climb the long ladder into the craft. As the ship flew off, water splashed against the portholes. Guimaraes asked if it was raining, and he got a telepathic reply. For the forty minutes they flew in the upper atmosphere he felt pain, along with a cold feeling in his genitals. He was then dropped off at the same spot he was picked up.

John A. Keel, *Why UFOs* (New York: Manor, 1970), pp. 187–88, also published as *UFOs: Operation Trojan Horse* (New York: Putnum's Sons, 1970).

43. August 20, 1957, near Quilino, province of Cordoba, Argentina, evening

On a mission with two other officers to guard a downed air force plane until proper men and equipment could reach the site and recover it, an unnamed male officer was left alone in a tent while his companions went for supplies. He heard a high-pitched hum; and a large, bright metal disc was hovering above him. The disc slowly descended, causing grass and plants to flutter wildly. Frantically tugging on his gun, the officer could not unholster it. A gentle voice (in Spanish) said not to fear, explaining that the interplanetary spaceship had a base in the nearby province of Salta. "We intend to help you," it said, "for the misuse of atomic energy threatens to destroy you." The voice then predicted that the entire world would soon know of the saucers. Bushes and trees rustled as the craft flew off.

Gordon Creighton, "The Humanoids in Latin America," in Charles Bowen, ed., *The Humanoids* (Great Britain: Futura, 1977), p. 100, citing *Diario de Cordoba*, August 22, 1957; *Flying Saucer Review* 11 (July/August 1965): 30; John A. Keel, *Why UFOs* (New York: Manor, 1970), p. 183, also published as *UFOs: Operation Trojan Horse* (New York: Putnum's Sons, 1970).

44. September 7, 1957, near Runcorn, Cheshire, England, 2:15 A.M.

James Cook saw a luminous object change from blue to white to blue and finally dark red. It then landed a few feet from him. A ladder came down and a voice said, "Jump onto the ladder. Do not step onto it. The ground is damp." Leaping on, he climbed into an empty room filled with a bright light. The voice instructed Cook to disrobe and put on plastic coveralls. He was asked to enter another nearby craft, agreed, and found twenty occupants there, all much taller than he. During the ride, Cook was told that the craft is from Zomdic, located in another galaxy, and that the ship can't operate in damp weather as it's surrounded by a type of electrified field. "The inhabitants of your planet will upset the balance if they persist in using force instead of harmony," the beings said. "Warn them of the danger." They also explained that their vehicles were used only in Earth's vicinity and couldn't function in outer space.

John A. Keel, *Why UFOs* (New York: Manor, 1970), pp. 185–86, also published as *UFOs: Operation Trojan Horse* (New York: Putnum's Sons, 1970).

45. October 15 and 16, 1957, near São Francisco de Sales, state of Minas Gerais, Brazil, night

During the night of October 15 and 16, farmer Antonio Villas Boas reportedly witnessed a birdlike object land nearby as he was plowing with a tractor. The craft stood on three legs and emitted a blinding red light and was covered with small purple lights. After his tractor engine stopped Boas ran, but he was grabbed by four people in rough, gray, one-piece garments and helmets. He was taken aboard, undressed, and seduced by an extremely fair-skinned, freckled young female with high cheekbones, a very pointed chin, and vivid "Chinese-type" slanted eyes. Regarding the sex act, Antonio said "It was a normal act, and she behaved just as any woman would. . . ." Shortly after the act, the woman "pointed at her belly and then pointed toward the sky." She stood five feet eight inches without a helmet.

Boas claimed they communicated to one another by a series of "barks," like a dog, but he couldn't understand it. They used strange instruments to take skin and blood samples, and then he was taken to the room with the woman, left alone, and they mated again. The rest of the crew (never seen without helmets or space-suits) were thought to be some five feet four inches. Boas was later let off the craft, and it flew away.

Gordon Creighton, "The Humanoids in Latin America," in Charles Bowen, ed., *The Humanoids* (Great Britain: Futura, 1977), pp. 101, 200–38, citing *SBEDV Bulletin*, no. 26/27 (April/July 1962); *Flying Saucer Review* 11 (January/February 1965, March/April 1965, July/August 1965); Antonio Villas Boas, "Declaration" (Depoimento), dated February 22, 1958, Rio de Janeiro, before Dr. Olava Fontes, M.D., and Senhor Joao Martins; Dr. Olava Fontes, M.D., "Medical Report on Antonio Villas Boas," Rio de Janeiro, February 22, 1958; Dr. Olava Fontes, M.D., Letter dated April 25, 1966, to Gordon Creighton; *Flying Saucer Review* 12 (July/August 1966), and various subsequent issues.

46. November 5, 1957, near Kearney, Nebraska, afternoon

Driving near Kearney, Reinhold Schmidt said his car quit while he saw a silver blimp-shaped object standing on four postlike legs twenty yards away. He approached the craft and a "staircase" came out, two middle-aged "men" emerged and searched him for weapons, then took him inside for half an hour, explaining they would be there for a while anyway, so he "might as well come inside."

The occupants, two men and two women (all middle-aged), wore ordinary clothing and were working on some wiring. Instead of walking, the beings "slid." Schmidt was told to tell people they meant no harm, and in "a short time" he might "know all about it." After being asked to leave, the ship silently lifted straight up and disappeared. After it left, Schmidt's car engine was able to be started.

Coral Lorenzen, "UFO Occupants in the United States," in Charles Bowen, ed., *The Humanoids* (Great Britain: Futura, 1977), p. 153, citing reports by United Press International, Associated Press, *Chicago Sun Times*, November 8, 1957.

47. November 6, 1957, near Playa del Rey, California, 5:40 A.M.

Richard Keyhoe claims that while driving along the Vista del Mar roadway, his engine stopped, as did those of three other cars. The drivers saw an egg-shaped object enveloped in a "blue haze" on the nearby beach. According to Keyhoe, two "little men" (five feet five inches tall) left the object and began asking questions of him and other drivers, such as "where we were going, who we were, what time it was, etc." Keyhoe said their skin was yellowish-green, but otherwise they were normal. They wore black leather pants, white belts and light-colored jerseys. After telling the beings he had to go to work, they reentered the ship and flew off. The presence of the other witnesses has never been corroborated.

Coral Lorenzen, "UFO Occupants in the United States," in Charles Bowen, ed., *The Humanoids* (Great Britain: Futura, 1977), pp. 156–57, citing *C.S.I. Newsletter*, December 1957.

48. November 6, 1957, Everittstown, New Jersey, evening

John Trasco walked outside to feed his dog and saw a brilliant egg-shaped object hovering in front of his barn. Confronted by a three-foot-tall being with large froglike eyes, Trasco thought the "little man" said, in broken English, "We are peaceful people, we only want your dog." Frightened, he replied, "Get the hell out of here."

Mrs. Trasco saw the object from inside the house, but the shrubbery prevented her from seeing the creature. It was dressed in a green suit with shiny buttons, a green tam-o-shanter-like cap, and gloves with a shiny object at the tip of each finger. His "putty-colored" face had a nose and chin. After Trasco yelled at the creature to leave, it fled into the craft, which took off rapidly. Trasco reportedly had a green powder on his wrist and under his fingernails, which washed off.

Coral Lorenzen, "UFO Occupants in the United States," in Charles Bowen, ed., *The Humanoids* (Great Britain: Futura), p. 156, citing the *Knoxville News-Sentinel* (Tennessee), 6, 1957; the *Delaware Valley News*, November 15, 1957; *C.S.I. Newsletter*, December 1957.

49. November 18, 1957, Cynthia Appleton house, Birmingham, England, 3 P.M.

While entering an upstairs sitting-room to check on her baby daughter, Mrs. Cynthia Appleton saw the figure of a "man" appear by the fireplace. The "image" appeared like a TV picture, first blurred, then clear. A whistling noise accompanied the materialization. The man was tall and fair, clad in a tight-fitting garb made of a plasticlike substance. He had shoulder-length hair and his lips moved as to speak, but she heard nothing. She then realized that questions in her mind were being answered telepathically.

The man said he was from another world and was looking for a certain substance, which Appleton thought sounded like "titium," but which her metal-worker husband later suggested might be titanium. She agreed that was the name. Through a mysterious process involving his hand, the stranger conveyed the picture of a saucer-shaped craft with a transparent dome. The visitor indicated that he came from a world of peace and harmony. At the end of the contact "suddenly he wasn't there anymore."

Appleton has since claimed several other contacts. During one encounter two beings appeared in her home and in a foreign-sounding English said they appear only to her because her brain was suitably fitted for such contacts. On one particular occasion she was told, "The Deity itself dwells at the heart and core of the atom."

Charles Bowen, "Few and Far Between," in Charles Bowen, ed., *The Humanoids* (Great Britain: Futura, 1977), pp. 17–18, citing "Birmingham Woman Meets Spacemen," *Flying Saucer Review* 4 (March/April 1958).

50. December 1957, El Cajon, California, night

Awakened by a roaring sound, Edmund Rucker saw an object land near his house. He saw four creatures with large heads through the lighted windows. When they emerged, he noticed they had domed foreheads and bulging eyes. They communicated to him in English their philanthropic and scientific motives.

Metempirical UFO Bulletin (MUFOB) 46, no. 12 (Autumn 1978): 9, citing *Flying Saucers Magazine* (July 1958). The account appears in MUFOB as part of Peter Rogerson's international catalogue of "type-1" UFO records.

51. December 1957, Snyders Lake, New York, night

Driving on Route 66 in the rain, Mr. L. Robinson saw an object fall into Snyders Lake. Investigating, he noticed a blue light being given off from a small semicircular object. A bluish-gold light flashed three times and three men of normal height appeared. They wore golden suits that radiated changing colors. One approached and talked to Robinson in "perfect English" for three hours. The men then left.

Metempirical UFO Bulletin (MUFOB), 14, no. 48 (Spring 1979): 10, citing *UFO Critical Bulletin* III 2: 5. Also, *Saucers, Space & Science* (March 1959). The account appears in MUFOB as part of Peter Rogerson's international catalogue of "type 1" UFO records.

52. 1957, Bayswater, western Australia, evening

Early one evening a "strange object in the sky" was seen by Mr. Laurie Campbell while he was driving with friends. Later the same evening, a five-feet two-inch being with "human features" came to his house and spoke telepathically "about various things." Campbell says, "Since then I have been obsessed with outer space."

Sunday Times (Perth), western Australia, September 16, 1984.

53. May 14, 1958, Sarandi, Brazil, 7 P.M.

Mr. A. Berlet was hitchhiking and saw a light on the ground. He approached it and found a round object (one hundred feet in diameter). When he was within about thirty yards of the object he was hit by a light and passed out. He awoke to find himself tied to a bed in the craft. He was untied and dressed in skin-tight clothing, then left the craft and walked through a city of large glowing buildings. He was fed meat and bread, felt unusually light, and given a bath in water that didn't feel heavy. After trying several languages, including Spanish and Italian, only German evoked a response. A guide called Acorc said that he was on Acart, thirty-one million miles from Earth. It has a population of ninety million in its capital city and is faced with serious overcrowding. They plan to colonize Earth soon, after we've destroyed ourselves. After eight days on the planet, Berlet was returned to Earth (three miles from Sarandi), but it took him three hours to walk home as he had to readjust to the heavy gravity.

SBEDV Special Bulletin, 1975, pp. 49–51, citing a publication by A. Berlet, *Discos Voadores da Utopia a Realidade*, published privately in Rio de Janeiro, 1967.

54. Approximately 1958, Miami Beach, Florida, night

Jessica Rolfe (pseudonym) was living at age five in Miami Beach, Florida, with her adoptive parents. One night three well-built, tall "men" with golden skin and brownish-gold hair materialized in her room. They lifted her from bed, telepathically saying, "Would you like to come with us now?" She replied, "No, I like it here." The men then returned her to bed and said it was okay, and then disappeared. Between ages five and fourteen, she claims various alien males from the same race would visit her bedside, teaching her many things. At age fourteen, she "chose" to ride in their spacecraft "powered by . . . magnetic energy and the energy of the navigator." The race of beings is highly evolved relative to Earth and often act as guides for other alien races visiting Earth. She decided to call them the Kuran race. According to their version of creation, several species of beings which once inhabited a planet in our solar system were offered the chance to be transported to other planets before their planet broke up into what is now the asteroid belt. Of the two races that agreed, Cro-Magnon was put on Earth; the other race went to a planet in the Pegasus constellation. Another alien race inhabited Earth at the time (known as Bigfoot today) but were unable to leave because of a transportation problem. Rolfe says she has read extensively in the paranormal.

Alan Gansberg and Judith Gansberg, *Direct Encounters: The Personal Histories of UFO Abductions* (New York: Walker & Walker, 1980), pp. 29–37.

55. April 18, 1961, Eagle River, Wisconsin, 11 A.M.

Watching a silvery object descend in his yard, chicken farmer Joe Simonton approached it without fear. A "hatch" opened and he saw three dark-skinned men inside. One of them handed him a silver-colored jug with two handles and made a motion like drinking, apparently indicating he wanted water. Simonton took the jug, filled it, and handed it back.

Looking into the object, he saw a man "cooking" or "frying" something on a flameless cooking apparatus. There were several small perforated cookielike objects beside the griddle, and Simonton motioned that he wanted some, whereupon one of the men handed him four. The craft then flew off rapidly. The beings appeared to be twenty-five to thirty years old and had dark hair. They were small (about five feet tall), wore dark blue knit outfits with turtlenecks and knit cloth (like that worn under race car drivers' helmets) covering part of the head. The entire episode lasted about five minutes.

An analysis of one of the cookies indicated it was made of corn, wheat flour, and other ordinary ingredients. Simonton tried a cookie and said it "tasted like cardboard."

Aerial Phenomena Research Organization Bulletin, May 1961, pp. 1–3.

56. Spring 1961, near Lake Huron, Michigan

An unnamed gas station owner near Lake Huron claims a flying saucer occasionally lands at a nearby island and beings from Venus talk to him, in English, sometimes in the presence of his wife and son. They are technologically advanced and visit Earth to promote lasting peace.

Aerial Phenomena Research Organization Bulletin, September 1961, p. 4.

57. July 1961, Massachusetts, night

Listening to various shortwave radio bands at home, Bob Renaud heard a "soft, warm, crystal-clear feminine voice" saying, "Bob, we'd like you to stay on this frequency for a while." During the next several months, space female Linn-Erri told him what was right and wrong with the world. He later claimed to talk with her over a TV set. She was a beautiful blonde of seventy-four years, "which in our society is the prime of life." On another occasion, three ordinary-looking men drove up and took him to a secret underground UFO base in Massachusetts.

John A. Keel, *Our Haunted Planet* (Conn.: Fawcett Gold Medal, 1971), pp. 183–84.

58. August 8, 1961, Alberta, Canada, 3:30 A.M.

Awakening from sleep, an unnamed man notices two small men standing next to his bed. He is suddenly paralyzed, but strangely content and fearless. The beings (four to five feet tall) were clad in dark-colored two-piece garments with a belt around the middle. One of the two "beautifully proportioned" men appeared older and had a receding hairline. They didn't walk, but floated. They spoke for about a minute, intimating that they would visit again. One of the visitors then said to the other, "I think he's waking up on us. We'd better go." The figures vanished while a hissing sound was heard. As soon as they disappeared the man was no longer frozen. His wife (also in the house) recounted a similar experience of seeing two men and being unable to move.

A neighbor claims at the same time the experience occurred to have seen a brilliant blue globe in front of the couple's house, which slowly flew off.

Aerial Phenomena Research Bulletin, April 1977, p. 6.

59. September 19–20, 1961, Indian Head, New Hampshire, about midnight

In what is perhaps the most well-publicized close-encounter case in UFO history, Betty and Barney Hill of Portsmouth, New Hampshire, were returning from a Canadian vacation. Driving on Route 3, Betty spotted a starlike object that began to pace their car, gradually growing in size. After watching it for about thirty miles, an unconcerned Barney was persuaded to stop, after Betty became hysterical. She believed the object to be of extraterrestrial origin. While Betty remained inside, Barney left the car and watched the "craft" seventy-five to one hundred feet off through binoculars. He saw a row of lights and six occupants. He ran back to the car, yelling to his wife that they were about to be captured. He sped off and they arrived home two hours late.

Ten days after the incident, Betty had a series of dreams which showed her and Barney being abducted by aliens and subjected to examinations aboard a spacecraft.

On February 22, 1962, Barney, after suffering from extreme tension and nervousness (apparently attributable to high blood pressure), sought prescribed hypnotic regression with Dr. Benjamin Simon, a psychiatrist and neurologist. Barney recounted how he and Betty had been escorted to a craft by short beings with large, hairless heads, slits for nostrils, and metallic skin. They were given medical exams and were told they would forget the experience and be released. Barney was given a posthypnotic suggestion by Dr. Simon that he would not be able to consciously recall the abduction. Then, unbeknownst to Betty, Simon regressed her and found a very similar abduction story. Betty was told the reason for her regression was medical in nature. She had no prior knowledge of Barney's story.

Betty told of having a needlelike instrument pushed into her navel during the alien exam. The beings said it was a pregnancy test. Barney had a cuplike device placed over his genitals and experienced coldness and pain there. After the incident he developed a mysterious ring of warts around his genitals.

Ronald Story, *Sightings* (New York: Quill, 1982); Coral Lorenzen and Jim Lorenzen, *Abducted!: Confrontations with Beings from Outer Space* (Berkeley, Calif.: Medallion, 1977); R. Sheaffer, *The UFO Verdict* (Amherst, N.Y.: Prometheus Books, 1981); J. G. Fuller, *The Interrupted Journey* (New York: Dial, 1977).

60. September 1961, near Salado River, Buenos Aires, Argentina

Fishing on a branch of the Salado River, a man saw an object (thirty-three feet in diameter) land nearby and approached it. Two beings (four and a half to five feet tall) wearing what appeared to be plastic diving suits came near him, inviting him aboard via drawings and signs. He was sprayed to protect him from the craft's interior atmosphere. The craft began whistling and rotating, then he was taken for a ride.

La Razon (Buenos Aires), October 3, 1961.

61. Late November 1961, northern plains of the USA, night

Returning from a hunting trip, four men were in a car driving through freezing rain and sleet. Only the driver was awake, who saw a brilliantly illuminated object descending one-half mile ahead to the right of the highway. They soon came upon the glowing tail of a silverish "silo-appearing type craft" protruding from the ground about one hundred fifty yards off and four "people" who were "standing around it." Thinking a plane had crashed, they pulled over and shone a flashlight on the scene. One of the "people" was close enough to be able to get a fairly good description—five feet five inches tall or less wearing a white coverall garment. They appeared to be humans. Surprisingly, "he made this gesture of, well, move back, or get out of here!" After summoning a highway patrolman they had passed earlier on the road, the men returned to the site to find everything gone. Seeing a taillight off in a field, they drove "right up behind this 'vehicle,' its lights went out and it vanished." There were no indications that any object had been there, despite heavy mud in the area. After the perplexed officer left, the men drove two miles and saw a glowing object land one hundred fifty yards away. One of the hunters then shot toward the object, hitting "the right shoulder of one of the 'forms.' " It spun to its knees, "got up with the other guys' assistance . . . and said, or hollered, 'Now what the hell did you do that for?' " The men ran back to the car and drove off. They also reported a period of lost time en route home.

J. A. Hynek and J. Vallee, *The Edge of Reality: A Progress Report on Unidentified Flying Objects* (Chicago: Henry Regnery, 1975), pp. 129–42, based on a transcribed taped interview with one of the witnesses, conducted by a U.S. Treasury agent who wished to be anonymous.

62. 1961, one hundred miles from Welland, Ontario, Canada

A Canadian now living in Auckland, New Zealand, Mr. I. Boyes claims he was telepathically attracted to a spacecraft one hundred miles from his Ontario home. He hitchhiked to the spot and was taken aboard a circular craft (one hundred feet in diameter). The three crewmen said they came from the Earth's "coniferous" age (coniferous refers to pine trees!) and time-traveled to the present.

They had white hair, bronze skin, and spoke highly accented English. Boyes says he was picked to help form a group, which he is presently promoting, called "Integral Structures Utopia."

Personal letter from John B. Musgrave, employee of the Mobile Planetarium Project at the Provincial Museum of Alberta, Edmonton, Canada, citing the *New Zealand Herald*, April 24, 1972.

63. Approximately 1961, Brown Mountain, near Morganton, North Carolina, night

Investigating the source of mysterious nocturnal lights often seen on Brown Mountain, Ralph Lael made contact with aliens. By asking questions, the lights moved up and down for "yes" and side to side for "no." Lael says one of the lights indicated that he should approach a concealed door in the mountainside. There, "intelligent beings" producing the lights were based. Inside the mountain, he was led to a room (eight feet square) with walls "clear as glass." Suddenly a voice said, "Do not fear; there is no danger here." The voice said Lael had been chosen to tell others about the true history of the lights. Lael says the voice claimed humans were created on the planet Pewam, which, he explained, is now a waste of asteroids between Mars and Jupiter.

In October 1961, Lael visited the mountainside, again entering the invisible door. This time he was offered and accepted a ride to Venus. Two days later he arrived on what he believed was Venus, and met direct descendants of people from Pewam. He described an attractive female named Noma, scantily clad in a bra and panties. While on Venus, he was also shown what appeared to be newsreels showing the destruction of Pewam, along with scenes of early humans on Earth.

Milt Machlin and Timothy G. Beckley, *UFO* (New York: Quick Fox, 1981), p. 108.

64. April 10 or 11, 1962, Cerbaia, Italy, night

Returning home from visiting a sick friend, tailor Mario Zuccula skirted a cemetery. Suddenly feeling a current of air from behind, he saw a gray or white metallic object hovering seven feet off the ground, from which a small metallic cylinder detached itself and landed. An intense bright light radiated from the door and two small men (about four and a half feet) emerged. The men, wearing hoods over their heads, approached, lifted Zuccula up, and carried him into the cylinder. They spoke in a serious tone (in Italian), which seemed to come from an amplifier. One of them said that "at the end of the fourth moon, about one hour from morning, we will return to give you a message to humanity." Zuccula next recalls standing near his house, where he was found.

Aerial Phenomena Research Organization Bulletin, January 1963, p. 6; *Flying Saucer Review* 8, no. 4 (1962). The accounts conflict slightly. FSR has the date April 10, while APRO gives April 11. APRO says the mother ship was white; FSR, gray.

65. April 30, 1962, Mount Manfre, near Sicily, Italy, night

Telepathically summoned to Mount Manfre, Eugenio Siragusa encountered two extraterrestrials of average height standing by a glowing saucer. They wore metallic clothes, helmets, and belts emitting flashing greenish-blue lights. He was given a message in Italian for "the most powerful man of Earth," warning countries to stop all H-bomb testing.

On the night of September 5, 1962, he was again mentally summoned to the mountain and beings (from a craft eighty feet in diameter resembling a spinning top) imparted a message for humanity.

Flying Saucer Review 9, no. 1 (1963).

66. August 19 and 20, 1962, Duas Pontes, near Diamantina, state of Minas Gerais, Brazil, night

In the early 1960s, several newspapers carried the fantastic story of twelve-year-old Raimundo Aleluia Mafra, who, after his father (Rivalino Mafra da Silva) was reported missing, claimed that he was abducted by a UFO. The boy says on the night of August 19, his family was in bed—himself, his father, and two brothers (six year-old Fatimo, two-year-old Dirceu)—when he heard a noise and saw a strange silhouette floating in the house. "It was a weird shadow, not looking like a human being." It looked at him and his two brothers "for a long time" before it left the room. Soon he heard a voice say, "This one looks like Rivalino." The boy says he then heard the entities talking outside the house, saying they were going to kill his father.

The next morning, two floating spheres were seen hovering near the ground by the house. One globe was black, while the other was black and white. Both had antennalike protuberances and gave off fire through an opening. The objects then merged and slowly moved toward his father, enveloping him in yellow smoke. "Then the yellow smoke dissolved. The balls were gone. My father was gone."

Aerial Phenomena Research Organization Bulletin (September 1962): 1, 3, 4, 5; and Gordon Creighton, "The Humanoids in Latin America," in Charles Bowen, ed., *The Humanoids* (Great Britain: Futura, 1977), pp. 103–104, citing *Diariode Minas*, Belo Horizonte (Brazil), August 26, 1962; *Ultima Hora*, Belo Horizonte, August 28, 1962; *Tribuna da Imprensa*, Rio de Janeiro, August 29, 1962; *Flying Saucer Review*, November/December 1962.

67. September 5, 1962, Wasserbillig, West Germany, night

Bound for Luxembourg on a coal train, Hans Klotzbach jumped off just before reaching Wasserbillig, suffering severe leg injuries. Crippled and losing blood, he lost consciousness but regained awareness inside a saucer-shaped craft in a room drenched in opal-blue light. A voice said in German that it had found him and felt sorry for him and also predicted future world disasters. Klotzbach fell asleep and awoke four days later, his legs healed, but with dried blood on them.

Gordon Creighton, "Healing from UFOs," *Flying Saucer Review* 15, no. 5 (1969): 20.

68. October 1963 Whidbey Island, Washington State, 9 A.M.

A woman saw a gray object hovering off the ground. Three occupants were visible through a transparent front section. One of the entities was suddenly standing outside the craft, wearing "asbestos-textured coveralls." Its face, hands, and feet were not visible. After asking, "What do you want?" the entity replied in English: "One of our party knows you; we will return." The object began to get smaller, tilted, sank partially into the ground, expanded to its earlier size and flew east, giving off steam, a flash, and noise.

Jacques Vallee, *Passport to Magonia* (Chicago: Henry Regnery, 1969), p. 294.

69. December 1963, Japan

A flying saucer landed near a man's farm and he conversed with the lone occupant.

Vaughn Greene, *Astronauts of Ancient Japan* (Millbrae, Calif.: Merlin Engine Works, 1978).

70. April 24, 1964, Tioga City, New York, approximately 10 A.M.

Farmer Gary Wilcox was spreading fertilizer in an open field when he stopped to check on another field nearby. Approaching the field, he saw a tiny egg-shaped object on the ground. He saw two small men (about four feet) clad in seamless outfits with hoods completely covering their faces. Each carried a tray with what appeared to be soil. One of them told Wilcox they were from Mars and that he need not be afraid, as they had talked to people before. The man's voice (he spoke smooth, effortless English) seemed to come from his body rather than his head. They then discussed organic material, including fertilizers. Wilcox was told that on Mars, food was grown in the atmosphere. The being said they could travel to Earth only every two years. They then asked for fertilizer, but when Wilcox went to get it, the craft flew off. Wilcox got a bag of fertilizer and left it in the field; he claimed it was gone the next day.

Coral Lorenzen, "UFO Occupants in the United States," in Charles Bowen, ed., *The Humanoids* (Great Britain: Futura, 1977), pp. 163–64, citing *Sun-Bulletin* (Binghamton, N.Y.), May 1, 1964.

71. June 5, 1964, Pajas Blancas, province of Cordoba, Argentina, 4 A.M.

While driving near Pajas Blancas International Airport, an unidentified couple's car engine failed, and they were soon confronted by a large machine blocking the road. The craft's powerful light went out, leaving only a mild violet-colored illumination. They watched it for twenty minutes, when suddenly a figure approached their car, asking (in Spanish), "What's the matter, my friend?" The driver replied that his engine quit. The being suggested that he try again, which he did, and the engine started. The stranger then said, "Don't be afraid. I am a terrestrial. I am carrying out a mission on Earth. My name is R. D. Tell mankind about it in your own fashion." He then walked slowly away, joining two other beings (all dressed in gray) who had now appeared. They entered the craft, which rose rapidly and vanished from sight, leaving a violet-colored trail.

Gordon Creighton, "The Humanoids in Latin America," in Charles Bowen, ed., *The Humanoids* (Great Britain: Futura, 1977), p. 108, citing *Cordoba pub. Cordoba,* November 29, 1964; *Flying Saucer Review* 12 (March/April 1966): 25.

72. June 15, 1964, near Arica, Chile

Rafael Aguirre Donoso, a Chilean miner, saw a strange object land near a road where he was driving. Two fair-complexioned men, speaking a mixture of Spanish and English, asked for water. After he gave them some they reentered the object, which rose and disappeared.

Gordon Creighton, "The Humanoids in Latin America," in Charles Bowen, ed., *The Humanoids* (Great Britain: Futura, 1977), p. 108, citing *La Razon* (Buenos Aires), June 21, 1964; *Flying Saucer Review* 11 (March/April 1965).

73. June 1964, Sagrada Familia, Brazil, night

While lying down, Luis Muzio Ambrosio, a medium, saw a yellow-orange light come into the room and heard a voice state, "We are friends and we are in our spaceship on the roof of your house." Nearby children reportedly said they saw a bright object land on his house. He also claims a series of later contacts.

Flying Saucer Review 17, no. 1 (1971).

74. July 16, 1964, Conklin, New York, 3 P.M.

Several boys saw a human-looking dwarf in a black suit with a helmet and glass in front of his face. He spoke in a strange voice "as if it came from a pipe." He walked into a shiny object in some nearby brush as the boys raced home. The witnesses were Randy Travis, age nine; Edmund Travis, age nine; Floyd Moore, age ten; and two other boys.

Jacques Vallee, *Passport to Magonia* (Chicago: Henry Regnery, 1969), p. 301.

75. Summer 1964, Little Lever, England, night

After seeing a glowing orange sphere silently explode near her house earlier in the evening, an anonymous woman later encountered a five-foot-tall being without a face in her bedroom. It wore an outfit composed of small rings. She was told telepathically not to be afraid, that a group of such entities was temporarily stranded on Earth.

In a later contact, three beings appeared in the bedroom, thanked her for not being afraid, and said that they were leaving soon.

Flying Saucer Review 22, no. 3 (1976): 27; *Northern UFO Network News*, no. 25 (1976); *Awareness* (Autumn 1976): 9.

76. August, 1964, northern New Jersey, afternoon

During the morning, a group of thirteen people, including Robert A. Wilson, saw a saucer-shaped object land on a hill. Some of the witnesses saw what appeared to be humanoid occupants wearing silverish suits. During the afternoon, Wilson's five-year-old son, Graham, met an "extraterrestrial" in a wooded area near the same hill. She had silverish skin and told him he should become a medical doctor as an adult.

Robert A. Wilson, *The Cosmic Trigger* (Berkeley, Calif.: And/Or Press, 1977).

77. Approximately 1964, Pittsburgh, Pennsylvania

Philip Osborne watched a 1979 NBC-TV documentary on UFO abductions featuring researcher Budd Hopkins. A few weeks later he became paralyzed for about a minute in the middle of the night. He called Hopkins and told him of a similar experience in 1964, while at Carnegie Tech in Pittsburgh, Pennsylvania, when he awoke during the night paralyzed with the feeling that someone was watching him. He recalled another childhood experience (at age six or seven) while vacationing in the Tennessee Smoky Mountains. He became frightened while searching for his brother's lost jacket at night near a remote picnic site.

On April 28, 1979, he underwent regressive hypnosis by New York psychologist Dr. Aphrodite Clamar. He told of having been in a large, illuminated "dome" and experiencing a floating sensation.

The next week, during another hypnosis session, he said that he thought he was carried to "a large, illuminated, round spherical" object. He felt calm and saw "a large eye . . . staring at me," possibly suspended overhead. During the incident he also saw a metallic arm which he associated with a cut on his leg.

Regarding the Carnegie Tech incident, he told of walking outside after the one-minute paralysis and being "led" to the remote grounds of the Heinz mansion. He saw a light and was drawn to a group of beings behind the mansion who had big foreheads and "metallic" eyes.

A third session with Dr. Clamar occurred June 7, 1979, again concentrating on this experience. He described seeing a being with pinkish skin. Then he "suddenly . . . felt much more calm." The being's eyes were deep-set under its protruding forehead. A voice said, "Everything will be all right."

He had a fourth hypnotic session April 12, 1980, and remembered that a "flying saucer" was near the Heinz mansion and he soon realized he was inside a dome-shaped room with two glowing spheres hovering on each side of his head, apparently calming him. In addition to the large-headed humanoids, there was at least one tiny robotlike figure present.

Budd Hopkins, *Missing Time: A Documented Study of UFO Abductions* (New York: Richard Marek, 1981), pp. 154–83.

78. Early 1965, Brasilia, Brazil

Abducted by a UFO crew and taken to their cold, thin-aired planet pocked with craters, an unnamed male claimed to see thousands of UFOs that were to be used in "a peaceful invasion" of Earth in 1966.

Coral Lorenzen, *Flying Saucers: The Startling Evidence of the Invasion from Outer Space* (New York: Signet, 1966), p. 80, originally published as *The Great Flying Saucer Hoax* (Tucson: William-Frederick Press, 1962).

79. January 30, 1965, near Monterey, California, early morning

Walking along Manresa Beach, Mr. S. Padrick came upon a landed object, and a voice invited him inside. He met a man about five feet ten inches tall with short auburn hair, a pale face, sharp chin and nose, and long fingers. He called himself Zeeno.

John A. Keel, *Why UFOs* (New York: Manor, 1970), p. 212, also published as *UFOs: Operation Trojan Horse* (New York: Putnum's Sons, 1970).

80. February 21, 1965, Chalac, near Formosa, Argentina-Paraguay frontier

One of several saucers seen in flight landed. About fifty Toba Indians, along with Argentine police, allegedly watched as three tall beings descended from the craft and slowly approached. The Indians knelt, praising them with uplifted arms in the traditional sun-worshiping ceremony of their ancestors, when they heard a voice from either the beings or their craft. It said they should not fear, for the space people would soon return to convince Earthmen of their existence, and bring peace. One Indian attempted to approach the machine but was dissuaded by gestures. The creatures (all the time enveloped in luminous halos) then slowly returned to the saucer. Luminous beams seemed to emanate from small wings on the craft. The luminosity became blinding as it took off. Several photos were reportedly taken.

Gordon Creighton, "The Humanoids in Latin America," in Charles Bowen, ed., *The Humanoids* (Great Britain: Futura, 1977), p. 110, citing *Cordoba pub. Cordoba*, February 25, 1965; *Flying Saucer Review* 11 (July/August 1965): 30.

81. April 24, 1965, near Scorition, South Devon, England, 5:30 P.M.

While walking in the country at Scorition Down, E. A. Bryant, a retired prison officer, suddenly encountered a large object which soon hovered some three feet off the ground. An opening appeared in the side of the saucer, and three human-shaped figures in "diving gear" appeared. The beings removed their helmets, and two of them had very high foreheads, blue eyes, and fair hair. The third, who was smaller, looked about fifteen years old and had normal features with dark hair and brown eyes.

A conversation in English ensued, and the dark-haired man said he was Yamski or a similar-sounding name. Yamski said it was unfortunate that someone called Des or Les wasn't there to see the visitation as he would understand. The occupants told Bryant they hailed from Venus and would return in a month bringing with them "proof of Mantell" or a similar name. (Mantell apparently refers to the highly publicized, January 7, 1948, death of U.S. Air Force Captain Thomas Mantell, who died after his plane crashed while pursuing a UFO.)

Charles Bowen, "Few and Far Between," in Charles Bowen, ed., *The Humanoids* (Great Britain: Futura, 1977), pp. 20–21, citing an address given by N. Oliver and E. Buckle at a public meeting of the British UFO Research Association (BUFORA), February 26, 1966; *Plymouth Independent* (Devon), August 8, 1965.

82. April 1965, near Monte Grande, province of Entre Rios, Argentina

Shopkeeper Felipe Martinez claims to have seen a large egg-shaped craft while hunting. It was hovering silently just off the ground, and as he rushed enthusiastically toward it, shouting "Amigo!" (Spanish for "friend"), he suddenly became paralyzed. A door in the object opened, and a man (three feet tall) wearing a "diver's costume" stepped out. Two cables ran from his helmet to the saucer. As they talked, the entity spoke slowly, with difficulty. He said his people were friendly and "came from near the moon." He called his machine a "sil" and told Martinez they would meet again May 3, 1965. He also said they needed help from us. Martinez replied that he wasn't in a position to give them much help, but that he'd report the contact to the local radio station. "Yes, we know," the little man said, extending a clammy hand and promising to see him again May 3.

Martinez claims to have met with aliens on May 3 and several occasions since. After a third alleged meeting (11 P.M. on July 21, 1965), he told the same little man his difficulty in finding anyone to believe him, to which the being replied they would soon show themselves to people everywhere on Earth. He was then warned if he failed to keep a December 3, 1965, rendezvous, they would take him and his family away, then burn Earth as punishment for failing to accept their existence.

Gordon Creighton, "The Humanoids in Latin America," in Charles Bowen, ed., *The Humanoids* (Great Britain: Futura, 1977), pp. 111–13, citing *Sydney Herald*, August 2, 1965; *La Cronica Matutina* (Buenos Aires), October 8, 1965; *La Cronica* (Buenos Aires), August 8, 1965.

83. Early August 1965, Paraiba, Cruzeiros, state of São Paulo, Brazil

While quietly fishing in the River Paraiba, Joao do Rio, a railway worker, noticed a saucer land nearby. A strange man, just over two tall feet with large luminous eyes, approached him. Speaking perfect Portuguese, he said he was from a flying saucer from another world and told him to relate his contact to fellow countrymen. Before reentering the saucer, he gave the man a piece of metal, which was later analyzed with inconclusive results.

Gordon Creighton, "The Humanoids in Latin America," in Charles Bowen, ed., *The Humanoids* (Great Britain: Futura), pp. 115–16, citing the *Yorkshire Post* (August 1965); *Jornal do Brasil*, Rio de Janeiro, August 13, 1965; *La Cronica* (Buenos Aires), August 14, 1965.

84. August 7, 1965, Venezuela

A UFO landed and two occupants seven to eight feet tall with long hair and big eyes conversed with three humans. They wore coverall-like clothes and communicated telepathically. When asked if any aliens live among us, they replied yes: "Two million, four hundred and seventeen thousand, eight hundred and five."

John A. Keel, *Our Haunted Planet* (Conn.: Fawcett Gold Medal, 1971), p. 123.

85. August 23, 1965, near Mexico City, night

Three students of La Salle University claim to have seen a shiny 160-foot disc emitting an intense white light land just outside Mexico City. The fair-haired, blue-eyed beings looked entirely like Earthlings, but towered over seven feet high. They wore seamless one-piece garb, metallic in appearance. The students were invited into the ship and taken for a three-hour journey to a large space station. The saucer ride was exceptionally quiet, and the beings said they communicated with each other telepathically. Their instruments were also operated by thought-power. The space station was occupied by aliens of different sizes and appearance from various parts of our solar system. The students also claimed to have met aboard the space station a Brazilian family who became lost in the jungles of their own country whom the aliens picked up. The beings who picked the students up hailed from Ganymede, the third moon of Jupiter. The visitors said they were a thousand years ahead of Earth and that they knew seven hundred Earth languages in addition to Spanish. The aliens said they would make a mass landing on Earth in October 1965 to effect a peaceful conquest and teach us how to use the power of thought properly and constructively, not destructively, as we presently do.

Gordon Creighton, "The Humanoids in Latin America," in Charles Bowen, ed., *The Humanoids* (Great Britain: Futura, 1977), pp. 118–19, citing *Ultimas Noticias* (Mexico City), August 22, 1965; *Ultima Hora* (Buenos Aires), August 22, 1965 (which gives full names of all students); *Noticias Populares* (São Paulo), August 23, 1965; *La Montagne* (France), August 23, 1965; *Bayreuther Tagblatt* (Germany), September 28, 1965.

86. August 23, 1965, near Mexico City, night

A trio of boys from a secondary school claimed to have contacted occupants from a saucer which landed by a road outside Mexico City, on the same night, time, and location as the three La Salle University students in the previous case. Their stories are identical in every respect.

Ibid.

87. About September 15, 1965, near Lima, Peru, night

A popular musician and a companion were driving when their car stopped and rose into the air. A voice said, "We come from a distant star . . . know your . . . languages. . . . We like music very much, and . . . especially esteem yours." They also said, "We believe in God." The car was then returned to the ground.

Listing of "Type 1" Cases, compiled by Richard Heiden, date unknown.

88. November 9, 1965, New York City, night

Trapped in his room on the twelfth floor of a hotel during the famous 1965 power blackout, actor Stuart Whitman heard a "whippoorwill" whistling sound outside the window where two luminous discs, one blue, one orange, hovered. A voice told Whitman, "They were fearful of Earth because Earthlings were messing around with unknown quantities and might disrupt the balance of the universe and their planet. . . . The blackout was just a little demonstration of their power, and they could do a lot more with almost no effort. They said they could stop our whole planet from functioning." No one else reported seeing or hearing the object or voice.

John A. Keel, *Why UFOs* (New York: Manor, 1970), p. 184, also published as *UFOs: Operation Trojan Horse* (New York: Putnum's Sons, 1970).

89. About February 15, 1966, Ballard, Washington State, night

Helping another man deliver oil barrels by truck, an unnamed mechanic claims to have set a homing device in a field. He said then a saucer-shaped object (thirty feet in diameter) set down on three legs. The five-foot-tall pilot inside allowed him to come aboard, telling him in Spanish that the craft was used only for travelling on Earth and that it took eighteen to twenty years to reach Earth. The witness also claims to have received letters from an alien living in Seattle, Washington.

Times (Seattle, Washington), March 21, 1966 (column by Donald Duncan).

90. July 31, 1966, between Chatham and Rochester, England, 12 P.M.

Kevin Kane heard a hum and saw a round object (about sixty feet in diameter) with wings and an antenna. "Everything glowed" upon the craft's landing. A six-foot-tall man dressed in black "told me to say no more than I have said," and snatched his camera. Male crew members wore black; the women, white. The craft then flew off.

A report by Kevin Kane to the UFO Investigation Centre (Sydney, Australia).

91. August 11, 1966, Victoria, New South Wales, Australia, night

Walking to a local shop, Miss M. Travers noticed a humming sound accompanied by the landing of a luminous silvery disc (fifty feet by ten feet). A door slid open and a tall, handsome man wearing a loose-fitting, metallic green tunic emerged. He spoke telepathically. He touched her, and she felt compelled to obey. She was taken inside the craft where the man allegedly had sex with her. After being released, she tripped and burned her ankle, losing consciousness. She awoke in a paddock where the encounter originated, and the object was gone. Travers later claims to have become pregnant.

Keith Basterfield, *An Indepth Review of Australasian UFO Related Entity Reports* (Australian Centre for UFO Studies, June 1980), p. 34; Otto Binder, *Unsolved Mysteries of the Past* (New York: Tower Publications, 1968); Frank Edwards, *Flying Saucers Here and Now!* (New York: Lyle Stuart, 1967), p. 147.

92. October 2, 1966, Cincinnati, Ohio, 8:20 P.M.

Inside her home, Mrs. Everett Steward smelled a bad odor, felt someone was watching her, and went to the bedroom where she saw an egg-shaped object with revolving red, green, and white lights and portholes. Several other people claimed to have seen it (seventy-five to one hundred feet off the ground).

After she went to bed, a bright white light filled the room, then vanished. Suddenly, a glowing globe appeared at the end of her bed, containing five "non-human" beings with bald heads and oval sunken eyes. They had slits for noses, appeared mouthless, and repeated the mental "We have made contact" message several times.

Leonard Stringfield, *Situation Red: The UFO Siege!* (Garden City, N.Y.: Doubleday, 1977), pp. 33–36.

93. November 2, 1966, between Mineral Wells, West Virginia, and Marginia, Ohio, night

Woodrow Derenberger was driving home to Mineral Wells when something "like the chimney of a kerosene lamp" landed on the road ahead. He stopped and saw a six-foot-tall, dark-skinned man with slightly elongated eyes approach him. His dark coat and blue pants were shiny. He also had a fixed grin. The man spoke telepathically, asking him to roll down the window, saying his name was Cold and he was from "a country much less powerful" than the United States. The man said he would return, reentered the craft, and flew away.

Derenberger claims several visits with Indrid Cold since. Cold and companions often arrive by car. They hail from Lanulos in "the galaxy of Genemedes." Derenberger says he was taken there and saw many cities and people with "colorful shorts" and signs written in Chinese-type script. The air and climate are identical to Earth.

John A. Keel, *Why UFOs* (New York: Manor, 1970), pp. 178–80, also published as *UFOs: Operation Trojan Horse* (New York: Putnum's Sons, 1970).

94. November 17, 1966, Gaffney, South Carolina, 4 A.M.

Two Gaffney, South Carolina, police officers (Charles Hutchins and A. G. Huskey) were patroling an isolated road when they saw a gold metallic sphere with a wide flat rim hovered just above the ground. A small door opened and a tiny ladder came down. They had a conversation with a four-foot-tall man. Hutchins said, "He talked real good . . . like a college graduate . . . acted like he knew exactly what he was saying and doing . . . didn't make any quick or false moves . . . just stood there and talked to us." Hutchins asked what he was doing and where he was from, but "he just laughed . . . a funny kind of laugh." The being asked "why we were both dressed alike. . . ." The conversation lasted two or three minutes. Speaking slowly and precisely, the small man declared, "I . . . will . . . return . . . in . . . two . . . days," climbed up the ladder, and took off with a noise "like an engine with a muffler on it." The being never returned.

John A. Keel, *Strange Creatures from Time and Space* (Conn.: Fawcett Gold Medal, 1970), pp. 149, 157–61.

95. January 25, 1967, South Ashburnham, Massachusetts, 6:35 P.M.

Betty Andreasson, a deeply religious fundamentalist Christian, was at her rural home with her parents and seven kids while her husband, injured the previous month in a serious car accident, remained hospitalized. Their electricity went out for about thirty seconds, during which time Betty saw a pulsating pink light outside the kitchen window. Her father saw "Halloween" creatures jumping "one after the other just like grasshoppers." Suddenly several aliens came through the wall, but Betty could recall nothing further. With the exception of her daughter Beckey, who saw an unusual light in the window, the rest of the family—in the TV room—saw nothing.

Under regressive hypnosis ten years later, Betty said she saw four aliens (about three feet tall) in dark blue uniforms and having big pear-shaped heads. Their outfits had a bird insignia on the left sleeve. They had gray claylike skin, slit mouths, and lined up one next to the other. The leader (taller than the rest—about five feet) telepathically communicated his name as Quazgaa. Like the others, he had two holes for a nose, a hole for each ear, and three-fingered hands covered with gloves. Betty offered them food, but Quazgaa said they needed mind food. Betty gave him a Bible, and in return she got a thin blue book. Betty was taken to an oval-shaped craft hovering in the back garden.

Inside the object, Betty saw a brilliant white light. She was told to undress, was given a white garment to wear, and was examined. A probe was pushed up her nose, while another entered her navel. They said she was being "measured for procreation."

Betty then passed through a glass wall with two humanoids to a red region where reptilelike beings were crawling everywhere. They next entered a very beautiful area where everything was green. Floating over a pyramid, she saw a crystal city where she was taken inside one of the structures. There she saw a large bird. The room was suddenly bathed in heat and light, hurting Betty. When the temperature dropped, the bird was gone, leaving only a mound of embers from which a "big fat worm" emerged. Betty then heard what she believed to be the voice of God.

The beings appeared to Betty in order to "reveal to man his true nature. . . . Man seeks to destroy himself. Greed, greed, greed . . . it draws all foul things. . . ." She says they want "the truth—freedom—love—to understand man's hatred—to deal with it righteously."

Under hypnosis, Betty's daughter Beckey also told of seeing the beings. Betty, who at the time of the original incident was thirty years old and unemployed, claims further contact since.

Raymond Fowler, *The Andreasson Affair* (N.J.: Prentice-Hall, 1979); John Rimmer, *The Evidence for Alien Abductions* (Britain: The Aquarian Press, 1974), pp. 69–71.

96. February 16, 1967, off Highway 70 near St. Louis, Missouri, morning

A 180-feet cigar-shaped object landed in a field, and three beings in silver suits invited Raymond Wettling inside for breakfast. They talked over coffee for an hour and forty-five minutes, and he was given a tour of the vessel's two rooms, one engulfed in bright red light and the other looking like an office. He left the craft, and it flew away vertically very fast.

Chicago American, February 16, 1967.

97. March 1, 1967, near Eden, New York, 1:30 A.M.

While racoon hunting in the woods, DeWitt Baldwin heard a buzzing sound and saw a gold-colored circular object land. A door slid open and a man in a tight-fitting suit with a helmet and some type of goggles "asked me what I was doing . . . he talked very plainly with no accent. I told him I was hunting. He asked if I was born here and I said no. . . . He told me he would be back." The man reentered the saucer and "seconds later zipped out of sight."

Baldwin claimed a second contact March 3, 1967, while returning to the site to get his wallet.

Buffalo Evening News (Buffalo, N.Y.), March 4, 1967, p. 1;. John A. Keel, *Our Haunted Planet* (Greenwich, Conn.: Fawcett Gold Medal, 1971), p. 110; also, a copy of a report by James Reed Jr. on the incident to the National Investigations Committee on Aerial Phenomena (NICAP), via Robert C. Girard, UFO book dealer, Scotia, N.Y.

98. March 20, 1967, near Butler, Pennsylvania, 10:45 P.M.

An anonymous Butler man saw an unusual aerial light and with his daughter left the house to investigate. He drove the family Volkswagen to the edge of town. Minutes after parking on a back road, they spotted two spheres of light, which rapidly picked up speed. The pair braced for a collision which never came. The globes changed and took the forms of five beings who stood only feet from the car. The humanlike entities had faces "totally devoid of expression. . . . Their noses were narrow and pointed, and their mouths were slits like the eyes." Their skin was like scar tissue or skin which has been severely burned. They wore grayish-green shirts and pants, helmets which were flat on top, and had blond hair. They stood five feet seven inches tall, although one was about five feet. The daughter said there was "no noise in connection with either the lights or the figures." The couple hurried into the car and sped away. The daughter later remarked that when the lights approached the car, she could hear a telepathic "chorus of voices" in her mind. "The voices said: 'Don't move . . . don't move.' They kept repeating 'Don't move . . . don't move,' but they dragged out the words—'Doooooonnnn'tttt Mooooove.' When the lights vanished, the voices stopped at once." Her father heard no voices.

Brad Steiger, *Alien Meetings* (New York: Grosset and Dunlap, 1978), pp. 52–54.

99. March 31, 1967, near Loco, Texas, 10:30 P.M.

While driving home, Carroll Watts saw an unusual light and turned his car off the main road to get closer. He came upon a craft (one hundred feet by eight to ten feet), left the car, and approached. A door slid open and a voice asked if he would submit to a physical exam. The voice said it was needed if he wished to take a ride—that any man passing the exam could fly with them—but women and children weren't allowed. Watts was asked to stand in front of a device in order to pass the test. He never saw an occupant, but just heard a voice: "They were stationed all over the world and could come and go as they pleased—no one could stop them. . . . When I declined the physical, they told me that several people had taken the test and made flights." Watts returned to his car, and the craft flew off silently.

Two weeks later, while driving near his home, Watts saw a light, and his pickup truck stalled. An egg-shaped craft landed, and he talked to four muscular men (five feet tall) with slit mouths and elongated eyes and wearing white coverall-type suits. When speaking, their mouths remained still. He was taken to a bigger craft and examined with a machine that probed his body with wires. Watts claims several contacts since.

John A. Keel, *Strange Creatures from Time and Space* (Conn.: Fawcett Gold Medal, 1970), pp. 155–57.

100. March 1967, Mexico City, midnight

While Maria Cristina Leguizamo listened to the radio, a flying saucer landed in her yard and an "extremely handsome man with green eyes" and shoulder-length silver hair invited her to take a ride. She was told to remove her shoes first. The being hailed from "the Green Planet" and said that the planet Arcobolus is pulling Earth "little by little toward the sun." He also said "neither Russians nor Americans will ever arrive at the moon."

General News (Mexico City), June 22, 1968.

101. April 21, 1967, near Rapid City, Michigan, 9 P.M.

The witness was returning from work and saw a round bluish-white object land in a wooded area. After alerting the sheriff's department, he drove to the area with his wife and kids. The man and officers split up and searched the region, and the witness saw a craft sitting in a swampy area and a man (five and a half feet tall) nearby. After yelling hello a couple of times, he got a telepathic message to "get away from here!" The witness fled back to the car.

Copy of a letter from the wife of the witness to the National Investigations Committee on Aerial Phenomena (NICAP), via Robert C. Girard, UFO book dealer, Scotia, N.Y.

102. June 9, 1967, Seattle, Washington, 9 P.M.

A red sphere came through the bathroom window, struck a six-year-old boy on the forehead, and then traveled "up through the ceiling." Outside the window there were bright red and blue lights and a lipless being with short horns and slanted eyes. The entity asked the boy about the composition of the garden soil, then asked him to "watch the rocketship" as he "would be right back." The being (with two tanks on its back jetting white exhaust) flew to the roof. There were two more beings in the ship. One of them came over and asked the boy what a tree was. When it pointed a gunlike object at him, the boy ran out of the bathroom, screaming.

Copy of a letter from the boy's mother to the National Investigations Committee on Aerial Phenomena, via Robert Girard, UFO book dealer, Scotia, N.Y. The letter is dated June 22, 1967.

103. Late June 1967, Wild Plum Campground near Downieville, California, evening

A group of tourists claim they were camping at the Wild Plum Campground and heard a high-pitched whistle. They saw a saucer-shaped object land in a gravel parking area. A mechanical voice then requested they "identify themselves from left to right," and they complied. The craft gave a whistling sound again and flew straight up.

Mountain Messenger (Downieville, California), June 29, 1967.

104. July 18, 1967, Boardman, Ohio, 1:30 A.M.

Awakened by a sound similar to background music in a science-fiction TV show, Reverend Anthony de Polo felt an "impulse" to go downstairs and look out the window. He did so and saw a figure in a luminous suit between his and the neighbor's house. He went outside, and the sound started again and he received the apparently telepathic message "You have nothing to fear. I shall not hurt you, and I know you will not harm me." De Polo moved closer, heard the sound again, and got another message: "Danger. I must leave." The figure turned into a shapeless glow and vanished.

Jacques Vallee, *Passport to Magonia* (Chicago: Henry Regnery, 1969), pp. 147–48, 347.

105. July 26, 1967, near Big Tujunga Canyon, California

Driving near Big Tujunga Canyon, Mrs. Maris De Long and Michael Kisner both heard a voice tell them to look for something unusual. They soon saw a flash, and a disc-shaped object appeared. A creature called Kronin emerged, saying he was "a space robot encased in a time capsule." He was very tall, boneless, eyeless, and was head of the Kronian race.

De Long later claimed several more contacts—including phone conversations with Kronin.

John A. Keel, *The Mothman Prophecies* (New York: Signet, 1975), p. 135.

106. Summer 1967, near Cochrane, Canada

A park ranger says he talked with friendly extraterrestrials and was taken on a spaceship ride. The man was a University of Toronto student manning a lookout post when he conversed with the furry, English-speaking visitors.

Personal letter from John B. Musgrave of the Mobile Planetarium Project at the Provincial Museum of Alberta, Canada, citing a Dusbury, Ontario (Canada), newspaper dated autumn 1967.

107. August 16, 1967, Caracas, Venezuela

A four-foot-tall being with a big head and big eyes and wearing a shiny outfit told Pedro Ramirez he was here because the Earth was "cracking and they wished to save it."

Allan Hendry, *The UFO Handbook* (New York: Doubleday, 1979), p. 141; also a copy of a letter to the National Investigations Committee on Aerial Phenomena written by Vladimir Scheffer, August 22, 1967, via Robert C. Girard, UFO book dealer, Scotia, N.Y.

108. August 29, 1967, Craddle Hill, Warminster, England

A fiery, cone-shaped object with a revolving rim landed, and Arthur Shuttlewood claims to have approached and talked with a being during a "reassuring meeting." The craft "blacked out" after six minutes, and he soon heard a thumping noise pass by and felt a gust of wind.

Arthur Shuttlewood, *Warnings from Flying Friends* (Warminster, England: Portway Press, 1968), p. 53.

109. September 3, 1967, Caracas, Venezuela

Suffering a bad headache, Paula Valdez came home after work and went to bed. Shortly after falling asleep, a whistling sound woke her. A small manlike being with a big head and bulging eyes was leaning over her and said, "I want you to come with us so that you will know other worlds. You will realize how small your world is." She screamed, and the figure floated from the room. Her family came in, but none saw the being.

Daniel Cohen, *Creatures from UFO's* (New York: Archway, 1979), p. 104.

110. September 9, 1967, Valencia, Venezuela, 5 A.M.

In front of city hall police officer Porfirio Andrade saw a four-foot-tall man with bulging, red glowing eyes wearing a silver uniform. He pointed his gun at it when a voice from a disc-shaped object overhead said, "Don't do him any harm. We are here on a peaceful mission. He'll do you no harm." Then the being on the ground began talking, first repeating that they were peaceful and saying "they" wanted Andrade to go with them to another planet where he would enjoy many benefits over being on Earth. Frightened, Andrade refused, saying he was on duty. The creature flew to the disc, into a door, and it flew away. The object emitted flame and noise as it left.

Daniel Cohen, *Creatures from UFO's* (New York: Archway, 1979), pp. 104–105.

111. September 14, 1967, La Baleia, Minas Gerais, Brazil

A domed object (sixty feet in diameter) with portholes landed on a football field. Underneath the object were red, blue, and yellow flashing lights. As Fabio Jose Diniz (age sixteen) approached, two men (seven feet tall) in tight-fitting, green "diver suits" emerged, saying (in Portuguese): "Don't run away—come back!" They said, "Appear here tomorrow, or we will take your family." They reentered the craft and flew away. Their suits obscured part of their faces. Their large round eyes were set far apart, and they appeared to have green skin and triangular-shaped eyebrows.

The next day Diniz returned to the site with a UFO investigator without incident.

Dr. Hulvio B. Aleixo, "Humanoids Encountered at La Balea, Parts 1 and 2," *Flying Saucer Review* 14, no. 6 (1968): 8–11, 20; 15, no. 1 (1969): 12–14.

112. October 6, 1967, Belfast, Northern Ireland, night

Walking home from a jazz club, Eugene Browne saw an object approach from the sky. Suddenly, a yellow light streamed out, the beam slowly intensifying. Within five minutes he lost consciousness. He awoke strapped to a table in a windowless room filled with blue light. Four friendly looking men and a girl, all in one-piece outfits, stood around him. The tallest—a six-foot-tall man—said, "At last, someone. You will do." Then he was freed from the table and led to the girl, who had blue eyes, long blonde hair, high cheekbones, thin lips, and freckled, fair skin. She initiated a sex act and explained they were from another galaxy and that they wanted the seed of Earth men. Eugene was returned to the table and told, "It will not be the last you will see of us." He soon awoke a mile from the original encounter scene and saw the ship fly off with a whistle.

Brinsley Le Poer Trench, *Operation Earth* (Aylesbury: Tandem, 1975), pp. 18–19.

113. October 10, 1967, Lakewood, Colorado, 12:45 A.M.

A six-foot-tall man with a goatee flagged down an anonymous male on his way home and telepathically asked the location of the North Star and the current date. He wore a jacket with four gold bars on both shoulders. He asked and was told that the witness had a cigarette in his mouth, and he said, "Oh, one of your primitive vices." After asking what the man was driving, the being responded, "Oh, your primitive mode of transportation." When the witness asked where he was from, the entity said he couldn't say, "but my colleagues and I will return." He then walked a few feet away and disappeared. The witness next heard a whining noise and saw an object (one hundred yards long) rise straight up to where two other objects were, and they flew off rapidly.

Project Bluebook, case investigated by Lieutenant Colonel A. P. Webb, U.S. Air Force.

114. November 28, 1967, near Americana, Brazil, 2:30 A.M.

Upon seeing a huge, bright metallic object with "enormous rivets on it" hovering fifty feet off the ground, an unnamed highway patrolman heard a humming noise and experienced a headache. His police car's engine and lights failed. When the object left, his vehicle acted normally. About forty-eight hours later, on November 28, the object returned, the officer again became paralyzed and two men in tight-fitting clothes with glowing belts emerged on a cylinder under the craft. The witness was told in Portuguese not to be frightened and to put away his gun. They said that they would return. The craft then flew away.

Aerial Phenomena Research Organization Bulletin (APRO) (September–October 1968): 5.

115. December 3, 1967, near Ashland, Nebraska, 2:30 A.M.

His patrol car engulfed in a bright light on the edge of town, Ashland police officer Herbert Schirmer recalls seeing a UFO fly away. Unable to account for missing time, he underwent regressive hypnosis, during which he recounted that his engine quit, his headlights and two-way radio failed. A football-shaped object with "tripod legs" landed in a nearby field. He was paralyzed, and several beings approached his car and invited him aboard. They communicated mentally, explaining they are from "a nearby galaxy," with bases on Venus and Jupiter. Climbing a ladder into the ship, he was taken into a room with red lighting. The interior contained computerlike machines and two triangular-backed chairs in front of a "vision screen." Inside the ship was cold. The four alien men (four and a half to five feet tall) had muscular limbs. Their "chest[s were] larger and bigger than you might expect on someone of their size." Their posture was rigid and they walked with a definite military motion. Their heads were long and thin, with "large Oriental eyes . . . more like cat's eyes." Their faces were "a pastry dough color." They had five fingers and wore silvery-gray gloves and boots. Seamless coverall garments "resembling a flight suit you buy at the Army surplus stores" covered their bodies, extending over their heads like a helmet with a little "antennae" protruding from the sides of the head. They had "funny-looking lips" and long, flat noses. Each wore a flashlightlike gun in a holster on the waist, capable of producing a paralyzing ray. While on board, two beings paced back and forth outside the ship "like regular soldiers on guard duty . . . looking as they walked." The ship was made entirely of magnesium, he was told. They landed to "take some electricity from the powerlines. . . . This is an observation ship . . . they have been observing us for a long time . . . they put out reports slowly to prepare us . . . for the invasion . . . not to conquer the world, just a showing of themselves. . . . He did not tell me why they are here." He was returned to the car as the ship emitted a reddish glow, followed by a high-pitched whine. The tripod legs retracted as the vessel rapidly flew away.

Warren Smith, *The Book of Encounters* (New York: Kensington Publishing, 1976), pp. 87–113.

116. December 12, 1967, between Ithaca and Auburn, New York, 7:00 P.M.

Driving home from visiting a friend in North Lansing, Rita Malley with her son Dana in the back seat were southbound on remote Route 34. Midway between North and South Lansing, the car was drenched in a red light from a circular dome-shaped object with brilliant red and green lights, moving as quickly as the car. Glancing back, Dana "was sitting straight up. His eyes were just bugging right out of his head. . . . I yelled at him. . . . His response was—nothing." The object "extended a white beam of light . . . and it was just completely right over the controls of my car. My car stopped. . . . I kept stamping the accelerator—but the car wouldn't move." Soon she heard a "low humming . . . like a whole swarm of bees." Suddenly the hum stopped and "voices came out of the . . . hovering object . . . my car windows were rolled up tight . . . they were all talking at the same time, saying the same thing, . . . as if what they were saying was being translated into English." The "voices were not impressions in my mind. They were external, coming from that hovering thing . . . like . . . they were talking through a loudspeaker, but not quite. I couldn't tell whether they were male or female . . . there were so many of them all at once." They said: "Paul Donalds, Moravia, killed . . . near or in Massena in a tractor-trailer owned by Joe Etinger, Moravia." The voices then said that Dana would not recall the incident. Malley gradually regained control of the car, and the object left. Both statements reportedly proved true. The next day she learned the man was killed exactly as predicted. Her son did not recall any of the experience.

The Official Guide to UFOs (New York: Ace, 1968), pp. 67–74. The case is written by and based upon a personal interview by Lloyd Mallan with Rita Malley.

117. December 1967, near Adelphi, Maryland

A psychology major in college, Tom Monteleone claims to have talked with a man, Vadig, from a grounded UFO on four separate occasions. During a later encounter Vadig came to a Washington, D.C., restaurant dressed in conventional clothes, where Monteleone was a waiter. Vadig appeared normal, except for bulging "thyroid eyes." Each encounter ended with the alien saying, "I'll see you in time."

John A. Keel, *Why UFOs* (New York: Manor), pp. 173–74.

118. May or June 1968, Buenos Aires, Argentina, after midnight

Walking home from a Buenos Aires theater in the fog, Benjamin Solari Parravicini, an Argentine painter/sculptor, encountered a man at the corner of Avenida Belgrano and Avenida 9 de Julio. He was a fair-skinned Nordic type "whose eyes were so light in color that it looked as though he were blind." The man spoke in an unintelligible guttural language, his manner "kindly and gentle." Looking upward, Parravicini saw an aerial ship without lights.

Overcome by dizziness, he awoke inside the craft, which was in flight, in the presence of three beings. A very handsome alien questioned him in an unintelligible language, yet he understood. He was told not to be alarmed; they would take him on a trip around the Earth, returning him precisely where they found him. He next found himself on the same street corner from where he left.

Charles Bowen, ed., *Encounter Cases from Flying Saucer Review* (New York: Signet, 1977), pp. 41–42.

119. June 1968, Carlos Paz, Argentina, 12:50 A.M.

Motel owner Pedro Pretzel saw an object with two bright red headlights on the road. Arriving home, he found his daughter unconscious. Upon reviving, she told of a blond man (about six feet five inches tall) in a bright blue outfit and holding a light-blue globe in his hand, who had talked to her.

Jacques Vallee, *Passport to Magonia* (Chicago: Henry Regnery, 1969), p. 357.

120. July 2, 1968, Sierra Chica, near Olavarria, province of Buenos Aires, Argentina, 11:30 A.M.

Riding horseback on his father's farm near Sierra Chica, Oscar Hariberto Iriart noticed three men (five and a half feet tall) standing near a wire fence, making signs which appeared to be encouraging him to approach. Thinking they could be bird hunters, he rode over. He found two white-haired men wearing red shirts. "Apart from the constant unblinking way in which they gazed fixedly at me with their deep-set eyes, they might have been just any ordinary men such as we see everyday," except they had transparent eyes. The boy could see through to the grass behind them. The following conversation ensued:

Visitor: "You are going to know the world."

Boy: "Yes, of course—when I have enough money."

Visitor: "No. We will take you. We cannot take you now, as we have a big load."

The strangers then showed him a silvery-colored elliptical-shaped craft standing on three legs in a muddy drainage ditch nearby. He was given an envelope, saying it was a message for him. The man told him to dip the letter in a nearby water puddle.

Upon doing so, he noticed that his hands and the envelope were entirely dry. The message was in Spanish (written in a childlike manner), saying, "You are going to know the world. F. Saucer." The word "you" was misspelled.

They climbed back onto the machine, lifted the top, and got in. Lights flashed as it shot up vertically, almost instantly reducing to a speck in the sky. Oscar felt "as though he had been asleep" and raced home. He noticed his horse and dog were paralyzed, remaining so for several minutes.

Charles Bowen, ed., *Encounter Cases from Flying Saucer Review* (New York: Signet, 1977), pp. 50–53.

121. July 22, 1968, St. Bruno, Quebec, evening

Six girls (ranging in age from seven to thirteen) claim they saw a dark hexagonal object in the sky. Inside was a figure wearing a white veil. Two of the six, Manon Saint-Jean and Line Grise, reported hearing a "soft and slow" voice advising them to pray and promising to return on Monday, October 7. The voice also promised that other signs would appear. The Virgin Mary also spoke to them concerning peace and brotherhood. Other UFOs were reported in the area at the time. It is unknown if the object and being reappeared October 7.

John A. Keel, *Why UFOs* (New York: Manor, 1970), p. 251, also published as *UFOs: Operation Trojan Horse* (New York: Putnum's Sons, 1970); personal letter from John B. Musgrave, employee of the Mobile Planetarium Project at the Provincial Museum of Alberta, Edmonton, Canada, citing *Montreal U.F.O. Newsletter*, no. 3: 18–19. It should be noted that *Saucer News*, no. 74 (Spring–Summer 1969): 34, describes the object as a cloud.

122. August 31, 1968, South America, early morning

Two unidentified male casino cashiers were driving home from work when their car quit. Investigating the cause, the pair found themselves surrounded by four small men who were entirely bald and stocky. They talked without moving their lips, and the men said they felt like a transmitter inside their heads was generating the words "Don't fear, don't fear." During their conversation, the little men said that the sun is "the reason for everything" and that mathematics is the universal language. Something resembling a

TV screen was then produced, which projected a scene resembling Niagara Falls, a giant descending cloud, then what appeared to be Niagara Falls but without water. The creatures took blood samples by pricking the middle finger of both men.

Although frightened, the pair could do nothing until the visitors finished, whereupon they disappeared into an illuminated disc hovering some three feet off the ground. After the object left, the car started without difficulty.

Aerial Phenomena Research Organization Bulletin (September-October 1968): 1, 3.

123. August 1968, Brasilia, Brazil, night

After claiming telepathic contact with extraterrestrials, Wilson da Silva says he predicted that a UFO would land on his property. A glowing disc landed while he was reportedly with a group of followers. He left the group and approached the disc, seeing a man of average height in a blue one-piece outfit and belt who emerged and contacted him. Upon returning, he told the group he could recall nothing but the following: "We are peaceful. Your atomic experiments are causing an imbalance in our world." The ship flew off rapidly. Da Silva claims additional contacts.

O Dia (Rio de Janeiro), a nine-article series by Eduardo Santa Maria between October 26 and November 4, 1970.

124. August 1968, near Toronto, Canada

In downtown Toronto, a car pulled up in front of "Mr. S" and the two men inside asked him by name if he'd like to go for a ride. He next recalled being left out in the country by a flying saucer. There were five men in dark brown clothing who said the craft was piloted by an unnamed female, whom he didn't see. They explained everything about the propulsion system. Mr. S declined an offer to ride in the saucer, saying he had to return to work. He was taken back to Yonge Street but couldn't recall the trip back.

Personal letter from John B. Musgrave, Mobile Planetarium Project at the Provincial Museum of Alberta, Canada, citing a letter from Vera Kolver to *Saucers, Space & Science*, no. 59 (1970): 15.

125. September 1, 1968, Mendoza, Argentina, 3:30 P.M.

Two men were returning home when their car's engine and headlights quit. After getting out and checking under the hood, they saw a large circular object hovering near them. They saw a trio of small humanoids, and the men suffered paralysis. Two other figures were seen near the object as well. The three communicated telepathically and showed pictures to them before reentering the craft and flying off rapidly.

Flying Saucer Review 14 (November 1968).

126. October 1968, Mar del Plata (Buenos Aires), Argentina, 3:00 P.M.

Ignacio Papaleo's small truck suddenly stopped on National Highway 2. Getting out to check the engine, he saw a glowing object just above his head and became paralyzed. Seconds later, a small ladder came out and a small man gestured for him to come aboard, then verbally asked him. He was told the contact was to see if he could be reproduced within the alien's atmosphere. He was helped up the ladder and passed out, later waking up in his truck with several puncture marks on his forearm.

Feomenologia, no. 41, citing *7 Dias Ilustrados* (Buenos Aires), December 1968.

127. December 28, 1968, Goulburn, New South Wales, Australia

An unnamed male carpenter encountered a craft in a rural area and approached it. The entity—human in appearance—stood four and a half feet, had long hair, young features, and silver clothes, and said it came from Saturn. The man talked with the being for three minutes before it reentered the object and flew off.

Ten years prior to this encounter, the same man, while foxhunting, says he shot at an aerial disc-shaped object near the same spot. After firing, there was a flash of light, and the man says he was burned.

Keith Basterfield, *An Indepth Review of Australasian UFO Related Entity Reports* (Australian Centre for UFO Studies, June 1980), p. 37.

128. February 7, 1969, near Pirassununga, state of São Paulo, Brazil, 7:00 A.M.

Tiago Machado was awakened by shouts from area residents who were watching a parachute-shaped object emitting a blue light. Running to where the object was seen, he reportedly encountered a disc from which two small men (three feet eight inches tall), emerged, clad in silvery-colored outfits, including gloves and boots. The faces looked yellow through their helmets and they had noses "squashed" at the ends. The men seemed to fly from the craft's opening to the ground. The figures spoke in unintelligible hoarse guttural sounds, which appeared to come from a tube projecting down from their chin. Nervous, Tiago then lit up a cigarette and began smoking, causing the creatures to laugh (when they did so, he noticed their teeth were black). He then laid the pack on the ground and pushed it toward them with his foot. One of them extended his hand above the cigarette pack, and it rose up into his palm. He then made a quick movement toward his body and the pack disappeared.

Appearing to converse by signs, the men made the outline of a sphere in the air, then indicated a motion which Tiago interpreted as denoting a craft falling or drifting to the ground. About this time, shouts of others could be heard, and the creatures drifted into the object. One pointed a pipe-shaped object at Tiago's legs, causing him to fall. The disc then flew away.

Aerial Phenomena Research Organization Bulletin (March-April 1969): 5.

129. Early May 1969, Brazil

A disc-shaped object landed, and three small yellowish-colored men with long hair and beards and prominent cheekbones emerged. They carried what appeared to be weapons, which were pointed at the legs of Brazilian army soldier Jose Antonio, paralyzing him. They placed a plastic helmet over his head and took him aboard. He was put into a seat, a safety belt was fastened, and he was taken for a ride. At one point the craft flew near something which was very bright, appearing to be the sun.

After the craft landed (not on Earth), Antonio was taken into a brilliant gray room where bodies of humans were lying at one side.

He was forced to drink a greenish liquid and asked many questions about Earth conditions. Once he drank the liquid he was better able to understand what they were saying. They wanted his help in staying on Earth, but he refused, pointing to his rosary. Then a Christlike man appeared and gave him a message in Portuguese, which Antonio promised not to disclose. The disc then returned to Earth, and he was let out in the darkness about two hundred miles from the original incident. The encounter lasted forty-eight hours, but he claims four and a half Earth days had passed during the period.

He claims another contact May 21, 1969, in which the beings wanted him to "work against my own people." He became scared that the world was in grave danger.

Aerial Phenomena Research Organization Bulletin (May–June 1969): 8; H. B. Aleixo, "Abduction at Bebedouro," *Flying Saucer Review* 19, no. 6 (1973): 6–14; Gordon Creighton, "Forty-Eight Hours in a Flying Saucer," *Flying Saucer Review* 17, no. 6 (1971): 15–17.

130. Summer 1969, Utah, midnight

Bill, Nora, and her two-and-a-half-year-old son, Alan, had driven continuously for thirty-six hours on a trip from western Minnesota to Los Angeles. Suddenly, while driving at ninety m.p.h., Bill was unable to control the steering wheel, and the car veered into a road post. All were shaken but uninjured. Bill fixed the flat tire and drove on. Feeling they were being followed, Nora looked in the rearview mirror and saw what appeared to be a motorcycle light in the distance, but on the wrong side of the road. She called it to Bill's attention, and he soon noticed it was flying in the air. Soon the object (fish-shaped with a fin and a red light on top) came within two hundred feet and emitted a humming sound. They felt unusual vibrations in the car. Alan began crying, and Bill and Nora were soon hysterical. Despite flooring the accelerator, the car would not top fifty-five m.p.h. They soon came upon a parked, lighted camper on the roadside, and pulled over. Bill was about to approach the camper and point out the UFO to the occupants, but decided to stay in the car after seeing a bony-faced, inhuman being peering out the window. Bill then saw an entity in a white, rubberish outfit and no apparent arm or leg joints approaching the car from near the camper. Nora saw nothing, but she noted that Bill appeared in a trancelike state. He experienced timelessness and a blank mind. Nora drove off, and the object finally flew away at about 6:30 A.M.

Later in the morning they passed what appeared to be the same camper. Nora became hysterical when she saw two inhuman entities inside the cab wearing black suits and gloves. They appeared almost headless, with vague outlines where the heads should have been and big "Cheshire catlike" grins.

Under regressive hypnosis five years later, Bill and Nora recounted similar stories of being taken aboard a ship and seeing grasshopperlike creatures with large heads, huge eyes, and telepathic communication. The beings apparently examined them as they were placed on a reclining chair or table.

J. Clark, "The Ultimate Alien Encounter," in D. S. Rogo, *UFO Abductions: True Cases of Alien Kidnappings* (New York: Signet, 1980), pp. 191–209.

131. October 17, 1969, Helsinki, Finland, evening

An anonymous Helsinki man was in his kitchen and was suddenly pulled backward by a beam of light. He saw a shapeless glow one and a half feet off the floor and twelve feet away. Above the light a voice said in Finnish that he had been chosen for contact as he would not be frightened. The voice said they "wished the people well." The voice said he wouldn't reveal himself because their teleporting device gave off a sound that infuriated dogs. The voice then said he would visit again in two years.

Pyhala Timo, "Contact in Helsinki," *Flying Saucer Review Case Histories*, no. 8 (December 1971): 7–8.

132. About 1969, Belfast, Northern Ireland

A married mother of three claims to have been taken aboard a spaceship several times by "perfect human beings" with shoulder-length hair. The inside is white, has large rooms with circular furniture, and a kitchen. She was actually "shown some cooking methods that she has since tried with success." The aliens speak English and proposed a peaceful solution to the Northern Ireland fighting and asked her to write a book on it. The beings are here to aid humans. They hail from different planets, some from the dark side of the moon.

Northern UFOlogy, no. 1 (October 1976).

133. 1970, near East Lancashire, England

An anonymous East Lancashire woman's car stalled while she watched a red and blue UFO. Soon after, "UFOs started talking to me. They said they had been watching me. I had been ill but they made me well by operating on my brain" telepathically. They made contact because of her telepathic abilities. "They . . . watched me from birth. It took them six years to sort out our language—they whistle to communicate to each other and hoot in case of danger. I have seen them through my telepathic eye. They have large heads . . . high foreheads. Beauty to them is a large brain."

She claims "they gave me a boyfriend in space and we made love by telepathy—I seemed to leave my body and then come back." It took three months for the crew to reach Earth at the speed of light. She also said they have cured cancer and study us like we study animals.

Lancashire Evening Telegram (Blackburn, England), August 29, 1980.

134. June 15, 1971, Alton, Illinois, 8:55 P.M.

Anthony Wilkens reported to the Alton police that a silver craft emitting green lights appeared by his back porch and two humanoids inside telepathically gave him a formula giving him "the universe at his fingertips," which was in turn given to police. After he refused an invitation to ride in the craft, they left, promising to return August 3. No contact was reported on that date, however. Wilkens was a patient in Alton's state mental institution at the time.

Evening Telegraph (Alton, Ill.), June 16, 1971, p. 1; various wire sources, June 1971.

135. August 17, 1971, Palos Verdes, California, 2:00 A.M.

Leaving a friend's house at 2 A.M., John Hodges, a twenty-nine-year-old security officer, pulled out of the driveway in the fog and saw two extraterrestrial beings in the headlights. They were shaped like human brains, one the size of a human body trunk, the other the size of an overgrown softball. Companion Peter Rodriguez, an operating room technician in his twenties, saw only the larger one. After dropping Peter off five minutes later Hodges could not account for two and a half hours.

Under regressive hypnosis, Hodges recalled being taken to a room containing several telepathic brainlike creatures who warned him that Earth would be destroyed in 1971 by atomic bombs "if we don't take the time to understand ourselves." Rodriguez underwent one reluctant and limited hypnosis session, generally corroborating Hodges's hypnotic account.

D. S. Rogo, *UFO Abductions: True Cases of Alien Kidnappings* (New York: Signet, 1980); A. Hendry, *The UFO Handbook* (New York: Doubleday, 1979); J. Rimmer, *The Evidence for Alien Abductions* (London: Aquarian, 1984).

136. November 1971, Kansas

Luke saw a silvery saucer while driving. It descended and hovered twelve feet above a field. He approached it, and a door opened, a ramp came out, and two beings (four and a half feet tall) with big hairless heads and wearing white robes emerged. They telepathically relayed feelings "of calm security." After asking to see the ship's interior, he was given a tour. It was brightly illuminated with control panels and buttons, including two chairs on invisible swivels. He was later walked down the ramp, and the ship flew off.

He claims to have contacted the aliens via astral projection since, but not in person.

Beacon (Wichita, Kansas), June 2, 1978, article by J. Roe.

137. December 5, 1971, Rio Carangula, Brazil, 7:00 P.M.

After claiming to have seen a UFO and occupants on three previous occasions, Paulo Caetano Silveira, a twenty-seven-year-old typewriter repairman, says that he was invited inside a craft and heard the beings speaking in an incomprehensible language to one another, without moving their mouths. He was made to understand (apparently telepathically) that they were peaceful and planned to prepare Earth for contact. The beings (twenty inches tall) had slanted eyes, fair skin, spiked "Roman helmets," and one-piece blue outfits. The craft gave off multicolored lights.

Dr. Walter Buhler, *Flying Saucer Review Special Bulletin,* no. 5 (November 1973): 11–25; *Aerial Phenomena Research Organization Bulletin* (September–October 1971): 1, 3; *Ultima Hora* (Rio de Janeiro), October 2, 1971; Gordon Creighton, "Uproar in Brazil," *Flying Saucer Review* 17, no. 6 (November–December 1971): 24–26.

138. 1971, Cairns, Queensland, Australia

While looking for mushrooms, a young man came across a landed object and talked with its humanoid occupants, who gave him a ride. He was let out on the other side of Cairns. The conversation was apparently spiritual, with the beings saying that Cairns, Byron, and Coff Harbour were the "greatest centers of religion," implying such religion was due to UFO activity and "mushrooms" of a hallucinogenic nature.

Keith Basterfield, *An Indepth Review of Australasian UFO Related Entity Reports* (Australian Centre for UFO Studies, June 1980), p. 41, citing personal communication of Bill Chalker, who got the story from a reporter.

139. 1971, Hamilton, Bermuda

While in Hamilton, Bermuda, orchestra leader Harry Nixon met an elderly man at a park, who claimed to talk regularly with aliens, usually at night. He described them as "men with wings and [three-toed] horses' feet." The beings said that "Britain would again be the most powerful country in the world; and that the Atlantic sea-floor was rising, and Bermuda would rise six hundred feet. . . . The visitors are from a planet ninety-five million miles away and they go around just as we do—in their own cars, too."

Arthur Shuttlewood, *The Flying Saucerers* (London: Sphere, 1976), pp. 87–88, quoting a letter from orchestra leader Harry Nixon, dated July 4, 1971.

140. March 16, 1972, Granadero, Argentina, dawn

Seeing a sparkling cloud in a field, truck driver Luis Bracamonte stopped his truck and watched the cloud change form into a blinding light. He next saw a rimmed oblong object one hundred yards off. Three broad-shouldered Chinese-looking men walked out and approached Bracamonte, and one of them grabbed his elbow. He was told telepathically not to be afraid.

La Union (Catamarca), March 22, 1972.

141. May 5, 1972, Imjarvi, Finland, 10:15 P.M.

Aarno Heinonen heard a noise in his house, and then a female voice told him to go to a crossroad—which he did—where he found a four-foot eight-inch tall, blonde-haired female in a luminous yellow outfit and silver-colored shoes. She held a silver ball with three projections resembling antennas. The witness was told in Finnish that the woman and her race hail from the other side of the Milky Way, that she was 180 years old, and that aliens had landed at Imjarvi before. He was told to keep silent about the encounter. He later reported further contacts with the female alien.

On January 7, 1970, he reportedly saw a three-foot-tall being at Imjarvi, wearing a light green one-piece suit and a cone-shaped helmet, and having a pale face and thin appendages. He later experienced vomiting and numbness in his right leg.

Ufoaika (Finland), October 1972; *Aerial Phenomena Research Organization Bulletin* (July–August 1970): 6–7; and *Flying Saucer Review* 16, no. 3 (May–June 1970): 23–24; 16, no. 5 (September–October 1970): 14–18; 16, no. 6 (November–December 1970): 22.

142. May 1972, near Volgograd, Soviet Union

Several people were in a car twelve miles west of Volgograd. After the engine stopped, they saw a large "metallic mass" and heard a mental voice say, "We come in peace. Do not fear us." The object flew off rapidly, after which the car engine started by itself.

H. Gris and Dick William, *The New Soviet Psychic Discoveries* (New York: Warner, 1979).

143. July 25, 1972, Frankston, Victoria, Australia, about 9:15 P.M.

On the evening of July 3, 1972, a thirty-seven-year-old housewife watched a large silverish-blue iridescent disc hover over the car she was driving. On July 25, a similar object appeared over the road as the woman was driving home. While she attempted to speed away, the engine stopped but the headlights stayed on. She pumped the brake, changed gears, tried moving the steering wheel, but all without success. The car then "controlled itself" off to the side of the road. A voice gave her three messages, after which her vehicle started by itself and the object flew off.

She later returned to the location of the encounter after hearing a mental voice tell her to do so. While she was driving there, a man "materialized" and later "dematerialized" inside the car. She met two other people at the encounter site and became unconscious upon seeing a strange man. She told of being taken inside an illuminated room. She later regained consciousness in the car. Neither of the two people who were with her the entire time of the reported encounter observed anything unusual, besides the woman lying unconscious.

Keith Basterfield, *A Catalogue of the More Interesting Australian Close Encounters* (Australian Centre for UFO Studies, October 1981), citing personal investigation by Garry Little and Bill Stapleton. Also Keith Basterfield, *UFOs: The Image Hypothesis. Close Encounters of an Australian Kind* (Sydney: Reed, 1981), p. 95; Keith Basterfield, *An Indepth Review of Australasian UFO Related Entity Reports* (Centre for UFO Studies, June 1980), pp. 97–98.

144. November 26, 1972, near Cash Creek Bridge, West Woodland, California, evening

Returning home from an outing with two women companions, legal secretary Judy Kendall, recalls driving but "we didn't seem to be getting anywhere." They remembered seeing a disc-shaped craft with bright lights hovering nearby. Under regressive hypnosis she told of how the trio were abducted by aliens. She described being physically examined by three types of creatures. One was humanlike, while another group appeared to wear gas masks. "And then there was one I nicknamed the witch doctor," Kendall said. "He was huge looking and he had a large bulbous-type head and grasshopper-type eyes and no ears. There were holes on the sides of his head. He had a small nose and I couldn't see much of a mouth. The only thing he said to me was, it will be OK." They expected to arrive home at 8:30 P.M., but didn't make it until past midnight.

The Bee (Fresno, California), November 3, 1979.

145. September 1973, Ivy Tanks, South Australia, 3 A.M.

A thirty-two-year-old woman was asleep in the passenger seat of a semitrailer for about one hour while crossing the remote Nullarbor Plains. She heard a voice call her name, telling her to awaken and look out the side window. Upon doing so, she saw a stationary egg-shaped object (about ten feet high by twenty feet long) on the ground which appeared to have a "force field" around it. The object glowed and was semitransparent. She saw two entities—a man walking in the direction of the object and a man sitting inside the craft. The illumination engulfing the egg decreased in intensity until no glow existed, while a single white light could be seen coming from the object. The figures were indistinguishable from normal humans. The walking being was wearing a loose-fitting white or silverish one-piece outfit which puffed up around the ankles and wrist.

Keith Basterfield, *An Indepth Review of Australasian UFO Related Entity Reports* (Australian Centre for UFO Studies, June 1980), pp. 8, 47, 71–73, 97, also personal notes of Keith Basterfield on the case, based on his direct investigation.

146. September 1973, near Atlanta, Georgia

An unnamed Georgia woman claimed to begin receiving communications with Zandark, a "member of the United Cosmic Council; a Commander in Chief in Charge of Directing Technical Transmissions Via Mental Telepathy of the Combination of Mediumistic Telepathy under the Direction of the Confederation of Cosmic Space Beings." He said they "come to bring peace" and claim to have built structures such as the sphinx and the pyramids.

John A. Keel, *The Mothman Prophecies* (New York: Signet, 1975), p. 137.

147. Sometime after October 11, 1973, Pascagoula, Mississippi, 8:00 P.M.

Fishing on a Pascagoula River pier, Charles Hickson and Calvin Parker watched a bright object descend. Three five-foot-tall entities with pointed ears, sharp noses, crablike hands, and elephant-like skin emerged and approached. Parker fainted and Hickson was floated aboard, examined by an eyelike device, and twenty minutes later said that he and Parker were deposited outside.

Both passed polygraph exams, and Hickson underwent regressive hypnosis. Although there was no apparent communication between the beings and the witnesses during this encounter, Hickson later claimed to have been in contact with telepathic extraterrestrials who claimed they would make themselves known in 1983.

Coral Lorenzen and Jim Lorenzen, *Abducted!: Confrontations with Beings from Outer Space* (New York: Berkley, 1977); M. Sachs, *The UFO Encyclopedia* (New York: Perigee, 1980); Ronald Story, *The Encyclopedia of UFOs* (New York: Doubleday, 1980); Ralph Blum and Judy Blum, *Beyond Earth: Man's Contact with UFOs* (New York: Bantam, 1980).

148. October 16, 1973, Lehi, Utah, night

Patricia Roach was asleep during the first night in her new house with her kids. She had been aware of reports of a local prowler. She awoke frightened with vague memories of an intruder in the house. Suspecting a prowler, she notified police and spent the rest of the night with a friend. The next day her daughter Dottie (age seven) said, "It wasn't a prowler, Mama, it was a spaceman." Nearly two years later, under regressive hypnosis, Roach told of being abducted by a "bright light" with "two figures over me." She saw three of her children "floated" into a bright room containing four or five beings and a lot of "machines and buttons." They were just over four feet tall, very thin, with large slanted eyes, long arms, and clawlike hands. They wore fluorescent clothing with belts and gloves. Roach said "they wanted to know how our minds work . . . to give them certain information that they don't have yet. . . . How we think. How we feel. Our emotions."

Dottie hypnotically recalls seeing a dark Indian girl wearing a dress on the UFO. She said "they put a needle in and they took my mind, my thoughts." A regular-looking man participated in the exam. He was five feet five inches tall, bald on top of his head with a fringe on the sides, dressed in black, wearing horn-rimmed glasses and a rubber glove. The alien asked "what I love, what I hate. What animals I like. They asked me about my family. They manipulated me." At one point during the exam a needle was pushed into her abdomen without pain. Daughter Betty also recalled her mother lying nude on the table surrounded by three aliens and a tall human male.

Coral Lorenzen and Jim Lorenzen, *Abducted!: Confrontations with Beings from Outer Space* (New York: Berkley, 1977); John Rimmer, *The Evidence for Alien Abductions* (London: Aquarian, 1984); Ronald Story, *The Encyclopedia of UFOs* (Garden City, N.Y.: Doubleday, 1980).

149. October 25, 1973, Uniontown, Pennsylvania, 9:00 P.M.

At least sixteen people saw a red sphere of light hovering high above a field. "Stephen" and two ten-year-old male friends drove out to investigate. His car headlights weakened as they approached. They walked over a hill crest and saw a domed-shaped object (one hundred feet in diameter) "like a big bubble . . . making a sound like a lawnmower." One of the young boys spotted the silhouette of a hulking creature nearby. Stephen fired a tracer bullet above two figures. In the light they could see two similar-looking seven- to eight-foot-tall creatures walking along a fenceline. They had long dark hair and green eyes. The arms were so long they almost touched the ground. The creatures were apparently communicating to each other with sounds similar to a baby crying. A burned rubber smell was also present. After Stephen fired three rounds of bullets into the bigger creature, it whined, moved its right shoulder close to the other creature, and the glowing object above the field vanished. The beings then turned and slowly walked into the woods.

By 9:45 P.M. state trooper Byrne arrived. He and Stephen soon started walking near the scene and heard a rustling. About a half hour later Stephen saw something coming from the woods, and the pair drove off. Just prior to this the officer let Stephen shoot his gun at a brown object nearby.

By 1:30 A.M., after being contacted by the police, a team of five UFO investigators, Stephen, and his father were on the scene. At about 2 A.M. a bull in a nearby field and Stephen's dog became excited. "Stephen began shaking back and forth as if he were going to faint. George Lutz asked him if he was OK, and Stephen then began shaking back and forth. . . . He began breathing very heavily and started growling like an animal. . . . Stephen was running around, swinging his arms, and loudly growling like an animal." After collapsing, he soon regained consciousness, saying: "Get away from me. It's here. Get back. . . . Keep away from the corner. . . . It's in the corner!" He later said during an interview that he saw a man dressed in a black hat and coat, carrying a sickle. "I kept seeing the date 1976. It popped out of my mouth: "If these people don't straighten out, the whole world will burn." He continued:

"I'm living in hell now. What I'm telling you happened before. This is how the world was destroyed. It will be very soon, and this world will be gone."

B. E. Schwarz, "Berserk: A UFO-Creature Encounter," *Flying Saucer Review* 20, no. 1 (1974); B. E. Schwarz, *UFO Dynamics Book I: Psychiatric and Psychic Dimensions of the UFO Syndrome* (Florida: Rainbow, 1983), pp. 195–213. Schwarz received his M.D. degree from New York University College of Medicine and is a fellow in psychiatry at the Mayo Foundation. Schwarz based his articles on an in-depth personal interview with Stephen and UFO investigators on the scene, including Stan Gordon, head of the Westmoreland County (Pennsylvania) UFO Study Group.

150. October 29, 1973, Toronto, Canada, 10:00 P.M.

While walking his dog in a park, a man watched a fluorescent blue-green light forming a circle on a brick wall. Inside this illuminated circle was a TV screen that emitted images, including that of alien entities. The man then communicated with the screen images. The witness became physically sick, and his dog was very frightened.

J. B. Musgrave, *UFO Occupants & Critters: The Patterns in Canada* (Amherst, Wis.: Amherst Press, in conjunction with Global Communications, 1980), pp. 51, 60, citing an investigation by Henry McKay.

151. November 2, 1973, between Manchester and Goffstown, New Hampshire, early morning

Shortly after leaving work as a masseuse at the Swedish Sauna in Manchester, Lyndia Morel noticed a big yellow light skyward while driving on Route 114A. The bright light flashed green, red, and blue. After the light went out and came back a couple of times, Morel saw it hovering in front of her. It was an orange and gold sphere covered with honeycomb hexagons with an oval window in the upper left. She heard a high-pitched whine, coinciding with a tingling through her body. Suddenly her eyes were drawn to it, her hands glued to the steering wheel as she lost control and was drawn to the object. She saw a being through the craft window. The face was lighter than the rest of the body, with a grayish, circular head. Its face had elephantlike wrinkles, and egg-shaped eyes with dark pupils that grabbed her attention. It had no nose or ears and a slitlike mouth. At this point she felt something was telling her "Don't be afraid."

Morel managed to pull off the road, run to a nearby house, and summon help. She told the startled couple inside, "Help me! I'm not drunk! I'm not on drugs! A UFO just tried to pick me up!" Although the couple could not hear the noise, Morel says the whine and tingling sensation continued for another two minutes. The investigating police officer, the couple, and Morel later saw a vague light in the sky, matching the appearance and location of Mars.

Aerial Phenomena Research Organization Bulletin (January–February 1974).

152. 1973, near Frederick, Maryland, night

"Steven Kilburn" said that while he was an undergraduate arts student at the University of Maryland he had had a strong feeling that "something happened to me . . . when I was driving home." He couldn't be more specific, "but something has always bothered me about a certain stretch of road I used to pass through whenever I left my girlfriend's house in Maryland." More specifically, it was ten to fifteen miles of desolate Route 40 between Frederick and Baltimore, Maryland. He consciously recalled the car stopping, getting out and feeling being watched. After discussing the incident with UFO researcher Budd Hopkins, psychologist Girard Franklin put Kilburn under regressive hypnosis. He told of the car stopping and getting out. His recall of the experience was very intense at this point, and tears streamed down his cheeks. An object clamped onto his body, immobilized him in pain, and turned him around as a very bright light and at least three beings "all dressed in black" were seen.

Seven months later he underwent another hypnotic session with psychologist Aphrodite Clamar. He told of the car moving by itself "like a magnet just sucked it over to the right." He now states that he previously had seen two hazy, whitish UFOs high over the road. At least three beings approached, but he no longer feared them. They had "chalky" or "putty" skin. He was touched with "white plastic tubes," causing him pain. One of the beings appeared to be "the boss." He had big black almond-shaped, shiny eyes without pupils and walked "like he had two really bad knees. He was hobbling almost . . . shifting his weight to the left and right. He had a very skinny build, extremely thin arms, legs, club feet, a pointed chin, thin neck and slit mouth."

By the fall of 1979, Kilburn could consciously recall being taken aboard a UFO and examined. During a fourth hypnotic session (January 1980), he said the beings gestured to him to enter a saucer where he was escorted through a tunnel to a white room with several beings inside. He was put on a table. He next realized he was clad only in a diaperlike outfit and apparently examined by a device from the ceiling. They then asked him to turn on his stomach. Two days after the hypnosis session he consciously recalled feeling "physically dirty, and wanted very much to shower," although he was too tired and went to sleep instead.

Budd Hopkins, *Missing Time: A Documented Study of UFO Abductions* (New York: Richard Marek, 1981), pp. 51–88.

153. April 6, 1974, Kitami City, Japan, 3:00 A.M.

Checking on his barking dog, Yoshiro Fujiwara claims to have seen a three-foot-tall "starfish" creature which held out an appendage, resulting in Fujiwara's being pulled about seventy feet off the ground and into a hovering object. After passing out, he awoke to see two beings with toadlike skin and a bad odor holding him down. After being told not to be frightened, he remained panic-stricken. Soon the craft landed, and a door opened, and he left.

That same evening he was in mental contact with "spacemen." Two evenings later, the beings returned in a craft, taking him around Earth twice and the moon once. After the trip, he was found partially conscious on the ground. During a later contact, he claims to have been taken to Jupiter and given a rock. Analysis showed it was limestone.

Copy of a letter stating details of the report by Junichi Takanashi for the Mutual UFO Network via Robert C. Girard, UFO book dealer, Scotia, N.Y.; also *Caveat Emptor* (September–October 1974).

154. June 1, 1974, Fort Victoria, Zimbabwe, 2:00 A.M.

While driving from Salisbury, Zimbabwe, to Beitbridge, South Africa, "Peter" (twenty-three) and his wife, Francis (twenty-one), saw a metallic figure crouching by the road. A half-hour later, a light on a distant hill approached the car, and their vehicle's headlights dimmed, but Peter continued using the "intense blue-white light around the car" to drive by. He was no longer controlling the car, and it gradually gained speed as the inside grew cold. This continued for two hours, until they neared Fort Victoria, when the light left and they regained control of their car. Soon two objects appeared, and the entire scenario was repeated, until they reached the Zimbabwe border, well after 6 A.M. The pair then realized they had traveled 170 miles at an amazing speed on just a half gallon of fuel.

Under regressive hypnosis, Peter said, "A space being was projected to the back seat of the car and sat there for the entire journey." Although he never left the car, he saw a similar type of being above in the ship. The figure in the car told Peter in English, "I would see the being only as I wanted to see it. If I wanted to see the being resemble a duck, it would look like a duck." The being said, "Because as we look at a dog in comparison, saying, 'Stupid dog,' so they look at us, saying, 'Stupid humans.' "

The two beings had "large chests, necks—[were] hairless, [had] two arms, two legs, no toes" and no visible sex organs. The friendly figure came from the "Outer Galaxy" and told Peter "they are time travelers, not space travelers." They speak all languages and come from a system of twelve planets of the Milky Way. "They don't fight, they have no wars . . . they are 2,000 light-years ahead of us." Peter also said there are thousands of them living with us as apparently normal humans to "direct the Earth."

C. Hind, *UFOs—African Encounters* (Zimbabwe: Gemini, 1982); C. Bowen, ed., *Encounter Cases from Flying Saucer Review* (New York: Signet, 1977); Dr. Carl Van Vlierden (Mutual UFO Network representative) conducted an in-depth interview with the witnesses; hypnosis by Dr. Paul Obertik.

155. October 25, 1974, Medicine Bow National Forest, Wyoming, 4:00 P.M.

While hunting in the Medicine Bow Mountains, Carl Higdon spotted five elk. He fired his rifle, but "the bullet only went about 50 feet and dropped." Retrieving the bullet, he saw a six-foot two-inch, 180-pound "man" in a black outfit and black shoes, wearing a belt with a star in the center. The bowlegged man had human facial features, except for a slanted head, no chin and his hair stood straight up. He called himself Ausso. Higdon said, "He asked me if I was hungry and I said yea . . . he tossed me some pills and I took one. I don't know why I did it—I never take pills of any kind unless a doctor prescribed them, not even aspirin." Another man appeared, asking if he wanted to go with them, and Higdon said yes. A helmet was put over Higdon's head and he was told they were going "home," 163,000 "light miles" away in a cubicle. He was taken to a room with a ninety-foot tower, where a shield came out from the wall and stayed in front of him for three to four minutes before retracting. Higdon was told he wasn't what they needed and would be returned. He was floated back to the ship and next found himself on a mountain slope. He fell on loose rock, injuring his head, neck, and shoulder. He managed to walk back to his truck and call for help on the C.B. radio, although he didn't know who or where he was. By 11:30 P.M. sheriff's officers found him and brought him to the Carbon City Memorial Hospital, where a physical exam by Dr. R. C. Tongco found nothing unusual besides amnesia. Dr. Tongco stated that Higdon's eyes "could not be examined properly because [Higdon] claims that the light is just too bright." Some of the details of his experience were brought out under regressive hypnosis.

Rawlings Times (Wyoming), October 19, 1974, and June 7, 1978; Jim Lorenzen and Coral Lorenzen, *Abducted! Confrontations with Beings from Outer Space* (New York: Berkley, 1977). A copy of the original medical report on Higdon by Dr. R. C. Tongco, dated October 26, 1974, appears in Leo Sprinkle, "Investigation of the Alleged UFO Experience of Carl Higdon," in Richard Haines, ed., *UFO Phenomena and the Behavioral Scientist* (Metuchen, N.J.: Scarecrow, 1979), pp. 225–357.

156. October 27, 1974, Aveley, Essex, England, late evening

"John" and "Elaine Avis" and their three kids were returning home after visiting Elaine's parents, when their son "Kevin" noticed a pale blue, oval-shaped aerial object. The object was soon lost to view. Suddenly they drove into a green mist, the car engine quit, the radio began smoking, and the car shook violently. Upon arriving home at 1 A.M., they were unable to account for two and a half hours of missing time. The family, especially John, began having dreams involving strange creatures. John soon became obsessed with these dreams. After hearing a UFO radio program, he contacted a UFO researcher and underwent regressive hypnosis, during which he told of encountering apelike humanoids with beaklike noses, triangular eyes, slanted mouths, pointed ears, and clawlike hands who gave him a medical exam. They verbally communicated that Earth would be destroyed by pollution. He was later returned to the car. Elaine later said she could consciously recall generally similar details. She initially refused, but later underwent limited hypnosis.

Andrew Collins, "The Aveley Abduction," *Flying Saucer Review* 23, no. 6 (April 1978), and 24, no. 1 (June 1978); Ronald Story, *The Encyclopedia of UFOs* (Garden City, N.Y.: Doubleday, 1980); Hilary Evans, *UFOs—The Greatest Mystery* (Albany: London, 1979).

157. October 28, 1974, near Bahia Blanca, Argentina, 1:15 A.M.

Argentinian truck driver Dionisio Llanca was admitted to Bahia Blanca Hospital at 7:45 A.M. Sunday morning, October 28, 1974, in a state of amnesia, after being found stumbling about the Bahia Blanca railyards. Three days later he related a fantastic story.

Llanca claims he was changing a tire outside Bahia Blanca on Route 3 when a bright yellow light illuminated the area. He became paralyzed and noticed "a plate suspended in the air." Three beings appeared, who watched him for about five minutes. There were two men and one woman. He was sure one was female "because of the form of the breast" and long blonde hair. The two men had short blond hair. All stood about five and a half feet tall and wore tight-fitting, single-piece, smoky-gray coverall suits. "Their faces were like ours except for high foreheads and elongated eyes, like the Japanese, and a little tilted." They wore long gloves and yellow boots, speaking "like a radio badly tuned with chirps and buzzes." One held him while another placed an "apparatus" in the base of his index finger. After it was removed there were two drops of blood on his finger. He next remembered awakening among the railcars and was later found by a motorist and taken to the hospital.

Aerial Phenomena Research Organization Bulletin (November 1973): 7–8; (December 1973): 5–8.

158. January 28, 1975, near Hinwel, Switzerland

Swiss farmer Eduard Meir's first contact occurred after acting on an urge to go to a place where a flying saucer later appeared. The beings were from the planet Erra, in the star group Pleiades. They look similar to humans. Most of Meier's contacts have been with a Pleiadian called Semjase, who appears "as a small Nordic girl with fine features, eyes that are slightly slanted but not Oriental, a slender figure, slender hands, skin that is very delicate and whiter than ours, thin lips, small straight white teeth and shell ears . . . set slightly lower than ours and blend right into the neck." The aliens view Earth as an insane society, rushing to our own suicide, and warned that the ionosphere is being destroyed by pollutants.

Arizona Republic (Phoenix), December 16, 1979.

159. May 1975, Cali, Columbia

German Navarrete claims two Martian scientists, Ran Kar and Kepton, each with an average life span of two hundred Earth years, telepathically told him many large-scale natural disasters would occur over the next ten years. Among them, most of Africa, North and South America, the Caribbean, and Pacific Islands would sink. They also predicted atomic war between three superpowers in 1977 and that by 1983 two new planets would be identified, resulting in a new series of "telluric movements" and "a verticalization of the terrestrial axis." By 1988, the vast geophysical destruction will have spared Australia and a few other areas. They also said Mars has two humanoid races—one of tall, thin, and powerful beings; the other having almost transparent skin, fair hair, blue eyes, and advanced brains. The two Martian languages are Sans and Iridin, which are communicated telepathically.

Ultima Hora (Buenos Aires), Argentina, evening edition, May 21, 1975; *El Cronista Comercial* (Buenos Aires), Argentina, June 10, 1975; *Flying Saucer Review* 21, nos. 3 and 4 (1975): 62.

160. June 9, 1975, Tenerife, Canary Islands

Spanish psychologist Emilio Bourgon claimed he and two others were taken into an alien craft at Tenerife Beach. The group of aliens, tall males in black and white outfits, huge gloves, and helmets, were "friendly," wanting "to help man." They were "very concerned with misery, ignorance and insalubrity" on Earth.

Cronica (Buenos Aires), Argentina, April 12, 1978.

161. August 13, 1975, near Alamogordo, New Mexico, 1:20 A.M.

Watching a meteor shower on a deserted dirt road, U.S. Air Force Sergeant Charles Moody claims to have seen a dull metallic object giving off a high-pitched sound, which suddenly stopped when he felt numb, peaceful, calm. He was taken aboard and met several beings (about five feet tall) looking "much like us" except they had large hairless heads, small ears and noses, big eyes and thin lips. "There was speech, but their lips did not move." They wore black skin-tight clothing, except one being "had on a silver-white-looking suit." They seemed to read his mind "and called me by my proper name—Charles—and did not use my nickname, Chuck." Inside the craft was very clean.

At the end of the meeting, the leader or elder placed his hands on the sides of Moody's head, said it was time to leave and asked him not to recall his experience for two weeks. (Two weeks later he claims to have remembered.) The being said they would meet again shortly and that he should see a doctor soon. When asked why he was contacted, he was told that in time "you will understand."

Moody later said a group of races is studying us and within three years would make themselves known to all mankind. "It will not be a pleasant type of meeting, for there will be warnings made to the people of this world. Their plan is for limited contact and after twenty years of further study and only after deeper consideration will there be any type of closer contact. They fear for their own lives and will protect themselves at all costs. Their intent is a peaceful one, and if the leaders of this world will only heed their warnings we will find ourselves a lot better off."

Aerial Phenomena Research Organization Bulletin (June 1976): 6 (July 1976): 5–6.

162. October 12, 1975, Maple Ridge, British Columbia, Canada, evening

Mr. and Mrs. David Hamel were watching TV when it went "snowy." Two beings emerged in "a silver dust." The entities—one male, one female—resembled humans and wore one-piece suits. Coming to where David sat, they touched his arm and telepathically explained they intended to elevate him to a spaceship above his home, then did so.

Personal letter from John B. Musgrave, employee of the Mobile Planetarium Project at the Provincial Museum of Alberta, Edmonton, Canada, citing *Canadian UFO Report*, no. 34 (Spring 1979): 8–10.

163. October 27, 1975, Norway, Maine, 3:00 A.M.

David Stephens suggested to his friend "P" they take a ride. A few minutes later P suddenly lost control of the van. Both panicked and soon saw multicolored aerial lights nearby. When P regained control of the vehicle, they stopped, but seeing aerial lights, they soon panicked and sped off. The van skidded sideways, and the two lost consciousness. Upon regaining awareness, they drove on, then returned to search for the lights. They saw an aerial object and P again lost control of the van, which then stalled out. The vehicle was enveloped by a fog and several objects were seen, which eventually flew off. Soon the van restarted. Stephens experienced a series of nightmares after the incident. Both noticed a period of missing time.

Under regressive hypnosis, Stephens said he was taken by a humanlike creature with slanted eyes and was telepathically told not to worry. He was taken to a room where his blood was extracted, and was later returned to the van. P refused hypnosis.

B. E. Schwarz, *UFO Dynamics: Book 1* (Florida: Rainbow, 1983); Coral Lorenzen and Jim Lorenzen, *Abducted!: Confrontations with Beings from Outer Space* (New York: Berkley, 1977); J. Rimmer, *The Evidence for Alien Abductions* (London: Aquarian, 1984).

164. Approximately November 3, 1975, Bokoel, Florida, 2:00 A.M.

Richard Jackson awoke, went out of his trailer, and saw a domed craft and a set of steps extending up to a door. He was invited inside by a five-foot-tall, chubby, dark-skinned man with no shirt and wearing brown coveralls. He said in English that they hailed from Planteh and were preparing a "neighboring planet" to be colonized by Earthlings. Jackson was asked to assist them in recruiting volunteers; in return he would be given perfect health. After an hour and a half, he left the craft, which shot off. He next recalls being in his trailer.

News-Press (Fort Meyers, Florida), December 15, 1975.

165. December 2, 1975, Fargo, North Dakota, 4 A.M.

Sandra Larson awoke to see two beings with luminous, mummy-like heads and brown "vinyl" bodies standing at her bed. She was floated through a wall into a nearby ship. When she was escorted from the craft, she was on another planet, where she was taken to a square building, questioned telepathically, and later taken home, floating through a closed door. As she began considering taking a bath, one being asked what soap was. At this, she gave him a cup of laundry detergent.

A report investigated by Jerome Clark in *UFO Report*, August 1976, pp. 21–23, 46–53.

166. January 6, 1976, near Hustonville, Kentucky, 11:15 P.M.

Driving down a highway, three women saw what they thought was a plane on fire. Mona Stafford was the first to spot the object. She became frightened, as did the others. Stafford says the car then drove by itself and accelerated to eighty-five m.p.h. Soon the car slowed, and she gained control of it. Stafford suffered severe eye irritation and red marks on her body, while Louise Smith suffered minor eye irritation and red marks. Elaine Thomas reported minor eye irritation. Unable to account for two hours and ten minutes of time in the auto, the trio agreed to undergo regressive hypnosis.

Mona Stafford recounted lying alone on a white table or bed while a large "eye" watched. She was then examined by four or five short humanoids wearing "surgical masks." During this time a "power" transfixed her to the bed/table.

Elaine Thomas recalled being separated from her companions and taken into a "chamber" containing a window. Humanoids with dark eyes and gray skin moved back and forth in front of the window, appearing to watch her. A bullet-shaped object (an inch and a half in diameter) was placed on her chest, causing discomfort.

Louise Smith described being examined while lying down. The aliens communicated telepathically. Specific details of her experience were withheld, since she wanted to write a book outlining the incident.

Ronald Story, *The Encyclopedia of UFOs* (Garden City, N.Y.: Doubleday, 1980), based on a report in the *Aerial Phenomena Research Organization Bulletin* (October 1976).

167. January 21, 1976, near Matias-Barbosa, Brazil, 11:30 P.M.

Driving the Rio de Janeiro-Belo Horizonte Highway, Erminio Reis felt "sleepy" and pulled off to nap. Minutes later, his wife, Bianca Reis, saw a bluish light illuminate the landscape. It advanced, and their Volkswagen "was absorbed as if through a chimney" into "a kind of circular garage, intensely lighted." At this point, Erminio was awake. Two dark male beings (about six feet six inches tall) approached and signaled for them to leave the car. Bianca said "the ground seemed to move." She also "felt as if drunk without having had anything to drink." The two men talked in a strange language. They were then taken up a staircase to a large room with many instruments. She said, "One of the strangers gave us headsets, put a pair over his ears" and "plugged" them into a device. A voice in Portuguese proclaimed, "My name is Karen, calm down. . . ."

Bianca was given a series of medical tests. Later they were made to drink an ill-tasting liquid substance. Then others, including a female, arrived. Karen said, "We also perform medical research. Old age continues being an illness, but we have been about to conquer it. In our world death does not exist." They were later instructed not to "talk about what has happened," as people would think they were crazy. "If you wish, we have a method to erase memories." The pair declined. Since the incident, Bianca claims to have been contacted by a small device the aliens use to measure brain waves.

La Nueva Province (Bahia Blanca, Argentina), September 17, 1978.

168. January 2, 1976, near Las Vegas, Nevada, 10:30 P.M.

Driving north toward Las Vegas after a singing performance in a nearby town, country singer John Sands noticed an aerial light following him, slowly getting closer. His car engine died as the object hovered one thousand feet above the car, then slowly disappeared over a nearby mountain. He soon saw two motionless figures in his headlights two hundred feet down the road. Suddenly, "I couldn't move my body." The figures approached. One of the males was described in detail: bald, of average height, without eyebrows or eyelashes, and pointed skin flaps for ears. His eyes were sunken, his chin strong and squared, his mouth tight-lipped. He wore a seamless black-silver skin-tight suit. "He started to talk, but he didn't use his mouth. It sounded like two people talking on the telephone long distance . . . muffled and a little slower than our speech."

Sands was told Earth's nuclear explosions created serious lapses in time sequences as we know it, resulting in faster aging and more disease. The situation was also creating problems for the aliens' planet. They warned, "We are going to stop it one way or another." They asked him what he was doing there, why there were so many people in Las Vegas, and what our means of communication is. To the last query, Sands said he didn't understand the question, as there are many means of communication. Apparently irritated, one of the humanoids replied, "Answer the question!" After Sands repeated that he didn't understand, the questioner turned to his companion, and they silently gazed at each other for two or three minutes. The questioner then extended his left hand, brushed Sands's left hand, and said, "We know where you are and will see you again." They turned and walked into the desert; a flash of light "came up" and they were gone.

John Wallace Spencer, *The UFO Yearbook* (Springfield, Mass.: Phillips, 1976), pp. 65–69.

169. March 3, 1976, near Refrigerio, Brazil, 4 P.M.

Walking home from school in a wooded area, twelve-year-old Francessco Ojeda came upon a clearing and saw a shiny round craft (forty feet in diameter) sitting on a small metal platform. Two beings (under five feet tall) in shiny suits were apparently making repairs. Upon seeing Ojeda, they entered the ship, and a blinding light hit him, knocking him partially unconscious. He vaguely recalls being taken aboard, having his clothing removed, and being placed on a table under a bright amber light. A telepathic voice reassured him of no harm, then said, "We are coming here in great numbers to visit your planet." The boy was later found by his parents, blind and with a "sunburn," wandering one mile from his house. The following day his sight was restored.

Gray Barker in *UFO Report* 4, no. 2 (June 1977), quoting *La Nacion*.

170. August 22, 1976, Egg Harbor, Wisconsin, 4:15 A.M.

Using a riding lawn mower on a golf course, Dean Anderson stopped after seeing a big orange object land nearby. Two beings floated out a door on a "band of light." As they approached, the object left. They extended their hands, shaking Anderson's hand, and the male said, "We come in peace. I am Sunar, from Jupiter. This is Treena; she comes from Saturn." They said they were on a scientific specimen-gathering mission. Treena had shoulder-length hair, bluish-gray eyes, a light tan, stood five feet two inches tall, and resembled Elizabeth Taylor. She wore a one-piece, skin-tight light green suit of a "glistening metallic material." Sunar has copperlike skin and claimed to be over two hundred years old.

After talking for twenty minutes, Anderson was given an envelope and asked not to open it for five Earth days. They then left. When Anderson opened it, it contained a golden "amulet" with a dovelike bird on one side; on the other were the words "Peace and friendship forever, Treena and Sunar." Beside the names were depictions of Saturn and Jupiter. Anderson will not allow the amulet to be photographed. During the encounter, Sunar claimed to have once met the Baha'u'llah, who founded the Baha'i religion (Anderson is chairman of the local Baha'i chapter).

Keta Steebs, writing in *The Advocate* (Sturgeon Bay, Wis.), March 31, 1977.

171. December 1976, Ossining, New York

Self-proclaimed psychic Greta Woodrew claims that while in a deep hypnotic trance during an experiment with parapsychologist Dr. Andrija Puharich she contacted beings from the planet Ogatta, light-years away. She passed through a long, shadowy tunnel which was guarded by Hshames, a humanlike being, along with a pair of birdlike entities. Hshames was covered with tiny feathers and stood just over five feet, had glowing, gold-speckled eyes with no lashes and an upper lip that resembled a bird beak. They communicated telepathically, the being telling her about Ogatta.

In a later contact, during her next hypnotic trance session, she says her soul separated from her body and traveled to Ogatta, the surface of which was covered with small glistening points of light that had a fluidlike appearance.

During the third experiment, a figure named Ogatta spoke, telling her that "beings had set up a way-station on the minor planet Vesta in our solar system, which will be used to help Earth. An armada of spacecraft would come down to Earth after drastic changes occurred. Their preparations were well under way." She was then showed scenes of the destruction to follow in the coming decades, such as earthquakes, volcanic displays, floods, hurricanes, droughts, and magnetic storms. Woodrew also said, "I was told by the extraterrestrials that they were survivors of what could come."

N. Blundell and R. Boar, *The World's Greatest UFO Mysteries* (New York: Exeter, 1983), p. 189.

172. 1976, British Columbia, Canada, night

Helene was dying of pancreatic cancer. She says a voice called her out of bed two months before doctors predicted she would die. Called from her house to a clearing several miles away, she came to a brilliant light and a spacecraft. "From the center of this large craft came a cylinder of light, and in this cylinder these two beings came down." The "small humanoids" wore "tight-fitting suits." She was floated to the ship where another being used several unusual instruments to cure her. This was done, they said, because they might need her help in the future. She was apparently still living in 1983.

Personal letter from John B. Musgrave, employee of the Mobile Planetarium Project, Alberta, Edmonton, Canada, citing *Arizona Daily Star* (Tucson), September 4, 1983.

173. 1976, Guadalajara, Mexico

Dr. Leopoldo Diaz claims two contacts with aliens. One day in 1976 a normal-looking man walked into his office and insisted on a complete physical exam. Diaz found him healthy, and the man said he was an alien. "He showed me a great wisdom . . . knowledge," and warned that humans are about to destroy themselves because of divisions and separations which lead to selfishness, envy, and deceit, resulting in war and death. Diaz says there are ten thousand space beings living among us because "they want to help us." They will "speak more and more. It is important to understand this."

During a second visit, Diaz claims he was instructed to proclaim the truth far and wide. His message is that "God is everywhere . . . all . . . religions you profess on Earth . . . are only roads to the same purpose—to know God."

Daily Press (Virginia), April 11, 1980.

174. January 27, 1977, near Clarksville, Tennessee

Driving on I-40, fifteen miles from Clarksville, farmer Donald Fender felt "like someone wanted to talk to me." He traveled on a side road and encountered an egg-shaped "spaceship." Beings emerged, saying they were from an unknown planet and were here as emissaries of peace. They stopped near Clarksville, the only place they can enter Earth's atmosphere, for they travel via a space vacuum, which is aligned where the road runs north and south through Clarksville. The visitors told Fender that because the location is the only place where the time-warp vacuum can be created, it will become a place from where all space travel will originate. "They said they were coming back . . . they didn't say when."

Timothy Green Beckley, *Timothy Green Beckley's Book of Space Contacts* (New York: Global Communications, 1981), pp. 41–42, citing the *Clarksville Leaf-Chronicle* (Tennessee), February 2, 1977.

175. Approximately February 7, 1977, near Warminster, England

In November 1976, Mrs. Joyce Bowles was driving in a rural area with a family friend, retired farm manager Ted Pratt, when she says the car suddenly seemed to float before it stopped. Bowles started screaming in response to seeing a large creature with pink eyes that were "horrible, as bright as the sun." The craft then quickly rose and flew off.

In early February the pair were again driving in the country when they heard a whistling sound. The car rocked and Bowles said, "Suddenly we were both inside this machine. . . . One of the spacemen standing a few feet from me was the same man I saw the first time. Lights were blinking and flashing everywhere. The man told us this was his field, whatever that meant." The beings wore luminous silvery suits and "high jackboots with pointed toes." At the center of their belts was "a glittering stone, and the man next to me kept pressing his stone or touching it." Suddenly they were back in the car.

Bowles claims at least two later contacts, one with sixty-five-year-old Ann Strickland on March 7, 1977, and the other with Ted Pratt in June of 1977.

N. Blundell and R. Boar, *The World's Greatest UFO Mysteries* (New York: Exeter, 1983), pp. 128–31.

176. March 12, 1977, Gisborne, New Zealand, 1:00 A.M.

Camping on a steep hill to watch for UFOs during a wave of sightings, three women ("B," "S," and "I") talked intermittently and dozed. They recall simultaneously waking in panic and fleeing to their car. Unable to account for two hours, B said under hypnosis that she suddenly awoke at 1 A.M. and touched a metallic boot. She turned away so as not to see the figure, looked at her sleeping friends, remained calm, and fell back asleep. B was taken to a small multicolored room and telepathically communicated with normal-sized human-looking male beings wearing white coveralls and boots. She also saw S in the craft. B was beamed back to the hill and began kicking in her sleep, waking her companions. They all panicked and fled.

M. Dykes, *Strangers in Our Skies: UFOs Over New Zealand* (Lower Hutt, Wellington, New Zealand: INL Publications, 1981).

177. August 6, 1977, near Pelham, Georgia, between 6 A.M. and noon

Mr. Dawson was walking his two dogs near a cow pasture when a circular object suddenly appeared in the sky and hovered above the ground. Paralyzed, he noticed his dogs and some forty nearby cows were also "frozen." The craft landed and a door opened; three men and two women emerged. They had pale white skin, pointed ears, sharp turned-up noses, and no necks. Two were nude, having hairless bodies. Clothing on the three other beings was "beautiful" and both sexes dressed alike in "silky" shoes with toes pointing upward. Dawson was given what he believes was a medical exam. He was fitted with a "skullcap" with cords extending into a ringlike device containing dials. Near the end of the exam, Dawson says a voice from inside the craft shouted, "I am Jimmy Hoffa! I am Jimmy

Hoffa! I am—" The cry abruptly stopped in mid-sentence. After the exam, the beings got together and talked in unintelligible, shrill voices. They then reentered the craft and flew off.

Milt Machlin with Timothy Green Beckley, *UFO* (New York: Quick Fox, 1981), p. 48.

178. September 4, 1977, Barrio Abr Centro, Puerto Rico, 3:30 P.M.

Lying in a hammock, Luis Sandoval (a seventy-four-year-old farmer) felt an urge to go to a nearby hill, where he heard a bang and saw a flash and a blue candle-shaped object. A three-foot-tall humanoid with a round, unattractive face, long pointed ears, big lips, a small mouth, and flaring nostrils emerged wearing what appeared to be a jacket and small tie. It told him in Spanish to "have courage," then examined his body. Sandoval was not scared. The being claimed to be an extraterrestrial, and said, "How nice Puerto Rico is." He stepped back and immediately vanished in a blue fire that rapidly flew off.

El Vocero de Puerto Rico (San Juan), September 19, 1977.

179. 1977, near Bulloo River, southwest Queensland, Australia

Three slim cylinders landed near a remote camp, and humanlike beings with blue-gray skin emerged and began playing games with lightning spheres. A prospector was told the beings hailed from Begua. Their women wore summer clothes, while the males dressed in gray business-style suits. They left after two days.

The prospector claims several UFO sightings in the vicinity, and on one previous occasion he saw a male and a female being in an aerial object.

Keith Basterfield, in the *Aerial Phenomena Research Organization Bulletin* (April 1979): 7–8.

180. 1977, near Paciencia, Brazil, 2:20 A.M.

Leaving his house at the usual hour of 2:20 A.M., Antonio La Rubia walked to a nearby field where he noticed a gray object on the ground. As a bright blue light enveloped the area, he became paralyzed as he suddenly noticed three "robots" (four feet tall). They each had a single antenna jutting from the top of their heads, which looked like a football placed sideways. A band of small, blue-shaded mirrors extended across the middle of their heads. They had two long armlike appendages (compared to an elephant's trunk) which narrowed to pointed tips. Their bodies were covered with scales, and they had only one leg, extending down from the center of the trunk. They didn't walk, but floated. One robot pointed an instrument at Antonio, and he involuntarily moved toward the disc, where inside he was shown a series of color pictures:

(1) Antonio naked, being examined by two robots.

(2) Antonio standing, still nude.

(3) Antonio clothed, carrying a shopping bag (his teeth were noticeably chattering).

(4) A horse and cart being pulled over a dirt road.

(5) Antonio inside a light orange-colored sphere.

(6) A blue sphere with one of the beings inside.

(7) A dog angrily barking at one of the beings.

(8) An apparent UFO factory where "millions" of "beings" or "robots" milled around.

(9) An old windowless train disappearing into a tunnel.

(10) An avenue jammed with cars.

Antonio also told of being struck with a syringe in the middle finger, removing some blood. Later he was thrown overboard and fell into a street near the abduction site. The entire episode lasted about thirty minutes.

Aerial Phenomena Research Organization Bulletin (October 1977): 1–2.

181. Early January 1978, Iran

A twelve-year-old girl, Sara, claims to have communicated with a space being five times over a seven-day period. The creature (about six feet seven inches tall) had arms three times the length of humans and was covered with black fur. It identified itself as "HONOR," who hails from a place that is ten light-years ahead of Earth. The creature apparently gave Sara strange abilities, as she is allegedly able to unplug wall sockets, move furniture, and turn the radio on and off without touching any of the items.

Rhein Neckar (West Germany), January 10, 1978.

182. February 1978, Ermington, Devon, England

While pressing clothes in her backyard, Mrs. G. noticed a shining blue shape approach her home from the north. She was soon engulfed "in bubbles of light." Three apparently male beings (about five feet tall) wearing bluish-metallic clothing approached. "They grasped me by the arms and we were lifted up [by] a beam of light into a kind of room. There were more of the men there. I was given the impression—I don't know how—that I would come to no harm." Later, "I found myself back on my lawn. I felt a sharp blow on the back of my neck. I was stunned but not hurt. When I looked around, the thing set off at great speed and disappeared."

Nigel Blundell and Roger Boar, *The World's Greatest UFO Mysteries* (New York: Exeter, 1984), p. 54, quoting an interview based on an investigation by the British UFO group Contact UK.

183. March 18, 1978, North Charleston, South Carolina, night

Investigating a UFO in a field, auto mechanic William Herrmann left his mobile home and next recalls being in a strange area with an object whirring overhead. After flagging a car, he found it was several hours later than he thought. Herrmann didn't recall the abduction until nearly a year later, when he says a UFO raced toward him, projecting a blinding aquamarine light. "I tried to run, but my legs wouldn't move . . . I was paralyzed. I couldn't yell. I thought, oh God, I'm going to die."

Later, he was "on this low examination table only two feet above the floor." Three strange-looking beings watched him. "Their skin was the color of a marshmallow. Their eyes were long and dark with a brown iris. Their heads looked like overgrown human fetuses with no ears or hair. I heard a voice telling me to have no fear." The aliens said there are three races of intelligent space beings that visit Earth, conduct experiments, and observe life.

On April 21, 1979, he says a metal bar bearing the letters "MAN" and mysterious symbols suddenly materialized in "a globe of blue-green light" in his bedroom. On a second trip aboard the UFO (May 16, 1979), he was told the bar "was a gift . . . signifying they were thankful for and appreciative of the way I handled the situation" after the earlier abduction. A Massachusetts Institute of Technology analysis of the bar revealed ordinary elements (a cast alloy of lead and 6 percent antimony).

News and Courier (Charleston, South Carolina), November 18, 1979.

184. May 15, 1978, near Caujimolpa, Mexico

Walking along a road, Ignacio Sanchez Munoz saw a hovering multicolored luminous cube emitting a buzzing sound and a yellow beam. He then received telepathic thoughts saying the cube was empty, but soon humanlike beings would arrive on Earth. After conversing with the voice for an hour, he was told, "Soon we shall return to chat with you."

International UFO Reporter 3, no. 7 (July 1978): 2.

185. May 17, 1978, near Lublin, Poland, 8 A.M.

Driving a horse-drawn carriage in a wooded region, a seventy-one-year-old farmer saw at least two men in smooth, black, tight-fitting "diver suits." They had green faces, slanted eyes, webbed hands and moved in a jumping motion. He was invited inside the white "bus-shaped" craft hovering close by. The inside was entirely black and had benches. After being examined by an X-ray-like device, he declined an invitation to eat a transparent material which the beings consumed. Rectangular footprints were later reportedly found at the site. A separate UFO sighting took place in the area at about the same time.

International UFO Reporter 3, no. 7 (July 1978): 2, citing Polish newspaper, *Kurier Polski*.

186. June 19, 1978, near Brockworth, Gloucestershire, England, 10:15 P.M.

John Mann and his family were driving home after visiting John's mother in Reading. John noticed a light one mile ahead. The family soon all saw a huge, multicolored, saucer-shaped object near Stanford-in-the-Vale, and they briefly stopped to watch. Everyone became frightened by the sight. John panicked and sped off. He then lost control of the car, which began driving by itself. The car then slowed down, and John snapped out of a "dream" state. Within twenty minutes they arrived at home, at 10:35 P.M., only to find the forty-five-minute trip took an hour longer. John developed skin irritation and itching. Soon, his daughter Natasha dreamed about UFOs, and John and his sister Francis sought and underwent regressive hypnosis. John described how the family was abducted when they stopped by the road to watch the UFO. Everyone floated upward in a "light beam" to a circular room where there were three men in metallic suits with blue eyes and pale faces. They were given medical exams. A man called Uxiaulia had a disc insignia on his uniform and told Francis that their planet, Janos, was devastated by meteorites from nearby Sarton, a planet that got too close to their sun and broke up. They escaped to a huge base ship which now sends out explorer ships—like the one they were on—to find a suitable planet to inhabit. She was told they "would like to live here." They were given fizzy drinks as they left the ship "to help you forget . . . you must forget because you will be exploited. In time you will remember. We will meet again, and you will know us." John's wife and two daughters did not undergo hypnosis, but Natasha later consciously recounted details similar to the story told by John and Francis.

F. Johnson, *The Janos People* (London: Neville Spearman, 1980); N. Blundell and R. Boar, *The World's Greatest UFO Mysteries* (New York: Exeter, 1984).

187. September 14, 1978, near Belden, Nebraska, night

While driving on Interstate 20, a prominent businessman watched a bright object land on the road ahead. He stopped his car twenty yards from the object, which closely resembled an army tank. As the witness began to exit the car, a door in the craft opened and a man stepped out. He appeared normal in every respect—dark-haired, of normal size, wearing white duck pants and a white shirt. He then spoke, addressing the witness by his first name: "Well, Bob—what do you think of this?" The man then reentered the object, which left the same way it came: ascending on a brilliant column of light. A high-pitched whine was heard as the object left.

Aerial Phenomena Research Organization Bulletin (December 1978): 1, 3.

188. November 1978, near Trier, West Germany, about 10:15 P.M.

Driving home after visiting friends, Pam Owens, her husband and son saw a rotating "oval-shaped" object with a red flashing light hover above the car. Arriving home an hour and twenty minutes late from what is usually a thirty-minute drive, Pam later underwent regressive hypnosis, recalling being "lifted" by the UFO and examined by two aliens. "When the object appeared, I got off the road" and stopped on the side. "The next thing I remember is lying on a table . . . paralyzed, without being able to move arms or legs, only the eyes, . . . looking in fright at the two beings. . . . They are bald . . . their cranium was enormous . . . they had enormous, very deep-set eyes." Green skin covered their eight-foot-tall bodies. "It seemed rough, like the wrapping of a mummy. They had four fingers on each hand . . . double as long as human fingers." As she wondered where son Brian was, a thin voice replied, "We are taking care of him." Asking about her husband, Chris, "the voice repeated that everything was all right. Then the two creatures appeared. One told me all would be fine but did not move his lips. They lifted my shirt and touched me as if trying to determine the size of the baby and its position. I was five months pregnant. I then saw the needle." It was inserted just above the navel. She next recalls being in the car and watching the UFO leave. Four months later she gave birth to a normal girl.

El Independiente, January 22, 1980.

189. December 6, 1978, Torriglia, Italy, 11:30 P.M.

Fortunato "Piero" Zanfretta, an on-duty private security guard near a small house in Marzano, observed four lights in a garden. Thinking they were thieves, he tried to radio for help, but his car's radio, engine, and lights failed. He then investigated with a flashlight and gun. Piero came face to face with a monsterlike creature at least ten feet high with undulating gray skin. Fleeing, he noticed a bright triangular object bigger than a house fly off.

Under regressive hypnosis, he told of being taken to a luminous hot place to be examined and interrogated by creatures with pointed ears, dark green skin, and dark gray tubes wrapped around their bodies. Each had a head two feet wide with spines or thorns for hair, two triangular eyes, something like a human eye in the center of the forehead, along with hands with fingernails. Although they didn't speak Italian, they translated with a "luminous device." They hailed from the "third galaxy" and wanted to talk. They said they will soon return in greater numbers.

Three days later, at 11:45 P.M., Piero was driving and couldn't control the car. After driving on its own for a mile and a half, the car suddenly stopped, and Piero struck his head on the steering wheel.

During another hypnotic session, he said, "I know that you need me, but I won't . . . I'm not the qualified people you need! Why are you undressing me? I won't. . . . This thing on my head . . . it's hurting me. . . . You are telling me that next time you'll bring me away. I won't. I won't. I'm well here with my wife and sons."

International UFO Reporter 4, no. 5 (November 1979): 13–15, citing *Gente* magazine, January 20, 1979, and *Skywatch: Shado Italy News* 1 (1979).

190. December 18, 1978, Guadalajara province, Spain, after midnight

Miguel Herrero Sierra's pickup truck suddenly lost its lights and radio, so he pulled off the road to wait for daylight. A man in a diving suit approached him and invited him into a nearby hat-shaped craft. He stayed for three hours, conversing telepathically with the crew before leaving.

Cronica (Buenos Aires, Argentina), January 26, 1978.

191. December 1978, between Harold Hill and Essex, England, 12:45 A.M.

John Day (thirty-three) and his wife, Sue (twenty-nine), were driving home after visiting her parents, who lived thirty minutes away. They left at 9:20 P.M. and arrived home at 12:45 A.M. During the trip the couple drove into a thick green fog. Unable to account for two hours fifty-five minutes, and both suffering recurrent nightmares of beings examining them on tables, John contacted a UFO group and underwent regressive hypnosis. He told of a white light following the car and landing by the road. John found himself in a large room with three entities (seven feet tall) wearing one-piece, silver-gray clothes similar to body stockings. Hoods covered the bottom parts of their faces, and they looked at him with bright pink eyes which had no eyelids. They communicated telepathically, asking him to lie on a table, which he did. "A metal arm swung over me, scanning my body. Then, three other beings, squat and ugly like dwarfs, appeared. One started to prod me with a pen-shaped object." They later agreed to let him tour the ship. He was left alone in a room with "an incredibly beautiful woman" who was surrounded by a gray mist and golden hair. She walked in but soon vanished. He next recalls being back in the car and driving on the road.

Sue declined hypnosis. Later, when discussing John's statements, she claims to have recalled part of the experience. "When I lay on the operating table they painted me with a mauve liquid. Then they washed it off. They prodded me all over with a penlike object and didn't spare my blushes. Then I screamed." A tall being put his hand on her forehead and she lost consciousness. "Later they took me on a tour round the ship . . . I told the beings I didn't want to go back. I asked if I could stay on the craft and they agreed. I saw John climb into the car and it started to vanish. As it disappeared, I said I had changed my mind and wanted to go back. Then I found myself sitting in the car."

Nigel Blundell and Roger Boar, *The World's Greatest UFO Mysteries* (New York: Exeter, 1984); *News of the World*, England, 1980; article by John Clare, specific date unknown.

192. 1978, Torrente, province of Valencia, Spain

Francisco Ramon Jimenez, age fourteen, says a dream about aliens while hospitalized in Alencia Clinical Hospital at age eleven changed his life. He claims to be an extraterrestrial and that he needed the successful leg operation because "they crippled me coming out, with the forceps." While he was hospitalized, aliens appeared in a dream and have appeared every night since. "When I sleep, my body remains on earth and I go to the planet Canymede. . . . They have explained to me how to cure people . . . given me . . . energy. . . ." He claims to cure all diseases by passing energy to the sick. He sees many patients and takes donations. He claims his energy is something we all have but don't use. It comes from another galaxy. Each night he "charges the batteries" by visiting Canymede. Many cures, usually in the form of gradual improvements, are claimed. Yet, Francisco says, "I cannot even cure myself of a simple cold. All the energy I have I must use for others."

CAMBIO 16, August 10, 1981.

193. January 4, 1979, Krugersdrop, South Africa, just after midnight

Meagan Quezet and her son Andre were looking for their dog and were driving on a rural road when they noticed a strange aerial glow. They found the pet twenty yards from an egg-shaped, lead-colored "spaceship" that gave off a pink glow and had spiderlike legs. Near it stood five or six olive-skinned beings. Two of the men (all just over five feet tall) approached. One, assumed to be the leader, was bearded. He looked at her with a penetrating stare, bowed at the waist, and appeared to greet her, speaking in a high-pitched, unintelligible, Chinese-sounding voice. The figures wore white suits tinted pink. She told Andre to get her husband. By the time Andre returned, he saw the ship flying off in the distance.

Later, under regressive hypnosis, she revealed that the bearded entity asked her in English to go away with him in the ship. "You know we'd like to take you away. It's a lovely place where we are. Very nice. You'll be happy there." She declined, saying, "I've got children. I don't think my husband would mind, but what about the child . . . I can't leave him." Inside the ship were chairs and panels, along with a table in the center. She said she and Andre jumped from the vessel, and Andre ran off to get his father. She was told she would receive a message and "then you'll forget about it afterwards. You'll never remember." They tried to persuade her to go, and then the legs of the craft retracted, and it flew off.

Cynthia Hind, *UFOs—African Encounters* (Zimbabwe: Gemini, 1982), 172–98; personal interview with witnesses by C. Hind; also personal interview between Bob Bartholomew and C. Hind at the annual Conference of the Massachusetts chapter of the Mutual UFO Network, August 1984.

194. Early January 1979, Rowley Regis, West Midlands, England

Jean Hingley was at her Bluestone Walk home when a flying saucer landed on the lawn. "I opened the back door and there was a blinding light. Then these three men bombed past me and went into the lounge. The little green men had wings and horrible waxy faces, like corpses." She offered them coffee, but they asked for a glass of water. Upon leaving, they took her mince pies and said they would return some other time.

Northern Ohio UFO Group Newsletter, issue 12 (June 1979): 8.

195. July 25, 1979, near Canoga Park, California, night

Under regressive hypnosis, Shari N. said she left her car to get a better look at a bright light. She claims to have been taken aboard an alien craft, strapped to a metal table, and examined by a slimy robot-like "thing" with a small head, and no shoulders, nose, or mouth. The creature poked at her with three-fingered appendages. When it touched her she felt an electric shock. She noticed other creatures in the background, although she didn't describe them in detail.

Chronicle (Canoga Park, California), October 18, 1979.

196. August 28, 1979, near Winchester, Virginia, about 11:00 P.M.

Southbound on U.S. Route 17, just past Paris Mountain (seventeen miles from Winchester, Virginia), in his tractor-trailer loaded with ketchup and mustard, truck driver Harry Joe Turner noticed a bright illumination "like a helluva light bulb" behind him. His rig "was vacuumed up into this thing" and taken to an unidentified galactic community 6.8 light-years away and returned to a Fredericksburg warehouse several hours later. His captors "were like you or me, only dressed in white clothes like a surgeon." They also had white caps, and "when they lifted up the fronts of them there were numbers, like identification numbers, written across their foreheads." Turner felt he was taken to a city 2.5 light-years beyond Alpha Centauri. He also stopped on the moon and saw astronaut Neil Armstrong's footprint. He said the alien city had undergone an apparent nuclear holocaust long ago and that their mission was to prevent an occurrence on Earth. "They want to help us, but . . . things have gone pretty far here and . . . the end is coming soon." Before the ordeal, Turner never read "anything but the *Winchester Evening Star* and *Hustler* magazine, but now reads a variety of literature and has 'a craving' for bananas, coconut and deer, items he never liked before."

Timothy G. Beckley, *Timothy Green Beckley's Book of Space Contacts* (New York: Global Communications, 1981), pp. 13–15; *Times-Dispatch* (Richmond, Va.), September 23, 1979.

197. November 30, 1979, near La Palma, Oaxaca, Mexico, 5:00 P.M.

Manuel Fidel Cruz Lopez was weeding his father's palm grove when eight armed men approached after exiting a hovering saucer-shaped object. They looked like tall Africans, were well dressed, had green lenses and radio transmitters, and touted machine guns. Lopez was ordered to cut off his penis, which he did with his machete. He got medical aid the next day after wandering that night in shock.

Four hours after the encounter, two schoolteachers saw a green object race across the sky then back again within seconds.

Lopez, who has a wife and three kids, said, "I am not ashamed of being castrated. That was fate and it could happen to anyone."

Probe (September 1980): 79, quoting *Carteles del Sur*, December 11, 1979. The case is part of an article called "UFO update," written and researched by Allan Hendry and J. Allen Hynek of the Center for UFO Studies.

198. December 4, 1979, Vastervik, Sweden, 1:00 A.M.

Taking an early morning walk in the Brevik Hills recreation area, Lilli-Ann Karlsson was suddenly paralyzed. Ahead was a luminous object hovering above the ground. A pair of five-foot-tall beings appeared from behind the object. "I couldn't hear it, but in a strange way I sensed that they were discussing my person. I felt ridiculous in their presence but suddenly heard a voice beside me saying I shouldn't be afraid." They approached and one outstretched its hand to her, but she remained paralyzed. They talked among themselves for a while and returned to the craft, disappearing behind it as they had appeared. Smoke came from the bottom, then suddenly it was not there.

UFO Journal (Cleveland, Ohio), issue 35 (July 1981), citing the *Nyhetsblad Newsletter* (Sweden), April/September 1980, citing an investigation by Tor Wiklund who wrote a report on the case in the publication *UFO-Information* (Skanninge, Sweden), issue 4 (1980).

199. 1979, state of Parana, Brazil, night

On her way to chat with a neighbor, Yolanda Kmiecik, mother of six, claims she was engulfed by an eerie foggy light that lifted her up and into a hovering disc. The crew, "resembling earth men, but with leather clothes," treated her well, serving a "viscous, tasteless liquid" before returning her. The crew said they weren't hostile, but concerned by the "contamination of our race by pollution, especially by the cigarette."

Milt Machlin with Timothy Green Beckley, *UFO* (New York: Quick Fox, 1981), p. 77; *Scientific Bureau of Investigation Report* 1, no. 10 (1978): 49. The S.B.I. account says it occurred in November, while Machlin dates it as August.

200. November 1980, near Rio de Janeiro, Brazil

Concert pianist Luli Oswald was driving with her male companion, Fauze Mehlen, when several unusual crafts emerged from the ocean. The car became uncontrollable: weaving, doors opening and shutting. Suddenly the car stopped. When they later arrived at a restaurant, they couldn't account for two hours. Under regressive hypnosis, Oswald said the car was floated into the bottom of a black disc. She next found herself out of the car and "They are putting a tube in my ear . . . tubes everywhere . . . they are pulling my hair. . . . They look like rats . . . have huge horrible rat ears and their mouths are like slits. They are touching me all over with their thin arms. There are five of them, their skin is gray and sticky."

Oswald could also see Mehlen being examined on a table with a light ray. The beings communicated telepathically, saying they were from Antarctica, claiming, "There is a tunnel that goes under the South Pole, that's why they came out of the water. Others are extraterrestrials." Two hours later they found themselves back in the car on Earth.

Nigel Blundell and Roger Boar, *The World's Greatest UFO Mysteries* (New York: Exeter, 1984), pp. 67–68.

201. Late November 1980, Braganca, Para, Brazil, dawn

A luminous dot grew in size as it approached at an incredible speed and landed on a nearby beach. Two beings resembling normal men emerged from a disc, asking farmworker Domingos Monteiro Brito several questions in his native language, including if there were large uninhabited areas in the neighborhood. Paralyzed with fear, Brito says he couldn't remember how or if he replied. He only recalls that before entering the craft, they promised to reappear at dawn on November 25 for another contact.

O Dia, December 14, 1980.

202. January 2, 1983, Chillan, Chile, night

Chilean schoolteacher Sergio Baeza claims telepathic communication with extraterrestrials after "a powerful light descended" and came "to rest on the ground" in a forest on the outskirts of Chillan. "When I thought of running away, there was something that stopped me from doing so; it was as if it was unnecessary, as if I knew that to attempt it would be useless." He says he felt the presence of unseen aliens, and their intention was to make contact. "[They were] asked mentally about the things I wanted to know, and they responded by turning lights on and off in the negative or affirmative." He determined "their intentions are peaceful" and they wish "to establish contact with us."

La Razon, January 8, 1983.

203. August 2, 1983, Aldershot, England, 1:15 A.M.

While fishing near Government Bridge over the Basing-stoke Canal, Alfred Burtoo saw a flying saucer land and two forms (four feet tall) emerge. They wore pale green suits, and dark visors covered their faces. After following them inside the ship Burtoo was asked to stand under an amber light, and they told him, "You can go. You are too old and too infirm for our purpose." Burtoo was seventy-seven at the time.

Aldershot News (England), November 25, 1983.

204. August 7, 1983, Winifreda, Argentina

Opening a ranch gate on a farm where he was working, Julio Platner was blinded by a bright white light. He lost consciousness and awoke in a room on an "operating table" with four beings around him. They talked telepathically, saying, "Don't be afraid. We would not harm you. What you are experiencing now has happened to thousands of people before. You can reveal it if you wish." He became "calm and comfortable." They took some blood from his left arm. The entire experience lasted fifteen to twenty minutes. At the end of the encounter, "I was told to stand up" and "the four beings disappeared and I found myself sitting beside my van." The beings were humanlike with hairless heads, small mouths, short noses, and flat ears hugging close to each side of their head. They stood between five and five and a half feet tall. The female being was thin and had what appeared to be breasts.

La Reforma (Buenos Aires, Argentina), August 12, 1983.

205. December 14, 1983, Chapeco, Santa Catarina, Brazil

Antonio Nelso Tasca was returning to Chapeco from Colonia Cella on highway BR-282. While passing a Coca-Cola factory, he felt an urge to stop. Looking up, he saw a luminous bus-shaped object. A band of solid light struck and "caught" him, pushing him into the craft. After losing consciousness, he awoke naked, and two or three small creatures were examining him in a dark area. They left and the place lit up. A door opened and a beautiful, small woman in light-colored clothes entered, explaining telepathically she was Cabala from Agali. "Her eyes were widely placed apart . . . slanted. . . . She was wearing slippers . . . and something like a nightgown." He was chosen to warn mankind of the Earth's destruction.

Eight hours after first seeing the object, he awoke, lying beside highway BR-282 near the Electro-Diesel Batistella works. He also claims to have discovered a "W" with an exclamation mark imprinted into his back.

O Estada (Florianoplia, Sta. Catarina, Brazil), date unknown.

A note about cases from 1984 to present: This list of contact cases since 1900 is relatively comprehensive until 1983. However, since the early 1980s, UFO groups, researchers, and authors have compiled thousands of claimed abductions and contacts with aliens. To list them all is not necessary to the central purpose of the catalogue. It is intended to show the content and form of the UFO contact narrative over eight decades.

Appendix B

Bibliography for Chapter 12

Adamski, G. 1955. *Inside the Spaceships*. New York: Abelard-Schuman.

———. 1961. *Flying Saucers Farewell*. New York: Abelard-Schuman.

Adamski, G., and D. Leslie. 1953. *Flying Saucers Have Landed*. New York: British Book Centre.

Anderson, C. 1956. *Two Nights to Remember*. Los Angeles: New Age Publishing.

Angelucci, O. 1955. *The Secret of the Saucers*. Amherst, Wis.: Amherst Press.

Barker, G. 1956. *They Knew Too Much About Flying Saucers*. New York: University Books.

———. 1977, June. *UFO Report* 1, no. 2. Cites *La Nación* (Buenos Aires).

———. 1983. *Men in Black: The Secret Terror Among Us*. N.p.: New Age.

Bartholomew, R. E. 1989. *UFOlore*. Stone Mt., Ga.: Arcturus Books.

Basterfield, K. 1980, June. *An Indepth Review of Australasian UFO-Related Entity Reports*. N.p.: Australian Centre for UFO Studies.

———. 1981a. *The Image Hypothesis: Close Encounters of an Australian Kind*. Sydney: Reed.

———. 1981b, October. *A Catalogue of the More Interesting Australian Close Encounters*. Australian Centre for UFO Studies.

———. 1987. "Your Mind: The Final Frontier." Unpublished manuscript, pp. 58–59.

———. 1988. *Abstracts of Possible Abduction Cases Where the Percipient Was in Bed/Asleep*. Adelaide, Australia: K. Basterfield. See page 4 citing *Aerial Phenomena Research Organization Bulletin* 26, no. 5 (1977): 1–3.

Beckley, T. G. 1980. *Psychic and UFO Revelations in the Last Days*. New York: Global Communications.

Bender, A. 1962. *Flying Saucers and the Three Men*. Clarksburg, W. Va.: Saucerian Books.

Bethurum, T. 1954. *Aboard a Flying Saucer*. Los Angeles: DeVorss. Reprint, Clarksburg, W. Va.: Saucerian Press, 1970.

———. *Facing Reality*. Prescott, Ariz.: Author.

Binder, O. 1968. *Unsolved Mysteries of the Past*. New York: Tower Publications.

Blum, R., and J. Blum. 1980. *Beyond Earth: Man's Contacts with UFOs*. New York: Bantam.

Blundell, N., and R. Boar. 1983. *The World's Greatest UFO Mysteries*. New York: Exeter.

Bowen, C., ed. 1977a. *Encounter Cases from Flying Saucer Review*. New York: Signet.

———. 1977b. *The Humanoids*. Great Britain: Futura.

Brinkerhoff, M. 1979, April. "The Incredible UFO Photography of Mark Brinkerhoff." *UFO Review*, No. 3.

Brownell, W. S. 1980. *UFOs: Key to the Earth's Destiny*. Lytle Creek, Calif.: Legion of Light Publications.

Buhler, W. 1973, November. *Flying Saucer Review Special Bulletin*, no. 5: 11–25.

Bullard, T. 1987. *UFO Abductions: The Measure of a Mystery*. Mount Rainier, Md.: Fund for UFO Research.

Clark, J. 1976, August. In *UFO Report*: 21–23, 46–53.

Clark, J., and L. Coleman. 1975. *The Unidentified: Notes Toward Solving the UFO Mystery*. New York: Warner.

Creighton, G. 1971, November/December. "Uproar in Brazil." *Flying Saucer Review* 17, no. 6: 24–26.

Dickhoff, R. 1964. *Homecoming of the Martians*. Makelumna Hill, Calif.: Health Research.

Drake, W. 1974. *Gods and Spacemen in the Ancient West*. New York: New American Library.

Dykes, M. 1981. *Strangers in Our Skies: UFOs Over New Zealand*. Lower Hutt, Wellington, New Zealand: NDL Publications.

Edwards, F. 1967. *Flying Saucers Here and Now!* New York: Lyle Stuart.

Evans, H. 1979. *UFOs—The Greatest Mystery*. Albany: London.

———. 1984. *Visions, Apparitions, Alien Visitors*. Wellingborough, Northamptonshire: Aquarian.

Ferguson, W. 1954. *My Trip to Mars*. Potomac, Md.: Cosmic Study Center.

Festinger, L., H. Riecken, and S. Shacter. 1964. *When Prophesy Fails*. New York: Harper and Row.

Flournoy, T. 1963. *From India to the Planet Mars: A Study of a Case of Somnambulism with Glossolalia*. Hyde Park, N.Y.: University Books.

Fowler, R. 1979. *The Andreasson Affair*. New Jersey: Prentice-Hall.

———. 1982. *The Andreasson Affair: Phase II*. New Jersey: Prentice-Hall.

Fry, D. 1954. *The White Sands Incident*. Los Angeles: New Age Publishing.

Fuller, C., comp. and ed. 1980. *Proceedings of the First International UFO Congress*. New York: Warner.

Fuller, J. 1966. *The Interrupted Journey*. New York: Dial.

Gansberg, A., and J. Gansberg. 1980. *Direct Encounters: The Personal Histories of UFO Abductees*. New York: Walker & Walker.

Girard, R. Truman Bethurum's personal scrapbook (original copy), courtesy of Robert C. Girard, UFO book dealer, publisher, Scotia, N.Y. Published by Arcturus Books, 1982.

Girvin, W. 1958. *The Night Has a Thousand Saucers*. El Monte, Calif.: Understanding Publishing.

Haisell, D. 1978. *The Missing Seven Hours*. Markham: Paperjacks.

Hartman, T. 1979. "Another Abduction by Extraterrestrials." *Mutual UFO Network Journal* 141: 3–4.

Harris, L. 1976. *Flying Saucer Review* 22, no. 5: 3.

Hendry, A. 1980. *Frontiers of Science* 2, no. 4.

Hind, C. 1982. *UFOs: African Encounters*. Zimbabwe: Gemini.

Holzer, H. 1976. *The UFOnauts*. New York: Fawcett.

Hopkins, B. 1979. "Possible Abduction in New York State." *Mutual UFO Network Journal* 137: 10–12.

———. 1981. *Missing Time: A Documented Study of UFO Abductions*. New York: Richard Marek.

Jacobs, D. 1975. *The UFO Controversy in America*. New York: Signet.

Johnson, F. 1980. *The Janos People*. London: Neville Spearman.

Jung, C. 1959. *Flying Saucers: A Modern Myth of Things Seen in the Sky*. New York: Harcourt, Brace & World.

Kask, G. 1976, March 31. "Introducing David Hamil—He Rides in Flying Saucers." *Maple Ridge Gazette* (British Columbia).

Keel, J. 1970. *Why UFOs*. New York: Manor. Also published as *UFOs: Operation Trojan Horse* (New York: Putnam's Sons, 1970).

———. 1971. *Our Haunted Planet*. Connecticut: Fawcett.

———. 1975. *The Mothman Prophecies*. New York: Signet.

Kinder, G. 1988. *Light Years—The Best Documented, Most Credible UFO Case Ever*. London: Penguin.

King, G. 1962. *My Contact with the Great White Brotherhood*. Los Angeles: Aetherius Society.

Klarer, E. 1980. *Beyond the Light Barrier*. Cape Town, South Africa: Timmins.

Kraspedon, D. 1959. *My Contact with Flying Saucers*. London: Neville Spearman.

Lee, G. 1959. *Why We Are Here!* Los Angeles: DeVorss.

———. 1962. *The Changing Conditions of Your World*. Los Angeles: DeVorss.

Little, G. 1980. Personal investigation report by the author.

Lorenzen, C. 1977. *Abducted!: Confrontations with Beings from Outer Space*. Berkeley: Medallion.

Lorenzen, C., and J. Lorenzen. 1976. *Encounters with UFO Occupants*. New York: Berkeley.

Machlin, M., and T. Beckley. 1981. *UFO*. New York: Quick Fox.

Maria, E. S. *O Dia* (Rio de Janeiro), series of nine articles appearing between October 26 and November 4, 1970.

Martin, D. 1959. *Seven Hours Aboard a Space Ship*. Detroit: Author.

Menger, H. 1959. *From Outer Space to You*. Clarksburg, W. VA.: Saucerian Press.

Menzel, D. 1953. *Flying Saucers*. Cambridge, Mass.: Harvard University Press.

Michael, C. 1955. *Round Trip to Hell in a Flying Saucer*. N.p.: Vantage Press. Reprint, Auckland, New Zealand: Phoenix, 1971.

———. 1977. *Signs and Wonders*. Reseda, Calif.: Mojave Books.

Miller, W., and E. Miller. 1959. *We of the New Dimension—Communications with Other Worlds*. Morongo Valley, Calif.: Authors.

Moore, R. 1977. *In Search of White Crows: Spiritualism, Parapsychology, and American Culture*. New York: Oxford University Press.

Mundo, L. 1956. *Flying Saucers and the Father's Plan*. Clarksburg, W. Va.: Saucerian Press.

———. 1964. *Pied Piper from Outer Space*. Los Angeles: Planetary Space Center Working Committee.

———. 1970. *Our Trip to the Moon and Venus*. N.p.: Author.

———. 1983. *The Mundo UFO Report*. N.p.: Vantage Press.

Musgrave, J. B. 1980. *UFO Occupants & Critters*. Amherst, Wis.: Amherst Press and Global Communications. Cites a personal phone conversation between Musgrave and the witness, in addition to a letter at the Center for UFO Studies, Evanston, Ill.

———. 1984. Personal communication citing a letter received from the percipient, dated March 16, 1976. At the time of this correspondence, Musgrave was employed at the Mobile Planetarium Project at the Provincial Museum of Alberta, Edmonton, Canada.

Nebel, L. J. 1961. *The Way Out World*. Englewood Cliffs, N.J.

Nelson, B. 1956. *My Trip to Mars, the Moon, and Venus*. West Plains, Mo.

———. 1960. *Souvenir of Buck's Spacecraft Convention*. West Plains, Mo.

Noonan, A. 1967. "I Went to Venus—And Beyond." *New Report on Flying Saucers*, no. 2.

Norman, R. 1980. *Have You Lived on Other Worlds Before: An Emissary for Thirty-Two Worlds Speaks to Earth*. N.p.: Unarius.

Norman, R., and T. Miller. 1974. *Telsa Speaks*. N.p.: Unarius.

Owens, T. 1968. *How to Contact Space People*. Clarksburg, W. Va.: Saucerian Press.

———. 1972. *Flying Saucer Intelligences Speak*. Cape Charles, Va.: Author.

Painter, R. 1973, January 26. "Youth Claims 'Saucer' Landed on Highway 18." *Gaffney Ledger* (S. C.).

Press. 1957a. *Sociedade Brasiliera de Estudoes Sobre Discos Voadores Bulletin (SBEDV)*, periodical of the SBEDV UFO research group, Rio de Janeiro, Brazil, no. 4, July 1.

———. 1957b. *Flying Saucer Review*, September/October.

———. 1965. *La Cronica Matutina* (Buenos Aires), October 8; *La Cronica* (Buenos Aires), August 8.

———. 1968. *La Razon* (Buenos Aires), June 4; *Correio do Povo* (Porto Alegre, Brazil), June 11.

———. 1971a. *Lancashire Evening Telegram* (Blackburn, England), August 29, 1980.

———. 1971b. *Ultima Hora* (Rio de Janeiro), October 2.

———. 1972. *La Union* (Catamarca), March 22.

———. 1975. *Ultima Hora* (Buenos Aires), evening edition, May 21; *El Cronista* (Buenos Aires), June 10; *Flying Saucer Review* 21, nos. 2 and 4 (double issue): 62.

———. 1977. *El Vocero de Puerto Rico* (San Juan), September 19.

———. 1978a. *Rhein Neckar* (West Germany), January 10.

———. 1978b. *La Cronica* (Buenos Aires), January 26.

———. 1979. *Arizona Republic* (Phoenix), December 16.

———. 1981. *Cambio* (Spanish magazine), August 10.

———. 1983a. *La Razon*, January 8.

———. 1983b. *Aldershot News* (United Kingdom), November 25.

Randles, J. 1976. "Two British 'Psychic Contactee' Cases." *Flying Saucer Review* 22 (6): 18–20.

———. 1983. *The Pennine Mystery*. London: Granada.

Randles, J. 1988. *Abduction*. London: Robert Hale.

Rawcliffe, D. H. 1959. *Illusions and Delusions of the Supernatural and the Occult*. New York: Dover.

Reeve, B., and H. Reeve. 1957. *Flying Saucer Pilgrimage*. Amherst, Wis.: Amherst Press.

Rimmer, J. 1984. *The Evidence for Alien Abductions*. Great Britain: The Aquarian Press.

Roe, J. 1978, June 2. "Are You Ready for Another Close Encounter?" *Wichita Beacon* (Wichita, Kans.).

Rogo, D. S. 1980. *UFO Abductions*. New York: Signet.

———. 1987, July/August. *International UFO Reporter*: 4–13.

Rowe, K. 1958. *A Call at Dawn*. El Monte, Calif.: Understanding Publishing.

Sachs, M. 1980. *The UFO Encyclopedia*. New York: Perigee.

Schmidt, R. O. 1958. *The Kearney Incident and to the Arctic Circle in a Spacecraft*. Hollywood, Calif.: Author.

Schwarz, B. E. 1983a. *UFO Dynamics Book 1: Psychiatric and Psychic Dimensions of the UFO Syndrome*. Florida: Rainbow.

———. 1983b. *UFO Dynamics Book 2: Psychiatric and Psychic Dimensions of the UFO Syndrome*. Florida: Rainbow.

Short, R., ed. N.d. *SOLAR SPACE—Letter.* Joshua Tree, Calif.: Blue Rose Ministry.

Smith, W. 1976. *The Book of Encounters*. New York: Kensington.

Spencer, J. W. 1976. *The UFO Yearbook*. Springfield, Mass.: Phillips.

Sprinkle, L., ed. 1981. *Proceedings of the Rocky Mountain Conference on UFO Investigations*. Laramie: University of Wyoming.

Steiger, B. 1978. *Alien Meetings*. New York: Grosset and Dunlap.

Steiger, B., and J. Whritenour. 1969, June. "The Contact Enigma: The Flying Saucer Missionaries, Part Three." *Flying Saucer Review,* special issue no. 2: 53–54.

Stevens, W. C. 1982. *UFO Contact from the Pleiades: A Preliminary Investigation Report*. N.p.: Author.

Stevens, W. C., with W. Herrmann. 1981. *UFO Contact from Reticulum*. Arizona: Authors.

Story, R. 1980. *The Encyclopedia of UFOs.* New York: Doubleday.

Strieber, W. 1987. *Communion*. Melbourne: Hutchinson.

Stringfield, L. H. 1977. *Situation Red: The UFO Siege!* New York: Fawcett.

Suares, J., and R. Siegel (with text by David Owen). 1979. *Fantastic Planets*. New Hampshire: Reed.

Swedenborg, E. 1758. *Heaven and Its Wonders and Hell*. London: The Swedenborg Society.

Swedenborg, E. 1860. *Earths in the Universe.* London.

Tarleton, V. 1967. Original transcript of his personal investigation of the case, courtesy of Robert C. Girard, UFO book dealer, publisher, Scotia, N.Y.

Tongco, R. C. 1974, October 26. Copy of Dr. Tongco's original medical report on Carl Higdon, at the Carbon County Memorial Hospital (Wyoming), appearing in Leo Sprinkle, "Investigation of the Alleged UFO Experience of Carl Higdon," in *UFO Phenomena and the Behavioral Scientist*, edited by R. Haines (Metuchen, N.J.: Scarecrow, 1979), pp. 225–357.

Vallee, J. 1969. *Passport to Magonia*. Chicago: Henry Regnery.

———. 1979. *Messengers of Deception*. Berkeley: And/Or Press.

Van Dusen, W. 1975. *The Presence of Other Worlds: The Psychological/Spiritual Findings of Emanuel Swedenborg*. New York: Harper and Row.

Van Tassel, G. W. 1952. *I Rode a Flying Saucer.* Los Angeles: New Age Publishing.

———. 1958. *The Council of Seven Lights*. Los Angeles: DeVorss & Co.

———. 1976. *When Stars Look Down*. Los Angeles: Kruckberg Press.

Vorilhon, C. 1974. *Le Livre qui dit la Verite* (The Book which Tells the Truth). France: Editions du message.

———. 1978. *Space Aliens Took Me to Their Planet*. N.p.: Canadian Realian Movement.

———. 1986. *The Message Given to Me by Extraterrestrials: They Took Me to Their Planet*. Tokyo: AOM Corporation.

Whiting, F. 1980, March. "The Abduction of Harry Joe Turner." *The Mutual UFO Network Journal (MUFON)*, no. 145: 3–7.

Wiklund, T. 1980. *UFO-Information*, issue 4. Skanninge, Sweden.

Williamson, G. H. 1954. *The Saucers Speak*. Los Angeles: New Age Publishing.

About the Authors and Contributors

About the Authors

Robert Bartholomew is a researcher in sociology at James Cook University of North Queensland, Townsville, Australia, with a special interest in mass social delusions and popular culture.

George S. Howard is professor of psychology at the University of Notre Dame, Notre Dame, Indiana. His research and teaching interests are varied and include narrative psychology, philosophy of the social sciences, and improving research methods in several applied areas of psychology. Both have an enduring interest in the UFO phenomenon.

About the Contributors

Clas Svahn is a journalist with Sweden's largest morning newspaper, *Dagens Nyheter*.

Anders Liljegren is the director of archives for UFO Research.

Bryan Dickeson is a computer specialist.

Keith Basterfield personally conducted investigations of two Australian UFO cases in chapter 10.

Index